Born a Slave, Died a Pioneer

BORN A SLAVE, DIED A PIONEER

Nathan Harrison and the Historical Archaeology of Legend

Seth Mallios

berghahn
NEW YORK · OXFORD
www.berghahnbooks.com

First published in 2020 by

Berghahn Books

www.berghahnbooks.com

Library of Congress Cataloging-in-Publication Data

A C.I.P. cataloging record is available from the Library of Congress

Library of Congress Cataloging in Publication Control Number: 2019033237

British Library Cataloguing in Publication Data

A catalogue record for this book is available from the British Library

ISBN 978-1-78920-347-9 hardback
ISBN 978-1-78920-430-8 paperback
ISBN 978-1-78920-348-6 ebook

For Jim

❦ Contents

🔥 Illustrations

Tables

🌿 Acknowledgments

The problem I have with the *Indiana Jones* movies is not that archaeology gets sensationalized. I, too, run kicking and screaming from snakes on a regular basis. My beef with Dr. Jones is that he is typically portrayed engaging in the archaeological process alone. His moments of discovery are usually in isolation, which is the opposite of how archaeology truly works. It is always a group effort. For every project director, there are hundreds of others who played a key role in uncovering archaeological insights. So, Indy, keep your stylish Fedora and bull whip, but I beg you: share the spotlight with your unsung archaeological team. Without mine, there would be no project.

For those who have worked with me on Palomar Mountain, in my laboratory, or in archives across the nation, I am indebted for your efforts. I offer sincere thanks to Esther Aguayo, Melissa Allen, Christian Allen, Chuck Ambers, Micaela Applebaum, Melissa Ayala, Joe Ball, Joseph Barca, Jamie Bastide, Alison Bell, Saz Benchekroun, Lisa Bender, Nicole Benson, Meredith Blake, John W. Bond, Brandon Booth, Elyse Bradley, Deborah Sullivan Brennan, Meagan Brown, Peter Brueggeman, Shirley Buskirk, Donna Byczkiewicz, Brenda Cabello, Vic Camp, Richard Carrico, Maren Castañeda, David Caterino, Stephanie Chavez, Chanthy Choeum, Steph Colvin, Ed Costa, Chris Coulson, Annemarie Cox, Maggie David, Kat Davis, Eduvijes Davis-Mullens, Richard Day, Lia Dearborn, Joseph DeWolf, Nick Doose, Kyle Dolph, Herbert P. Douglass, Connie Vinita Dowell, Cynthia Eischen, Sarah Elkind, Iris Engstrand, Shannon Farnsworth, Christopher Fennell, Jordan Finch, Lluvia Flores-Renteria, Maria Franklin, Richard Fritz, Natalia Galeana, Yesenia Garcia, Caeli Gibbs, Forrest Goodwin, Tim Gross, Cole Giurlani, Henry Glassie, Shelby Gunderman, Leah Hails, Michelle Hammond, Michelle Hart, Kristi Hawthorne, Consuela Hedrick, Kjrsten Hefty, Jackie Herrera, Robb Hirsch, Michael Hoke, Brandi Holcomb, Cece Holm, Fred Holt, Everett Hunt, Natalie Jackson, Shelby Jenkins, Gregory Jones, Alan Kezele, Erika Kleinhans, Hank Koerper, Ken Kramer, Alexia Landa, Monique Larragoitia, Jaime Lennox, David Lewis, Megan Libby, Kent Lightfoot, Lauren Lingley, Hilary Llamas, Gabby Mallios, Scott Mattingly, Matthew Maxfeldt, Ron May, Jason Maywald, Kim Mazyck, Molly McClain, Glen McClish, Anamay Melmed, Henry Mendoza, Monse Meza, John Michener, Anne Miller, Rayna Milloy, Onika Miyashiro, Isabella Montalvo, Hilary Moore, Cecil Munsey, Therese Muranaka, Marlo Nalven, Peter Nelson, Kurt Olney, Jason Peralta, Andrew Phelps, Bonnie Phelps, Shannon Pierre, Misty Plotner, Elizabeth Pollard, Trevor Prough, Jon Putman, Anna Quimson, Martin Ramirez, Orlando Ramos, Robert Ray, Denise Redden, Randy Reinholz, Dominique Rissolo, Jodi Roberts, Leigh Robertson, Laura Roderickz, David Ross, Aaron Sasson, Amethyst Sanchez, Kimberly Scott, Leland Searl, Carol Serr, Steve Shackley, Ninveh Shamoon, Blue Sheppard, Katherine Sholan, John Smiley, Kim Smiley, Olivia Smith, Justin Sorensen, Thomas Sowles, Kathleen Stanford, Cindy Stankowski, Samantha Stevens, Hannah Stover, Sarah Stroud, Hillary Sweeney, Kristin Tennesen, Matthew Tennyson, Cole Tepper, Robert Tews, Mariz Timog, Aldo Torales, James Turner, Raven Tyson, Isaac Ullah, Stephen Van Wormer, Josiah Walker, Susan Walter, Timothy Ward, Barbara Anne Waite, Steve Weber, Laura Weide, Matt Werle, Andrew Wiese, Michael Wilken-Robertson, Lisa Woodword, Nichelle Worthington, and Elizabeth Yamaguchi.

I am grateful to have worked with two supportive sets of landowners during the project. Jamey and Hannah Kirby first gave us permission to dig in 2003, and then Elisa Kisselburg, Vicki Morgan, and Susie Silvestri continued to champion our archaeological endeavors in 2007. Vicki is now the sole owner of the property; her passion for today's Harrison Serenity Ranch, along with the tireless work of Jackie Martin and April Walsh, has propelled us past seemingly insurmountable obstacles. I also want to express my gratitude to my San Diego State colleagues, staff members at the region's historical archives, and the outstanding people at Berghahn Books. In addition, I offer special thanks to Jaime Lennox, Fred Conway, David Lewis, Tobin Vaughn, Jim Herrick, and Kit Sickles. Gretchen and Gabby Mallios could not have been more supportive, helpful, and inspiring at every twist and turn; I can only hope to repay the enormous debt I owe them with my continued adoration. Lastly, I am most appreciative of my extended family of Emmetts, Schmidts, Pecks, Henkles, Hopkins, Dahl-Mallioses, Mallioses, Winchesters, and Swifts.

This book is in honor of Nathan Harrison.

 Prologue

August 1897, late morning

High up a dusty and desolate mountain road stands a lone figure, unmoved by the dry wind and searing sun. Wildlife pulsates around him. A jittery lizard pops up on its forelegs, hungrily eyeing an oblivious beetle, only to be skewered by the talons of a hawk diving silently from above. The man's attention is focused far from these ever-present natural rhythms of predator and prey. His gaze is fixed on a slow-moving horse-drawn wagon five miles below, creeping along the serpentine path. As the sounds of creaking axles and groaning wagon-wood echo across the valley, a team of sweat-soaked horses snorts, wheezes, and sighs in weary response to the unrelenting terrain. A half-dozen passengers chatter nervously, warily eyeing the precipitous drop along the side of the narrow and shoulderless rutted road, eagerly anticipating the exotic world at their alpine destination. Hours drift by with little apparent change. The wagon inches up the mountain, and the man rarely stirs, except to take a slow drag from his crusty applewood smoking pipe, adjust his weathered dungarees which are missing their top button, and wave away the incessant gnats flitting about his tattered cowboy hat. Though strangers, the wagon-borne visitors are coming to see him, like so many others before them. He will likely greet and delight them with free water—for both human and beast—and a recitation of tales regarding the natural wonderland that is his home, although he always maintains the option of disappearing into the surrounding woods long before their arrival. Yet now, as the wagon-driver scolds his stubborn horses for resisting the steepest pitch of the grade, the deliberately inert figure on the barren overlook makes no effort to ease their journey or hasten their arrival. His own path to this very spot decades ago had been fraught with unimaginable hardship, and he is content to sit back, wait, and watch . . .

❧ Introduction

Nathan Harrison, an African American born into slavery in Kentucky decades before the Civil War, endured some of the most treacherous times in US history for anyone who was not white. Despite this, he grew into a permanent and prominent fixture thousands of miles from his birthplace on a remote mountain in Southern California. Confronted with unfettered violence and bigotry in nearly every stage of his life—be it enslavement in the Antebellum South as a child, the hazardous trek across country as a subjugated teenager, Gold Rush exploitation as a young man, or the chaos of the Wild West as a newly emancipated free person—Harrison survived, persevered, and adapted. Although he ultimately lived alone, high up on Palomar Mountain in rural San Diego County for nearly half a century during the late 1800s and early 1900s, Harrison was deeply enmeshed in multiple local communities, including nearby Indigenous groups, an extensive network of Mexican ranchers, and burgeoning Anglo populations in both rural and urban San Diego. Harrison did not sound, look, or act like any of his Southern California neighbors during his lengthy time in the region. Despite these pronounced differences and the lethal racial turmoil of the early US period in California, he gained widespread acceptance and was celebrated by his contemporaries for his extraordinary longevity, resourcefulness, regional knowledge, and charming demeanor.

Regardless of this past acclaim, most people alive today have never heard of Nathan Harrison. Those relatively few individuals who do recognize his name have likely encountered a wide array of tall tales, rife with far-fetched fabrication. While Harrison's actual life story was a microcosm of the diverse cultural heritages and volatile histories of the nineteenth-century United States, a wealth of enticing exaggerations with tantalizingly unverified secondhand details have elevated his already significant biography into something more. They exalt Harrison, transforming this unsung migratory laborer of humble origins into a legendary western trailblazer and an enduring American pioneer. As such, Nathan Harrison has become larger than life.

The list of entertaining yet often highly inaccurate anecdotes about Harrison is so lengthy and broad that it covers nearly everything from his time in bondage before the Civil War to his later years at a rustic cabin high up Palomar Mountain in the southwest corner of the United

States. Below is a sampling of some of the most conspicuous claims that were found in the historical research about him. Allegedly, Nathan Harrison:

- perilously escaped slavery, floating down the Mississippi River in the 1840s,
- fought with Frémont's Battalion in the Bear Flag Revolt in the summer of 1846, helping the United States defeat Mexico and acquire California,
- joined the Mormon Battalion in 1846–47 as it made the longest infantry march in US history,
- sailed in treacherous waters around South America's Cape Horn on the way to California in 1849,
- jumped ship at San Pedro (Los Angeles) in the 1850s as a fugitive slave,
- encountered notorious gold-country bandit Joaquin Murrieta in 1853,
- drove an ox team with the first wagon train over Tejon Pass in 1854, opening the primary route to Southern California,
- narrowly averted being scalped by tomahawk-wielding Native Americans in 1864 while traveling via covered wagon from Missouri to California,
- had multiple Southern California Indian wives in the 1880s,
- was the consummate Wild West mountain man—he rode a radiant white horse, could tame any wild stallion, had "owl eyes" (the ability to see in total darkness), and once killed a mountain lion measuring over 14 feet in length,
- hid a sizable stash of gold from his mining days near his cabin; it has never been found,
- lived to be 107 years old, finally succumbing to natural causes in 1920, and finally . . .
- to this day, Nathan Harrison's ghost morosely wanders his Palomar Mountain home, distraught that his body was placed in an unmarked grave, over 100 miles away from his beloved hillside homestead.

Some of these embellished stories have slivers of actual bygone realities in them. Others are entirely false. Nonetheless, the collective lore can be used to reveal important hidden truths about Harrison and his times. Like elusively shifting flames in a campfire, these mythical accounts hint at some greater understanding of days gone by, but then flicker away into the darkness of the disappearing past.

The enduring stories of Nathan Harrison are reflections of generations of people who told these accounts and the many audiences who continue to bear witness to such narratives. As author Tony Horwitz noted, "History is arbitrary, a collection of facts. Myths we choose, we create, we perpetuate . . . The [mythical] story may not be correct, but it transcends truth" (2008: 37). Lasting stories, such as the ones told of Harrison, result from a series of intricate performances that contain insights far beyond the original subject matter, narrator, or audience member. The collective lore can act as a prism of wisdom when observed from informed perspectives by bending and transforming singular understandings of the past into broader and better-contextualized knowledge.

Aside from being born enslaved in the early nineteenth-century American South and dying in San Diego as the region's first African American homesteader, there are few incontrovertible historical facts of Harrison's existence. The lone verifiable details of his life pale in comparison to the often deliberately sensationalized stories featuring his exploits. Truth rarely impedes the telling of an entertaining tale. Generations of narratives of Harrison's adventures, eccentricities, and personal charms—told and retold long after his death—have grown his biography from a relatively obscure historical footnote into a captivating figure of local mythology. As such, Harrison's legend has been far from static. The widespread tales of his origin story, his path to emancipation, and even his place in history have changed with great regularity in the century since his passing.

Nathan Harrison's mixed legacy, until now, has been both as an untold and a mis-told account of American history. If it were not for the many tall tales, he likely would have been forgotten long ago. This book offers a new narrative of Harrison. It is informed by a critical reading of past records and accounts, broadened by an appreciation of multiple cultural perspectives, and most importantly, fueled by an entirely new data source of over 50,000 recently uncovered archaeological artifacts. These unearthed fragments from the late nineteenth and early twentieth centuries include the ordinary and the extraordinary. In the same deposit of everyday smoking pipes, sheep shears, and leather boot fragments, excavators found numerous ornate goods, including a stylish pocket watch, gaudy "President" suspender clips, and nickel-plated sock garters. We were even able to identify and pull a 100-year-old thumbprint off of one of the fired rifle cartridges uncovered at the site! This text is a study in history, anthropology, and archaeology; yet over the course of the analysis presented here, the reader will be drawn into discussions from a wealth of additional fields, including mathematics, chemistry, physics, biology, geology, architecture, literature, philosophy, performing arts, and many others. Insights from the sciences, social sciences, humanities, and arts all contribute to greater understandings of Nathan Harrison's particular past and how people like him helped shape the present.

Nathan Harrison is both a subject and an agent of the past. He actively made history, and his story has also been repeatedly used by others to remake history. In fact, Harrison's alleged actions often heighten intrigue into the nostalgic narratives surrounding his life. Nowhere is this more apparent than in the exact words he purportedly spoke. According to dozens of accounts, Harrison would routinely greet visitors to his remote Southern California hillside property with the introductory quip, "I'm N——r Nate, the first white man on the mountain."[1] This is by far the most common direct quote in all of the extensive Harrison lore (Mallios and Lennox 2014). If it is possible to get past current-day shock and outrage over the inflammatory racial epithet, one can begin to contextualize and appreciate the ironic humor, ethnic insight, and dualistically crafted identities Harrison employed in this profound statement.

These dualisms were not subtle. At the turn of the nineteenth century, he was both white (non-American Indian) and non-white (African American). He was liberated (legally emancipated) and bound (overtly disempowered by racist Reconstructionist policies and rampant discrimination). He was private (living alone and apart on a remote mountain) and public (on display for frequent visits from tourists). Harrison managed to broach such polarizing societal issues in a nonthreatening fashion, with disarming humor and charm. Furthermore, he used a titillating phrase[2] visitors were certain to remember and repeat. His bold yet playful proclamation teemed with individual agency, multivalent symbolism, and strategic identity-politics of the late 1800s and early 1900s. Through his distinctive and memorable greeting, Nathan Harrison firmly established his right to be—and his right to be *right there* on the west side of Palomar Mountain in particular—yet successfully elicited a smile from nearly every guest to his homestead. This hard-to-forget and oft-repeated phrase is one of numerous story elements that reveal as much about the life and times of the Postbellum West (1865–1914) as the individual biography of Harrison itself.

Harrison's noteworthy introduction toyed with established notions of race and ethnicity. Every individual experiences, constructs, and exhibits a sense of self, which often develops in complexity over time. Shared identities result through connections with others and can draw on anything from a common religion, language, ancestry, activity, etc. Ethnicity, being a concept that unites identity and community, is a prominent part of an individual's sense of being. It connects that person with others who share common history and culture. These connections are clearly distinguishable by a literal or figurative boundary dividing one group from another (Barth 1969: 13). Origin myths are a tool often used in the construction of ethnic identity as these stories both underscore a common history and express shared values. Though commonly tied to shared heritage and ancestry, ethnicity also includes important cultural differences from nonmembers (Voss 2008: 27). Despite these marked divisions, ethnicity is a fluid construct continually altered through situational interactions. The origin (ethnogenesis), development, and growth of ethnic groups are often tied to interaction with other groups in a setting that was intense, volatile, or oppressive (Penner 1997: 259).

Race is not the same as ethnicity. Race is a social grouping based on a loose, superficial, and scientifically unrigorous set of physical traits. Furthermore, race is often imposed onto groups of people by others, especially outsiders. It is a product of the human mind—a decision—not the human body. Racialization involves the process of deliberately assigning people into groups in order to fabricate the biological or social superiority of one set of people over another (Miles 1989: 75). Racialization was integral to Nathan Harrison's life and times as he suffered great hardship as the result of a race-based system of slavery that had ramifications well beyond the Emancipation Proclamation. These highly nuanced issues of group affiliation, evolving identity, and social hierarchy were of major consequence to Harrison, and much of this book is geared to examining how he managed to follow rigid societal norms yet still live a life that transcended established racial and ethnic groups.

Government documents in the form of census and voting registration records made it clear that Nathan Harrison was black because all official forms asked for identification by race. However, he regularly redefined his ethnicity, immersing himself in a wealth of different communities. Harrison's shared history and culture evolved over the course of his adventurous life, intersecting at times with Native Americans, Mexicans, and many other marginalized non-Protestant groups in the Old West. He also won favor with dominant white populations, both rural and urban. Harrison was not just liked by these different groups, he was an active member in their communities.

Few people in US history embody ideals of the romanticized American Dream more than Nathan Harrison. His is a story with prominent and celebratory themes of overcoming staggering obstacles, forging something from nothing, and evincing gritty perseverance. In a biography of hard-fought and hard-won progress, Harrison survived the horrors of slavery in the Antebellum South, endured the mania of the California Gold Rush, and prospered in the rugged chaos of the Old West. Each of these mini-eras resulted in incredibly short lifespans for most people, especially those who were not white. By nearly all measures, Harrison would have been expected to die young. His achievement of such Jeffersonian principles of life, liberty, and the pursuit of happiness was even more impressive when one contextualizes his accomplishments in the times in which he lived.

Nathan Harrison succeeded against nearly impossible odds and seemingly insurmountable barriers, yet his biography also brings readers face to face with certain harsh realities. The glorified ideals inherent to his American success story were compromised by the despondent manner in which he met his end. Harrison's final year and ultimate demise were shrouded in sadness. For all he achieved during his near century-long lifespan, Harrison died alone in a public hospital surrounded by neither friends nor family. Furthermore, his remains were unceremoniously placed in an unmarked grave, far from the communities and the natural mountain environment he purportedly cherished most. Harrison's life saga, though rife with impressive real and embellished accomplishments, was no fairy tale, especially at its conclusion.

Historical Archaeology

The field of historical archaeology is optimally suited to examine the complexities of Harrison's biography. It specializes in both documents (words) and artifacts (things). Few disciplines are so dualistically aligned with famed lexicographer Samuel Johnson's poetic declaration that, "Words are the daughters of the earth and . . . things are the sons of heaven" (1755: paragraph 17). Historical archaeologists find new clues by locating previously undiscovered and often buried materials through excavation. We also piece together insights from written records of the past with a careful eye on the social and political context in which they were first created. We must be versatile because archaeological science and text interpretation are very different tasks. On the one hand, it is necessary to employ relatively standardized field methodologies to pinpoint material realities of the past through long-established archaeological dimensions of space, time, and form (Spaulding 1960). On the other, we must be keenly aware of humanistic biases inherent to written records, oral accounts, and other kinds of narratives. As this discipline routinely employs disparate lines of evidence—through artifacts, primary historical documents, oral histories, secondary narratives, photographs, etc.—its practitioners need be especially attuned to contradiction, revision, and omission in widely accepted stories of the past.

Despite this diverse analytical tool kit, historical archaeologists are far from immune to the myth-making process. In fact, we occasionally contribute to biographical exaltation by privileging certain insights while dismissing others. When uncovering historical complexities and pointing to the flaws in one-dimensional truths about the past, it is imperative that historical archaeologists do not fall into a similar trap by presenting our own conclusions as exclusive, all-encompassing, or absolute. Human activities of the past were intricate performances that have been further complicated by subsequent generations of historical revisions and reconstructions, including the most current interpretations from the edge of the archaeologist's trowel (Hodder 2004). Our intention to be as accurate as possible in our methodologies and interpretations should never be conflated with insisting a singular technique and theory is sufficient or the final word on the subject. We must keep in mind Alison Wylie's observation that artifacts "do not speak for themselves" (1989: 2). On the contrary, archaeologists speak for artifacts.

Many historical archaeologists, including myself, maintain a most democratic fixation on the everyday detritus and details of the past. Old garbage, mundane bureaucratic documentation, and other ordinary materials can be used to challenge traditional one-dimensional histories that tended to privilege the elite, the white, the male, or those with some sort of inherited status. We often emphasize that corporeal demise and daily refuse are the tangible end-products of every human existence regardless of societal privilege in all of its guises. With a deferential nod to Benjamin Franklin, nothing is certain except death and garbage.

Every person who has ever written a narrative had a particular perspective that included innate biases, but these types of inevitably distorted literary lenses are not necessarily present in the garbage of the past as it rests in the ground awaiting discovery. Whereas only wealthy individuals often had access to the supplies, abilities, and circumstances to perpetuate and curate grand stories of their past, everyone produced refuse. Furthermore, few people ever had a particular agenda, especially one that considered personal legacy, when dumping their trash. Though archaeological narratives are constructions like any other story,[3] and occasionally stray far from any established notions of a factual past, they often start anonymously and posthumously with a collection of disassociated and fragmented artifacts pulled from the earth long after the demise of their original owner.

The Nathan "Nate" Harrison Historical Archaeology Project

Working on the Nathan "Nate" Harrison Historical Archaeology Project meant striving to learn everything possible about Harrison's life, legend, and legacy. Simultaneously, I wanted to disseminate these insights broadly and engage all of those who were interested in meaningful discussions about the multiethnic history of the United States in which Harrison lived. From its outset, the project united research, teaching, and community engagement. At its analytical core, the endeavor was driven by a research design with specific questions that would be best answered by archaeological fieldwork, rigorous historical studies, and multicultural perspectives. University students, many of whom were training to be professional archaeologists, executed the fieldwork as part of their undergraduate or graduate curricula. They were involved in each aspect of the field project (Figure 0.1). In addition, public history was a priority of this project, resulting in annual technical reports, a complete artifact catalog on the project website (http://nathanharrison.sdsu.edu), and extensive community outreach through presentations, open houses, and school lesson plans.

Excavations during the Nathan "Nate" Harrison Historical Archaeology Project (2004–08 and 2017–present) were the core of our research endeavor, and they were entirely dependent on archaeological field schools. Our primary classroom was the site, and in a broader sense, Palomar Mountain. In exchange for getting trained in how to dig and being included in cutting-edge research, dozens of undergraduate and graduate students lived in tents on the former Harrison property, toiled long hours at the high-elevation site, ate camp food, and shared a makeshift latrine. Over the years, many of the field-school participants would stay on with the project, engaging in further site-specific research, analysis, and other archaeological internship and volunteer roles. In addition, eight graduate students—Sarah Stroud, Matthew Tennyson, Jaime Lennox, Shelby Castells (Gunderman), Kristin Tennesen, Katherine Collins, Rachel Droessler, and Cecelia Holm—wrote Master's theses on research relating to the Harrison site.

Extensive historical research was conducted before, during, and after the excavations. At the outset of the project, the land owners gave us what was thought to be a comprehensive catalog of all of the historical records, accounts, and photographs of Harrison. Our digging

Figure 0.1a/b. Field-school students actively participated in all phases of the archaeological process, including placement of the datum (*top*) and site excavation (*bottom*). (Courtesy of the Nathan "Nate" Harrison Historical Archaeology Project.)

was not just in the dirt, as significant archival investigations turned up numerous additional materials relating directly to the life and times of the famed Palomar pioneer. Furthermore, the excitement and attention the excavations brought to the site and the intriguing subject matter inspired other community members to share their personal historical collections with us. One of the more spectacular rediscoveries included a cache of original documents that were first found in the Harrison cabin years after his passing, forgotten, but then found, scanned, and sent to us. Known as "The Cabin Collection," these materials included personal letters, receipts, and a photograph. Rediscovering the long-lost items was nothing short of thrilling. We suddenly could read the handwritten words of Harrison's stepson in a lengthy correspondence, see the face of his step-granddaughter in a faded picture, witness the racism of poll taxes through a voter-registration receipt, and follow the detailed business squabbles of everyday frontier life. Throughout our research, we continued to include new information in our quest to assemble every contemporaneous record relating to Harrison, classify them according to type and content, examine how they changed over time, trace patterns of invention, evaluate most likely scenarios, and construct multiple plausible narratives.

Community outreach and public history were an inseparable part of this project at nearly every step. Not only did many Palomar Mountain locals grant us access to their property, turn over their archival material to us, and welcome us into their homes, but they also shared important insights into the quirky history of the region and its long-time inhabitants. With unwavering ideals of inclusion, transparency, and sustainability, the Nathan "Nate" Harrison Historical Archaeology Project continues to rely on collaboration and cooperation in order to make progress towards finding ways to share Harrison's story with all.

Archaeological projects often evolve over the course of the excavations. In living and working up on Palomar Mountain each summer, witnessing the awe of first-timers at the site and surrounding environs, and engaging local residents in a research project that involved complex issues of historical identity, agency, and community, I began to develop a different and deeper appreciation for the importance of place—this particular place—in history.[4] The natural beauty, the tranquility, the isolation, the security, the community . . . these innate qualities of Palomar Mountain make it more than a simple place of residence for today's inhabitants. They hint at the profound effect it might have had on past occupants.

Harrison's time on the mountain cannot be separated from the mountain itself. After decades of nomadic travel—migrating across the country and throughout California, first as a slave and later as a laborer—Harrison arrived at Palomar. Repeated clues in the historical records suggest that it was a highly meaningful space for Harrison and one with which he deeply identified. His many years of drifting and wandering concluded at this place where he finally was able to take root and make a permanent home. Philosopher Simone Weil emphasized that rootedness in a place is "the most important and least recognized need of the human soul" (1971: 43). Furthermore, the road winding up the west side of the mountain, which has borne his name for over a century, was the only non-Indigenous route up Palomar during his lifetime. In addition, one of the area's well-established Native American trails—still actively used during Harrison's time on Palomar Mountain—also ran through his property, right by his front door. It was no exaggeration or mere poetic figure of speech to state in the late nineteenth and early twentieth centuries that nearly all Palomar Mountain roads went through Nathan Harrison. He was an intrinsic part of the land, and I believe that the land became an intrinsic part of him (Figure 0.2).

There are important differences between space and place. Whereas *space* merely designates location, *place* is imbued with a sense of meaning. Palomar Mountain was more than a space to its past inhabitants and to Nathan Harrison in particular. It transcends simple literal descriptions. Scholars can offer a wealth of emotionless details about the area. Geographers can tell you Palomar Mountain rises northeast of San Diego at 33 degrees, 21 minutes, 22.82 seconds north by 116 degrees, 51 minutes, 56.34 seconds west. Prehistoric archaeologists can report

Figure 0.2. This undated photograph of Nathan Harrison at his Palomar Mountain cabin captured the dramatic canyon view and the rise of Boucher Hill to the east. Look closely: he is holding a puppy. (Courtesy of the Nathan "Nate" Harrison Historical Archaeology Project, Kirby Collection.)

that it has been occupied by local Native American groups for many thousands of years as bedrock mortars, created gradually over millennia, still cover much of the landscape. Linguists can explain that the Indigenous population first knew this place as "Paauw," Spanish explorers labeled it "Palomar Mountain,"[5] and American settlers renamed it "Smith Mountain."[6] Furthermore, geologists will insist Palomar Mountain never be called "Mount Palomar" because it is not a peak; rather, it is part of a range (the In-Ko-Pah Mountains) with a rolling plateau extending twenty-five miles along the northern boundary of San Diego County (Beckler 1958: 6). These facts, no matter how interesting or informative, fail to get at the far more profound question of what the mountain signified and continues to symbolize for its many residents.

The stories Palomar Mountain inhabitants tell are far different from such sterile academic descriptions; they are far more deeply connected to the land and get at the environmental relationship between human and earth. For example, the first people of Palomar—the Luiseño Indians—refer to the mountain as "Paauw." It is a blend of the words "mother" and "mountain." For many Luiseño, Palomar Mountain is a sacred place, where Paauw rose above a flooded earth and saved her children, the Luiseño. Paauw maintains great prominence in traditional Indigenous stories.

Early US American pioneers also expressed tales of reverence for Palomar Mountain. Regional historian Ed Davis avowed of local settler Theodore Bailey:

> This mountain [Palomar] meant more to him than so much cattle range and so much timber. The soul of the mountain spoke to him in the crooning of the pines, the murmuring brooks, the rustling leaves, the massive oaks, the fragrant flowers, the whistle of the mountain quail, the coo of the wild pigeon, the coughing squirrels, all in a language he loved and understood. (1938: no page numbers)

These descriptions go beyond lifeless portraits of space and shed light on the meaning of place. This is a paramount issue for the Nathan "Nate" Harrison Historical Archaeology Project to address. Specifically, what did it mean for Harrison to call this land home? Relatedly, when did he become a *permanent* resident, one who was seen as inseparable from these environs? Furthermore, how did he tie his identity directly to Palomar Mountain and to the diverse local communities that maintained a special connection with the immediate terrain? These were just some of the intricate inquiries that the study of Harrison's life and legend elicited.

A Brief Overview of Theory in Historical Archaeology

I stated earlier that the field of historical archaeology was particularly well-suited to analyze Nathan Harrison's intricate biography. In parallel fashion, I believe that this project—due to the dynamic intersection of rampant myth-making, fluid identity politics, and rigorous archaeological science—has the potential to influence how scholars at different sites interpret the past. Over the past eighteen years, careful examination of all things relating to Harrison gradually drew me toward ideas that allowed for multiple perspectives and disparate theories. Even though historical archaeologists, past and present, are far from uniform in thought or practice, I found myself especially receptive to envisioning how certain profoundly different interpretations could coexist. I gravitated away from prizing singular theories that necessitated isolating a unique correct explanation at the expense of all others. As a result, this book is both my statement on the historical archaeology of Nathan Harrison and a case for more inclusive ideas about how we think about the human past. However, before proceeding with Harrison's story and the different interpretations I propose, some context is needed for past and current anthropological theories in historical archaeology.

Simply stated, theory is used in anthropology to frame interpretations in broader context and to explain why humans act the way we do. Historical archaeology (study of recent past peoples, often those with some sort of associated documentation) is a subset of archaeology (study of past peoples), which is itself a subfield of anthropology (study of people). As a result, anthropological theory is often employed by historical archaeologists to interpret people, behaviors, and events of the recent past, no matter how seemingly bizarre, unique, or disconnected they may seem. Over time, scholarly theories have tended to come and go, eventually replaced by a newer approach; each has proved to be susceptible to waves of curious initial engagement, widespread popularity, and later critical dismissal.

When early historical archaeologists from the late 1800s and early to middle 1900s dug and analyzed sites, they often constructed descriptive chronologies that defined and classified people of the past by the artifacts found at their sites. This "Humanistic Historical Archaeology" focused on questions of who, what, where, and when; the answers were then used to create classifications of past cultures, often with a singular label and associated list of traits. This approach was also called "particularistic" because it focused so closely on the unique (or highly particular) circumstances that occurred at an individual site or complex of sites. Like anthropologist Franz Boas's theory of Historical Particularism, it did not necessarily seek comparisons with other cultures or investigate change over time. Sites already established as historically important, like Jamestown, Virginia,[7] the Miles Standish House in Plymouth, Massachusetts,[8] and President Abraham Lincoln's house in Springfield, Illinois, were dug by archaeologists funded by antiquarian, preservation, public works, and touristic cultural-heritage sources. These sites were already famous due to existing historical accounts and lore; the excavations served primarily to expand insight into the exalted landmarks. History, and more specifically historians, had already set the narrative process in motion long before the first trowel hit the ground as the sites were predetermined to be archaeologically important because they were historically famous, instead of being famous because they were archaeologically important (on the basis of what was excavated). The primacy of the historical record led some of the field's leading practitioners to relegate archaeology to secondary and tangential status. J. C. Harrington, for whom the Society of Historical Archaeology's lifetime achievement award is named, called historical archaeology "an auxiliary science to American history" (1955: 1121). Ivor Noël Hume took it a step further and insisted archaeology "was a handmaiden to history" (1964: 224). This Culture History approach emphasized that archaeology's purpose was merely to augment history.[9]

Scientific revolutions overtook many scholarly fields in the 1960s and '70s, and archaeology did not escape this intellectual firestorm. Dissatisfied with the subjectivity inherent to a humanistic approach, advocates of a more scientific historical archaeology toiled to construct a theoretical framework based on objectivity, analytical rigor, and scientifically controlled comparison. It was highly positivistic, focusing on what could be observed, tested, and later, predicted. This new approach[10] attempted to move beyond descriptive questions to arrive at a more robust research issue of explaining human processes[11] of the past. It applied deductive reasoning to formulate laws of human behavior. Seeking to elucidate nuanced ways of life in place of producing highly particularistic histories, the query of "how" transcended "who," "what," "when," and "where." This approach was strikingly different as were the decisions on which groups to study. Many historical archaeologists began to take interest in past peoples who did not appear in the written records, including non-elite, nonwhite, nonliterate, nonmale groups for whom archaeology might have been one of the only empirical voices to speak their often lost and overlooked history. Instead of reinforcing or substantiating historical facts, scientific historical archaeologists developed narratives based in material remains (empirical data) and saw historical accounts as subjective and secondary. As a result, archaeology was no longer presented as peripheral, secondary, tangential, or auxiliary to history. In fact, historical archaeologists such as Stanley South explicitly exalted archaeological analyses over related historical studies (1977: 12).

Cognitive historical archaeologists shifted intellectual discussions in the 1970s and '80s from the "how" to the "why," insisting that differences in material culture over time were the results of changing past mindsets. Rather than focusing on external processes, they started in the minds of historical peoples — specifically in binary mental structures that are a unique trait of the human brain — and developed elaborate grammars establishing time-sensitive cultural norms across all aspects of society. Drawing heavily on the social science theories of Structuralism and Symbolism, these historical archaeologists looked for material parallels between people in a given culture, positing broad explanations for cultural transformations independent of established general histories or universalistic laws of human behavior.[12] The meaning of artifacts was linked to how they were cognitively conceived as opposed to what they were and how they were used. Though presented as a compromise between humanistic and scientific historical archaeologies of the time — deemed "Scientific Humanism and Humanistic Science" (Deetz 1983) — it soon became clear this was an entirely different theoretical framework as opposed to a paradigmatic midpoint or compromise.

Other historical archaeologists also searched for explanations of "why" that were not necessarily tied to mental structures. For example, in the late 1970s, '80s, and '90s, various historical archaeologists began to employ Marxist historical materialism in their work, prioritizing discussions of class over culture when studying and interpreting actions, events, and items of the past (Leone 1977, 1982; M. Johnson 1995; Mullins 1999). Marxist thought brought attention to differences in class position into historical archaeology, distancing itself from previous theories that treated highly hegemonic cultures as cohesive wholes. It emphasized the agency of individuals who created a world on their own terms and reacted to the spread of capitalism and its concurrent issues of inequity, exploitation, and commodification.[13] Historical materialists also often highlighted repeating cycles of change, noting recurring themes of the human condition (Cannon 1989). Marxists were far from alone in breaking down holistic concepts of culture and recognizing meaningful internal divisions. Other archaeologists, regardless of theoretical orientation, began to focus on gender, ethnicity, age, religion, and other important intracultural differences (Deagan 1983). These distinctions often reflected tensions related to power discrepancies and struggles among diverse historical groups.

During the same time, feminist archaeologists both examined new issues and offered a significant challenge to archaeology's scientific approach. These scholars investigated a variety of qualitatively different topics, such as social constructions of gender, parenting and childhood issues, and gender inequity in studies of the past (Conkey and Spector 1984; Little 1994; Beaudry 2006; Wilkie 2014). In addition, they effectively challenged the singularity and exclusivity of many previously established archaeological theories. Two scholars in particular, Margaret Conkey and Joan Gero, though not historical archaeologists, exposed often unaddressed agendas in science and debunked the practice of presenting archaeological conclusions as absolutely correct or final (Conkey and Gero 1991).[14] They demonstrated that feminist thought in archaeology was not just about gender. It questioned purportedly value-free objective archaeological science and the premise that the past was singular (Conkey and Gero 1997; Gero 2015: 12).

Likewise, the late 1980s, '90s, and early 2000s saw historical archaeologists draw on Ian Hodder's postprocessual ideas concerning contextualized and interpretive archaeology (Hodder 1985, 1986). These practitioners focused on studies of identity, grounding their investigations in how distinct groups negotiated daily life in volatile historical and cultural contexts. They also focused on the experience of individuals, expounding on the role and importance of personal agency in history, often on a small scale (A. Praetzellis and M. Praetzellis 2001). A highly interpretive and contextualized historical archaeology resulted. Scholars such as Mary Beaudry, Adrian and Mary Praetzellis, Laurie Wilkie, and Julia King used multiple perspectives and disparate lines of evidence to show how archaeological insights were empirically, yet subjectively, constructed as opposed to objectively discovered, observed, or extracted (Beaudry 1996; M. Praetzellis and A. Praetzellis 2004; King 2012; Wilkie 2014: 60). These constructions fit multifarious archaeological insights into an interpretive whole.

Interpretive historical archaeologists were often highly reflexive and engaged deconstructionist thought. Like many contemporary critical theorists, these scholars were adept at acknowledging their own agendas and biases as well as pinpointing those of their peers, archaeological predecessors, and the writers of the historical records relevant to the sites under study. They employed multiple perspectives of past events and were especially successful at exposing and dismantling dominant assumptions of marginalized groups. Although the specific theory of "Critical Historical Archaeology" was deeply rooted in Marxism (Leone 2010),[15] contextual and interpretive approaches to historical archaeology employed many of the same "critical" approaches. Consequently, current critical, contextual, and interpretive historical archaeologies remain highly varied. Many ongoing practitioners prioritize a highly contextualized approach, some emphasize alternative narratives, and others focus on the feminist-identified fallacy of objectivity (Trigger 2006: 455–71).

To complicate matters further, the early 2000s has also witnessed controversial claims that the field has experienced "the death of archaeological theory" (Bintliff 2011; Pearce 2011; J. Thomas 2015a). Scholars have taken many figurative suspects into custody for the murder of theory. Some blame technological advances, some eye the political agendas of individual practitioners, and others depict a "post-ideological 21st century" of practicing nontheoretical archaeologists (J. Thomas 2015b: 14). When it comes to theory in today's historical archaeology, there is little consensus. As a result, it is futile to suggest a singular theoretical label for the field, be it interpretive, critical, or even nonexistent (atheoretical). Rather than lament this chaos, Charles Orser explained that it is precisely the fact that historical archaeology is "not a conceptually unified field of inquiry" that makes it so "contentious and alive" (2001: 625–26). Likewise, Julia King optimistically observed that, "interpretive diversity presents exciting opportunities for accessing an ultimately inaccessible past and, in so doing, revealing avenues of inquiry that may have previously gone unnoticed or unexplored" (2012: 11).

Simply put, theory in historical archaeology went from descriptions of what happened, to explanations of how it happened, to appreciations of why it happened. We are now coming out of a period in which every previously established theoretical construct has been contextualized, picked apart, and deconstructed. Given the name of one of the latest paradigms (Critical Theory), it should come as no surprise that critical theorists were so thorough in their critique of all theories. This process included not only the archaeological literature in question but the scholars themselves. Deconstructionist thought has expanded significantly in academic disciplines across early twenty-first-century universities; seemingly no theory has gone unscathed under the postmodern lens.

Rather than dwell on the shortcomings of our collective predecessors, I propose an approach that engages the contributions of each, be they humanistic, scientific, cognitive, materialist, feminist, interpretive, contextual, critical, or other. At various times, humans of the past were functional, rational, symbolic, idiosyncratic, or contrarian. As a result, I am drawn to ideas that allow for this versatility and offer a more complete picture of human experiences, especially through multiple perspectives. Likewise, we all know people who have a wealth of cultural, historical, and anecdotal information (humanists); who can eliminate distractions, see intricate patterns, pinpoint cause-and-effect relationships, and successfully predict coming actions (scientists); who can deduce uncanny insights into the mindsets of others (cognitivists); who can identify inequity and oppression even when well-cloaked (materialists); who appreciate the diversity of experience and the fluidity of perspective and are not frozen by interpretive ambiguity (feminists); who are sensitive to individual motivations even in group settings (agency specialists); and who emphasize the futility of reducing complex human systems, events, and actions to general categories, causes, or characteristics (postmodernists). Let us invite them all to our analytical party and embrace Laurie Wilkie's declaration that "no one set of theory can contain us" (2014: 375).

Toward an Orthogonal Historical Archaeology

I am not the first person to call for pluralistic approaches to archaeological theory.[16] Famed archaeologist J. O. Brew wrote in the 1940s on the dangers of classifying artifacts in a singular manner. In a time when his peers often defined and charted culture groups as monolithic blocks that were fixed by conceptions of a static artifact type, Brew demanded additional classificatory systems based on new research questions. He declared:

> We need more rather than fewer classifications, different classifications, always new classifications, to meet new needs. We must not be satisfied with a single classification of a group of artifacts or of a cultural development, for in that way lies dogma and defeat. (1946: 65)

While many archaeologists are familiar with Brew's bold statements and embrace the importance of new and innovative classifications, his insistence on inclusion of *existing* classifications has been often overlooked. It is worth emphasizing that Brew wanted more, not just new.[17]

We can draw parallels between new analytical questions that inspire new classificatory criteria and those that provoke new theories explaining the human experience. Brew's ageless call for continual growth in a classificatory method is extended here as a plea for the development of new theories for historical archaeology that are equally innovative and inclusive of past ideas. Likewise, archaeologist Alison Wylie emphasized the need for scholars to tack back and forth between polarized scientific and humanistic models when constructing their interpretations (1989).

I believe that now is an optimal time to employ new anthropological theories governed by different themes and explanations while still evaluating and incorporating important insights from past theories. Anthropologist Bruce M. Knauft recently suggested that this inclusive move is already starting to occur. In a 2006 article, he noted that many scholars have increasingly given up grand theoretical debates—many of which were mutually exclusive and thus highly polarizing in nature—and "now weave together approaches and perspectives from a toolbox of possibilities" (407). Accordingly, Alison Bell recently transcended a dualistic debate in historical archaeology regarding Vindicationist and Diasporic perspectives by insisting on inclusion of both approaches (2008). Knauft celebrates emergent anthropology as "mosaics of part-theoretical assertion, part-subjective evocation, part-ethnographic and historical exposition, and part-activist voicing" (2006: 411). I am heartened by Knauft's observations and Bell's approach, yet I propose the field take it a step further. It is not enough to have access to a diverse analytical toolbox, each of the tools needs to be employed purposefully.

The current moment of paradigmatic chaos and deconstructionist anti-theory creates an opportunity to apply a deliberately inclusive type of omni-theory, one that brings together all established and relevant models of the human experience on the same archaeological data set and historical records. I call this approach "orthogonal" (pronounced "awr-**thog**-uh-nl") though I acknowledge at the outset that some may be tempted to dismiss this as merely a new title for an already existing practice.[18] In fact, the term is not new at all and has already come to mean different things among distinct disciplines, but each involves an act that broadens, deepens, or expands.[19] In meditative philosophy, orthogonal thought connotes a mental spaciousness that results from unfolding one's mind to contemplate greater breadth and depth of meaning (Kabat-Zinn 2012: 72). Across disciplines, the word orthogonal generally refers to a deliberate movement for additional perspectives that is expansive yet still measurable from its origin.

Applying this approach to historical archaeology involves, but is not burdened by, perspectives from each of the field's earlier prominent theories. It starts with attention to site-specific historical descriptions and assemblage-specific material classifications that are humanistic and particularistic. However, there is no insistence on a singular story, typology, or cultural pattern. It does use rigorous, repeatable, and scientific methodologies based on empirical realities in the ground and in the associated historical documentation. Instead of attempting to generate universal behavioral laws and assuming objectivity, the interpretations of past human acts are culturally and historically contextualized, as are the analytical frameworks of the archaeologists. In addition, this approach appreciates how the collective mindsets of groups of past people can be a driving force in organizing and participating in the world. While acknowledging that individuals often carried formative blueprints in their minds for mediating everyday life, this omni-theory is also closely attuned to the role of individual agency, reflexivity, and resistance and the remarkable diversity of expression. Likewise, orthogonal perspectives employ analytical techniques sensitive to marginalized populations within larger cultures and detail exploitative processes when empirically based, but do not start with the assumption of material expressions of inequity at all sites. Furthermore, critical theory is used to examine all narratives in context, be they historical, archaeological, or analytical, in an effort to be thoroughly transparent. It also pays close attention to issues of identity creation, maintenance, and negotiation. Embracing orthogonal thought means not being defined by a single theory, which enables historical archaeologists to acknowledge the value of a particular paradigm and then move on, instead of dwelling in it. That is the mindful spaciousness of this approach: the ability to appreciate something fully and in a most open-minded manner, which can facilitate the process of transcending it.

When examining Harrison's life and legacies, the approach described here opens the interpretive floodgates to a deluge of different and often cacophonous narratives. Rather than assess them along a single measure of plausibility and seek to eliminate all except the seemingly truest explanation, I endeavor to accept and embrace the multiplicity of perspectives. In addition, although an evaluation process is inevitable, it can be applied deliberately using what I call the saturation process. It is a sequence of immersion in as many viable interpretive potentialities as possible. This inundation of multiple perspectives, multiple explanations, and multiple experiences greatly resembles the performance, reception, and interactive quality of the human past itself. It embraces complexity instead of automatically seeking to reduce, order, and simplify it. In his iconic novel, *If on a Winter's Night a Traveler*, Italo Calvino captured the literary inundation that transforms a mass of seemingly rival explanations into an orthogonal presentation of experience. He wrote directly to his audience:

> What I want is for you to feel, around the story, a saturation of other stories that I could tell and maybe will tell or who knows may already have told on some other occasion, a space full of stories that perhaps is simply my lifetime, where you can move in all directions, as in space, always finding stories that cannot be told until other stories are told first, and so,

setting out from any moment or place, you encounter always the same density of material to be told. (1981: 105)

Calvino's saturation of narratives transcends a gravitation toward singular stories with inherently isolated and privileged truths. It enables his audience to embrace multiplicity without being overwhelmed by the din of different narratives.[20] In fact, the din becomes the melody, or at least melodic. The work presented here emulates Calvino's approach but endeavors to balance narrative inundation with archaeological rigor.

Documentary Evidence, Contextualized Histories, and Seriations

History is a record of past events and times. Traditional chronological accounts are linear, customarily starting with births and ending with deaths. Einsteinian relativity and *Terminator* movies aside, they correspond with the assumed steady forward movement and singularity of the current timeline. Even in this postmodern age of seemingly omnipresent relativity, there still is an expectation of basic historical facts about a given subject matter. We may anticipate great debates about the "how" and "why" of history, but the opening statements about the "who," "what," "when," and "where" of our primary topic are typically straightforward and easily answered with direct and definitive evidence.

Despite the abundance of existing information about Nathan Harrison, there is great confusion. There is extensive historical documentation about him, with well over one hundred records and accounts of his life (Mallios et al. 2017a; Mallios et al. 2018). In addition, there are thirty-one different historical photographs of Harrison (Mallios et al. 2017b). As a result, it would seem as though we have great insight into his story. For example, numerous official documents definitively state that Harrison was born in 1833. In scrutinizing all of the evidence, however, we see other seemingly reliable sources affirm 1831 as his date of birth. There is also a good chance he was born sometime in the late 1820s . . . or perhaps the early '20s. In fact, it is not entirely possible to rule out the late 1810s. Likewise, many records make it clear that Harrison was a native of Kentucky. Others list Virginia as his home state. There is evidence he was born in either Missouri or Mississippi as well . . . or perhaps Tennessee. It is even difficult to be definitive about his very name. San Diego County's Nathan Harrison was listed in the historical records under a variety of aliases, including Nat, Nate, Nath,

Nathan, and Nathaniel Haris, Harris, Harrisen, and Harrison. We archaeologists base most of our insights on established dimensions of space, time, and form, and yet it is impossible to be certain of Harrison's state of origin (inaugural space), date of birth (inaugural time), or given name (inaugural titular form). As a result, there is no simple empirical starting point for our study. With such rampant inconsistencies about the most basic of historical facts, one cannot help but ask: how can there simultaneously be so much assertive historical clamor about Nathan Harrison's life and so little verifiable information or agreement?

The extensive documentary evidence concerning Nathan Harrison falls into two nonexclusive categories: primary and secondary sources. Primary sources are experienced; they were created contemporaneously and included such items as governmental records (historical censuses, registers, certificates, receipts, maps, and other official forms) and newspaper clippings, letters, photographs, primary oral histories, and written accounts from individuals who personally knew Harrison and had firsthand interaction with him.[21] Secondary sources are interpretive; their information came from a distance, often either second-hand or after-the-fact and traditionally consisted of oral histories and written accounts from individuals who knew of Harrison but did not have direct dealings with him.[22]

Primary sources are often privileged over secondary sources because of their immediacy and interactivity with the subject in question, but both types of sources have inherent individual biases by the author and reflect broader cultural perspectives of the era. Historical inaccuracies abound in the stories of Nathan Harrison and take many forms. Some were clerical errors, some were sympathetic reflections by members of the tight-knit mountain community, and some were deliberate historical revisions for political gain.

Historiography is more nuanced than history; it is contextualized history. Historiography is a narrative presentation of multiple histories that includes a critical examination and evaluation of primary and secondary sources. This process employs significant scholarly attention to differing agendas, biases, and perspectives. The resultant narrative flows back and forth between straightforward chronicles of the past and discussions of the historical, cultural, and individualistic contexts of the source material. There are many Nathan Harrison stories, but an overwhelming majority of them are not contextualized. In essence, this history is in dire need of historiographic insight.

Due to the seemingly mercurial nature of the many existing biographies, those of us working on the archival aspects of the Nathan "Nate" Harrison Historical Archaeology Project had to embrace a wealth of perspectives and allow for multiple plausible alternatives. We employed fluidity and flexibility in reconstructing the past, always ready to appreciate complexities and nuances of differing and often evolving perspectives. We were aided by experts in many different and nontraditional academic disciplines. For example, conflict resolution specialist Marguerite Yourcenar provided insight as to how one turns contradiction into reconciliation. She offered a broad overview, which included the following detailed directions:

> The rules of the game: learn everything, read everything, inquire into everything . . . when two texts, or two assertions, or perhaps two ideas, are in contradiction, be ready to reconcile them rather than cancel one by the other; regard them as two different facets, or two successive stages of the same reality, a reality convincingly human just because it is complex. (Quoted in Cloke and Goldsmith 2000: 1)

We endeavored to apply these goals and ideas of narrative intersection and union to apparent historical discrepancies. For example, when one reliable source claimed Harrison never married and another well-informed narrative insisted he was a "squaw man" (married to a woman of Indigenous descent), both perspectives could be incorporated in multiple empirically-based yet nonexclusive manners (Asher c. 1938: no page numbers). As will be detailed in the coming chapters, perhaps Harrison had been married, but it was not necessarily a traditional Western union of which all in the area would know, acknowledge, or publicize; or perhaps he chose to keep his nuptials from some audiences. The lack of documentary evidence of the marriage in the form of a certificate from a church (or other official institution) might be attributable to the informality of the union, the fact that all Pala Indian Reservation records from 1886–92 were destroyed in a fire, or some other factor. Regardless of our self-professed dedication to narrative inclusion, glaring contradictions—those clearly at odds with other accounts—had to be evaluated on the basis of the best evidence.[23] Harrison could only be born in one year, be a native of one particular southern state, and first arrive at Palomar Mountain at one particular time.

Harrison's status as a former slave complicated the process of evaluating and assembling competing narratives. Even though he was not enslaved during his time on Palomar Mountain, Harrison had survived the institution that treated people as property and interacted out west with many individuals who had owned slaves. Disparate views of slavery and former slaves abounded in the region, especially considering the fundamental question of whether enslaved individuals were people or property. Awareness of strikingly different viewpoints on such a cornerstone issue required paying additional attention to the racist rationalizations and biases of those who defended and identified with slaveholders and constantly considering how enslaved people asserted their humanity in various ways.

While attention was now paid to the historical and cultural context of each source, the process was further complicated by the ways in which the content in these documentary accounts changed over time. Fortunately, archaeologists are especially skilled at noting how things change over time, so much so that we even created our own word for the study of materials in a sequence: "seriation."[24] Traditionally, seriations are employed to determine chronology at a site; for example, types of stone tools—based on their relative frequency and gradual changes in style—can be placed in order to show which areas were occupied earliest, latest, and in between.[25] They have been used with great success on a wide variety of archaeological material culture from strikingly different eras, including famous studies on ancient Egyptian pottery vessels and relatively recent colonial gravestones in New England (Petrie 1899; Deetz and Dethlefsen 1965). About a decade ago, I started employing this archaeological technique on the historical records themselves (Mallios 2007). These nontraditional seriations of past written accounts treated the documents as artifacts in order to examine how they changed over time. Simply put, these seriations allowed us to observe how stories evolved. It was not as much historical archaeology as it was archaeological history.

Archaeological seriations are rigorous tools for showing how items of the past changed. If the selection process of traits for these items is explicit, transparent, and justifiable, then the resultant pattern pinpoints meaningful and precise transformations.[26] Although seriations can be especially effective at demonstrating how things evolve, they do not answer the much more difficult question of why these particular things were altered. To answer the question of "why" requires the process of interpretation, which requires an entirely different set of analytical tools. In the words of Erwin Chargaff, the famed biochemist who led the discovery of the double helix structure of DNA, "Science is wonderfully equipped to answer the question 'How?' but it gets terribly confused when you ask the question 'Why?'" (1977: 8). Likewise, formulating explanations as to why social phenomena changed in such a peculiar manner can benefit greatly from an approach that transcends science by employing multiple perspectives, measures, and scales. There can be multiple valid explanations for why stories changed even if the transformation appears singular in nature.

One of the analytical benefits of having so many narratives told of Harrison in the century since his passing is the remarkably detailed resolution of how these tales changed over time. There are multiple accounts from nearly every decade, and numerous narratives contain rich descriptions of his life and legend.[27] Temporal patterns, although not necessarily evident when reading a single narrative, become clear when viewing all of the accounts in their entirety. It was in this dual approach of discerning macro-scale assemblage-wide historical patterns and scrutinizing micro-scale individualized historiographic insights that we sought to understand and appreciate the histories of Nathan Harrison.

The Evolution of This Project

When I first set out to find the Harrison site, I was met with skepticism. During my initial years in San Diego (2001–03), I heard comments such as: "There already is an article on blacks in San Diego," "African Americans did not impact San Diego history," and "you really should just focus on the missions; they were first." In addition, I witnessed how San Diego's past was regularly told and taught as a series of four culturally monolithic historical periods—California Indian (pre-1769), Spanish (1769–1820), Mexican (1820–46), and American (1846–present)—and capped by Kevin Starr's dismissive claim that, "From a historian's point of view, nothing much happened in San Diego before the Second World War" (Reid 2003: 6). These factors pushed me to investigate the context behind them and helped me present a much more comprehensive study into the life and legacies of Nathan Harrison, especially in terms of multicultural perspectives on the Gold Rush, the Old West, and the emergence of Modern America.[28]

While the past half-century has produced important archaeological research on slave experiences at sites in the Antebellum South, far less attention has been given to analyzing the lives of African Americans after emancipation. Recent work at places like Annapolis, Maryland (Mullins 1999); New Philadelphia, Illinois (Fennell 2011); the Harriet Tubman home in Auburn, New York (Armstrong 2011); and Boston Saloon in Nevada (Dixon 2011) has made important contributions in presenting post-emancipation African American life as "more than a history of victimization" (Cobb 2011: xii). These current scholars and others have blended discussions of race and racialization with other prominent issues of the time period, including Reconstruction, migration, and industrialism. Despite this progress across the US, little work has been undertaken on these sorts of sites in California (M. Praetzellis and A. Praetzellis 1992, 2004; Carrico et al. 2004).

As I started writing this book, I wanted to create a simple text about Nathan Harrison. I failed in that endeavor. In my defense, little about Harrison's life and legend is straightforward. I abandoned my initial goal of simplicity, and instead, now hope to have written with clarity about a most complex topic, allowing for exploration of the subject matter's most intricate nuances. Yes, this book meanders; it includes forays into everything from landmark Supreme Court cases to *Alice in Wonderland* symbology to individual vials peddled by scheming snake-oil salesmen. However, it is united on a distinct theme of inquiry: how did Nathan Harrison achieve acceptance from both his contemporaries as well as subsequent generations of people following his death? He experienced a remarkably full and widely embraced life, and once gone, he evolved from person to myth to legend.

Nathan Harrison's extraordinary existence was defined not by privilege, inheritance, or providence, but by the journey to liberation and expression of his ultimate acceptance by many different groups. He succeeded where many others failed. Close historical, anthropological, and archaeological examinations of his particular survival strategy revealed an odd mix of interpersonal relationships, self-deprecating performances, and socioeconomic opportunism through strategic gift-giving. Throughout this book, different lines of evidence repeatedly emphasize Harrison's ability to gain support from disparate communities, tailor his identity for distinct audiences, and acquire acclaim through purported generosity. Harrison moved forward under a guise of backwardness; he befriended the disenfranchised, tactically played the fool, and publicly gave away wealth. In doing so, he managed to make great social strides without ever appearing presumptuous.

This text includes three chapters: the first concerns the history of Nathan Harrison, the second focuses on the many myths surrounding his life story, and the third centers on what was learned through archaeological excavations at his former Palomar Mountain home. Most readers would expect the history chapter of the book to consist of truths, the myth-making chapter to be full of falsities, and the archaeology chapter to be the final and most empirical word on Harrison's life, legend, and legacy. Contrary to these expectations, many pages in the history chapter are spent on fallacious accounts, the discussion of myth-making reveals a great many truths about the creators and tellers of the fictions (including Harrison himself), and the archaeology chapter evokes as many questions as it answers. As tempting as it is to privilege all things archaeological—would anyone dare contradict Franz Boas's alleged proclamation that, "Man never lies to his garbage heap"?—it is essential to contextualize the interpretation of material remains as yet another narrative. Despite purportedly rigid disciplinary boundaries, I propose that the processes of engaging in history, anthropology, and archaeology are each, in the end, acts of story-telling (Isaac 1993). This book is about stories and more stories. Rather than lament any inconsistencies among them, I eagerly present them all as part of the saturation process that is necessary to amass appreciation for the many perspectives, interpretations, and realities of Nathan Harrison.

Notes

1. The N-word is quoted over fifty times in this book. Although this racial epithet is highly offensive and one of the most provocative words in twenty-first-century American speech, it is also an integral part of Nathan Harrison's story. Nearly every early narrative includes the word, and even the title of the county road that bore his name was officially labeled "N——r Nate Grade" until 1955. Quite frankly, the N-word is too important to discussions of the life and times of Nathan Harrison to ignore or avoid. Out of respect for modern-day sentiments, the word is always placed in quotes and veiled with interior dashes even though none of the historical sources treated the word in this fashion.
2. The N-word was not as inflammatory in the late nineteenth century as it is today, but even then it was often used and interpreted in a charged and disempowering manner.
3. Archaeological data might be immune to the biases of written documentary evidence, but it does suffer from its own biases, starting with what fails to preserve in the ground. Furthermore, the interpretations of archaeologists are rife with agenda, perspective, and bias.
4. There is something about uninterrupted weeks of hearing mountain critters scurry by your head in the middle of the night as you sleep in a tent, watching the sun rise over the cloud-covered valley below as if the mountain floated on air, roasting dinner over an open fire as the nighttime temperature suddenly plummets, and avoiding poison oak, rattlesnakes, and other maladies when looking for a safe place to do your business that draws one closer to what certain aspects of daily life might have been like for people of the past.
5. In Spanish, "paloma" translates to female pigeon, a common site in the area during the nineteenth century. "Palomar" is a common reference to "the place of the pigeons" or to a dovecote, a structure for housing domestic pigeons. An 1846 Mexican land grant was the first written account of the name "Palomar."
6. This short-lived name change occurred after the 1868 murder of pioneer Joseph Smith; locals successfully petitioned to change the name back to "Palomar" in 1901 (Wood 1937: no page numbers).

7. Jamestown, and more specifically "1607 James Fort," was the first permanent English settlement in the Americas.
8. Captain Myles Standish was one of the original *Mayflower* pilgrims, a leading English settler, and the first commander of the Plymouth Colony militia.
9. The Culture History approach, also called the "Classificatory-Historical Period" in American Archaeology, was a dominant theory in all of archaeology during much of the first half of the twentieth century (Willey and Sabloff 1971: 88–130).
10. The "New Archaeology" and its allegiance to a more scientific approach was paralleled in many other intellectual disciplines, even those that would traditionally be seen as more humanistic, like literary theory and its "New Criticism" (Ransom 1941).
11. This emphasis on "process" led to the new theory to be labeled as "Processual Archaeology," used interchangeably with the "New Archaeology."
12. Structuralists argued that these changes often shifted from one abstract extreme to the other, transforming conceptually from public to private, natural to artificial, asymmetrical to symmetrical, etc. (Deetz 1977; Glassie 1971, 1975).
13. Whereas choice merely reflects the decision-making process of individuals, the term agency implies "the struggle from freedom of action within systems of inequality not of their making" (Orser 2007: 53; Silliman 2005: 281).
14. Feminist thought significantly influenced archaeologist Ian Hodder's ideas regarding deconstructionism and contextual archaeology; he cited Conkey's work in his seminal 1985 article, "Postprocessual Archaeology."
15. Critical Theory's reflexivity centers on exposing political and economic inequity and exploitation.
16. Deetz's 1983 plea for paradigmatic pluralism was, in fact, a case for Structuralism. Instead of finding common ground between particularistic approaches and the New Archaeology, he developed a cognitive theory for Historical Archaeology that was distinctively different and shared little with the other theories (Deetz 1983).
17. In my mind, new ideas will always have a lure that engages scholars and students; the real challenge is appreciating past insights and contributions while being impressed by never-before heard theories.
18. There is obvious overlap between contextual archaeology and my calls for an orthogonal archaeology as both draw on insight from contextual meanings of artifacts and constantly moving hermeneutic circles of interpretation (Hodder 1986: 150–53). However, I see orthogonal thought as less reliant on deconstructing the work of others, and more drawn to the inclusion of past theories and the cumulative nature of archaeological research. Furthermore, my emphasis on a union of different paradigms echoes Conkey and Gero's observation that "feminist practice . . . might coordinate multiple strategies and objectives of different co-investigators into the research of nonrenewable archaeological resources (1997: 429). Even my coming invocation of Italo Calvino's story saturation could be framed as the "thick description" of cultural anthropologist Clifford Geertz (1979).

19. In the sciences, orthogonality denotes the creation of right angles from a single point, vector, or function. The etymology of the word orthogonal comes from "ortho" (meaning rectangularly straight) and "gony" (meaning knee); together the terms relate to the right angle formed by a bent knee. The literal meaning ties to exact 90-degree rotations. In mathematics, it refers to a process of rotation that creates right angles and results in perpendicularity. This rotation produces in a pair of vectors having a defined scalar product equal to zero or a pair of functions having a defined product equal to zero. Likewise, in general science, orthogonal has been expanded to describe any matrix composed of right angles. However, psychologists have come to use the phrase "orthogonal contrasts" in reference to a group characteristic that does not overlap with and is totally unrelated to another. Likewise, in colloquial speech the term has become synonymous with "irrelevant to," especially in reference to expanding into highly tangential and off-topic material. I find it ironic that a scientific term that originally referred to a strictly controlled 90-degree rotation would later be used to describe uncontrolled mental meandering.

20. This saturation of stories is an ongoing and gradual process. Since second readings of a given tale inevitably lend additional insight, it can seem endless. Nevertheless, once all current narratives are assembled, read, and appreciated in context, it is possible—in Calvino's terms—to set out from any moment or place and encounter the same density of historical and biographical material. Like the satisfaction of binge-watching an entire television show series after being piqued, puzzled, and perplexed by a few out-of-sequence episodes, the saturation from an orthogonal approach allows us to see the current totality of a storyline. While numerous questions remain regarding certain characters, plot developments, and future directions, these queries are no longer based on the partial sampling of the performance.

21. These sources included firsthand accounts by Harrison acquaintances Robert Asher (Asher c. 1938), Edward Davis (Davis 1932, 1938), Abel Davis (Davis c. 1955), Bessy Ormsby Helsel (Day 1981a), Max Peters (Day 1981b; Ryan 1964h), Jim Wood (Day 1981c), Chris Forbes (Day and Melvin 1981), Winbert Fink (W. C. Fink c. 1931), Adalind Bailey (Hastings 1959a), Louis Salmons (Hastings 1959b; Ryan 1964b), Harry Jones (Hastings 1960a), Joseph Reece (Hastings 1960b), Clarence Rand (Ryan 1964a), Clyde James (Ryan 1964c), Thekla James Young (Ryan 1964d), Frank Jones (Ryan 1964e), Wallace Stewart (Ryan 1964f), Donald Jamison (Ryan 1964g), Mary Beemer (Ryan 1964i), and Fred Blum (Ryan 1964j), in addition to a variety of contemporary newspaper articles (Van R. 1912; "Memorial Fountain" 1921; Heath 1921; and "West Palomar Grade May Be Abandoned" 1938). There was no standardized manner in which these accounts were originally recorded. They were amassed whenever a local historian was inspired to record testimonies from elderly pioneers, and, as a result, are located in historical societies across the county. Some of the interviews were structured by a specific set of questions, others were simply presented as a lengthy narrative of one's life story (Mallios et al. 2006, 2007).

22. These sources ranged from popular magazine pieces to academic journal articles and included the following sources: "Palomar Mountain" 1958; "Pioneer's Grave to Have Marker" 1972; "Pillar of Palomar" 1982; . "North County Yesterday" 1986; "Historic Quotes" 1993; "Front Pages: Did You Know?" 2002; Bailey 2009; Bartlett 1931; Beckler 1958; Bevil c. 1995; Bostic c. 1964; Bryson 1962; Carlton 1974, 1977; Craine c. 1963; John Davidson 1937; G. Fink 1979; Fleisher c. 1963; Frazee-Worsley c. 1960; Heath 1919; Helsel 1998; B. Jackson 1971; James 1958; Kelly 1978; Lockwood 1967; Lynch c. 1990; Madyun and Malone 1981; Melvin 1981a, 1981b, 1981c, 1981d, 1981e, 1982a, 1982b; B. Moore, n.d.; Eloise Perkins 1971, 1972; Ross 1998, 2005; Rucker 1951; Rush 1952a; J. Stone 1972; Strain 1966; Stuart 1966; Taye c. 1940; N. Thompson 1961; S. Thompson 1972; Waite 2015; Wood 1937; and Yamaguchi 1998 (Mallios et al. 2006, 2007).

23. I define "best" as firsthand, corroborated, and from a reliable source with relatively few blatant fallacies.

24. Even though this word is not in the dictionary, it is nevertheless a mainstay in the field of archaeology and has been for over a century.

25. As we noted elsewhere, "Seriations are especially useful in isolating the inception, growth, peak in popularity, decline, and disappearance of a cultural trait that follows a unimodal distribution" (Mallios and Lennox 2014: 59).

26. Since there are an infinite number of possible traits and an infinite number of types based on these traits, the selection process is critical and worthy of scrutiny.

27. Brad Bailey proclaimed that Harrison was "undoubtedly the most beloved and well-known figure associated with early Palomar Mountain" (2009: 46).

28. It also helped me understand how my own work is situated among my regional colleagues. Archaeologist Kelly Dixon detailed a recent shift from the classic "Old West of mountain men, cowboys, Indians, gunfighters, prospectors, and outlaws" to the "counterclassic history of wage earners, women, minorities, urbanization, industrialization, and colonialism" (2014: 179). Of course, the approach advocated here involves both classic and counterclassic themes.

1

History, His Stories, and Historiography

When local author Laura James related that, "Nate was a friendly person . . . but his life story was never told, even by his best friends," she pinpointed the primary difficulty in trying to write an authoritative Harrison biography—there is remarkably little reliable information (1958: 5). In fact, there are struggles of many types in any attempt at constructing an accurate history. Carl Becker insisted nearly a century ago that, "[History is] an unstable pattern of remembered things redesigned and newly colored to suit the convenience of those who make use of it" (1935: 253–54). Despite the many inherent challenges in its construction, the following overview of Nathan Harrison's life is offered as a starting point for detailed discussion of who he was, how he came to California, and why he became revered as a legendary pioneer of the Old West.

Biographical Synopsis

The child of Ben and Harriet Harrison, Nathan "Nate" Harrison was born into slavery in Kentucky in the 1830s. Virtually nothing is known of his childhood. As a young man, he traveled west with his owner, Mr. Harrison, during the early years of the Gold Rush (1848–52). Nathan Harrison worked as a miner in Northern California's motherlode region in the 1850s and early '60s. Following the death of his owner, Harrison migrated southward toward Mission San Gabriel in the 1860s, working as a rancher, timber man, and laborer. In the 1870s, he frequented many parts of San Diego County, including Pauma Valley and other northern inland areas, as well as the city of San Diego; Harrison found regular work all over the region as a rancher, timber man, laborer, cook, and shopkeeper. It was during this time that Harrison married an Indigenous woman with children from a previous union; their marriage was brief, although he would remain close to her family. From 1879 to 1882, Harrison patented and lived on land at Rincon, near the base of Palomar Mountain and adjacent to Pauma Indian territory; this acquisition made him the first African American homesteader in the region. In 1882, Harrison sold his property to Andreas Scott and left Rincon, although he stayed in the general area and worked at Warner's Ranch and in Temecula for a few years. Harrison married again in the late 1870s or early '80s, this time to an Indigenous woman named Dona Lavierla; they were not together long. In the late 1880s, Harrison made his home two-thirds of the way up the west side of Palomar Mountain; he claimed the tract's water in 1892 and homesteaded the land in 1893. Harrison lived on Palomar Mountain from at least the late 1880s through 1919. During his early years on the mountain, Harrison was busy in many local industries, including shepherding, cattle tending, bee keeping, and horticulture. In his later years on Palomar—especially after the county widened his road and made it a public highway in 1897—he became a popular attraction for tourists, visitors, and friends, who helped to sustain him with regular gifts of food and other supplies. During a visit by acquaintances in October of 1919, an ailing Harrison was convinced to leave the mountain and receive medical attention. Now in his eighties, he lived for an additional year in the San Diego County Hospital before dying there on 10 October 1920. Harrison's body was immediately interred in an unmarked grave in Mount Hope, the city cemetery.

The Nathan Harrison Historiography

A key step of contextualized history or historiography is transparency, especially with regard to chronologies involving contradictory elements. The process employed here involved separating probable histories from obvious fiction while incorporating a majority of plausible options. Once all of the accounts were meticulously inventoried, dissected, and studied, we could evaluate each story and even individual narrative elements. This level of analysis makes it possible to ascertain the most likely scenario while still incorporating multiple perspectives.

The historiographic process also involved noting how authors of individual accounts apparently drew information from others. This was often the first step in pinpointing when historical fallacies started and mapping their consequent growth. Alternative histories were not entirely eliminated from Harrison's biography; however, they were explicitly de-emphasized due to certain dubious details. Whereas the next chapter on myth-making explains how and why certain fictions became told as historical fact, the remaining historiographic section of this chapter focuses on which narratives were seemingly the most accurate and why. Individual sentences from the biographical synopsis introduce each historiographic section to ground the discussion in the ultimate conclusion.

The child of Ben and Harriet Harrison, Nathan Harrison was born into slavery in Kentucky in the 1830s.

The most reliable historical sources, which include censuses, great registers, and other government documents, placed Nathan Harrison's year of birth between 1822 and 1835 (Figure 1.1). Even during his lifetime, there was a clear pattern of Harrison's exact age being disproportionately exaggerated over time. Whereas the rest of us age one year with each passing twelve-month period, Harrison's birth year was recorded significantly earlier with each new calendar. Close examination of the curious case of Nathan Harrison revealed that, according to government documents, his alleged age unnaturally accelerated with each subsequent record. During the 1870s and '80s, he was purportedly born in the 1830s; however, censuses taken in the 1900s claimed a birth year in the 1820s.[1] It is worth noting that these were official and contemporaneous government documents, not embellished mountain fables told generations after his passing. The "historical facts" were already clearly under manipulation during Harrison's lifetime, especially in his last few decades on the mountain.

Nathan Harrison was most likely born in Kentucky. Fifteen of sixteen contemporaneous government records pinpointed Kentucky as his state of origin, whereas the lone outlier listed Alabama.[2] Although Virginia, Mississippi, Missouri, and Tennessee were mentioned in secondary accounts, none of these states were corroborated in the more reliable historical sources.[3] Harrison's state of origin was an important foundational fact for his biography. Successful identification of it was also a key element in evaluating competing stories regarding the identity of the slave-owner who brought Harrison to California as the two distinct alleged owners were from different states. Ironically, only the last official record—his death certificate—included the names of Nathan Harrison's parents, Ben and Harriet. All other census records, registers, and other governmental receipts failed to identify them.

Virtually nothing is known of his childhood.

Contemporary mountain residents who knew Harrison well emphasized that he rarely spoke of his pre-California life. They repeatedly alleged that Harrison was especially recalcitrant about his ordeals as a slave. Harrison friend and Palomar neighbor Robert Asher avowed

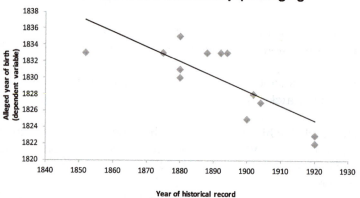

Birth year	Source	Date recorded
1822	1920 San Diego County Census (San Diego Township)	8/9 January 1920
1823	1920 San Diego County death certificate	1 January 1920
1825	1900 San Diego County Census (Smith Mtn. Township)	1900
1827	1904 Great Register, San Diego County (Jessie)	~1904
1828	1902 Great Register, San Diego County (Jessie)	~1902
1830	1902 Great Register Index, San Diego County (no record)	?
1830	1880 San Diego County Census (Bear Valley Township)	28/29 June 1880
1831	1908 Great Register, San Diego County (no record)	?
1831	1904 Great Register Index, San Diego County	~1904
1831	1880 Great Register, San Diego County	11 August 1880
1831	1882 Great Register, San Diego County	11 August 1880
1833	1852 California Census	14 October 1852
1833	1875 Great Register, San Diego County	30 June 1875
1833	1877 Great Register, San Diego County	30 June 1875
1833	1879 Great Register, San Diego County	30 June 1875
1833	1888 Great Register, San Diego County	25 August 1888
1833	1890 Great Register, San Diego County	26 August 1888
1833	1892 Great Register, San Diego County	3 August 1892
1833	1894 Great Register, San Diego County	19 October 1894
1833	1894 San Diego County voter registration form	22 October 1894
1835	1880 San Diego County Census (San Jacinto Township)	22 June 1880

Figure 1.1. A table and scatterplot of contemporary government records show that during his lifetime Harrison's accepted birth year gradually changed from 1835 to 1822. (Courtesy of the Nathan "Nate" Harrison Historical Archaeology Project.)

with unwavering certainty, "Of one thing I am sure, however; not one word did Nate say about his old Kentucky home, or of the trek to California" (c. 1938: no page numbers).[4] Secondary sources also related Harrison's reluctance to discuss his antebellum past. Virginia Stivers Bartlett quoted a rancher named "Jack" as declaring that, "Give Uncle Nate a drink . . . and he would tell you more about the county than anyone in it. But never a word about himself" (1931: 23). Extensive research into slave records, censuses, and other historical sources failed to locate any information that offered direct insight into Harrison's pre-adult years. This was hardly surprising as most African Americans did not appear in federal censuses until the end of the Civil War, and various slave schedules of the middle-nineteenth century were often irregular and fragmentary.

As a young man, he traveled west with his owner, Mr. Harrison, during the early years of the Gold Rush (1848–52).

One of the most important discoveries of the Nathan "Nate" Harrison Historical Archaeology Project was not a rare artifact but a recently scanned and uploaded census record that was not known to project researchers until the spring of 2018, a decade and a half after our work began. The 1852 California census for Santa Clara County listed Nathan Harrison as a nineteen-year-old black male, born in Kentucky but having last lived in Missouri. Santa Clara County was one of the original counties in California at statehood and stretched from Santa Cruz in the west to Merced and Stanislaus to the east; it was adjacent to many areas that produced sizeable veins of precious metals and saw expansive growth during the California Gold Rush. Each of these four traits listed for Harrison in the record—his name, year of birth, state of origin, and gateway state to the West—was echoed in the most reliable historical sources. Of course, presence on that census record did not establish when Harrison arrived in California, just that he was living there in 1852. Furthermore, the 1850 California census did not include an entry for Nathan Harrison. These crucial pieces of information suggested Harrison came to California between 1850 and 1852.

While all histories of Harrison agreed he migrated from the American South to California, there was significant debate as to when the westward trek took place. Many primary and secondary narratives suggested he and his owner were part of a team that joined the California Gold Rush (1848–55), but others put Harrison in the West for the first time either before 1848 or after 1855. Overall, there were six general scenarios for Harrison's journey across the US; they are discussed in chronological order and evaluated for accuracy on a case-by-case basis (Figure 1.2).[5] The first posited a mid-1840s pre-Mexican-American

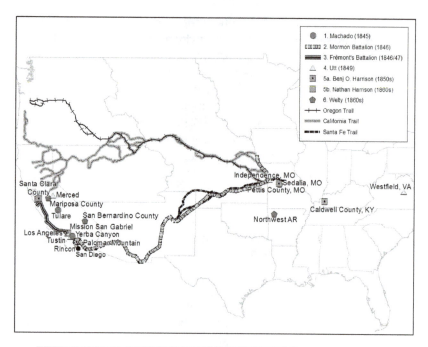

Figure 1.2a/b. Maps of different potential Nathan Harrison migration scenarios against a backdrop of the United States in 1850: the first offers an overview of the different scenarios on a nationwide level, and the second focuses on Southern California. (Courtesy of the Nathan "Nate" Harrison Historical Archaeology Project.)

War arrival date. The second specified an 1846 journey that ultimately united Harrison with the Mormon Battalion that marched from Iowa to San Diego. Similarly, the third denoted a late 1840s Mexican-American War period/pre-Gold Rush cross-country trip that ended with Harrison joining Frémont's Battalion sometime between 1846 and 1848. The fourth involved a Virginia-to-Los Angeles journey that ended on Christmas Eve of 1849. The fifth and best-corroborated scenario claimed a late 1840s/mid-1850s heart-of-the-Gold-Rush trip that brought Harrison to California's mother-lode region. The sixth placed Harrison on an early 1860s wagon train from the Midwest. Since each trip was largely tied to different routes, personnel, and purposes, it was often difficult to combine narrative details and find inclusive historiographic compromises.[6] As a result, certain scenarios just seemed more likely than others.

The tales of Harrison's life were not told in a vacuum. Many of the mountain's best storytellers were well aware of rival narratives and the rampant creative license frequently employed in such chronologies. For example, in a 1959 interview, Harrison friend Louis Salmons poignantly justified his biographical account over others with the following opening proclamation: "Well, I'm not as big a liar as some of the rest of them. All I know is what the old man [Harrison] told me a thousand times" (Hastings 1959b: no page numbers).[7] This statement simultaneously emphasized the degree of invention and exaggeration in many accounts of Harrison and avowed Salmons's alleged authentic firsthand knowledge of Harrison's past.

Scenario #1: Pre-1845 Arrival

Harrison friend Robert Asher wrote a series of unpublished manuscripts during the 1930s and '40s. Many of his descriptions included eye-witness accounts of life on the mountain during the nineteenth century. Asher quoted former Nathan Harrison nephew Frank Machado with the earliest claim of Harrison being in California. In an extended passage, Asher related that, "Machado is an Indian owning a bit of farm land lying between the Indian Reservation of La Jolla and the Henshaw Dam . . . He is a very interesting talker and is well posted on the mountain's history for some time back" (c. 1938: no page numbers). Asher specified in one Sunday afternoon interview with Machado:

> We got [Machado] started talking about "Mister Harrison," as he called Nate. Said Machado: ". . . Mr. Harrison was working in Tulare County in 1845, was threatened with death, so went to [Yerba] Canyon near Santa

Ana. Married Fred Smith's mother, a Lake Pechanga[8] woman, then Dona Lavierla, my aunt, in 1882." (c. 1938: no page numbers)

This brief and disjointed two-sentence summary contained a wealth of important information. Furthermore, other reliable sources echoed the overall sequence of Harrison moving southward from a mining community (like Tulare County) in the center of the state to south-lying Yerba Canyon near Santa Ana.[9] In addition, some of Harrison's closest friends insisted he had married multiple Indigenous women in succession, although his exact matrimonial history would be a subject of great debate.

The initial date of 1845 in the Asher/Machado passage was potentially problematic. Semantically, Tulare County was not officially created by the US government until 10 July 1852, and the town of Tulare was not founded until 1850. Furthermore, there was very little pre-Gold Rush (pre-1848) industry in this particular area of Mexican territory in 1845. While it is true that in 1841 the Mexican government began to allow foreigners to apply for land grants, the Tulare region was not in high demand (Engstrand 1993: 65–66). The Asher/Machado narrative offered no other details supporting why Harrison would venture to Tulare and end up working there in the early to mid-1840s. Less than a decade later, however, Tulare County would be a hotbed for mining activity. Asher was usually a reliable source, but in this case, he was quoting someone else and did not comment as to the veracity of the information. Furthermore, none of the other accounts supported an early or mid-1840s presence of Nathan Harrison in California. The combination of a seeming geographic non sequitur in the yet-to-exist Tulare County, a lack of supporting information for the early date, and a wealth of competing narratives undermined the credibility of this particular scenario.

Scenario #2: 1846 Arrival

Bertram Moore, an Assistant San Diego County Engineer from 1922–50, scoured County Supervisor records for interesting historical notes and identified an unattributed and unverified account of Nathan Harrison joining the Mormon Battalion on its famed trek across the western US to San Diego. He reported that, "In 1846—Nate was about 16 years old— Harrison landed in one of those towns along the route followed by the Mormon Battalion on their march to Calif. He joined as a helper (servant to some officer)" (B. Moore, n.d.: no page numbers). The Mormon Battalion primarily consisted of over five hundred Latter-day Saints in

Iowa who formed the only religion-based unit to serve in the United States military. Starting in July of 1846, they marched nearly two thousand miles to San Diego to support the US in the Mexican-American War of 1846–48. The battalion never saw action because the peace treaty was signed twenty-six days in advance of their 29 January 1847 arrival. Nevertheless, their march remains one of the longest in US history.

The story of the Mormon Battalion has come to represent two important ideals in early US American history: 1) religious freedom and 2) the arduous trek westward. Though Harrison's celebrated biography embodied similar themes of liberty and death-defying challenges in the Old West, there was no supporting evidence of his joining the Mormon Battalion in any capacity. No other sources confirmed this narrative and many countered it. Furthermore, thorough historical documentation on the Mormon Battalion offered no evidence of him being on any company roster, arrival list, or record of any kind.

Scenario #3: 1848 Arrival

Author Virginia Stivers Bartlett claimed that Harrison came to Southern California "in 1848 with Frémont's Battalion" in her article, "Uncle Nate of Palomar" (1931: 23). Bartlett's statement was a reference to the famed California Battalion formed during the Mexican-American War led by US Army brevet lieutenant colonel John C. Frémont.[10] Frémont's group consisted of soldiers and a bevy of outriders, hunters, cartographers, couriers, and scouts. The multicultural crew included missionized Indians, Spaniards, and future frontier legend Kit Carson. Many members of Frémont's team were explorers and emigrants who came to California before John Sutter discovered gold in Coloma in January of 1848. The battalion's first official action against the Mexican government involved assisting in the capture of San Diego. Frémont and his men landed in San Diego on 29 July 1846, left behind about forty individuals to garrison the town, and then proceeded to Los Angeles and later to Monterey. When Frémont led the California Battalion back from Monterey to Los Angeles (December 1846 to January 1847), it marked the end of the Mexican-American War. In fact, the last battle of that conflict was fought in San Pasqual Valley—east of Escondido and south of Valley Center—on 6 December 1846. The war officially ended with the signing of two treaties, the Capitulation of Cahuenga on 13 January 1847 and the Treaty of Guadalupe Hidalgo on 2 February 1848.

The members of Frémont's Battalion were some of the first celebrated US heroes in what had been Mexico's Alta California territory. Placing Harrison amongst the soldiers that defeated Mexico—especially in San Diego, the oldest Spanish settlement in California—gave his life story great pizazz and ascribed to him pioneer status. Like the previous Mormon Battalion claim, it forever linked him with the inception of the United States in San Diego. The attribution was dubious, however, as none of the other contemporary historical sources corroborated it, and many disputed it.[11] Furthermore, none of the existing rosters of the California Battalion included Harrison's name.[12] In addition, if Harrison had arrived in Southern California in 1848, as Bartlett claimed, he would have missed the 1846 arrival of Frémont's Battalion in San Diego by two years. Even though there were multiple conflicting facts in Bartlett's account, her arrival-date declaration for Harrison went seemingly unquestioned and was reiterated numerous times.

The purported association between John C. Frémont and Nathan Harrison might have been a case of mistaken identity. James Duff, a Missouri native with African American and American Indian heritage, arrived in California with Frémont on one of his four westward expeditions in the 1840s. Frémont would secure a Spanish land grant during this time that gave him ownership of a large area near Yosemite. Duff was instrumental in helping Frémont establish the state's first quartz-crushing stamp mill[13] on this land in 1849; it was specifically located near Mariposa, California (Chamberlain 1936: chapter 3). Duff often declared that, "I was the first white man to settle on Mariposa Creek," an ironic phrase remarkably similar to Nathan Harrison's assertion of being "the first white man on the mountain."[14] Perhaps Bartlett quoted someone or made the mistake herself of confusing Duff with Harrison, as both men were African American settlers in California during the Gold Rush, and both used the memorable label "first white man" to self-describe and justify their particular settlement claim in the Old West.

Scenario #4: 1849 Arrival

Despite the fact that the most reliable historical accounts insisted a man named "Mr. Harrison" owned Nathan Harrison and brought him west from Kentucky to gold country in Northern California, there was a rival narrative positing a different owner, departure state, and California arrival region. Local writer Philip S. Rush insisted in the 1952 issue of the regional magazine *Southern California Rancher* that when Lysander Utt left his native Westfield, Virginia, for the Old West in the late 1840s, he brought with him a slave named Nathan Harrison. Utt's party stopped in Independence, Missouri, along the way and ultimately reached Los Angeles on Christmas Eve of 1849. According to Rush, Utt released Harrison from bondage when California was admitted to the Union as a free state, soon after their arrival. Although Rush did not specify how and when Harrison ventured to San Diego County, he affirmed this was the same Harrison who would later become a celebrated Palomar Mountain pioneer.

Unlike the scarcity of historical records regarding the early years of Nathan Harrison and the paucity of details about his family, the life and kinship relations of Lysander Utt were very well documented. There were numerous census records for him, his parents, and generations of his offspring; multiple local history books described his business ventures; and family members penned two different biographies feting the Utt patriarch's accomplishments. The wealth of sources and family members interested in detailing relative history resulted in a high-resolution chronology that ultimately undermined Rush's celebrated assertion of a meaningful link between Lysander Utt and Nathan Harrison.

Lysander Utt was born to parents John Wesley Utt and Mary Creager on 1 June 1824 in Wytheville, Wythe County, Virginia. Lysander was the third of their thirteen children. In 1840, the family uprooted and moved to Jackson County, Missouri, where John died in 1849. Lysander worked the family farm until 1849, when he decided to venture west, crossing the plains with an ox team and coming to Los Angeles via the Santa Fe Trail. Lysander then traveled north and spent two years mining gold in Mariposa County; this venture peaked with Utt and business partners pooling all of their resources to pay for the construction of a dam to divert a local waterway for panning. Much to their chagrin, a massive storm erupted, flooded the region, and carried away the dam and their life savings. Leigh Robertson succinctly noted in her Utt family history that following this catastrophe, "They were busted and broke!"[15] As a result, Utt turned his attention to farming and freighting supplies to the railroad under construction in the nearby Sierra Nevada Mountains. Both ventures were successful over the next two decades, as was an additional lucrative foray into supplying wood for steam engines. Lysander married Arvilla Platt in 1864; she gave birth to their son, Charles Utt, a year later.

By 1874, Lysander was ready to retire to Southern California. As a result, the Utt family loaded their belongings into a horse-drawn lumber wagon and moved four hundred miles south to Tustin City, near Santa Ana. Soon after arriving, Lysander used some of his cash reserves to purchase a large abandoned structure that would soon become the "L. Utt Pioneer Store." Utt's building stocked supplies of every kind imaginable and offered upstairs rooms to rent for travelers. Lysander, wife Arvilla, and son Charles worked long hours and built the venture into a thriving business. They used the profits to purchase many other parcels of land in Tustin as well. Lysander died in Tustin in 1890, before any of his grandchildren were born, and Charles took over the store and his other holdings. Charles had a son named James B. Utt, who would eventually become a California Congressman.

The biographies of Lysander Utt were detailed and fascinating; they noted everything from his nickname ("San") to his spending habits ("very frugal") (Hess, n.d.: no page numbers). As far as the work presented here, there was only one problem: they never mentioned Nathan Harrison! Page after page of his life's intricacies and receipt after receipt of his business ventures and possessions failed to include even a single entry for Harrison. No one had ever connected Lysander Utt and Harrison until Rush wrote his story thirty-two years after Harrison's passing and over a half century after Lysander's death. It was hard to believe that such nuanced accounts would have made this sort of omission, especially considering Harrison's growing status in early twentieth-century Southern California. There were other inconsistencies between the established Utt biographies, fragmentary Harrison records, and Rush's assertions as well. For instance, Lysander Utt traveled from Missouri, not Virginia, to California in 1849; and Harrison was from Kentucky, not Missouri or Virginia. Overall, Rush's narrative was holistically different from any other pre-1952 Harrison history.

Part of the confusion with Lysander Utt likely stemmed from the fact that there was another Utt who did regularly interact with Nathan Harrison. Major Lee Utt lived for many years near the base of Palomar Mountain at Agua Tibia Ranch during the late 1800s. In addition to being a prominent lawyer and politician, Major Lee Utt also oversaw a large farm that frequently employed, housed, and fed Nathan Harrison. A brief letter written from Lee Utt to Harrison on 1 January 1884, found in the Cabin Collection corroborated their business dealings; it stated:

Agua Tibia

Jan. 1, 1884

Nathan Harrison:

Dear Sir: I will take forty (40) Cedar Posts to be delivered at Scott's Store in the Rincon: and I agree to pay you 15cents each for said goods, it is to be understood that "Said Posts" are of good quality and size and proper length. Let me know by mail through Mr. Ruff (or by any other means you think best) when the Posts are ready and I will send you the money. I want the Posts soon.

Lee H. Utt[16]

According to Harrison acquaintance W. C. Fink, Major Lee Utt had a strong affinity for Harrison and especially enjoyed hearing stories from him about his adventures at various local Indian reservations. When tracking Harrison historical narratives, *it was imperative not to mistake Lysander Utt for Major Lee Utt*, even though the details of their respective biographies were often confused, reversed, or amalgamated in the existing records.

Unlike Lysander's roots in Virginia, Levi "Lee" H. Utt was part of a northern Utt contingency traced through his grandfather to Pennsylvania and Ohio. Lee was born in 1840 in Illinois, a free state. He enlisted in the army at a very young age and lost a foot while fighting in the American Civil War. Undeterred by this injury, Lee immediately re-enlisted in the cavalry, serving as Captain of Company A of the Seventh Kansas Regiment. Lee Utt's war wounds were severe and resulted in him spending extensive amounts of time at various army sanitariums before moving west to California in the mid-1860s.[17] Once out West, he would accrue significant wealth and social connections. Local pioneer and future business partner Herbert Crouch recalled that, "Major Utt was the first settler [on the land grant near Mission San Luis Rey, Montserrate, and the San Luis Rey River] in 1867. He first stayed at [Rancho] Guajome with Colonel [Cave] Couts,[18] and afterwards with [Caves' brother, William] Blount Couts"[19] (1965: no page numbers). The 1870 Census listed Major Lee Utt's residence in San Luis Rey, but he had many holdings throughout San Diego County.

Lee Utt married Sarah Marston in 1875; she was from one of the most well-established families in San Diego.[20] There were multiple accounts of Marston women taking family trips to Utt's Agua Tibia Ranch (Marston 1959). For example, the autobiography of Sarah's sister, Anna Lee Gunn Marston, detailed:

All of my children remember their visits to the Agua Tibia ranch and the wonderful times they enjoyed there, but the older ones remember "Uncle Lee" [Utt]. . . He studied law and acquired a fine knowledge of history and general literature, and, owing to his retentive memory and natural gift of expression, he was a most interesting and entertaining talker. He bought the Agua Tibia, to which he was attracted by the warm Sulphur spring and the enormous fig trees, said to be the largest in the county. This ranch, on a spur of Palomar mountain, three miles above the Pala Mission, had been the home of an Indian chief. It had a comfortable adobe house of several rooms and a vineyard of mission grapes as well as fig trees. The view down the San Luis Rey valley was very fine. Major Utt so far regained his health that at the time of his marriage he had improved the ranch by the building of reservoirs and the planting of several large groves of olive and apricot trees. Here [their children] Anita and Lewis spent their childhood. Having an opportunity to sell the place in 1887, the family spent several years in the Eastern States and in Mexico and finally returned to make their home in Redlands, where Major Utt died in 1895. (Marston 1959)[21]

There were conflicting accounts as to whether Lysander and Lee Utt were related. Census information did not support that they were close relations. However, a separate article in the same 1952 magazine that insisted that Lysander Utt brought Nathan Harrison west also stated that, "Lysander Utt was an uncle of Major Lee H. Utt" (Rush 1952b: 29). It is worth noting that both Rush articles were rife with errors, including the false assertion that Lee Utt was a Virginia native. Even if Lysander and Lee Utt were kin, this familial connection did not necessarily strengthen the link between Lysander Utt and Harrison or undo the many historical contradictions between their biographies.[22]

Scenario #4, which featured Lysander Utt as Harrison's owner, was highly dubious. Nonetheless, close examination of its details led to an important clarification in the Harrison chronology between two acclaimed Southern Californian business leaders of the same surname (and first name, first initial) who had often been blended into one biography. In distinguishing between the principal characters in this tale of two Utts, Lysander Utt was a Virginia native (the South) who mined in Northern California during the Gold Rush before starting a prominent supply store business in the Tustin/Santa Ana area; in contrast, Lee Utt was a Civil War soldier from Illinois (the North) who was severely injured in battle and later went on to settle at Rancho Agua Tibia as a lawyer, politician, and farmer. Lee Utt was a friend, neighbor, and employer of Harrison for up to three decades (circa 1865–95). Certain historical accounts would even insist that Major Utt repeatedly paid Harrison's Palomar Mountain property taxes. Conversely, Lysander Utt had no apparent connection to Harrison until 1952 when an obscure magazine article claimed that he had once owned him over a century earlier and brought him to California.

Scenario #5: 1848–63 Arrival

Many sources suggested Harrison came west during the California Gold Rush (1848–55) and before President Lincoln's 1863 Emancipation Proclamation. This scenario provided an economic impetus for the westward trek and also accounted for Harrison's enslaved status throughout the trip and during the first part of his residency in California. Accounts alleging a pre-Gold Rush California arrival by Harrison were undermined by the question of what drew his coterie cross-country, and those indicating a post-1863 start for Harrison in the Old West could not address how and why he would make the trip while still enslaved. On the basis of these two factors alone, this timeline for Harrison's arrival seemed more plausible than others.

All of the different narratives that maintained Harrison's entry into California in the circa 1850s (1848–63) could be easily united into one general chronology, regardless of the occasionally disparate details they each provided. Catherine Wood's book, *Palomar: From Teepee to Telescope*, stated:

> As nearly as can be ascertained, [Nathan Harrison] and his master came from Kentucky by ox team, stopping three or four months at Sedalia, Missouri, waiting to join a wagon train west. About the time they reached California, a movement was on foot in Los Angeles to break a road over the Tejon Pass to the north. Money was subscribed and bullocks furnished, and Nate drove an ox team with the first wagon train over the Pass. (1937: no page numbers)

Although Wood did not assign a date to this trip in her initial description, she later explained, "Cleland's 'History of California' says: 'In September, 1854, [the] people of Los Angeles raised $6,000 for the construction of a wagon road between their city and Ft. Tejon.' That seems to check with Nate's story" (1937: no page numbers).[23] Linking Harrison to the opening of Tejon Pass provided a concrete date for his arrival in the region as this route between the southern edge of the Central Valley and the northern extreme of Southern California has been well established in state history as 1854.[24]

Wood offered important additional details in sequence, the first and last of which were anchored by exact dates. She wrote that after leading the ox team over the pass (presumably in 1854), "[Nathan Harrison] and his master went up to the mining district near Merced, where his master died. Uncle Nate went down to the San Gabriel Mission for a time and later found his way to the foot of Palomar, where he took up a claim at Rincon" (Wood 1937: no page numbers). Wood's account specified in order that: 1) Harrison opened Tejon Pass, 2) Harrison mined near Merced, 3) Harrison's owner died, 4) Harrison spent time at the San Gabriel Mission, and 5) Harrison owned land at Rincon. The last of these details occurred in 1879 as a "Nathan Harris" completed a United

States Land Patent for land at Rincon on 10 November 1879. He sold this land to Andres Scott less than three years later.

At about the time Nathan Harrison likely arrived in California, it was a free state yet still very hostile to African Americans. In 1850, less than 1,000 of the state's 92,597 inhabitants were of African American or African descent (Savage 1976: 12). According to state law, slave owners already in California when it was admitted to the US in 1850 either had to free their slaves or return to the South. However, slaves who remained in California had to petition for citizenship; it was not automatically granted.

There are many modern misnomers about the plight of enslaved peoples in California from statehood in 1850 to the ratification of the Thirteenth Amendment in 1865. Quite simply, the Golden State was no land of equality for African Americans. California did outlaw slavery in its first state constitution (1849) and entered the union as a free state. However, much of the state's purported abolitionist sentiment was driven by white miners who fretted over direct competition with slave owners; they agreed to California being a free state only as a means to excluding blacks altogether (Carlton 1974: 8; Lapp 1977: 128; Wheeler 1993: 52). Furthermore, Democrats from the South were prominent in the California legislature during this time and passed many statutes that explicitly discriminated against African Americans.[25] Historian Malcolm Edwards unambiguously described these policies as "an appallingly extensive body of discriminatory laws" (1977: 36). For example, the new state was adamant in its compliance with the federal Fugitive Slave Law of 1850, which mandated the immediate return of all runaway slaves to their owners. This required that escaped slaves living in California, regardless of from where they ran away or were captured, were returned to their slave state of origin instead of being treated as free people. It also explicitly denied the freedom claims of enslaved African Americans brought into California by gold-seeking whites. Since Nathan Harrison came as a slave to California during the pre-Emancipation Gold Rush, he was not free. In fact, a majority of the 2,200 blacks in California in 1852 were still slaves (Goode 1973: 59). The state renewed its fugitive slave law in both 1853 and 1854 before allowing it to lapse in 1855 (Susan Johnson 2000: 190).

To make matters worse, some slave owners—even if they did not come west for the Gold Rush—simply refused to liberate their slaves. Historian William Katz explained that proponents of slavery managed to convince California legislators to leave many loopholes in the "broad and arbitrary fugitive slave law," the result of which was slave owners staying in the Golden State for over a decade and working their slaves just as they had in the South (1987: 134). Slavery was institutionalized in California despite being explicitly outlawed by the state constitution. One of the key factors undermining any abolitionist progress in California was that the state had failed to emancipate slaves when it entered the union. As a result, slave owners retained rights over the enslaved because the legality of this servitude trumped what they could claim was only temporary residence in a free territory (Goode 1973: 63). The same logic was upheld by the US Supreme Court in its 1857 *Dred Scott v. Sandford* decision, which insisted that since slaves were not citizens, residence in free territory did not make them free (De Graaf and Taylor 2001: 10). Clearly, slavery was alive and well in the Old West, even after California had been admitted to the union as a free state.[26]

While US lawmakers in California enacted nuanced compromises to cement the status of African Americans as secondary in the Golden State, their legislative actions and inactions concerning California's Indigenous population were far worse. Typified by clearly unambiguous racial hatred and unrelenting economic exploitation, the period of 1846–80 was especially brutal for local Indian groups (Carrico 1987; Forbes 1969; Heizer 1974). Members of San Diego County native tribes during Spanish and Mexican occupation (1769–1846) were treated as feudal slaves, forced to endure countless unprosecuted murders and rapes, and culturally devastated by nearly everything the Europeans brought, from their foreign diseases to their animals that over-grazed the local environment (Carrico 1987: vii, 13, 15; Jayme 1772: 43–44). US Americans were vocal in their condemnation of Spanish and Mexican colonial practices. For example, in 1846, US Lieutenant William H. Emory described in his diary the state of the local Indigenous population that, "This race, which in our country has never been reduced to slavery, is in that degraded condition throughout California, and do only the labor performed in the country. Nothing can exceed their present degraded condition" (US Congress 1848: 165). Despite the seemingly sympathetic tone of the account, the US would continue the outright open warfare on Indigenous lives and ways of life.

When US officials signed the 1848 Treaty of Hidalgo, they made far-reaching commitments to the Indigenous population that were never honored (Carrico 1987: 16). US settlers, propelled by self-serving rights of conquest as opposed to legal accord, were especially adept at annihilating nearly every aspect of native life, from unapologetic murders to sophisticated denials of Indigenous land claims (Trafzer and Hayer 1999: vii, 17). They had all the power and little incentive to work with California Indians. Land-hungry US settlers pushed natives off their lands, prevented Indigenous people from testifying against them in the courts, reneged on numerous treaties, and incessantly exploited the Indian work force.[27] Historian Brendan C. Lindsay summarized:

> Thousands of white men [in California] certainly went so far as to participate directly in genocide by murdering thousands of Indian men, women, and children. But perhaps the more important story to share is that of the hundreds of thousands of white citizens who, through apathy, inaction, or tacit support, allowed the extermination to proceed directly by violence or indirectly though genocidal policies of cultural extermination and planned neglect. (2012: 9)[28]

Local California Indians had little recourse; for example, Cave J. Couts, Jr., the first federal Indian agent of San Diego County, was repeatedly accused—but never tried or convicted—of killing native people in his employ through inhumane punishment. Even when the Indigenous population did manage to eke out a political victory, like in 1870 when they convinced President Ulysses S. Grant to set aside extensive land for reservations at Pala and San Pasqual Valley, the benefits were often short-lived. Historian and archaeologist Richard Carrico explained that, "President Grant revoked his own executive order [in 1872], returning over 69,000 acres to the public domain without any assurances that the Indians would ever receive title to one single acre" (1987: 69).[29] Chauncey S. Goodrich offered a stark conclusion in his 1926 study of California Indian legal status, stating, "The swift economic development of California was bought at a certain cost of human values. It was the Indian who paid the price" (1926: 94).

Although some contemporary California settlers would lament the Euro-American annihilation of the Indigenous groups, few intervened in any meaningful manner. Elected officials wavered between fomenting rampant aggression toward California Indians and philosophically bemoaning it while doing virtually nothing about it. For example, California's first US governor, Peter H. Burnett, stated in his 1852 "Address to the Legislature":

> That a war of extermination will continue to be waged between the two races until the Indian race becomes extinct, must be expected; while we cannot anticipate this result with but painful regret, the inevitable destiny of the race is beyond the power and wisdom of man to avert.

Not only were Native Americans in San Diego County denied equal rights with white settlers, they were incessantly antagonized by squatters on traditional Indigenous lands. To make matters worse, cash-strapped San Diego County governmental officials insisted local Indians be taxed because their cattle grazed public lands (Harrison

2004: 67). In fact, in 1850 San Diego Sheriff Ágoston Haraszthy issued an ultimatum demanding that the Indigenous population either pay taxes or forfeit the cattle to the new US government. Violence soon erupted between the two sides at Warner's Ranch (just thirty miles east of Palomar Mountain), culminating in what historians have deemed "The Garra Uprising" (Carrico 1987: 46). There were less than a dozen casualties, and after the skirmishes, local Cupeño tribal chief Antonio Garra,[30] former whaler Bill Marshall,[31] and Juan Verdugo, were captured, tried, and executed for treason. American officials pointed to this incident to ramp up hysteria in the region against the Indigenous population and proclaim that "an Indian war is upon us" (Lindsay 2012: 158). Though formal war had not been declared, US Americans used these sorts of events to justify any and all brutal treatment of native groups.

US pioneers at Palomar Mountain noted the harsh conditions the local Indigenous population faced across Southern California and especially in and around the missions. Will Dyche, son of George Dyche[32] and a Palomar native who grew up fluent in various Indigenous dialects, vividly recalled his friend Mata-qua-whee, an elderly San Pasqual Indian, showing him the numerous scars on his back from being whipped dozens of times in a row with three-quarter-inch leather thongs at the mission at San Luis Rey and the *asistencia* at Pala (E. Davis 1938: 3). In fact, one of George's most prominent memories was of seeing the whipping post at those two nearby missionary settlements (E. Davis 1938: 3). Likewise, Nathan Harrison—a man who had experienced the horrors of slavery firsthand—succinctly told Robert Asher that, "The Indians were treated like slaves" (c. 1938: no page numbers).

California's ethnic tumult during the 1850s and '60s was important context for the Harrison timeline. Furthermore, ascertaining the date of death for Nathan Harrison's owner was critical for understanding the state and degree of his emancipation. If Harrison the owner died before the slaves were first federally emancipated in 1863—regardless of California's status as a free state—Harrison would have likely been sent back to Kentucky to continue his enslavement. Therefore, if Wood's timeline was correct, it would be expected that Harrison and his owner lived in Merced for at least the nine years between 1854 and 1863. Other sources included supporting assertions of this sequence, but none of them had explicit dates. For example, San Diego County pioneer John Welty stated that, "[Harrison] came from Kentucky to Sedalia, Missouri, where he waited for several months while a wagon train was being made up to come overland to Merced and on to the mines" (James 1958: 6). Other sources made it clear that Harrison and his owner came to California as part of the Gold Rush; John Davidson avowed that, "[Nathan Harrison] and his master were '49ers at which time he was a grown man and claimed to be the best man among his master's slaves" (1937: 2). Furthermore, some accounts corroborated the general chronology but did not specify the initial Los Angeles arrival. Harrison friend Ed Davis wrote:

> Nate Harrison as a young man came to California with his master, a Mr. Harrison, before the Civil War, crossed the plains and went north into the mines. From there he drifted south and when his master died in Los Angeles, Nate came down to Rincon, in San Diego County, and took up a homestead now owned by the Golsh family. He sold out, lived on the Warner Ranch for a while, then on to Palomar and at last settled in the canyon, where he built his cabin and lived for many years. (1938: no page numbers)

Davis' account not only gave a complete chronology, it was also the first to specify the name of Nathan Harrison's owner as "Mr. Harrison." It was common for slave owners to assign their last names to their slaves. Ed Davis, Catherine Wood, and Abel Davis specified that the death of this Mr. Harrison resulted in Nathan Harrison's freedom. The authors differed on where the slave-owning Mr. Harrison died; Ed Davis stated that he died in Los Angeles whereas Wood and Abel Davis wrote that Nathan Harrison's owner, not specified by name, passed away in Merced.

Learning more about slave-owning Mr. Harrison was key to deciphering the tangled web of contradictory historical details concerning Nathan Harrison. In the 1852 California census for Santa Clara County, a listing for a 55-year-old white male named B. O. Harrison, also originally from Kentucky and a recent resident of Missouri, immediately preceded the entry for Nathan Harrison. It was unlikely these two individuals were listed together due to alphabetical order as other people on the same census page were not listed by letter. These records were commonly compiled in the order in which the census taker encountered the individuals, meaning that adjacent people were often living or traveling together. It was also common for slaves to be listed immediately following their owners.[33] Their common state of origin and previous residence further supported the theory that B. O. Harrison was Nathan Harrison's owner.

Additional pre-1850 census records included information on B. O. Harrison. The 1840 federal census contained an entry for a white 40–49-year-old male named Benj O. Harrison in Pettis County, Missouri; this record listed seven other individuals in the Harrison household, including a black male slave under ten years of age. Nathan Harrison would have been approximately seven years old in 1840. In addition, the 1830 US census contained an entry for a 20–29-year-old white male named Ben O. Harrison in Caldwell County, Kentucky. Furthermore, the 1810 federal census for Livingston County, Kentucky, listed a white male named John Harrison as head of household with a son, presumably Ben O. Harrison, between the ages of sixteen and twenty-five. Each of these records coalesced to present a narrative of a slave-owning Harrison family from Kentucky during the early 1800s that had one son (Benj. O. Harrison) venture west, first to Missouri and later to California, during the Gold Rush with one of the family slaves (Nathan Harrison).[34]

Slaves in Kentucky during the first half of the nineteenth century faced some of the harshest conditions and strictest laws in the Antebellum South (Lucas 2003). For example, at the time when the Harrisons likely left for California, state lawmakers approved a constitutional amendment that unambiguously declared "an iron-bound guarantee of the preservation of slavery in Kentucky" (S. Moore 2016: 36–37). Furthermore, Kentucky refused many rights that certain other slave states granted. It did not recognize slave personhood, personal property rights, or the ability to testify in court. Border States in the South, those closest to the North, often had and enforced stricter rules oppressing enslaved African Americans than those located farther south.

There was general relative chronological agreement in this scenario, but just as multiple sources omitted Harrison's initial Los Angles stop before traveling to Merced, others left out descriptions of his time mining in Northern California. They did not deny this earlier work; their narratives just flowed directly from his initial California arrival to his subsequent San Diego County settlement. For instance, J. H. Heath wrote that, "The story is that Mr. Harrison, who before the Civil War was a slave, came into northern San Diego county soon after the negroes of the south were freed" (1919: 8). Edmund Rucker stated that, "Nathan Harrison was born a slave in Kentucky and was brought to California as a youth in a party of which his owner was a member. He lived for a time near Temecula" (1951: A12). John Davidson noted:

> "N——r Nate" was brought to California as a slave by his Master. He stayed with his Master and mistress for several years. They however became very dissipated[35] so that he finally ran away. They had all come from Kentucky and from there had gone to Los Angeles. When Nate left them he came to Palomar to live. (1937: 2)

In addition, anthropologist J. P. Harrington wrote in 1932 that, "A 30 year old negro named Harrison came with the very first Americans that reached Palomar Mountain and later lived downslope . . . and hence called it N— —r Grade" (Harrington 1986: no page numbers).[36] Overall, there was nothing in these passages contradicting the Scenario #4 sequence established by Davis and Wood.

Another succinct summary of Harrison's westward migration came from an interview Ed Hastings conducted with Harrison friend and neighbor Louis Salmons in 1959. Salmons stated:

> [Harrison] come from Kentucky to Sedalia, Missouri, and that was where they all congregated there. And they had to make a big wagon train for the Indians—stand the Indians off. So he came there up to Fort Stockton, up by Sacramento and was there for several years. And finally the man that. . . . His master that brought him out, he died and old Nate drifted on down this way then. . . . [Harrison came to California] before the Civil War. Oh, yes, it was—he was still a slave when he came. He came here in the early day. I don't know what year. He didn't know what year himself that he came[37]. But he was a slave when he came across. Then when his master died, he was free. Well, by that time I think they'd freed the slaves. The war was over by that time. (Hastings 1959b: no page numbers)

Salmons was elderly at the time of the interview, and his narrative was disjointed. Nevertheless, his account both corroborated the general timeline of temporary residence in Sedalia, Missouri (which was in Pettis County, MO—listed in the 1840 census for Ben O. Harrison), a pre-1861 (pre-Civil War) arrival, an extended stay in mining country, and the death of Mr. Harrison. Salmons offered a slightly later date for Mr. Harrison's passing than others, opining that at this time "they'd freed the slaves [post-1863]" and "the war was over [post-1865]." It was important to note that with the exception of Rush's seemingly error-filled narrative (Scenario #4), none of the historical accounts of Nathan Harrison suggested that he became a free man when California was admitted to the Union on 9 September 1850.

Scenario #5 included a distinct order of events augmented with certain temporal anchors. Although few exact dates were specified by the many sources that could be synthesized into this collective history, mini-date ranges could be established for each of the key events. For example, Mr. Harrison likely brought Nathan Harrison from Missouri to California in the late 1840s or '50s, they mined in and around Merced and other mother-lode regions during the 1850s and early '60s, and Mr. Harrison died in the early to mid-1860s, at which time Nathan Harrison migrated southward. Unlike the previous three scenarios, there were no glaring problems or inconsistencies with this general timeline, and it was supported by the majority of historical narratives, especially those written by people who knew Harrison personally, like Ed Davis and Louis Salmons.

Scenario #6: 1864–68 Arrival

There were a few additional narratives that presented entirely different scenarios for Harrison's trek to California. These remaining accounts posited a post-Gold Rush 1860s arrival date for Nathan Harrison. In general, the stories in this group suffered from three deficiencies: 1) they were uncorroborated, 2) they were from obscure secondhand sources, and 3) there were clear contradictions with certain established elements from primary sources, especially the 1852 Santa Clara County census record. Nonetheless, there were important parallel events worth keeping in mind for later comparisons with the myth-making process.

In her *Journal of San Diego History* article, "Palomar's Friendly Hermit," Laura M. James reported an extended story told to her by Elsie Crooks, granddaughter of San Diego County pioneers John and Mary Welty, who first arrived in Southern California in 1864. Crooks explained to James:

> John Welty brought his family to California in a covered wagon train. At one point they met another party at a river, and the two outfits helped each other to cross. When they were across, the Welty's train came right on. They wanted the others to come with them, but for some reason the other group wanted to lay over a day. They laid plans to overtake the Welty train at a place where the two outfits planned to rest for several days. When they did not arrive as planned, Grandfather Welty rode back to see what was delaying them. He found that the Indians had killed them all, burned their wagons, and made off with their stock. As he was returning to his outfit, he came upon a woman, a baby, and a Negro. They had managed to escape by hiding in some tules [a giant species of sedge native to the western United States] and willows. For fear the Indians would track them, they had put some of their clothing over their shoes, and were endeavoring to reach the others on foot ... Later, when the Welty train reached a fort, the woman and baby were left in order that they might return to the East with the first outfit going that way, but the Negro came on to California. He was Nate. (1958: 7)

There was a glaring problem with this account. It specified that the African American traveling with them was a child, not a man. The transcript stated: "Early the following morning, a colored boy, who had miraculously escaped the tomahawk and had been hiding in the willows, crept into camp. . . . They learned from the Negro boy that there had been seven men in the party with their wives and children" (Morril 1942: 209). This qualification greatly undermined the Welty assertion that the "colored boy" in question was Nathan Harrison. As Robert Asher previously calculated, "[Nate Harrison] would have been eighteen years old in 1849, a grown man, and thirty years old in 1861" (c.

1938: no page numbers). Since the Welty wagon train arrived in San Bernardino in 1864, Nathan Harrison would have been in his mid-30s and clearly no longer a boy. None of the other accounts stated that Harrison was born in the 1840s or '50s.

There were even claims that Harrison did not arrive in California until the late 1860s. For example, North County local Bessie Helsel wrote that, "Uncle Ed says that Nate was among those on Grandfather's wagon train in 1868, but I am not sure" (Helsel 1998).[38] This was almost certainly untrue as multiple accounts verified Harrison's role on the makeshift jury of a very public Palomar Mountain murder case in 1868. Clearly, Harrison was already a well-established part of the trusted mountain community by the mid-to-late 1860s. Helsel was a child when she retold the family story that Harrison was on her grandfather's caravan. There was clearly some truth in her wagon train account, but it was most likely a different wagon train than the one that brought Harrison to California much earlier. Overall, none of the Scenario #5 accounts seemed probable.

It would be easy to dismiss Scenarios 2, 3, 4, and 6 as entirely flawed because of significant inconsistencies, especially since a cogent argument could be made that these seeming fabrications explicitly served the purpose of placing Harrison at a celebrated California event (e.g., the Bear Revolt, the Mormon Battalion march, etc.) or with a particular family (the Utts, Weltys, Ormsbys, etc.) instead of relating a reliable history. Nonetheless, there were repeated peripheral elements to the largely discredited stories that might still have had relevance for Harrison's biography. For example, Missouri was mentioned as a gateway to the west on Harrison's migration in multiple accounts from Scenarios 4, 5, and 6. Rush specified Independence, Missouri, and Wood, James, and Hastings pinpointed Sedalia, Missouri,[39] as a staging or departure point for the Harrison journey. Both locales were at or near the head of the Oregon, California, and Santa Fe Trails, three of the most prominent routes to the West (see Figure 1.2a). Even the dubious accounts supported the notion that Nathan Harrison traveled to California through Missouri and along these famed land routes.

Nathan Harrison worked as a miner in Northern California's mother-lode region in the 1850s and early '60s.

Overall, Scenario #5 established the most likely timeline for Harrison, placing him in California's mining country in the late 1840s or 1850s.[40] Accordingly, Nathan Harrison and his owner, Mr. Harrison, labored in the mother-lode region for up to a decade, working in multiple towns like Merced, Placerville, and others. There was debate in the historical narratives as to how Nathan Harrison gained his freedom. Although many sources emphasized that he was emancipated through the combination of the passage of the Thirteenth Amendment and the death of his former owner in the 1860s, isolated accounts offered other uncorroborated explanations. For example, John Davidson recalled:

> At the time the Lincoln pennies were minted [circa 1909], I gave [Nathan Harrison] a bright penny and told him what Lincoln done for the slaves: he said, "I know about Abe Lincoln. I had my freedom long before that [1863]." We knew that, for it was a subject he would not talk about. He had escaped from his master in the gold diggings. (1937: 2)

The veracity of Davidson's account was undermined by the oxymoronic phrase, "we knew that. . . [because] he would not talk about [it]." In addition, another narrative insisted the Nathan Harrison purchased his freedom from Mr. Harrison ("Front Pages: Did You Know?" 2002). Despite the multiple explanations surrounding how he was emancipated, almost all historical sources agreed that a newly freed Nathan Harrison promptly left mining activities in the environs of northern and central California in the 1860s and ventured toward Los Angeles. None suggested that he was still enslaved in Southern California.

Arrival in Southern California

Following the death of his owner, Harrison migrated southward toward Mission San Gabriel in the 1860s, working as a rancher, timber man, and laborer.

Harrison's north-to-south migration during this time paralleled the movement of many freed blacks in California. Most started in the gold country but left as ethnic tensions rose and white miners enacted ways to restrict the mining activities of black, Chinese, and Mexican prospectors (Lapp 1979: 4; Carlton 1974: 8; Savage 1945: 41; Soulé, Gihon, and Nisbet 1855: 412; Chiu 1967: x, 10–15; Bean 1973: 164–65; Pitt 1966: 48–68). Although some black miners concentrated in Sacramento and San Francisco, far more headed south to Los Angeles by the 1880s. The irony of this decision was that these African Americans were headed directly into areas of California that were far more dominated by migrants from the former Confederate US South as opposed to Northern California, which included far more settlers from north of the Mason-Dixon line.

Mission San Gabriel[41] was mentioned repeatedly in reliable historical accounts as Harrison's first Southern California destination following his mining days in the north. The name "Mission San Gabriel" was likely a broad term for the entire Chino Rancho,[42] a land grant originally connected to Mission San Gabriel. John Davidson stated that, ". . . [Harrison] found refuge in the south part of the state among strangers and at one time was a wood cutter at San Gabriel Mission. He saw some adventurous times there and El Monte by the night robbers" (1937: 2). Now a free person, Harrison likely had some control over his labor. This time at the mission marked a transition from his mining activities to those more attuned with ranching, like cutting timber, herding livestock, etc.

In the 1860s, El Monte was at the treacherous crossroads between Los Angeles, San Bernardino, and San Pedro. The town had a notorious reputation, even for the Old West, with regular knife and gun fights in its gambling saloons and lynchings on the outskirts of town. The disputes between lawless settlers, raiding Indigenous groups, bandit gangs, and others were frequent and deadly. The primary defense against El Monte's rampant criminal activity was the formation of a local militia company called the "El Monte Rangers," and later, a local vigilante group known as the "El Monte Boys." El Monte justice was often just as brutal as the crimes prosecuted. Further inciting civil unrest was the fact that by 1861 El Monte had become a hotbed of secessionist sympathizers.[43] Although Davidson did not specify the particular "adventurous times" involving Nathan Harrison or the ne'er-do-wells of El Monte, there were numerous other contemporary accounts of criminal behavior in the region that amply described the murder, mobs, and mayhem.

Louis Salmons related stories from Harrison's early days in Southern California; he stated:

> [Harrison] lived on San Gabriel for a long time before he came down here. And he used to go to Los Angeles . . . [which] was just a little runt of a Mexican town then and he always called it the "Pueblo."[44] He went to the Pueblo occasionally and when he was there he never slept in Los Angeles[45] overnight. He'd saddle his horse and go out on the hills. He said they was killing people every night.[46] (They had a sign up, "N— —r don't let the sun set"). (Hastings 1959b: no page numbers).

Signs like this that attempted to intimidate African Americans by insisting that they would be persecuted if found in a town in the evening were common. These "sundown towns" established a temporal segregation, allowing ethnic minorities to be in a locale during the day but enacting discriminatory local laws and threatening violence against the same group at night. There were thousands of sundown towns in the United States as late as the 1960s. Local Frank Axe told his son Fred that

Escondido, one of the closest settlements to Palomar Mountain, was a sundown town; he stated that, "No blacks were allowed to stay there. No one fed them in restaurants or gave any black shelter. They were run out of town" (Fred Axe, email to author, 21 February 2005).

The previous Salmons's quote about opting against spending the night in Los Angeles offered insight into early lessons Harrison learned about settlement strategies in Southern California. He saw firsthand reasons to fear urban areas at night. There were clear advantages to sleeping in the hills in nearby rural areas as opposed to city centers as the elevated remote areas were not patrolled by sundown racists. In addition, higher ground was almost always easier to defend in the case of an assault. In fact, choosing to sleep in the hills above Los Angeles might have been the harbinger to his decision to live above San Diego, Escondido, and Bear Valley on Palomar Mountain.

The 1860s were incredibly volatile times for the United States, from coast to coast. Abolitionist John Brown and his followers, black and white, attacked a federal arsenal at Harper's Ferry, Virginia on 16 October 1859, in an attempt to destroy slavery by freeing and arming slaves. It was one of the sparks that ignited the Civil War, which officially erupted on 12 April 1861, when Confederates bombarded Union soldiers at Fort Sumter, South Carolina. Likewise, Harriet Beecher Stowe's 1852 book *Uncle Tom's Cabin* portrayed the horrors of slavery to mainstream white audience, further stoking abolitionist flames. The four-year US Civil War would claim approximately three-quarters of a million lives, nearly destroy the nation, and leave no American region unaffected by the carnage.[47]

It was also during this time in the 1860s that Los Angeles had descended into utter chaos and debauchery. The city averaged a dozen murders each month and was labeled by noted journalist Morrow Mayo as "The Hell-Hole of the West" (McDougal 2002: 9). The fact that nearly every denomination of organized religion besides Catholicism had abandoned the town led East Coast newspaper editorials to suggest that Los Angeles should change its name to the more accurate moniker of "Los Diablos" (McDougal 2002: 9). Historian Dennis McDougal noted:

> Most mayhem [in Los Angeles] took place along the quarter-mile corridor of brothels, bars, gambling houses, and opium dens known as Calle de los Negros. Anglicized to "N——r Alley," Calle de Los Negros was the heartbeat of LA and the Gomorrah of the Pacific. Located southeast of the central Plaza de Los Angeles, N——r Alley had evolved into LA's first Chinatown by the end of the century; it flourished until the 1930s, when it was razed to make way for LA's new Union Station. But in the mid-

1800s, all libidos could still be satisfied for the right price along N——r Alley, whether the drug of choice was cheap whisky, high-stakes poker, or the black-market purchase of another human being to serve as indentured servant, blood sacrifice, or helpless sex slave. Those who weren't felled by rape, homicide, or cirrhosis in downtown Los Angeles could generally count on expiring from the cholera, dysentery, or smallpox that brewed in the zanjas, or open sewer ditches, that fed directly into the city's water supply. (2002: 9)

Few sources gave any definitive dates as to when Harrison left the Chino area and the nearby chaos of El Monte and Los Angeles to settle in San Diego County. It is worth noting that he did not appear on the United States Census of 1860 for San Diego County, or anywhere else for that matter. Nevertheless, his overall migration seemed to follow the Southern Emigrant Trail from Chino southward through areas that today hold the towns of Murrieta, Lake Elsinore, Temecula, and Aguanga (A. Miller 2012: 2). The 1860s and '70s seemed to be a time when he had seasonal residences and many jobs. If Harrison truly was "the first white [non-Indian] man on the mountain," as he so often proclaimed, then one of his temporary homes would likely have been on or very near Palomar Mountain. Multiple sources identified Harrison as a migratory Southern California shepherd. W. C. Fink explained:

> ... the sheep men used the high pasture lands on [Palomar] mountain for summer and fall feed and kept them there if the snow held off till the pasture was good in low land and coast. N——r Nate, two dogs and a flock of sheep came to those vallies [sic] afterward known as French valley and Doane valley. There is where Nate was sheep herding. (c. 1931: no page numbers)

Likewise, Catherine Wood stated, "[Harrison] spent his summers in Doane valley" (1937: no page numbers).

Fink and Wood also mentioned Harrison's transition to living with local Indians at the Pauma Rancheria,[48] located at the base of Palomar Mountain, during this time. Fink stated:

> [Harrison] grew tired of being alone with only dogs and sheep for company. "I told those dogs to take good care of the sheep," he afterwards said and left for Pauma Rancheria, taking his roll of bedding and the little food, flour, and frijollies [sic] which would insure him a welcome with the Indians. His living with the Indians became so interesting he did not return to the sheep ... [nor] did he return home to the home Ranch at Chino. Nate ... ever afterward remained in [San Diego] County. (c. 1931: no page numbers)

Wood offered a similar description of her own, noting that, "[Harrison] lived with the Indians at times, and occasionally helped the early settlers with their sheep" (1937: no page numbers).

Many of the local Luiseño people were impacted by US executive orders in the 1870s and '80s that established reservations at Pala, Rincon, Pauma, and La Jolla. Although the initial 1870 executive order granting land for Pala and San Pasqual was revoked in 1872, President Grant successfully set aside lands exclusively for San Diego County Native Americans in 1875 that created reservations at Santa Ysabel, Pala, Agua Caliente, Sycuan, Inaja, Cosmit, Potrero, Cahuilla, and Capitan Grande (Carrico 1987: 84).[49] Many of these reservations and a variety of others created over the next century were within a few miles of Palomar Mountain.

During this time, Palomar Mountain was rocked by one of its most famous murders; the victim was Anglo-American Joseph Smith, deemed by some as the first white man on the mountain.[50] Smith, nicknamed "Long Jo" by his US friends and "Jose Largo" by his Spanish-speaking amigos because of his lanky 6' 4" frame, had been instrumental in opening Palomar Mountain to US pioneering through his role as overseer of the roads traveled by the Butterfield Stagecoach Line.[51] This route linked Palomar with the Warner's Ranch area and was the main conduit for immigrants arriving in the mid-to-late 1800s via covered wagon through the desert regions to the east. Smith was a keen and well-connected business man who built a spacious adobe house and lived on the mountain only a year after the stage road opened in September of 1858. He lavishly entertained at his villa, but it was Smith's gracious and gregarious nature that led to his demise. He picked up a drifter on the road to Temecula in 1860, was enthralled with the young man's back story as a deserter from a British ship in San Diego harbor, and hired him as a ranch foreman. Soon after, the man murdered Smith. Many motives have been suggested—a fight over winning attention from Smith's Indian wife, a desire to steal Smith's purported hidden stash of gold, or just simply a drunken argument—but none were corroborated by anyone close to the scene of the crime. Edward Davis gave the most detailed account of the nefarious 1868 incident, writing:

> Palomar Mt. Joseph Smith came to the Mt. around 1858 or 60—before the civil war and settled in the Geo. Cook valley back against the hills. ... During the war (civil) deserters began to come into the Mts. And one came from Arizona and went to Palomar and lived with Smith for a while. Smith had an Ind. Woman who at this time was visiting friends in La Joya and this deserter got Smith's gun and shot him at a work bench in back of his house. The man thought [Smith] had money hidden away and searched but did not find any. He then went to La Joya and told the Ind. Woman Smith was dead and returned with her to the Smith house. The day Smith was killed Bill Place came to Smith's and found his body shot[,] and when his murderer came back they arrested him and took him down to the Warner ranch store and called a jury together for trial. On

this jury were the Helms, Andrew Linton, Bill Place, Old Nate [Harrison] and other old timers. He was found guilty and sentenced. That night he was chained to the wheel of a big freight wagon with an iron ring locked about his neck. The next morning he was hanged to the tree on hill back of the old Wilson house in Warner Ranch. (1932: no page numbers)

Though explicitly forbidden by California Statue 133, Section 11, vigilante justice was common in San Diego County and much of the Old West during the mid-to-late nineteenth century. These violent acts were especially pronounced in the more isolated regions of the northern and eastern areas of the county, like Palomar Mountain. In most cases, those executed were drifters, Mexicans, and California Indians. Furthermore, the San Diego coroner's jury repeatedly refused to name or indict any people involved who perpetrated the vigilante justice.

Catherine Wood also detailed events immediately following the execution, noting that, "After Joseph Smith was murdered, a sale of his Palomar property was held at the ranch. Judge Witherby, prominent San Diegan, had charge of it, and Uncle Nate cooked for the visitors, who came far and wide" (1937: no page numbers). This was one of multiple references through the years mentioning Harrison's adroit culinary abilities. In fact, Asher once gushed in an undated reference to Harrison's cooking with the grandiose declaration: "And such a supper [Harrison prepared]! Beef stew with the beef done just right. Flaky white potatoes with gravy that couldn't be beat. And perfect home-baked bread. The loaves were very thick but thoroughly baked all the way through with a rich, brown crust" (c. 1938: no page numbers).

Harrison's well-publicized role in the capture and execution of Smith's murderer was the only verified account of him working to apprehend criminals. Nevertheless, Abel M. Davis insisted that, "Nate was always on the side of law and order. . . He helped the sheriff catch more than one rogue and was on the other end of the rope when the scoundrel was strung up" (c. 1955: 63). Davis also emphasized that Palomar Mountain during this time "was a refuge for outlaws [because] it was easy to hide out with stolen cattle in one of the secluded spots" (c. 1955: 63). Clearly, seclusion was a mountain characteristic that appealed to multiple individuals, be they rustlers or former slaves wary of sundown laws.

The area in and around Palomar Mountain—now named Smith Mountain after Long Jo's untimely demise—was still primarily wilderness in the late 1860s. Local rancher Herbert Crouch explained that, ". . . the whole country was a free range. People who did not own a foot of land owned cattle and just turned them loose, and were on the rodeo ground to brand whatever they could find and gather in. . . There were hundreds of mustangs, all pintos, roaming about" (1965: 7). Asher supplied additional rustic details of the region and noted how Harrison used savvy mountain-man skills to master the terrain; he stated:

> Nate had a horse story, or rather a wild-horse story. Nate had been called to San Diego on important business, but he had no horse, and did not want to walk. So he went out into the hills back of Elsinore Lake and located a band of wild mustangs. He rounded up the mustangs, and kept them running until they got good and thirsty, when they made a break for the lake, and had good drink. However, Nate managed to head them off before they could quench their thirst, and kept them going for a long while. Then he allowed them to go down to the lake and fill up. After drinking they just stood around, which Nate said was a bad thing for either horse or man. Then he scared them up again and kept them on the go for another long while. Then another drink, and some more standing around. Then Nate got really busy and soon ran down the nag he wanted. He had to let the animal rest for a few hours, but it was young and strong and quickly got over its cold-water jag. So Nate rode the sixty miles to San Diego and back. No; they didn't pinch him for horse-stealing. The mustangs were wild and didn't belong to anybody. All you had to do if you wanted one was to run him down like Nate had done. (c. 1938: no page numbers)

In the 1870s, Harrison frequented many parts of San Diego County, including Pauma Valley and other northern inland areas, as well as the city of San Diego; he found regular work all over the region as a rancher, timber man, laborer, cook, and shop keeper.

By 1870, Harrison was well established in Southern California, although he was still far from sedentary. Regardless, he still did not appear on the 1870 US Census for San Diego County. Harrison worked a variety of jobs in Riverside County, northern San Diego County, and the city of San Diego. Although not listed on the 1873 Great Register, Harrison was denoted on the 1875 and 1877 Great Registers at Monserate. These listings were recorded on 30 June 1875 and marked the first definitive, contemporaneous, and official records of Harrison in California. Monserate was a relatively new settlement located near present-day Fallbrook in northern San Diego County. A few historical descriptions detailed daily life at Monserate in the late 1800s, including the following passage from J. Smeaton Chase's *California Coast Trails: A Horseback Ride from Mexico to Oregon in 1911*:

> We found that the place was the old Monserate Ranchhouse, and as our host had lived here, boy and man, for thirty-eight years, many were the tales he had to tell of the days when Don Tomas Alvarado maintained here the traditions of the grandest of Spanish California ruling over a household of no mean dimensions [during the late nineteenth century].

... Thirteen thousand sheep, three thousand head of cattle, and three hundred horses could the don call his own. (1913: chapter 3)

Previous stories of Harrison's shepherding and his listing as a "laborer" on the registers might have alluded to working the massive amounts of livestock owned by the Alvarados out of Rancho Monserate.

In the early 1870s, Harrison gained employment with surveyors in the region as their cook.[52] Due to the odd shape of California, it required three north/south meridian-baseline sets for surveyors McIntosh,[53] Henry Hancock, and M. G. Wheeler to map the territory. Asher quoted Harrison as stating, "The Frenchman [put up] fifteen hundred dollars for the survey, Doane and Mendenhall wouldn't dig [pay] up. Charlie Fox was the surveyor and I was cook" (c. 1938: no page numbers). The names mentioned in the quote attributed to Harrison by Asher were well known in late nineteenth century Palomar Mountain history. McIntosh, Hancock, and Wheeler were prominent local surveyors who held public office. The Frenchman was one of the Nicolas brothers (Jean or Augusti), Harrison's future neighbors on Palomar Mountain. Doane was George Doane, close friend of Harrison and fellow Palomar Mountain resident. Mendenhall was Enos Thomas Mendenhall, the highly successful "Cattle King of Palomar" from North Carolina who founded the Mendenhall Cattle Company.

At the same general time that Harrison was busy on projects in northern San Diego and San Bernardino counties, he also worked in the city of San Diego for Louis Rose, one of the region's most well-known and respected businessmen. Rose, a famed pioneer developer, community advocate, and political leader, was born in Neuhaus-an-de-Oste, Germany in 1807, immigrated to the US in 1840, and came to San Diego a decade later as California became a state.[54] He was the city's first Jewish settler. In addition to serving on San Diego County's first grand jury, the county's first Board of Supervisors, and the 1853–55 City Board of Trustees as President, Rose built a successful ranch and tannery on 650 acres of land near San Clemente Canyon in 1853. This was the first and only tannery in San Diego County for many years. Cattle hides were so lucrative and prominent in the region during this time that those in the leather-manufacturing industry called them "California dollars" (Harrison 2004: 45). With help from the ample revenue that the "Rose Canyon" tannery provided—in addition to his nearby butcher shop in Old Town—Rose set about on an ambitious plan to develop "Roseville," a town in Point Loma next to the bay that he hoped would compete with San Diego's New Town in the late 1860s and early '70s. While Rose achieved great successes in San Diego, he also repeatedly over-reached and faced the wrath of creditors and embarrassment of bankruptcy. His story was synonymous with San Diego's boom-and-bust cycles during the second half of the nineteenth century.[55]

At the center of the recorded interactions between Nathan Harrison and Louis Rose was a pet Galapagos tortoise named "Chili." Rose obtained Chili around 1851; he likely purchased the beloved reptile from a whaler.[56] Rose's tenderness for animals was well known, and Chili figured prominently in narratives of the time. Benjamin I. Hayes, a San Diego judge and politician during the 1850s, '60s, and '70s, noted:

> I went to a stand at Mr. Rose's—to see the turtle [Chili]. It is six years old, came from the Galapagos Islands; weighed when brought here 35 lbs, now 100 lbs. We presented it a slice of bread; it quietly snapped off a piece. Hens and little chickens gathered around for a share, even picking at the crumbs in its mouth—to all which it paid no attention. Then the cook put a piece of pancake in its mouth. A little pet dog helped himself to part. It merely raised up on its feet, to let the dog play beneath . . . Rose has a great fondness for pets. I saw him go up and kiss a mule the other day. (Harrison 2004: 129)

Harrison worked for Rose in the mid-1870s, helping out as a shop-keeper at one of the stores in Roseville. Asher stated:

> There came a time [c. 1874], when Mr. Rose had to go north on a business trip to be absent from his store for two or three weeks. He left Nate in full charge of the store and the "turkle."[57] The turkle [Chili] was an immense Gulf of California creature and the apple of the storekeeper's eye. The turkle was somewhat given to wandering away from the Rose premises if given the least opportunity to get away. His boss's last instructions to Nate were warnings not to allow the turkle to get away. One morning, a few days after Mr. Rose's departure, the turkle was missing from its usual haunts. Nate hunted around for hours whenever he could leave the store. But he dared not leave the front of the store out of his sight on account of possible customers. Rose was gone two weeks. Nate said that he kept worrying about what Mr. Rose would say. But Mr. Rose never said a word. He just organized a posse, and the posse found the turkle where La Presa is now. (c. 1938: no page numbers)

This near disastrous sequence of events did not diminish the Rose-Harrison relationship; Harrison would later tell Asher that, "Louis J. Rose was the finest white man I ever knew" (c. 1938: no page numbers). Rose died in 1888.

During the same time period in the mid-1870s, Harrison also had work on an extended project near Palomar Mountain. Asher reported that Harrison told him in the early summer of 1901 that, "About twenty-five or thirty years ago [in circa 1871–76]. . . . I helped build thirty-two miles of two-wire fence on Pine Mountain. Mr. [James] McCoy had the contract. He lost a hundred dollars on the job" (c. 1938: no page numbers). Pine Mountain was about 10–15 miles southwest of the Agua Tibia area, home to Harrison friend, host, and occasional employer Major Lee Utt.

It was during this time that Harrison married an Indigenous woman with children from a previous union; their marriage was brief, although he would remain close to her family.

Historical narratives about Harrison's activities in and around Palomar Mountain in the 1870s typically began with details of the projects on which he worked but then often turned toward his interaction with local Indigenous women. For example, during this time, Harrison frequently visited Major Lee Utt at the Agua Tibia Rancho, which was just a few miles west of Palomar Mountain and where Harrison would acquire property at Rincon in 1879. Fink recalled:

> Many times [Harrison] turned up at Agua Tibia Rancho asking for work but meaning food and comfortable home and never was refused to be taken in and supplyed [sic] with clothes. . . . [W]hen the work became distasteful to him [he] left without notice to live among the Indians and later would return as glad as a lost pup to its mother. This amused Maj. Utt very much and was a pleasure to hear him tell his adventures with the squaws who had not been able to quell the manly spirit of Nate. (c. 1931: no page numbers)

Other historical accounts also listed Harrison's different mountain-based employment; Charles Mendenhall, grandson of cattle-baron Enos T. Mendenhall, remembered Harrison as "smart as a whip, a good wrangler and a pretty good timber man," and J. H. Heath noted that, "in [the] earlier years [Nathan Harrison] worked for the various ranchers of the mountain" (Bryson 1962: no page numbers; Heath 1919: 8).[58]

Although few of the Lee Utt–Nathan Harrison historical interactions were dated, the ranching partnership between Utt and Herbert Crouch that likely involved Harrison as a shepherd was fairly well chronicled, especially in terms of the regional transition from cattle ranching to sheep. Crouch emphasized the consequences of the drought on livestock strategies, stating, "Between '69 and '76, as the cattle went out, the sheep came in" (1965: 31). He also offered an overview of his time in the region that included reflections on the challenges of all San Diego County ranchers in the 1870s. Crouch noted:

> I landed in San Luis Rey March 25th, 1869. While in San Diego I met Major Utt, who, having found out that I understood about sheep, told me he had a number of ewes in a place called San Luis Rey [Agua Tibia]. . . . In those days land was considered worthless on account of the four dry

years, [18]70–71–72–73 which will never be forgotten by those who had stock at that time, and too many cattle to do much farming. . . . [59] A great many proved up on their land, sold out, and left. (1965: 33)

Herding sheep clearly loomed largely for Nathan Harrison; it was one of his most employable skills and seemed to influence where he chose to live. In addition, although the name and major details of Harrison's first wife seems to have escaped the annals of history, it is known that she had a son by the name of Frederick "Sheep" Smith. Born circa 1850 and later married to Maria Mogort, Fred Smith was best known for his business operations in Wilmington, located in south Los Angeles. True to his nickname, Fred Smith listed his occupation in the 1880 census as "sheepraiser." He lived in Southern California for all of his adult life and was especially prominent in Los Angeles. As noted by historian Tom Jacobs:

Frederick "Sheep" Smith owned about 360 acres in the vicinity of Norwalk Boulevard and Carson Street at the time [of the late 1800s and early 1900s] and . . . grazed flocks of sheep there. According to his grandson, John, . . . Sheep Smith drove his flock to markets as far away as San Francisco, grazing all the way and taking three months! John's father later donated a whole block of that same land for the Bloomfield School. (1976: 14)

Fred Smith seemed to be important in Nathan Harrison's life for multiple reasons. A recently rediscovered letter from the Cabin Collection verified the marital union between his mother and Harrison. Dated 13 June 1873, the six-page, handwritten correspondence from Fred Smith to Harrison began with the honorific "Querido padrastro," which translated to "Dearest Stepfather." The letter included important business details, corroborated Smith's prominent standing in the regional sheep industry, and coordinated a visit. In addition, it provided a voice for a close Harrison relative and firmly established that Harrison and Smith's mother had already married by 1873.

Other historical accounts added that Harrison's first wife—presumably Fred Smith's mother—had children from a previous marriage. A second spectacular find from the rediscovered Cabin Collection was one particular image of a young woman, presumably of California Indian descent, with an inscription on the back that read, "From your granddaughter Dory Mary Smith, Norwalk Route of Bloomfield District" (Figure 1.3). On the basis of this find, it became clear that the Harrison-Smith connection transcended multiple generations and reflected continued family ties.

When Harrison married Fred Smith's mother, he became Fred's stepfather and the step-grandfather of Smith's children. Dory Mary Smith

Figure 1.3. This picture of Nathan Harrison's step-granddaughter was intriguing for both the image on the front and the written clue on the back. (Courtesy of the Nathan "Nate" Harrison Historical Archaeology Project, Kirby Collection.)

was born to Fred and Maria (Mogort) Smith on 3 November 1882, at least nine years after the Harrison-Smith union. Based on the clothing in the photograph, the image of Dory Mary Smith was taken around the turn of the twentieth century; the fact that she would have been about eighteen years old at the time further supported this identification. Dory Mary Smith signed the photograph and listed her contact information as the Norwalk Route of Bloomfield District, which corresponded with the aforementioned land in the Jacob's passage that Fred Smith's son, presumably Dory Mary's brother, donated for a school. In addition, this address matched that of Fred Smith's at the time. Dory Mary Smith married Frank Carricaburu and, according to the 1930 Census, had seven children.[60] Dory Mary Carricaburu remained in the Los Angeles area for her entire life and was buried in the Artesia Cemetery District, only a few miles from where her father used to graze his sheep in the nineteenth century.[61]

The 1873 letter from Fred Smith to Harrison clearly had a secondary agenda in addition to setting up a visit. Although initially deferential, by the end of the correspondence Smith overtly chastised his stepfather for reneging on business responsibilities and implored him to change his ways. Smith expressed dutiful concern for how Harrison had shirked duties in the past, stating, "All this time that you have been in California, you have abandoned your work, and that is why you don't have anything now . . . if you don't maintain your job you still will never have anything." Fink's narrative offered details that confirmed Harrison's tendency to abandon work duties. When describing Harrison's shepherding skills, he stated that on one occasion:

> [Harrison] did not return to the sheep for some time and when he did, he found dogs and sheep gone. His job was gone as well as the sheep, and he was responsible for the flock of sheep. Responsibility sat very lightly on his shoulders, but what would happen when the owner came with supplies and to get the flock of sheep? He thought of safety for his hide and that safety lay in flight from the scene of the disaster. (c. 1931: no page numbers)

Smith was obviously frustrated with Harrison's tendency to bounce from job to job with little care or concern for past responsibilities. As a result, he was unapologetically direct in his critique of Harrison's poor work ethic. In addition, Smith stated that this behavior would ultimately impact himself, explaining that if Harrison failed to accumulate wealth he would have little inheritance to pass on to his descendants. Smith dramatically concluded, "And [then] I will end up with nothing."

Locating the links between Harrison and Fred Smith's family were like finding needles in a haystack, even for historical archaeologists who boast this sort of specialized skillset. At first, Machado's reference that Harrison married Fred Smith's mother was the lone piece of evidence. Then, the Cabin Collection produced the long correspondence from Fred Smith that addressed Harrison as "stepfather" and the handwritten note on the back of a photograph found at the cabin with the name "Dory Mary" and the family attribution "your granddaughter." In addition, a final scouring of Robert Asher's many manuscripts revealed the following passage: "[In 1918] a man named Smith stayed with Nate the greater part of one winter shortly before Nate was taken down to San Diego. I never saw Mr. Smith, but was informed that he was Nate's son-in-law" (c. 1938: no page numbers). Overall, the familial Nathan Harrison–Fred Smith bond, although well hidden in the historical records, stayed strong from at least 1873 to 1919.

From 1879 to 1882, Harrison patented and lived on land at Rincon, near the base of Palomar Mountain and adjacent to Pauma Indian territory; this acquisition made him the first African American homesteader in the region.

There were a handful of official documents that help establish the location of Harrison's home and his general range of activity in the late 1870s and early '80s. There were three Great Register entries (1875, 1877, and 1879) for Harrison, each of which placed him south of Los Angeles in Monserate. They showed he was still very mobile but also suggested a primary base near the mountain that would ultimately be his long-term home. On 10 November 1879, Harrison patented land in the Rincon area at the base of Palomar Mountain. He received a US land patent for 112.15 acres in lots 2, 3, and 4 of Section 22 in Township 10, South Range One West of the San Bernardino Meridian. Though no homestead certificate existed for this transaction, the Bureau of Land Management general land office records placed this title transfer under the authority of the 1862 Homestead Act. It was this transaction that resulted in Harrison being hailed as the first African American homesteader in the region. This land was not the property on which future archaeological excavations would be undertaken starting in 2004. Laura James specified that, "The first home that we hear of Nate having was in the Rincon Valley" (1958: 7). Likewise, local Louis Salmons recalled that, "Then [Harrison] drifted down here, and he was all around. He took up the hundred acres that the Rincon Spring's on" (Hastings 1959b: no page numbers).

One must not automatically equate a land claim with full-time residency. Herbert Crouch explained that for some individuals land-claiming in the late nineteenth century was just a way to make a fast buck. He noted:

> Buying and taking up land in the early days was a most harassing job, and got on my nerves a great deal. . . . People would not take up the land in the early days. They thought it was of no value . . . [Others] would take up a claim on purpose to sell it for what they could get, and move on somewhere else. (1965: 37)

The Homestead Act of 1862 had important ramifications for the northern inland territory of San Diego County. Most of this land was owned by the US government, which had a poor record of honoring stipulations in the 1848 Treaty of Hidalgo that guaranteed a continuance of Mexican landholdings and an even worse legacy with the Indigenous population. The US Homestead Act declared that unclaimed areas were public domain for American settlers willing to live on and improve the territory. In exchange for a modest $10 filing fee, the government allowed an individual to claim up to 160 acres of public land as long as improvements were made in the form of a house and the surrounding area was used for grazing or farming (McHenry 1997: 6). In addition, the person who filed the official claim had to be at least twenty-one years of age and listed as "head of household." Once homesteaders had resided on the property for five years, it was theirs (W. W. Robinson 1948: 168). Designed to encourage settlement of the Old West and passed during the middle of the Civil War, the Homestead Act enabled many families from east of the Mississippi River to accumulate vast land holdings in the Old West and accrue significant wealth for their descendants. The Homestead Act would not be replaced until 1976; by that time 10 percent of the government's land had been awarded through 1.6 million different claims.

Why did Harrison choose to patent land in 1879, and why at Rincon? These were difficult questions to answer. Harrison's continued southward migration through California and decision to settle in a rural area again paralleled statewide trends for African Americans. Whereas most other California cities maintained far higher percentages of blacks in urban areas during this time, San Diego stood out for having much higher rural settlement rates for African Americans.[62] There were many factors contributing to this phenomenon, including the city of San Diego's lagging pre-1880 growth and economic advantages of rural life for laborers.[63]

Harrison also might have chosen to live at Rincon because of his close ties to the local Indigenous community. Various sources emphasized his interactions with Rincon Indians in particular but offered no exact dates. Rincon Chief Juan Sotelo Calac baptized Harrison, and Calac's wife, Encarnacion Calac, was Harrison's godmother[64] (Figure 1.4). The Calacs' grandson, Max, recalled that when "Nate was baptized by Indians [he] became a member of the tribe" (Ryan 1964h: no page numbers). He also noted that, "[Harrison was] allowed to dance in [the] dance ceremonials. [He] tied a red bandana around his forehead [with] a feather stuck in [and] attended Indian fiestas" (Ryan 1964h: no page numbers). Furthermore, when Peters stated that, "Nate was married to an Indian woman for a while and lived in Rincon," he linked the union and residing at the bottom of Palomar Mountain (Ryan 1964h: no page numbers).

The 1880 San Diego County census recorded Nathan Harrison twice, once in the San Jacinto Township and once in the Bear Valley Township.[65] Both townships were in what was San Diego County in the late nineteenth century, but neither was directly adjacent to Palomar Mountain. They were each about ten miles from the mountain and in differ-

Figure 1.4. Anthropologist J. P. Harrington took this photograph of Chief Juan Sotelo Calac and his wife Encarnacion at the Rincon Indian Reservation in 1933; both individuals played significant roles in the life of Nathan Harrison. (Reprinted from John P. Harrington, *Explorations and Field-Work of the Smithsonian Institution in 1932* [Washington, DC, 1932]: 87. Public domain.)

ent directions. The censuses included a wealth of personal information about Harrison. The San Jacinto record listed Harrison as an illiterate married 48-year-old black male farm laborer. According to this document, both Harrison and his parents were born in Kentucky. Harrison's name appeared in conjunction with the Larson family, a Scandinavian husband (Elisha Larson), wife (Fredericka), and their two children. The Bear Valley listing reiterated that Harrison was a black male farm laborer, but it listed his age at fifty, his place of origin as Alabama, and his marital status as married. This record documented him in conjunction with the Juans. Angel Juan was a farm laborer and harness maker; he and his wife were California Indians.

As was the case with so many historical accounts concerning Nathan Harrison, the majority of similarities suggested that these government documents referred to the same individual but there were just enough differences to raise doubts. His name, sex, race, and occupation were identical; his age and geographic proximity to Palomar Mountain were within an expected variation for the time; but his state of origin and marital status were irreconcilably different, especially since the record that stated he was married pre-dated the account of his being single—not widowed—by a week. Already in 1880, Nathan Harrison's marital status was open to interpretation as was his birth state and age. Debates concerning these matters would continue for the next century.

It was difficult to be certain of the exact chronology of Harrison's marriage to Fred Smith's mother. The accounts mentioning this marital union offered no dates. Furthermore, there were few firmly established events to bookend their wedding date or her subsequent death. All that was recorded was that they married once he was in the region (post-1870), that Smith called Harrison his stepfather in an 1873 letter, and that Smith's mother died soon after the union with Harrison. The fact that one of the 1880 census records listed Harrison as single and the other as married might have suggested a relatively recent union or a recent dissolution. Harrison's departure from the immediate area and sale of the Rincon property in 1882 might have hinted he was moving on from his Rincon life, perhaps due to the loss of his wife or a burgeoning relationship with someone else. With so little evidence, it was hard to do little more than suggest a circa 1870–82 date range for the Harrison-Smith marriage.

Despite the fact that California was admitted to the Union as a free state in 1850, it enacted miscegenation laws during the late nineteenth century that explicitly forbade members of the purported white race from marrying those of African or Asian descent. The Golden State's most pronounced late nineteenth- and early twentieth-century anti-immigrant legislation focused more on restricting Asian populations than other groups, but its discriminatory laws also drew on long-established Southern sentiments that sought to criminalize black-white intermarriage (Kurashige 2008). As a black man in California, it was illegal for Harrison to marry a white woman. However, he could wed a Mexican, Native American, or Asian woman. In fact, Mexicans and Indigenous peoples in California could marry anyone. While legal precedents often placed Hispanics in the white category, many decades of intermarriage in California under Spanish and Mexican rule (pre-1850) offered numerous exceptions and cases of racial ambiguity that undermined the restrictions. Furthermore, "Indian wives" were relatively common in the Old West—Catherine Wood listed many examples in nineteenth-century San Diego County including Joe Smith's spouse and George Dyche's wife—a phenomenon often spurred on by the dearth of white women in the region during this time.[66]

The unique occupation pattern of Southern California—with thousands of years of Indigenous settlement, followed by quickly changing periods of Spanish (1769–1821), Mexican (1821–48), and US American (1848–) governance—led to some strange and contradictory rules concerning interethnic unions, especially for African Americans. Spanish exploration of the state brought many Africans and African Americans to the region; the result of which had been extensive interethnic marriage and general acceptance of blacks marrying non-blacks.[67] Although the Spanish colonial identity system did fixate on distinctions between the many different kinds of interethnic unions, it transcended singular color or nationality attributions and was far more complex than US American racial categories.[68] For example, Pío Pico, the last governor of Alta California under Mexican rule (1845–46) had a grandmother of African ancestry as well as Mexican, Indian, and Italian heritage (Gray 2002). Spanish norms counted him as a first-generation "Californio," even though later US American rules would have deemed him as black.[69] In fact, at the 1849 California Constitutional Convention Pío Pico's brother, Andrés, served as a delegate and holistically approved many anti-black provisions that were passed; quite simply, these laws had no effect on Californios, like himself (Carlton 1974: 11).

On the contrary, African Americans with similarly mixed heritage from the American South who migrated west were deemed black and faced severe discrimination in the form of restrictions, segregation, and widespread antagonism. The inconsistency was pronounced and exacerbated by the fact that racial categories and the resultant racial order were rarely static in the Old West (Schumann 2017: 101; Orser 2007). While nineteenth-century Southern California had long witnessed broad

Spanish and Mexican acceptance of Africans and African Americans, it was also the southern route for westward expansion frequented by pro-slavery settlers after the Civil War, who brought their extensive bigoted ethnic baggage to Southern California and magnified existing racial tensions. To complicate matters further, certain US presidents in the first few years of California's statehood, like Millard Fillmore and his "Know Nothing" nativistic platform of 1856 that "Americans [i.e., not Catholics, Jews, Indians, blacks, etc.] must rule America," offered highly constrained definitions of equality, integration, and personal liberty. Southern California's unique Spanish history, massive immigration from Southern states, and highly conservative politicians on issues of race made interethnic unions a complex and volatile matter for non-whites.

Marriage was not the only contemporary social institution layered with legalized racism. Despite the ratification of the Fifteenth Amendment in 1870, which gave African American males the right to vote, there were still numerous ways politicians found to disenfranchise blacks at the polls. An 11 May 1880 San Diego County poll tax receipt for $2 with Harrison's name offered insights into these practices. Poll taxes were fees all voters, regardless of property ownership or wealth, had to pay when casting a vote in an election. Although commonly associated with the American South as a tactic of Jim Crow discrimination, poll taxes were also common in the Old West. In fact, California had a poll tax until 1914, but it did not successfully block Harrison from voting in 1880.

The 1880 records also established that Harrison resided in San Diego County and was able to travel large distances between households working as a farm laborer. The 1880 and 1882 Great Registers, which included entries for Harrison, copied much of the information from the contemporary San Jacinto census. There was also a second letter in Spanish from Fred Smith to a Mrs. Lucía from December of 1880 that was part of the Cabin Collection and directly mentioned Harrison. It stated:

Anaheim, December 10, 1880

Mrs. Lucía,

I beg of you, do not play dumb regarding the mares that I sold to your deceased husband, Miguel. It was about 6 or 7 beasts that you yourself must have seen when he took them to Aguanga. And there is also a metal [a piece of iron] of which there are many eyewitnesses. Well, I sold you the beasts [mares] for the sum of 80 pesos. And I gave him a receipt [a paper] of said sales of the beasts to which he gave me a promise to pay back [IOU], which I still have. Now I want you to return the metal [piece

of iron] and 75.00 in cash or in animals. Give it to Mr. Ines Harrison, and
I will head over there to collect it.

Frederico Smith[70]

This letter corroborated Fred Smith's presence in both the Los Angeles area and at Palomar Mountain. It was sent from Anaheim and
ended with a reference to Smith joining Harrison, presumably near
Rincon where he owned land or at Bear Valley or San Jacinto where
Nathan Harrison appeared on two different 1880 census records. Furthermore, the letter referenced Miguel taking the mares to Aguanga,
which was located less than ten miles from Rincon, on the northern
base of Palomar Mountain. In fact, the mares might have initially belonged to Harrison.

There was also a 24 September 1881 record from Julian of Nathan
Harrison being arrested for public drunkenness. Though Julian maintained the largest African American community in the region and was
home to many successful entrepreneurs who were ethnic minorities, it
is noteworthy that Harrison's only historically verified time in Julian
ended in his arrest. The court proceedings stated:

> One negro Nathan Harrison Being Brought into Court this 24th day of
> September 1881 By Constable G. W. Dean on a Charge of Drunkness &
> Boyisters Conduct on the Streets of the Town of Julian. it is therefore or-
> dered By the Court a fine be assessed of Ten dollars against Nathan Har-
> rison and he be comited [sic] to the County jail[.] After Due consideration
> I hereby Remit [forgive] the above fine
>
> G. C. Daves
> Justice of the Peace
> (San Diego County Public Records Office)

One can only speculate as to why the Justice of the Peace waived Harrison's hefty fine. As far as we know, this was his only recorded run-in
with the law over the course of a near century-long life.

Located more than thirty miles from Rincon and Palomar Mountain,
Julian was a bustling town during the 1880s. Its growth was fueled by
a mini-gold rush that started after the discovery of the precious metal
by African American Fred Coleman in 1869. By 1872, Julian had a population nearly half the size of San Diego (Crawford 1995: 55; Harris
1974). Nearly two-thirds of the blacks in San Diego County lived in the
vicinity of Julian. Julian's high black population corresponded with its
distinctive settlement pattern; unlike many other Southern California
towns, over 60 percent of Julian's inhabitants were from the northern
US and Europe, as opposed to the South (LeMenager 1992: 145).

In 1882, Harrison sold his property to Andreas Scott and left Rincon, although he stayed in the general area and worked at Warner's Ranch and in Temecula for a few years.

After less than three years as owner of the Rincon land, Harrison sold the property. A deed of sale related that on 19 June 1882, "Andres" Scott purchased all 112.15 acres from Harrison for $300. The 1880 San Diego County census listed farmer Andreas Scott and his wife Elvira as California Indians living in the Bear Valley Township.[71] Many historical accounts verified this sale. Ed Davis explained that Harrison had an interim stop between his sale of the Rincon property and the homestead on Palomar Mountain, writing that, "He sold out, lived on the Warner Ranch for awhile, then on to Palomar and at last settled in the canyon." Warner Springs was a ranch with 25–30,000 head of sheep, cattle, and horses. In 1880, Andrew Linton was named overseer of the ranch. Harrison was well acquainted with Linton, as they had served together on the ad hoc jury that convicted, sentenced to death, and executed Joseph Smith's murderer in 1868.

Harrison married again, this time to an Indigenous woman named Dona Lavierla; they were not together long.

There were no overt explanations in the historical records as to why Harrison sold his land and left in 1882, although the move seemed to coincide with his marriage to a second Indigenous woman, Dona Lavierla.[72] As noted earlier, Frank Machado stated that Harrison married "Dona Lavierla, my aunt, in 1882" (Asher 1938: no page numbers). This assertion both anchored the union in time and established the kinship between Lavierla and the Machado family. It might explain why Harrison, and presumably Lavierla, moved to Warner's Ranch, as Frank Machado's farm was between the La Jolla Reservation and Lake Henshaw, right next to Warner's Ranch (see Figure 1.2b). Furthermore, an account by Bertram Moore linked Harrison's stay at Warner Springs with the Indigenous community; it stated, "[Harrison] worked his way north and west, finally stopping off at Warner's Spring where he lived with Indians until he moved to his humble stone shack on Palomar" (n.d.: no page numbers).

Warner's Ranch was southwest of Palomar Mountain, but Asher stated in a different account that Harrison lived in the *opposite* direction after leaving Rincon. In an extended and uncorroborated passage full of intrigue and bizarre details, Asher claimed:

Nate lived for a time near Temecula, northwest of Palomar Mountain. I think he said that he had seen Juan Murrieta, the famous bandit. At any rate, he knew a good deal about Murrieta and had several Murrieta stories on tap. He once told me about a "Big Snow" which had come about Thanksgiving time. As near as I could figure, it was probably the big snow year of 1882–83.[73] The late Warren Hackett of San Diego was driving stage between Temecula and San Diego that winter and I have heard him refer to his troubles in getting through the snow drifts at that time. Nate said that the snow piled up higher than the bottom of the window of Wolfe's store at Temecula, and that they had to shovel the snow away before they could get out of the door. (c. 1938: no page numbers)

This account did far more to complicate the Harrison timeline than simplify it. Asher's narrative selection contained three seemingly linked elements: 1) Harrison living in Temecula, 2) Harrison encountering Juan Murrietta, and 3) a massive snowstorm hitting the region in the early to mid-1880s. The individuals Asher mentioned in this brief passage—Warren Hackett, Harrison, and storeowner Louis Wolf—were all related by marriage. Perhaps Harrison and wife Dona Lavierla were in Temecula as invited family guests, and Harrison continued to labor in his usual ranching capacities.

The "Juan Murrieta, the famous bandit" reference was likely a red herring. I believe that Asher mixed up his Murrietas. Juan Murrieta was a major sheep rancher whose land became the city of Murrieta, just northwest of Temecula. By the 1880s, he had moved his massive sheep ranch down from Mariposa, near Yosemite, to northern San Diego County. Juan Murrieta was not a bandit, famous or infamous, but he did own over 100,000 sheep. On the contrary, Joaquin Murrieta Carrillo was a legendary outlaw in the California gold fields of the 1850s.[74] Harrison had undoubtedly heard many tales of the iconic thief during his time in mother-lode country, but according to most sources, by 1853, Joaquin had been killed and his head was pickled in a jar and on public display.[75] This Murrieta might have been dead even before Harrison arrived in California. The far less exciting Murrieta (Juan) and Harrison seemed to have had many opportunities to know each other. They likely arrived in gold country near Merced in the 1850s. Both were in the Temecula area in the 1870s. Furthermore, Harrison was a frequent visitor to Pala and patented land a few miles away at Rincon, and Juan Murrieta married Adele Golsh of Pala in 1873. If Harrison sold his property at Rincon in 1882 and went to work for Juan and Adele in the Temecula area, the employment would have been brief as Juan lost all of his sheep and sold out in 1884 (Crouch 1965: 22).[76]

Another reason that the story of Joaquin Murrieta and Harrison might have gained traction was that Palomar Mountain was allegedly home to various outlaws and desperadoes during the second half of the nineteenth century. One of these tales concerned Tiburcio Vásquez, an especially notorious lieutenant in Joaquin's gang. Vásquez purportedly had a hideout on or near Harrison's tract and used it while the authorities errantly searched for him in areas to the north (A. Davis c. 1955: 63).

By the mid-1880s, there was still nothing definitive in the historical records that pinpointed Harrison as living on the western slope of Palomar Mountain. In fact, some accounts questioned whether he was living at all (Figure 1.5). The *San Diego Union* ran a story on 21 March 1884, reporting that Harrison had died in the massive downpour—that would later be deemed "The Great San Diego Flood."[77] The newspaper article stated that, "Poor 'Nate' Harrison was drowned in the San Luis Rey River during the recent storm. He was a Southern slave and has resided here many years." Unfortunately, the brief article did not specify where "here" was, or how long "many years" constituted. Less than a month later, the newspaper recanted the story, asserting that, "N— —r Nath [*sic*] is not drowned as was reported in the Union; he still lives to vote the Republican ticket and beat his way through the world." Although neither of these brief accounts placed Harrison on Palomar

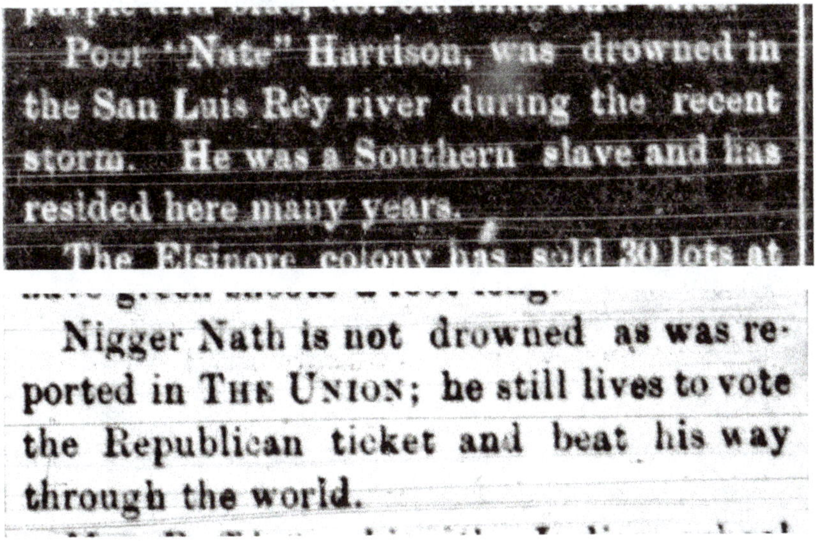

Poor "Nate" Harrison, was drowned in the San Luis Rey river during the recent storm. He was a Southern slave and has resided here many years.

Nigger Nath is not drowned as was reported in THE UNION; he still lives to vote the Republican ticket and beat his way through the world.

Figure 1.5a/b. Few historical contradictions of Nathan Harrison were more pronounced than these newspaper articles from the spring of 1884. (*San Diego Union,* 21 March 1884 and 20 April 1884. Public domain.)

Mountain, they did situate him in northern San Diego County, near the San Luis Rey River. In addition, they intimated that he was widely known in the local region and had lived there for quite some time.

In the late 1880s, Harrison made his home two-thirds of the way up Palomar Mountain; he claimed the tract's water in 1892 and home-steaded the land in 1893.

Government documents indicated that by the late 1880s Palomar Mountain was Harrison's home. The 1888 and 1890 Great Register list-ings, both based on information recorded on 26 August 1888, listed Harrison as a farmer at Pala, which was the district that included Palo-mar Mountain. The 1894 Great Register, which post-dated Harrison's official homestead certificate, also listed Pala as his "local residence." In addition, the San Diego County 1889/90 Ownership Map for the western slope of Palomar Mountain included the name "Harris" at the same location—Section 1 in Township 10 South of Range 1, west of the San Bernardino Meridian—that Nathan Harrison would later homestead in 1893. This hand-drawn plat map strongly suggested that by 1889 Harrison had already established a residence at the moun-tain location that would be his home for at least three decades. On the basis of historical records alone, however, it was difficult to deter-mine whether this residence was relatively recent (mid-to-late 1880s) or dated back decades.

On 26 May 1892, Nathan Harrison filed a water claim for the spring associated with his Palomar Mountain land. The hand-written claim gave him rights to the active springs and streams on his property for irrigation and stock purposes; he could also legally sell the water to his neighbors. Water would become central to Harrison's existence on Palomar Mountain. Mark Twain's alleged quip that, "Whiskey is for drinking. Water is for fighting over," was especially appropriate when discussing contentious disputes over this most valuable resource in the Old West. Differences in water use were prominent between the differ-ent groups inhabiting San Diego County during the nineteenth century as Indigenous peoples, Spanish, Mexican, and US American settlers each employed decidedly different goals, strategies, and tactics. In fact, non-Indigenous inhabitants quickly implemented key components of a hydraulic society for the region, including environmental manipu-lation, unequal distribution patterns, and emphasis on irrigation and agriculture over domestic use (Wittfogel 1957: 12). The stakes were high for water control. Historian Donald Worster emphasized that in the American West, a lack of water ". . . was a threat to an established standard of living, to a margin of wastefulness, and to a future of unrestrained economic growth" (1985: 312).

Whereas the region's Indigenous groups were intimately familiar with the fluctuation and unreliability of local rivers, colonial immigrants were often unprepared for the frequent periods of flood and drought, and the havoc these cycles would wreak on their capitalistic profits (Shipek 1981: 295–312; Brodie 2013: 17). Native peoples did engage in small-scale water management methods—riverine settlements that included adjacent plant husbandry, brush and rock dams, storage vessels, and erosion control; each of these actions reflected specialized regional knowledge (Shipek 1993). On the contrary, Spanish and Mexican missionaries created elaborate irrigation systems for agricultural fields, but the unreliable local water sources led to poor crop yields and disproportionately low Indigenous conversion rates (Engelhardt 1920; Lightfoot 2005). Spanish construction of a rock and concrete dam and aqueduct temporarily addressed these limitations, but secularization of the mission during the Mexican period saw these structures fall into disrepair with the primary economic focus on cattle grazing (Luksic and Kendziorski 1999: 5). US American water-rights rules, drawing on a common-law system maintaining that primary rights defaulted to the first resident to claim the adjacent waterway, directly contradicted Spanish law that prioritized community use and public benefit (Strathman 2005: 38). Specifically, Spain's 1783 "Plan of Pitic," which governed all of its pueblos, limited each individual's water use for what was needed for domestic and livestock purposes, whereas US practices for much of the second half of the nineteenth century privileged private ownership, consumption, and commerce without individual restrictions (Kanazawa 1998). During the late 1800s, multiple private companies engaged in elaborate projects, like mammoth dams and flues, in an effort to capitalize on their rural water holdings and the growing urban population. As a result, nearly every east-west running river in San Diego County was interrupted with dams and reservoirs financed by private individuals and companies, as opposed to public entities (D. Walker 2004: 19). In 1895, this situation was holistically reversed when the State Supreme Court ruled that California would revert to "pueblo water rights," insisting that municipalities, like cities, owned the water (Reich 2000: 132). Extensive litigation followed this dramatic decision as private companies fought desperately to reclaim waterways from local cities (Strathman 2005: 42).

Dynamic water-rights legalities during the late nineteenth and early twentieth century had important ramifications for Nathan Harrison and his mountain spring. He had claimed the water as an individual citizen in 1892, but public opinion of private ownership of the public water supply changed significantly during the first decades of the twentieth century (Courtemanche 1982: 150). Even though the water exclusively belonged to Harrison, he never explicitly charged for it. In fact, he deliberately offered it to his visitors as a gift. This approach suggested generosity, yet it implicitly required reciprocity. It was a social exchange as well as an economic transaction. Harrison managed to regale his guests and earned significant social capital as a generous host and community icon, all the while ensuring essential return offerings to sustain him at this remote locale. Contemporary Escondido native Mary Connaghan Newell described these activities, labeling Harrison "the Good Samaritan of Palomar," deeming his spring a "filling station," and stating in slightly exaggerated terms that, "Endearing himself to thousands of visitors over a period of more than 70 years, he was literally the man by the side of the road—watching the world go by" (A. Davis c. 1955: 62–64) (Figure 1.6). Frank Jones had a more capitalistic interpretation of Harrison's gifts of water and expected return offerings. Focusing on the profitable outcome, he declared, "That was Nate's racket!" (Ryan 1964e: no page numbers). These were two opposite interpretations of the same gift-giving sequence; Newell saw it as altruistic, and Jones deemed it opportunistic.[78]

Ed Davis offered a detailed account of Nathan Harrison's dedication to providing water to visitors, emphasizing that he almost always chose to deliver it personally. Davis wrote:

> When he heard a team far down the grade it was his invariable custom to come out and be waiting with a bucket of cool refreshing water for the thirsty horses. It was a steep hard pull up to Nate's place and he had the only water convenient to the road, so when the teams reached his place, they were tired, sweaty and thirsty. How grateful those horses must have been when they plunged their muzzles deep into a bucket of cool water. This was a self-imposed task, which he performed faithfully, from an innate deep sympathy for the weary horses and what a satisfaction it must have been to him, to realize what it meant to the horses. The County later took over Nate's task and put in a pump and water trough alongside of the road, but Nate was always there to pump the water in the trough whenever he heard a team on the grade. (1938: 11)

Nathan Harrison completed a homestead certificate on 27 March 1893 for his 45.55-acre Palomar property. Numerous historical narratives verified the timeline established by these official records from the early 1890s. John Davidson wrote that, "[Harrison] was persuaded to take a free homestead on the west end of Smith mountain, 60 acres next to the Pauma Grant line on Oat Ridge where [there] was a Spring and pasture land which he owned at the time of his death" (1937: 2). A

Figure 1.6. Harrison stood at his spring in this undated photograph; county supervisors furnished him with the pump and trough. (Courtesy of the Nathan "Nate" Harrison Historical Archaeology Project, Kirby Collection.)

peculiar issue surfaced in the brief Davidson passage about Harrison's homestead. Who "persuaded" Harrison to homestead the property, and why did he need to be prompted? Harrison had owned nearby land before; what was different about this transaction, or had he been "persuaded" then as well? Was it the homestead certificate itself that was the impediment? Was the fee an issue? Why did he only claim

45.55 acres when he was entitled to 60? Furthermore, why did he wait until 1893 to complete the certificate? One would expect application for land ownership to predate a map that designated ownership and the ability to own the land's water.

There was much debate as to why Harrison completed his homestead certificate so late. Much of the speculation started with the assumption that he had lived on the mountain for many decades before filling out the homestead certificate and had long been established as the rightful owner of the property. Some authors, such as Davidson, implied that Harrison needed encouragement to complete the paperwork. Others, such as Carlton, suggested that this was a strategic decision to wait "until long after the anti-black provisions of California's homestead laws had been repealed" in order to avoid seeming too audacious as an African American owning land in nineteenth-century San Diego County (1974: 13).

The 1893 date on which Harrison officially obtained the land from the US government might have been irrelevant in determining how long he had lived at his Palomar Mountain cabin. Many sources suggested he had resided at his hillside home for many years before 1893. Furthermore, it was local Luiseño Indians who were in control of the territory for centuries before the arrival of various missionaries and other settlers. Despite being decimated in the nineteenth century and relegated to reservations during the twentieth century, these Indigenous peoples had a direct tie to the local land and significant influence in settlement patterns. Accordingly, Max Peters Rodriguezés emphasized that, "Indians gave [Harrison] the land" (Day 1981b: no page numbers).[79] Although this passage did not specify a date, it emphasized that Nathan Harrison had Indigenous consent to live on Palomar and that the Luiseño locals chose to gift the land, as opposed to sell or trade it. It is important to note that gift giving, a socioeconomic norm in many non-Western societies, resulted in Harrison acquiring the land that would be his home for nearly half a century and provided an economic engine for his continued sustenance (water from the spring). Nevertheless, in order to have ownership of this land recognized by the US government, Harrison would ultimately have to file the homestead certificate.

Chronologically clustered in the early 1890s with his water claim and homestead certificate was another important government record. Harrison registered to vote on 22 October 1894. His voter registration form offered multiple personal insights into Harrison's life, including his relatively diminutive height—5'3"—and birth state of Kentucky (Figure 1.7). Like the many Great Registers of the late 1880s and early

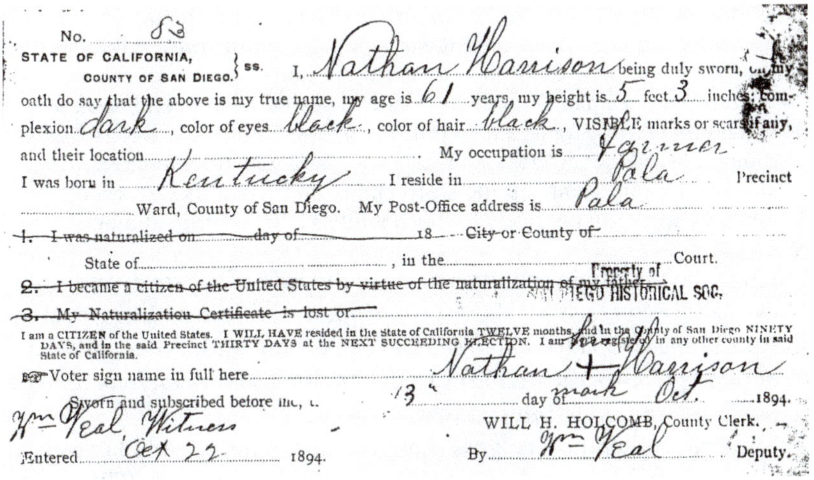
No. 83

STATE OF CALIFORNIA, } ss.
COUNTY OF SAN DIEGO.

I, Nathan Harrison being duly sworn, on my oath do say that the above is my true name, my age is 61 years, my height is 5 feet 3 inches; complexion dark, color of eyes black, color of hair black, VISIBLE marks or scars, if any, and their location / . My occupation is Farmer

I was born in Kentucky I reside in Pala Precinct

Ward, County of San Diego. My Post-Office address is Pala

~~1. I was naturalized on day of 18 City or County of~~

State of , in the Court.

~~2. I became a citizen of the United States by virtue of the naturalization of my father.~~

~~3. My Naturalization Certificate is lost or~~

Property of San Diego Historical Soc.

I am a CITIZEN of the United States. I WILL HAVE resided in the State of California TWELVE months, and in the County of San Diego NINETY DAYS, and in the said Precinct THIRTY DAYS at the NEXT SUCCEEDING ELECTION. I am not registered in any other county in said State of California.

Voter sign name in full here Nathan + Harrison

Sworn and subscribed before me, 13 day of Oct. 1894.

Wm Veal, Witness

WILL H. HOLCOMB, County Clerk.

Entered Oct 22 1894. By Wm Veal Deputy.

Figure 1.7. Harrison's 1894 voter registration also indicated that he was unscarred and that his primary occupation was farming. (Courtesy of the Nathan "Nate" Harrison Historical Archaeology Project, Kirby Collection.)

1890s, it listed his residence as Pala, which included Palomar Mountain. Just as he had done with the 1892 water claim, Harrison marked the form with an "x" in place of his signature, suggesting that he was illiterate. Although there was no definitive way of knowing how Harrison voted in the 6 November 1894 election, five interrelated factors suggested his alignment with the Republican party: 1) the *Union* retraction story from seven months earlier asserted his allegiance to "the Republican ticket," 2) African Americans of the time often associated the Democratic party with sympathies and policy agendas for former slave owners, an allegiance to which Harrison likely would not profess 3) the Republican party successfully branded itself as the "Party of Lincoln" and emphasized abolitionist accomplishments, 4) San Diego was home to many active local black Republican political clubs, and 5) the Republican party made the largest mid-term congressional gains in the history of the nation during this particular election.

During his early years on the mountain, Harrison was busy in many local industries, including shepherding, cattle tending, bee keeping, and horticulture.

Despite the revisionism that would occur in the twentieth century with regard to Harrison's purported life in isolation, Palomar Mountain in the 1890s was a busy community. Catherine Wood noted:

During the "gay" nineties [1890s], Palomar had enough families to support three public schools; since it was a popular summer resort for many
people of Southern California, it had three hotels in operation part of
the time, and a small tent city in Doane Valley each summer. It took the
better part of a day for a team to pull the N——r Grade, so travelers often
camped over-night at "Tin Can Flat" near the foot in order to provide for
an early morning start up the steep climb, and when they reached the
top, they were usually ready to stay a while. (1937: no page numbers)

Much of the mountain activity started at the base of the steep and circuitous road that passed by Harrison's property. Requisite slow travel up
the grade allowed Harrison to see travelers coming for miles and hours
in advance; it also allowed him to decide long before anyone arrived
whether he wanted to interact with visitors.

Multiple contemporary government records portrayed Harrison as
nearly inseparable from the road. For example, a December 1896 survey
map entitled, "Survey No. 94 Map of Road from a point in the Pauma
Townsite to the Summit of Palomar Mtn.," contained a section of the
road demarcated with "N. Harrison." The road surveyed for this map
was first known officially in San Diego County records as "N——r Nate
Grade"; the name was only changed to "Nate Harrison Grade" in 1955.
Close examination of the Sickler map showed that Harrison's property
was bounded to the south by the Pauma Indian Ranch, to the north by
Augusti Nicholas and William E. Boucher (see Figure 3.4b). The road
came to its terminus at the property of wealthy cattle rancher E.T. Mendenhall, where it joined the road to Warner's Ranch. In addition, on 12
February 1897, the County of San Diego asked for and received Harrison's consent in turning the aforementioned road that led up to the
mountain and to his property into a public highway. Various historical
accounts offered slightly different dates of construction for the grade,
each post-dating the Sickler map and the road-widening request. This
work from 1897 through 1900 transformed what was little more than a
trail into a hard-packed road that would soon be well-traveled. Despite
the modification, it still took a horse-drawn wagon an entire day to
ascend the west grade.

The 1900 San Diego County Census included an entry for Nathan
Harrison on Smith (Palomar) Mountain. This was the first census that
specified Smith Mountain as its own district, as opposed to the general
Pala area. Local pioneer and hotel owner Theodore Bailey, one of Harrison's closest friends, was the census taker. Although censuses were
taken every ten years during this time, there was no census information
on Harrison for 1890 or 1910. Unlike the conflicting 1880 censuses that
listed Harrison as single and married, the 1900 census stated that he

was a widower. Harrison's widower status in 1900 seemed to have been from the passing of his first wife (Fred Smith's mother), not his second (Dona Lavierla), who presumably divorced Harrison before marrying another man (William Veal) and divorcing him in 1891.

Using his Palomar Mountain cabin as a home base, Harrison was involved in many laboring ventures, including tending to cattle, cooking, house-building, hog-killing, and other odd jobs, during the early 1900s. Chris Forbes emphasized that during this time laborers were not paid with money but with food; he stated that, "[Harrison] did come into the Valley at times and work for several weeks helping to build houses and other jobs. He was not paid. No one got paid in those days. Money was hard to come by. All you received was your meals" (Day and Melvin 1981: no page numbers). Forbes's comments were revealing about the economic climate on the mountain and in the general area. With a scarcity of money, community members often traded services and paid each other in consumable goods. These sorts of arrangements often resulted in a tighter-knit community, despite the hardship, as bartered payment and gift exchange took the form of social engagement instead of being merely an impersonal and alienable economic transaction. Furthermore, there might have been inherent disincentives for separateness and economic independence; during these difficult times, it was likely often easier to survive as a hired hand than to try to be entirely self-sufficient on one's own land.

There were many references to Harrison's interactions with Jean and Augusti Nicolas, who were commonly called "the French brothers" or "the Frenchmen," because they hailed from France. Harrison and the Frenchmen were close, literally and figuratively; they were neighbors and friends. In fact, Chris Forbes thought there might have been a "Possibility that the Frenchmen got Nate to homestead the land with their help, in exchange for giving them part of it. Nate ended up with 45.75 acres. Jean Nicolas had the 40 acres to the east and Augusti had the 125 above him" (Day and Melvin 1981: no page numbers).[80] Harrison did not fence his property and almost certainly let the Nicolas brothers run their animals on his land, especially since he often watched their livestock. Forbes tended sheep for the Frenchmen as well; he explained that they "had 17,000 sheep at one time" (Day and Melvin 1981: no page numbers). Robert Dewey Kelly, who owned the Harrison property from 1946–56 and archived many accounts of the mountain, claimed that, "The Nicolases used to come down from French Valley and spend winters with Nate because it was milder at his elevation. They brought their grapes and used Nate's water to make wine, which they both drank" (Day and Melvin 1981: no page numbers). Forbes also related an ongoing good-hearted wisecrack between the Nicolas brothers and Harrison, stating that, ". . . they discovered that the property line went through Nate's house [and] joked with Nate a lot about 'owning half of his house'" (Day and Melvin 1981: no page numbers). The humorous reference would become a reality in 1921 when, after Harrison's passing, Jean Nicolas purchased the Harrison land.

Harrison engaged in many cottage industries on the mountain in the early 1900s, including ranching, horticulture, and tending to horses. James wrote:

> Later [Harrison] took up a homestead on the south slope of Palomar Mountain. Here he lived for years, clearing a small part of the land, planting an orchard, and raising horses. He had the one price of $150 for his horses, regardless of age, size, or kind. And he insisted he be paid in gold. He said he wanted no truck with silver or folding money. During the summer months he acted as herdsman for a Temecula man who ran a large herd of sheep on the mountain. During the winter months he did odd jobs for his friends in the valley, and was always in demand at hog killing time. (1958: 7)

Harrison was known for having reliable horses to sell and allegedly paraded about on a most distinctive steed. Forbes and others insisted that, "Nate truly rode a white horse. Real white. It was no tale" (Day and Melvin 1981: no page numbers; Day 1981b: no page numbers; Ryan 1964g: no page numbers).

Even though Harrison had officially sold his property at Rincon decades earlier and now lived high up Palomar Mountain, he still maintained a close connection with the Indigenous community at the base of the mountain. Max Peters Rodriguezés, grandson to Harrison's godmother Encarnacion Calac, visited him nearly every weekend during the early 1900s. Rodriguezés, a child at the time, explained that once he finished his schoolwork for the week on Friday he would venture up the grade and deliver Harrison food from his grandmother (Ryan 1964h: no page numbers). Furthermore, Harrison regularly came to Rincon. Rodriguezés recollected that, "Nate often visited with [my] grandmother] all day—talking and laughing. [I] remember hearing them when [I] came in from milking the cows after [my] school day" (Ryan 1964h: no page numbers).

In his later years on Palomar, Harrison became a popular attraction for tourists, visitors, and friends, who helped sustain him with gifts of food and supplies.

Various people regularly brought goods to Harrison. Forbes recalled:

> Nate used to get clothes brought to him by the Frenchmen, and he would put them on over his old clothes. He had as many as five layers on at once. The Frenchmen and the Indians going up to their summer acorns atop the Mountain brought him things. So did tourists and travelers along the Grade. He used to sit out at N——r Point (Billy Goat Point) often. (Day and Melvin 1981: no page numbers)

The big change during the early 1900s was in the ways these people ascended the mountain. Harrison's Grade, once an exclusive trail for horse-drawn vehicles, now was traversed by horseless carriages. The automobile age greatly affected Nathan Harrison and the lives of his neighbors. Catherine Wood explained:

> The first "horseless carriage" to ascend Palomar Mountain was that of L. O. Johnson of San Pasqual Valley, who in June, 1904, made a trip up the N——r grade, thus proving the feasibility of an auto stage. Before long, summer passenger service to Palomar was started consisting of three laps, first by train to Oceanside, thence to the mountain by auto stage, where a horse-drawn stage carried visitors to the top. The fare from San Diego was ten dollars each way. (B. Moore, n.d.: no page numbers)

Cars of the 1900s and '10s had many limitations that made the ascent (and descent) of Palomar Mountain a highly daunting endeavor. Brad Bailey detailed that, "With primitive mechanical breaks, vacuum fuel pumps, and straight-cut gears, many early automobiles were woefully inadequate for the challenge of scaling Palomar Mountain" and ocassionally ended up broken down or rolling off the side of the grade (2009: 60). Drivers up Palomar Mountain were often forced to be very innovative. For example, Wood explained that drivers regularly "had to back up the steep pitches in order that the engine might receive enough gas" and that it was "custom when descending the mountain to tie a tree to the back of the wagon to act as a brake" (1937: no page numbers). As a result, the Harrison grade became a well-known challenge for early automobile enthusiasts.[81]

The years of 1904–05 witnessed one of the more colorful episodes in Palomar Mountain history. In 1904, local mountain man and close Harrison friend, George Doane, finally succeeded in procuring a wife. With a long gray beard that covered nearly all of his face and reached his waist, Doane—whom Catherine Wood deemed, "truly the romantic character of Palomar Mountain"—had long experienced trouble finding a spouse despite the fact that he outright owned Upper Doane Valley and ample livestock (1937: no page numbers). Ed Davis mockingly summarized that, "George raised cattle, hogs, and whiskers, and he was successful in all lines" (1938: 20). Doane was especially enamored with local "school marms," allegedly proposing "to every teacher who ever taught on the mountain" (Beckler 1958: 19–20). George's lovelorn poetry—his favorite ditty was "Though I like doughnuts and clams, still better I like the school ma'ams"—was as distinctive and well known on the mountain as his beard. Deeply frustrated with his inability to find a mate in the San Diego community, Doane placed a nationwide advertisement for a wife and then narrowed the field to two finalists from Louisiana. They were a mother and daughter, and both were purportedly open to marrying him. Fifty-three-year-old George Doane promptly cleaned up—"washed, combed, dyed, and dressed with meticulous care, put a little fragrant bear grease on his whiskers and hair, [and] put on his dinky derby"—took a train to St. Louis, met with the women, and selected the daughter, a sixteen-year-old named Irene Hayes to be his bride (E. Davis 1938: 21A). George and Irene traveled back to Palomar Mountain together and brought along Irene's African American maid to live at his log cabin (Figure 1.8). The maid was named Amy; people in the area referred to her as "Amy N——r."

George Doane was well known across San Diego County, and his odd marital union made headlines. The 13 October 1904, *San Diego Weekly Union* reported:

Figure 1.8. Amy, Irene Doane, and George Doane pose together atop Palomar Mountain sometime in 1904/05. (Frances Beven Ryan Papers, Escondido Public Library Pioneer Room. Public domain.)

> Geo. E. Doane, of Doane valley, Smith mountain, one of the oldest native sons of the state, surprised his friends by coming in Wednesday evening with a young wife. Mr. Doane had never been east before, and has been a resident of this county for twenty-eight years. The bride does not look to be over 20 years old. She was Miss Irene Hayes, oldest daughter of Mrs. Dr. Hayes of Zwolle, Louisiana. ("Marriage Notices" 1904)

The newspaper mockingly labeled him "one of the oldest native sons" and repeatedly emphasized the age difference between bride and groom. Though many Palomar men were older than their wives, the Doanes' 37-year age gap was the largest in the region.

Within months, Irene's mother, Susan Hayes, and her youngest daughter, Ida, also moved to Palomar Mountain and homesteaded a nearby area today known as "The Hayes' Place." Following the Doane marriage, neither George, Irene, Amy, Susan, nor Ida would reside long on the mountain. In 1905, George and Irene sold their property and moved to Holtville in Imperial Valley.[82] Although the Doanes had a son in 1908, George and Irene divorced soon after their departure from Palomar. Susan Hayes and her daughter returned to Louisiana immediately after they had fulfilled the minimal years of residence required under the Homestead Act to sell. Amy was fired by George and Irene even before the Doanes left the mountain for allegedly attempting to poison the newlyweds. Wood provided the details, noting:

> One day the Doane group came to Bailey's store from which they bought groceries, complaining of the quality of the food they had purchased the day before, but they were assured that the groceries were all right when they left the store. They went on home and learned later that Amy had tried to poison the family by putting lye in the lard, because they made her work so hard. (1937: no page numbers)

Nathan Harrison and Amy were close friends; he even had a nickname for her that had nothing to do with her ethnicity. Louis Salmons explained:

> The maid [Amy] that came out, she was a big colored girl. She was about six feet; she wasn't fat, she was just big. Had a foot that long. Old Nate— the boys used to go around and measure her tracks, you know. And old Nate said, "I always call her my 'cubby.' She's got a foot like a cub 'bar.'" She helped him put up hay and bring in wood and things. (Hastings 1959b: no page numbers)

Despite her friendship with Harrison, "Cubby" was on borrowed time at Palomar Mountain after the alleged food-tampering incident. She was promptly sent back to Louisiana.

The first decade of the 1900s witnessed a general change in primary activities for Harrison. With the widening of the grade and the start of the Bailey hotel stage ferrying passengers up the mountain and by Harrison's place by car, the elderly African American homesteader seemed to have done as much entertaining as traditional laboring.[83] Allan O. Kelly told a story of visiting Harrison at his cabin around 1908. He recounted:

> When I was seven years old, my father decided that the family should take a camping trip to Smith's Mountain, now known as Palomar Mountain, to see the world and to visit the Bailey family. . . . We arrived at "N — —r Nate's" log cabin[84] about noon. . . . "N — —r Nate" was an old, white-haired Negro slave who had come to this spot some time in the 1850s or 1860s. . . . He had a lovely spot: a far distant view to the ocean, a fine spring and about an acre of good soil for a garden and a few apple and pear trees. He also kept a few pigs, which lived off the acorns. In addition, the people on the mountain brought him a sack of flour now and then so that he never lacked for food. . . . He was said to sometimes tell the summer tourists that came his way: "When I first came here dere was nobody but Injuns. I was de fust white man on dis mountain." (1978: no page numbers)

Kelly's passage was the first to emphasize that visits from tourists had become regular and expected occurrences. Now in his seventies, Harrison was clearly transitioning away from his traditional mountain-man ranching skills. In addition to being a one-stop water service station, he also seemed to perfect his role-playing and story-telling as a memorable character for sightseeing visitors.

Harrison benefitted greatly from the automobile stage that traversed the mountain. The cars brought numerous visitors by his property and multiplied his opportunities to provide services (water, entertainment, etc.) that were almost always reciprocated. Despite this economic reality, Harrison was no fan of motorized transport; in fact, multiple contemporary sources emphasized his disdain for the car. The 15 June 1912, *Oceanside Blade* reported:

> The many friends of the aged negro Nate, who lives at the head of N — —r Canyon, will be glad to hear that he is well and cheerful though he grows more and more feeble. A recent automobile accident has greatly cheered him and added to his fund of stories, and Nate looks with contempt on autos, and thinks them the work of the evil one. (Van R. 1912: no page numbers)

Close reading of this passage revealed that the nearby car crash pleased Harrison for multiple reasons; it substantiated his already established distrust of motorized vehicles and also gave him more entertaining tales to share with visitors. The newspaper's use of the phrase "fund of stories" subtly reflected how Nathan Harrison's tales were a marketable good that were consumed by visitors.

Harrison was not only a beneficiary of the close mountain community; he also came to the aid of many locals, despite his advanced age. For example, in the summer of 1909, Robert Asher's brother, Alpheus, embarked on a trip to Palomar Mountain. Unfamiliar with the terrain, "Alf" misjudged the steepness of the grade, got severely dehydrated, and passed out near Harrison's spring. Harrison rescued the weary traveler, nursed him back to health, and put him up for the night at his cabin. According to Alpheus, Harrison solemnly vowed that he "couldn't do too much for Bob Asher's brother" (Asher c. 1938: no page numbers). This near-death experience made a lasting impression. Robert Asher recalled that, "Alf never forgot Nate's kindness to him and often referred to it with gratitude" (Asher c. 1938: no page numbers).

There was an inherent irony in discussing the remoteness of mountain communities of the Old West. A lure of venturing westward for many people in the nineteenth century was in being able to take advantage of government claims that entitled individuals to never see their next-door neighbors (McHenry 1997: 20). Settlement was often predicated on open space and distance from other people, which is counterintuitive to most scholarly discussions of an inclusive community. However, the difficulty in self-sustainment in these remote rural lands resulted in well-established communal bonds, even if they covered very broad areas.

Phillip Stedman Sparkman, one of the more colorful characters in Palomar history, embodied this contradiction of simultaneously being a distant loner and community linchpin. From an historical perspective, his connection to Nathan Harrison initially seemed tangential at best. Sparkman, a native of England lived at Pala during the 1890s and early 1900s, ran multiple stores in the area, the first of which was on Harrison's former Rincon property. Asher recalled many accounts of personally hunting bobcats in and around Harrison's hillside homestead and selling the skins to Sparkman, who paraded around in an elaborate bobcat robe he made in part out of Asher's prey (c. 1938: no page numbers). Beyond his fancy coat, Sparkman was also a skilled anthropologist known for his expertise in Indian languages. With the help of many local informants, he wrote "The Culture of the Luiseño Indians" and "Sketch of the Grammar of the Luiseño Language"; both were definitive resources on the Indigenous population of the region and are still of value to scholars in the twenty-first century (Sparkman 1908b, 1905).[85]

Philip Sparkman was killed on 19 May 1907; his murder was never solved. Palomar old-timer Harry P. Jones recalled:

> I used to stop at Rincon quite often and buy a little lunch meat or something like that. At Rincon Mr. Philip Sparkman ran the store, a country store; they had everything for sale. Mr. Sparkman was a very, very quiet man, but after you'd get to know him you'd know he was a very fine man. One day an Indian came into Sparkman's store, drunk, and killed him. (Hastings 1960a: 8)

There was much debate as to the identity of Sparkman's murderer. Although the "drunken Indian" hypothesis came to be the accepted norm in San Diego histories, contemporaneous testimonies suggested otherwise. Neighbors insisted that Sparkman, who never married, had no enemies in the native community. His kind demeanor and high standing with the Indigenous population seemed to contradict the brutal manner in which he was murdered. Sparkman, who had recently sold over $1,500 in wheat, was found dead with two gunshot wounds and his throat slashed, yet nothing was missing from the store ("Philip Sparkman Obituary" 1907). Sparkman's blood was both inside of the store and outside where his corpse was found, suggesting that he was first shot in the building, a struggle ensued, and then he was shot a second time while trying to flee. Local authorities suggested that Sparkman had likely been slain by someone he knew, but the coroner's jury concluded that he died from wounds "inflicted by parties unknown" (Crawford 1995: 50).[86]

Unbeknownst to nearly everyone in the region, Sparkman had been fronting the money for Harrison's property taxes for many years. This economic nuance surfaced only after nobody filled that void following Sparkman's death. Six years after the 1907 murder, a despondent Harrison learned that the county had sold his homestead at a tax-delinquent sale to Palomar newcomer Nathan Hargrave. Asher recalled the situation in detail, including the fact that Major Lee Utt—who died in 1895—had been paying Harrison's property taxes before Sparkman as well. In a lengthy and highly enlightening passage, he wrote:

> I once found Nate in tears [in 1913]. Mr. [Bentley] Elmore[87] had sent me in to ask permission to make our road camp on the flat south of Nate's house. Nate said it would be all right and then told me about his present trouble. Nathan Hargrave had been down to see him and had told him that he had bought Nate's place at a tax sale[88] but that Nate could stay if he wanted to. Nate said that he couldn't understand how Hargrave could buy the place if he, Nate, didn't want to sell. And he didn't want to sell ever, complained Nate.
>
> [Harrison said,] "After I go I want my daughter to have it."

I inquired about the daughter, it being the first time he had ever said anything about a daughter, or even having been married. He said that the daughter was a trained nurse and lived in New York City. I next inquired about the matter of unpaid taxes. Nate contended that he had always paid the tax whenever anyone asked him for the money. I asked him if he remembered when he last paid over any money for the taxes. He said, maybe last year or the year before. I asked him if he was sure it hadn't been six years or more. No, it couldn't be that long since he had given money to Sparkman the last time he saw him, and nobody had asked for money since then. He said that Major Utt, of Agua Tibia, used to pay his taxes for him, and then he would pay the money to Major Utt the first time he would see him. After Major Utt died, Phillip Sparkman had been paying his taxes for him. I hadn't realized up to that moment that it had been fully six years since Sparkman's murder, but a quick calculation brought me to a realization of that fact, and the probability that Nate's taxes had gone unpaid for six years and that therefore Hargrave had obtained title by bidding in the property at the last tax-delinquent sale.

I explained as best I could to Nate, but he was inconsolable. I calmed him a bit by promising to do what I could for him. I did speak to Elmore about Nate's dilemma, and Elmore became quite indignant. He thought Hargrave incapable of doing such a thing. Later in the day, when Elmore came in for dinner, he said that Louis Salmons had just passed by, and that he had told Louis about Hargrave having bought the place over Nate's head and that Louis had gone right up into the air.[89] He added that he thought Louis was going to take the matter up with his brother Frank [Salmons], and that Frank[90] would speak to his partner, Congressman [William] Kettner, and that Kettner would do what he could for Nate in Washington [DC]. A couple of weeks later I was told that Hargrave had bid in the Negro's property for the sum of twenty-eight dollars.

Still later I heard that Nate had given one of his horses to Hargrave and that Hargrave had agreed to deed back the title to Nate. I can testify to the fact that Hargrave did deed back the property in accordance with the agreement. (Asher c. 1938: no page numbers)

In addition to recounting how Harrison almost lost his property to unpaid taxes, Asher's story contained many important insights, including: 1) Harrison had a daughter, 2) Major Utt had fronted Harrison's taxes before Sparkman, 3) Hargrave so infuriated the mountain community by covertly obtaining Harrison's land that the Salmons brothers were willing to use congressional connections to get the homestead back to its rightful owner, and 4) Harrison paid off Hargrave with one of his horses. These never-before told nuances are worth discussing one by one.

Harrison had a daughter? This was the first and only mention of it. The details of her being "a trained nurse in New York" were also surprising. Being situated on the East Coast until his late teens/early twenties could have resulted in Harrison leaving behind a child when he departed for California in the 1850s. A daughter from his early adulthood pre-Gold Rush Kentucky days—the late1840s/early 1850s—would have been in her sixties in 1913. Perhaps the child in question was from one of his marriages in California, although both Fred Smith's mother (presumed wife #1) and Dona Lavierla (presumed wife #2) were likely too old to bear children while with Harrison.[91] Or could this have been a reference to a daughter born out of wedlock, a stepdaughter, or even a daughter-in-law? This reference remained one of the most tantalizing, elusive, and frustrating loose ends of the Harrison biography and was difficult to reconcile with Chris Forbes' declarative statement that, "[Harrison] fathered no children" (Day and Melvin 1981: no page numbers).

The assertion that Major Lee Utt supplied payment up front for Nathan Harrison's property taxes for many years corroborated two important aspects of the Harrison biography. First, it seemed to support further the close bond between Lee Utt and Harrison.[92] Multiple sources posited that their relationship went beyond employer and laborer and that the two men had a genuine friendship. This might explain why Utt would agree to front what Harrison owed. Second, the need to have Utt first, and later Sparkman, pay for his taxes confirmed the dearth of available money—especially among the working class—in late nineteenth and early twentieth century rural San Diego County society. Harrison would have had to rely on select cash-rich individuals, like Major Utt, to pay his larger bills up front and then he would work off the debt.

The closeness of the mountain community was apparent in the reactions of Bentley Elmore and the Salmons brothers to Hargrave's property coup. They were outraged by the underhanded nature of the acquisition and prepared to call in favors from San Diego's recently elected US Congressman, William Kettner, to rectify the situation. Kettner's influence was unneeded as a core group of Palomar pioneers rallied around Nathan Harrison and insisted that Hargrave agree to accept a horse in exchange for the property. Hargrave, who had only recently moved to the mountain, was quickly condemned as "a hustler" by locals and shown that his manner of business dealings was not appreciated or condoned (Asher c. 1938: no page numbers).

Harrison paid off Hargrave with a horse. Harrison's horses seemed to be one of the only sources of alienable wealth for him during this time. He had few other material possessions. In addition, Harrison was regularly sustained by neighbors and visitors with various offerings. Not only were his horses a source of viable income, Harrison was encouraged by friends to keep prices high.[93] Furthermore, he insisted on gold for the horses in order to buffer himself against an environment in which money was scarce and food was often traded for labor. Gold had long been, and remains today, a most reliable universal equivalent, especially in comparison to paper money and perishable goods (Marx 1977: 159, 161, 180). In a community heavily influenced by gift exchange, short on money, and rife with trades for services, the horses were one of Harrison's most important assets; in this particular instance, these equine commodities ended up saving his homestead.

Though most narratives emphasized that Harrison survived on the handouts of others during the early 1900s, a few—like the previous horse story—pinpointed alternative sources of revenue. Another account that highlighted an entrepreneurial side to Harrison's character came from Thekla James Young, whose father Colonel James leased Doane Valley through 1916. Young explained that her father also rented land from Harrison, noting that, "Colonel James . . . leased for 2 years from Nate. 160 acres land on Palomar west end . . . Lease pay was 1 gallon whiskey and a sack of beans" (Ryan 1964d: no page numbers).

These two examples, the horse sale and the land lease, were two of remarkably few recorded commodity-based transactions involving Harrison. Both involved the simultaneous exchange of something for something with an emphasis on the equated values of those two items or services (Mallios 2006a). On the contrary, the historical accounts of Harrison's time on Palomar Mountain almost exclusively detail gift exchanges, which always took the form of something for nothing. Even though every gift implicitly required a later return gift, both offerings were made as purported generosity. Since there was a delay between the initial present and the reciprocal gift, trust was a key component of gift exchange, and successful gift giving strengthened the interpersonal bonds between the two parties involved.

During a visit by acquaintances in October of 1919, an ailing Harrison was convinced to leave the mountain and receive medical attention.

Well into his eighties and in failing health, Harrison struggled in his final months on Palomar Mountain. Chris Forbes first met Harrison around 1918, noting that, "Nate was old, very old" (Day and Melvin 1981: no page numbers). He recalled that, ". . . before his friends took him to the hospital, [Harrison] couldn't walk and was crawling around on his hands and knees" (Day and Melvin 1981: no page numbers). In this context, it seemed likely that Fred Smith's aforementioned extended visit with Harrison during the winter of 1918/19 was undertaken in order to care for his debilitated stepfather. Visitors often celebrated Harrison for his antiquity and self-reliance in such a difficult environment, but by 1919, it was clear that Harrison's cabin was no longer a viable residence for the pioneer. Though he had been a fixture on Palomar Mountain for many decades, Harrison's time at his hillside homestead was coming to an unceremonious end.

The 22 October 1919 *San Diego Union* reported that Harrison was admitted to the San Diego Hospital. Asher explained how it came to be that Harrison left the mountain, stating:

> ... Harry Hill and Ed Quinlan had informed the County Supervisors of Nate's plight and that the Board had ordered Constable Harry Hubble to go and get Nate and bring him down to the County Hospital. A Mr. Butler, who was in charge of the County Garage, accompanied Hubble on the trip. Mr. Butler told me about the trip himself. He said that Nate objected most strenuously against being taken away and had only consented after the two countrymen had succeeded in convincing him that a continued residence on his place would not be fair to his friends on the mountain. (c. 1938: no page numbers)

Asher's account of Harrison reluctantly agreeing to leave the mountain further emphasized the closeness of the Palomar community.[94] Not only did concerned neighbors insist on appropriate hospital care for their debilitated colleague, but Harrison only acquiesced when he was made aware of the toll his presence would take on his friends. This passage clearly revealed how Harrison and his neighbors put a premium on the well-being of each other instead of on themselves. Reciprocal care was a core trait of this cohesive community.

Now in his eighties, Harrison lived for an additional year in the San Diego County Hospital before dying on 10 October 1920.

Few details were written of Harrison's eleven-and-a-half-month stay at San Diego County General Hospital. Furthermore, virtually no accounts mentioned anyone visiting Harrison during this year.[95] The lack of details regarding Harrison's time off the mountain, especially when compared to the rich description of his daily activities from 1880–1919, suggested that either Harrison went largely unvisited or his guests did not want to talk about what they witnessed. The 1920 San Diego County census, taken 8/9 January, documented Harrison at the hospital. It also included a few details that strayed from other census records, namely that Harrison could now read and write. All previous census and great register entries had stated either that he was illiterate or left the column blank.

Nathan Harrison died at 2:20 pm on 10 October 1920, after nearly a year in the hospital. According to the death certificate, Dr. O. G. Wiskenski gave Harrison's cause of death as "Articular Rheumatism" and "Chronic Myocarditis" with a contributing factor of "Hypostatic Pulmonary Congestion." More simply stated, Harrison's severe joint inflammation was compounded by an inflamed heart muscle and blood pooling in the heart. When discussing a similar array of lethal medical conditions, journalist Jorge Ramos once wrote that these factors commonly stemmed from a lifetime of cigarettes, eggs, bacon, and butter, each of which Harrison had plentifully indulged (2007: 131). Harrison's death certificate also included some new information about his past. For the first time in any existing record, it listed the names of his Kentucky-born parents, Ben and Harriet Harrison.[96]

Harrison's body was immediately interred in an unmarked grave in Mount Hope, the city cemetery.

Harrison was laid to rest three days after his passing on 13 October 1920. To the chagrin of many of the mountain community, he was placed in an unmarked grave in the city cemetery, Mount Hope, instead of on Palomar Mountain. Virginia Stivers Bartlett emphasized that, "Not buried on the mountain, amid the lilacs and dogwood, with rabbits and quail to scamper over his grave, but in the pauper's field" (1931: 24).[97] It seemed clear that people who knew Harrison well would have preferred that his body be placed near his hillside homestead.

When Nathan Harrison died on 10 October 1920, he passed away without a will, known in legal terms as "intestate." As a result, there were numerous legal documents related to handling Harrison's final affairs. The official legal file for Case #9268: "In the Matter of the ESTATE of Nathan Harrison, Deceased (PLAINTIFF) vs. the Office of Clerk of the Superior Court of the State of California in and for the County of San Diego (DEFENDANT)" contained forty-five pages and detailed many of the nuances required to handle Harrison's estate in the two years between his passing and the final decree-settling account (Mallios et al. 2017a). The paperwork tracked a straightforward estate sale in which Harrison had no will, had his estate administered by the county, sold his 45.55-acre Palomar Mountain property to Frank Salmons for $607.50, and ended up with a net gain (once hospital and legal expenses were taken out of the sale price) of $145.78.

There were a few surprises in the documents. First, the final account spreadsheet revealed that Harrison had $69.44 in cash at the outset. This had never before been described in any narrative, meaning that no details remained as to whether he brought this money with him to the hospital in 1919, had it delivered by a friend some time in 1920, sold personal belongings to acquire the cash, etc. Second, of the $145.78 that remained in the Harrison estate after the sale, $100 was given to Theodore Bailey's "Uncle Nate" Memorial Committee to purchase a permanent marker for Harrison at the entrance to his former homestead. No mention was made of the fate of the remaining $45.78.

These legal documents marked the end of Harrison's immediate connection with the Palomar Mountain property. Salmons held on to the property for twenty days only. On 26 July 1921, he sold it to Jean Nicholas, one of the French brothers who owned adjacent land, for one dollar. Nicholas would own the Harrison property for over two decades.

Harrison's estate was minimal as his hospital bills nearly balanced out the worth of his property. It was important to remember, however, that Harrison's primary commodity—apart from land and water—was his herd of horses. Only one of the historical accounts discussed the fate of Harrison's horses. Chris Forbes recalled:

> Millard [Beemer of Pauma Valley] said later that Charlie Frye turned up with a strange herd of horses soon after Nate died. They were wild and always trying to go from the country club (now) area where Charlie kept them through Millards' crops and up Nate's Grade. They'd always wondered about that [why the horses headed up the grade]. Charlie was a kind-hearted fellow who would feed his animals even if he didn't have anything to eat. So they guessed that he rescued the horses after Nate was taken away and he fed them and took them over. (Day and Melvin 1981: no page numbers)

Immediately following Harrison's passing, his friends from the mountain community began to raise money to purchase a permanent monument in his honor to be placed near his spring. Theodore Bailey led the charge, even offering a photograph of Harrison to anyone that would donate 25 cents or more to the cause. The original memorial design included plans for the marker to be a functional drinking fountain, an homage to the central role that water—and more specifically, free water disbursement to visitors—played in Harrison's life on Palomar Mountain. Intended to be symbolic of how Harrison graciously quenched the thirst of all travelers up the precipitous grade, the design was abandoned for a far cheaper version with no flowing water. The monument, which was built by Ed Davis's son Stanley, was a granite and white quartz cairn with a bronze plaque in its top center niche; it was placed at the hairpin turn on Harrison's grade that intersected with the entry driveway to his cabin and property (Ross 1998: no page numbers; Mallios and Caterino 2011) (Figure 1.9).

Figure 1.9. A close-up photograph of the plaque revealed that it stated: "Nathan Harrison's Spring / Brought here a slave about 1848 / Died October 10th, 1920, aged 101 years / A man's a man for a' that." The original brass marker and a subsequent replacement plaque were both stolen, and today the memorial has no metal marker. (Courtesy of the Nathan "Nate" Harrison Historical Archaeology Project, Kirby Collection.)

In separate accounts, Ed Davis pinpointed 1923 and 1924 as the date this memorial was completed and dedicated in a public event honoring Harrison (Davis 1932, 1938). More than one hundred people attended the ceremony. Acquaintances from the mountain, valley, and adjacent areas flocked to pay their respects. Although Theodore Bailey had raised a majority of the money for the statue, he was too emotional about the passing of his dear friend to speak. Davis stepped in and addressed the crowd on his behalf. Robert Asher attended the ceremony and recalled that, "[Ed] Davis spoke very highly of the friend we had all known for so long" (c. 1938: no page numbers). Davis also played "My Old Kentucky Home" and other favorites of Harrison's on the violin to conclude the ceremony. The selection of "Old Kentucky Home" was seemingly an overt tribute to Harrison's birth state.

There was little recorded activity at the Harrison property through the 1920s. Though Jean Nicholas owned the land for over two decades starting in 1921, he apparently did not alter the cabin site. When visiting in October of 1931, Virginia Stivers Bartlett observed:

> The ridge pole of sycamore is still in place and from it hangs an old shovel handle, with a dangling collection of rusty wire hooks. These once supported Nate's flour, sugar, bacon, and surely "cawn[98] meal," and kept them out of reach of the thieving pack rats. Forlornly empty they rattle harshly in the sweet mountain breeze. No edibles about now to tempt the hungry little wood creatures. But I saw the hind leg of a rabbit in the fireplace. (1931: 25)[99]

Despite the fact that Harrison had died, a steady stream of visitors with cameras continued to visit his cabin.

During this time, many individuals began to make a push for protecting and preserving Palomar Mountain's natural beauty and bounty. By the early 1930s, these unified preservationists had made significant progress. Palomar State Park, which included 1,862 acres at an average elevation of 5,000 feet, was founded in 1933.[100] It bordered the former Harrison property to the north. Palomar State Park was part of the immense and noncontiguous open space that made up Cleveland National Forest, itself founded in 1908.

In 1934, a public works project came to the mountain. These kinds of government-sponsored projects endeavored to provide employment for a nation struggling with the Great Depression.[101] Catherine Wood wrote that, "In the spring of 1934, a CCC (Civilian Conservation Corps) unit was established in Doane Valley" (1937: no page numbers). She also noted in a postscript to the article that the CCC likely tore down Harrison's abandoned structure "as a safety precaution" (Wood 1937: no page numbers).[102]

Until it was announced in 1934 that Palomar Mountain would be home to the world's largest telescope, most Americans had never heard of it (E. Davis 1938: 48).[103] The California Institute of Technology purchased 160 acres from the US Forest Service and local ranchers in 1934 and began plans for a mega-telescope.[104] The building process was incredibly challenging and even required the building of a new road, dubbed the "Highway to the Stars."[105] Nevertheless, the celebrated end-product became operational and took its first astronomical image in 1949. *American Magazine* deemed it "the most significant scientific achievement of our time" ("Palomar Mountain" 1958: 13). By the 1950s, the telescope had become a major tourist site, making Palomar Mountain a household name and attracting nearly a half-million visitors on an annual basis.

Palomar Mountain history is commonly portrayed in a segmented fashion, with its chronology separated into bounded events. These narratives commonly isolate Luiseño occupation, pioneer settlements, and the emergence of an occupation oriented around the construction and use of the telescopes. On the contrary, Indigenous peoples still live in the region, there was great interaction between natives and settlers, and many long-time Palomar families, included those who regularly interacted with Harrison, were closely intertwined with the observatory-building process.

Despite the massive construction efforts on the nearby Caltech observatory, which involved a spectacular series of arduous astronomical deliveries up the south side of Palomar Mountain, the next twenty years saw little change on the west side of the mountain and at Harrison's cabin site. Although the San Diego County Board of Supervisors considered abandoning care on the west grade in 1938—it emphasized that, "[the] need for keeping the road open to public travel has ended with completion of the new road up the south slope of the mountain," and that, "the old route was hazardous and expensive to maintain"— the road was left intact ("West Palomar Grade May Be Abandoned" 1938). Over the years, various locals returned to Harrison's former abode and reported on the slowly vanishing ruins. Asher noted in the late 1930s:

> There is not much left of Nate's cabin now. Only a part of one corner of the fireplace is still standing, but the weeds are high over everything. Nearby are the charred remains of bits of lumber, probably piled there and burned by the present owner of the place. Around the site of the house a number of grape vines and fruit trees are still alive and vigorous. (c. 1938: no page numbers)

Though the property changed hands from Jean Nicholas to Dorothy Bowman in 1943, from Bowman to Thomas and Midge Colby in 1946, and from the Colbys to Robert Dewey Kelly in 1956, few alterations to the land occurred as Bowman and the Colbys were each absentee owners.[106]

The 1950s brought three major changes to the former Harrison homestead. First, new landowner Dewey Kelly, a member of a pioneer North County family with deep ties to the region, lived on the mountain and began various construction projects on the property. Second, Kelly used a tractor to flatten the area in and around the original cabin site. The back-and-forth blading of the site would prove to be a great challenge to archaeologists hoping to reconstruct activity areas through *in situ* artifacts. Third, the National Association for the Advancement of Colored People (NAACP) successfully petitioned San Diego County to change the name of the road up the west side of Palomar Mountain from "N——r Nate Grade" to "Nate Harrison Grade" in 1955. Despite the official renaming, adoption of the new moniker was slow.[107]

Richard and Lois Day purchased the Harrison tract from Kelly in 1969 and held it for over three decades. During the Day's ownership period, the original Harrison cabin was little more than a small and scattered pile of rocks. Kelly's blading of the site had nearly erased all aboveground markers of the former hillside homestead. Though a careful steward of the land in many respects, Richard Day routinely pothunted at the cabin site during his extended stay on the mountain (Ross 1998).[108]

Despite several decades of relative dormancy, the early twenty-first century brought dramatic changes to the Harrison property. On 9 June 2000, James and Hannah Kirby purchased the land from the Days. Three years later in 2003, the Kirbys gave permission to San Diego State University archaeologists to survey and begin excavations in search of the original Harrison cabin site. In 2007, the property was sold to three owners who transformed it into "Pacha Mama's Grove," marketed as "a place of laughter, love and healing [with a mission] . . . to bring together people from all walks of life for growing and healing." Since then, only one of the owners (Vicki Morgan) remains involved and brought the property back toward its historical roots, rebranding it as "Harrison Serenity Ranch." Grant-funded excavations resumed at the site in the spring of 2017 and are ongoing.

Despite every effort to make the history of Nathan Harrison as accurate and transparent as possible, the straightforwardness of the timeline presented in this chapter was deceptive in two manners. First, the vast amount of uncertainty concerning Harrison's past greatly outweighed the purportedly known events. Second, this relatively simple chronology stood in stark contrast to many of the stories that have evolved into local lore in the century since his passing. As will be discussed in the next chapter, the creation and perpetuation of legend was a powerful force that often obliterated any concerns for historical accuracy. Since regenerative waves of revisionism often played to and manipulated public sentiment, they regularly fed self-serving agendas, prioritized contemporary beliefs, and erased lessons from previous generations. Make no mistake, myth-making grows with such ferocity and conviction that we are left to wonder whether the past actually happened in a certain manner or is merely a malleable tool for the present.

Notes

1. The inverse relationship was clear, linear, and statistically significant. The correlation between when the record was taken and Harrison's purported year of birth had a value of -0.77, meaning that over two-thirds of the variation in when the document was recorded was inversely responsible for the variation in Harrison's purported birth year. The exact r-squared value was 0.71. The data in Figure 1.1 was edited to remove redundant cases. Great Register entries often copied information from previous years instead of procuring original or updated data. Therefore, when consecutive Great Registers merely transcribed the entries of previous years, this information was not included as a new entry. As a result, the statistical analyses only included only fourteen cases instead of the eighteen in the table. This trend is even more pronounced if one discards the initial outlier (the 1852 census) as it was recorded when Harrison was nineteen and well before any age exaggeration would bolster his status in the region.

2. While an overwhelming majority of direct historical evidence indicated that Kentucky was Nathan Harrison's state of birth, there were additional tangential clues that also pointed to the Blue Grass state as his place of origin. For example, Harrison was quoted as telling Robert Asher of an occasion when Palomar Mountain grizzly bears were so close to his cabin that "you could just hear them poppin' their teeth" (Asher c. 1938: no page numbers). Frederic Gomes Cassidy, in his *Dictionary of American Regional English*, noted that this particular phrase originated in Kentucky (Cassidy 1985; Gunderman 2010: 61). Furthermore, Harrison friend Chris Forbes recalled that "Nate's nickname was Inez" (Day and Melvin 1981). It was worth noting that the original male moniker "Inez" (Portuguese form of "Agnes") was also the name of a nineteenth-century town in eastern Kentucky, first settled in 1810 (Gunderman 2010: 61). Could Harrison's nickname name have been "Inez" because that was his Kentucky hometown?

3. Nathan Harrison was such a common name that various archives included entries for a nineteenth-century-born Nathan Harrison in each of the states mentioned on the list. However, this inventory of potential Nathan Harrisons was quickly culled using the census variables of "birth year" (1820–40) and "race" (black).

4. A Palomar Mountain resident for over three and a half decades, Robert Haley Asher was an expert on local history, horticulture, and geology. He was also an accomplished photographer and painter who captured much of the local history on paper, film, and canvas. Born in 1868, Asher homesteaded

Palomar Mountain land that he ultimately donated to the Baptist Church in 1933. This land would eventually host today's Palomar Christian Conference Center.

5. Since none of the existing sources suggested multiple trips for Harrison across the United States, no hybrid scenarios with repeated migrations were concocted for consideration.

6. To complicate matters further, few of the accounts specified which of the predominant contemporary trails (Oregon, California, or Santa Fe) were taken.

7. Born in 1876 in Atlanta, Georgia, Salmons spent much time on Palomar Mountain with Harrison as a neighbor. Salmons would eventually settle on nearby Dyche Valley; he married Theodore Bailey's youngest daughter, Hodgie (E. Davis 1982: 46–47; 1938: 38; Bailey 2009: 31).

8. There was no Lake Pechanga, but the Luiseño word for Lake Elsinore was Payyaxchi. Pechanga and Payyaxchi were pronounced similarly, especially in Anglicized contexts. The woman described as both Harrison's wife and Fred Smith's mother was likely from Payyaxchi (Lake Elsinore). The Machado family had a ranch near Lake Elsinore. Frank Machado was well-informed on matters involving Harrison during the 1860s, '70s, and '80s because Harrison was his neighbor and later married into the Machado family as his uncle.

9. In addition, this account was the first of many that might have referenced a possible incident of race-based hostility—specifically that he was "threatened with death"—that Harrison endured.

10. Frémont's volatile professional career included being named military Governor of California, a court martial conviction for mutiny and insubordination, and the distinction of being the first Republican Party candidate for president of the United States. He lost in 1856 to James Buchanan; Frémont ran on a campaign platform that sought to block the expansion of slavery.

11. For example, Nathan Harrison was not listed on the 1850 Census of San Diego County, California.

12. Fred Rogers' inventory of California military volunteers in 1846–47 did not include Harrison on the complete roster of the California Battalion (1950: 17–25; see also Manders and Colwell 1966: 14). There were seven documented African Americans—John Grider, James Duff, Jacob Dodson, Charles Gains, Billy Gaston, Joe McAfee, and "Ben," bodyguard of Lieutenant Archibald Gillespie—who were members of the Bear Flag Party (Goode 1973: 44; Forbes 2001: 87). Historian Delilah L. Beasley interviewed one of them, John Grider, in the late 1910s; it served as a case study for her text, *The Negro Trail Blazers of California* (Beasley 1919). Beasley's accounts of Grider paralleled tales of Nathan Harrison; Grider was a former slave from Tennessee brought west in bondage by George H. Wyatt in the 1840s, he allegedly purchased his freedom in 1850, lived in Vallejo for more than sixty years, and then died in Fairfield hospital at the age of ninety-eight (McGriff-Payne 2009).

13. A stamp mill served to separate gold from quartz.

14. Harrison might have known or heard of James Duff, or the parallel ethnic proclamations could have been coincidental. Regardless, they both

employed an effective strategy of declaring pioneer status by asserting primacy and non-Indianness. This type of statement effectively justified settlement rights to their respective areas in spite of black skin color. Of course, Harrison took the strategy a step further by adding a self-deprecating epithet that made a joke of his purported whiteness; he both claimed the land and coyly made certain no one would accuse him of overstating his rights. On the contrary, Duff was hardly deferential or timid in his push for equal rights. He owned a large house, adopted a Caucasian daughter, and fought for black progress and equality as a vocal member of the Mariposa School Board, the Colored Citizens Conventions, and many other organizations (Reader 2009).

15. Robertson was Lysander Utt's great-granddaughter, and she forwarded this family lore to me in a 1 September 2009 email.

16. The letter was found in digital form and donated to the project by Peter Brueggeman.

17. Levi (Lee) Utt had a pension record for 1866; it listed his address as Pala and his place of birth as Illinois. Major Utt was one of nearly two thousand Civil War veterans who would eventually settle in San Diego (Palmer 2006: xi).

18. Colonel Cave Couts, a West Point graduate, would become one of Southern California's wealthiest men. He ventured west in 1849 as a US Army lieutenant immediately following the Mexican-American War. Once he left the military, Couts settled in San Diego and took a job surveying local pueblo lands. In 1851, he married Ysidora Bandini, the daughter of Juan Bandini, a wealthy Mexican who had sided with the Americans during the war.

19. At separate times in the late nineteenth century, Cave and Blount Couts each managed to escape punishment for shooting and killing unarmed Mexican men (Crawford 1995: 53). Clearly, wealth and Anglo-American ancestry had its privileges in San Diego's Wild West, especially when it came to the murder of Mexicans (Knott 1991: 142). Noted humorist George Derby observed in 1853 how common murders of local Indians were as well, emphasizing further that whites accused of Indigenous killings were seldom brought to trial and almost never convicted (Carrico 1987: 22).

20. Marston family patriarch George Marston was a Wisconsin native who moved to San Diego at the age of twenty in 1870. He became a highly successful department store owner, an active politician, and a celebrated philanthropist. For his role in helping to establish Balboa Park, the San Diego Public Library System, and Presidio Park, he has often been hailed as "San Diego's First Citizen." Sarah and Anna were two of his five children.

21. Utt was buried in Hillside Memorial Park Cemetery in Redlands, California. When Lee Utt sold his Agua Tibia land and retired north to San Bernardino in the early 1890s, his family was only temporarily removed from the property. The buyers eventually defaulted, and Sarah Utt and the children returned to Agua Tibia soon thereafter.

22. Regardless of kinship, Lysander and Lee likely knew of each other through the agricultural business. Charles E. Utt, Lysander's son, published an article on avocados in *The Vista Press* in 1928, and Lee Utt's family ran an avocado orchard throughout the late 1800s and early 1900s. Furthermore,

Lysander owned a large all-purpose store, and Lee was a local farmer. Historical accounts also noted that Lysander once took a trip to Escondido and visited an orange grove, which might have been one of Lee's groves at Agua Tibia Ranch.

23. Wood referenced Robert Glass Cleland's 1922 *A History of California: The American Period*; the specific passage in question included the following piece of information that was relevant to the Harrison timeline: "The work [on Tejon Pass] was completed in December of the same year [1854]" (no page numbers).

24. Wood was the only source to insist that Harrison was present at the opening of the Tejon Pass. Although her general timeline of an arrival for Harrison in California and his initial work in more northern mining areas was corroborated by many other accounts, the placement of Harrison on the first ox team at Tejon was not necessary to the chronology. Simply put, the timeline appeared to be reasonably accurate regardless of whether Harrison was present at this famous historical California event.

25. As of the 1850s, blacks in California were not citizens, could not settle on public land, were unable to vote or hold office, and could not attend public school (S. Moore 2016: 44).

26. The duplicitous, disingenuous, and despicable conditions facing African Americans in the 1850s led black leaders to organize a series of three "Colored Conventions" in 1855, 1856, and 1857 that would become the West's first civil rights campaign (De Graaf and Taylor 2001: 10).

27. James J. Rawls identified three phases of Anglo-Indian relations in California: first, settlers claimed they were liberating the Indigenous population from Mexico; second, they exploited the natives as sources of labor; and third, once the need for labor had diminished, they sought to relocate or exterminate the Indians (1984; See also Carrico 1987: 42).

28. The word "genocide" is a powerful statement regarding the deliberate and systematic extermination of a group, and scholars for years were generally hesitant to label the US treatment of Native American peoples as such. Recent studies, however, like those by Brendan Lindsay and Benjamin Madley, openly employ and justify use of the term. In his 2016 book, *An American Genocide: The United States and the California Indian Catastrophe, 1846–1873*, Madley provided extensive details of widespread US violence against California's Indigenous population and discussed ways in which the government provided financial and legal support for the US Army and volunteer militias to exterminate native peoples.

29. The change in the President's decree was not due to a capricious mindset but extensive political lobbying. White landowners and San Diego newspaper editors were especially adept at swaying public opinion. Carrico stated that, "Stirred by sensational newspaper accounts and a sincere fear of another major uprising, much of the north county area was temporarily in the hands of the [purportedly] belligerent Indians who had never fired a shot" (1987: 81).

30. Garra, a highly intelligent person who spoke more than five different Indigenous languages as well as English, Greek, and Latin, was well aware that the US American government was taxing the local Indian population

without allowing any representation in the legislative system, and that this practice of taxation without representation was one of the most celebrated causes of the American Revolutionary War less than a century earlier (Mallios and Caterino 2007a: 36).

31. Marshall had married a Luiseño woman and worked at Warner's store. He was sympathetic to the native cause, and was later labeled as "California's wickedest man" (Mallios and Caterino 2007a: 36).

32. Dyche was a native of Berkeley Springs, Virginia (in today's West Virginia); he crossed the country via wagon train as a teenager during the Gold Rush (E. Davis 1938: 14). After clerking in Sacramento and a successful stint in the Northern California cattle business, Dyche moved to Rincon, where he built a cabin and lived for many years. He married a Cahuilla Indian woman, and they had three children. Their oldest child, Will (born in 1869), was a close friend of Ed Davis and an informant for many of his Palomar Mountain histories (E. Davis 1938: 14; B. Litchfield 1982a).

33. The 1852 California census form did not have a column for slaves, reflecting that it was purportedly a free state. As discussed earlier, the reality was that slavery still occurred, but that the government had no interest in tracking it. Therefore, the 1852 document that contained entries for both B. O. and Nathan Harrison could not distinguish whether Nathan was a former or current slave.

34. There were other white male Harrisons that appeared in the California census, but each of them failed to correspond with the predominant Nathan Harrison–owner chronology in at least one of the following key characteristics: 1) born in Kentucky, 2) lived in Missouri, 3) owned slaves, 4) came to Northern California during the Gold Rush, and 5) died circa 1855–70. For example, there was a forty-year-old white male named N. P. Harrison on the 1860 California census in Placerville (El Dorado County) who was also a Kentucky native. This entry led us down two different analytical rabbit holes, each of which proved to be unrelated to Nathan Harrison. Thirteen different California Great Registers listed a white male named Nathaniel Pickering Harrison born in 1831, but he was from Virginia and did not die until 1894. Interestingly, this Nathaniel Pickering Harrison was not the N. P. Harrison listed in the 1860 census in Placerville. Placerville's N. P. Harrison was born in 1820 (not 1831), and closer scrutiny of the original census listing—not the transcription—revealed that N. P. was not a Harrison at all; his name was N. P. Narrison! Clearly, neither Nathaniel Pickering Harrison nor N. P. Narrison was Nathan Harrison's original owner.

35. The term "dissipate" referred to wasting one's fortune on items of extravagance, and to become "dissipated" suggested that the Harrisons also forsook their morals while squandering wealth.

36. Assuming that Harrington was referring to Joseph Smith's party as the inaugural US settlers to ascend Palomar, this would place Harrison in San Diego County in the late 1850s as well.

37. Salmons's account was the only narrative suggesting that Harrison did not know the exact year of his own arrival in California.

38. The editor of the Helsel text included the following note: "Bessie's grandfather was Matthew Ormsby, a member of General Lee's Confederate army

that surrendered at Appomattox in 1865. He migrated in May of 1868 to Southern California with his family and others on a wagon train organized in Northwest Arkansas."

39. Independence and Sedalia are separated by only eighty miles.

40. Harrison's 1920 death certificate further supported this general chronology as it maintained that he first arrived in California in approximately October of 1850 and resided in the Golden State for seventy years.

41. San Gabriel Mission, the fourth Spanish mission built in California, was founded by Fathers Pedro Cambon and Angel Somera on 8 September 1771.

42. Chino Rancho, thirty-five miles east of Los Angeles and twenty-five miles southwest of San Bernardino, had earlier consisted of two Mexican grants, "Santa Ana del Chino" and "Addition to Santa Ana del Chino," the former containing 22,234 acres and the latter 13,366 acres ("Chino Ranch, San Bernardino County, California" 1889).

43. A. J. King, an Undersheriff of Los Angeles County and former member of the El Monte Rangers led the El Monte Mounted Rifles, a secessionist militia company established on 23 March 1861. Following the Civil War Battle of Fort Sumter in April of 1861, King and his followers marched through the streets of El Monte with a large portrait of Confederate General P.G.T. Beauregard. They were promptly arrested by US Marshals. As a result, Union troops established New Camp Carleton near El Monte in 1862 to prevent further insurrection. Historian Stuart McConnell summarized that, "Southern California was an open powder keg [during the 1860s]. All that was needed was an able leader to ignite the fuse which would rend the state asunder and bring the Civil War to the Pacific coast. There were many Southerners and their sympathizers in California, especially in Southern California.... Los Angeles, San Bernardino, El Monte and Visalia were hotbeds of succession rumors, and loyal Unionists appealed to the military authorities for help. They feared an open outbreak within the state and invasion from Lower California" (McConnell 1992: 3).

44. Los Angeles was one of two pueblos in Alta California during the region's Mexican Period (1821–48); the other was San Jose. Harrison's use of the term "Pueblo" was another subtle indicator of his great antiquity (or his adroit ability to fake great antiquity) in California. It was Mexican and Spanish nomenclature that referred to pre-US American settlements.

45. Pro-slavery sentiments were hardly confined to Los Angeles in Southern California during this time as many San Diegans were decidedly anti–African American. Judson Ames, editor of the local newspaper *The Herald*, actively lobbied for California to be split into two, with the north being free and the south being a slavery extension state. Furthermore, in the 1864 presidential election, San Diegans voted for General George McLellan, who refused to support the abolition of slavery, over Abraham Lincoln by the count of 180–51.

46. This may not have been an exaggeration as Robert Glass Cleland noted, "The year 1854 was one of the worst in the criminal annals of the south. Los Angeles city alone, it is said, averaged one homicide a day for every day in the year" (Wood 1937: no page numbers).

47. Slavery was intricately woven into the very fabric of the United States—all of it, not just the South. While the country's political unrest could be divided along the Mason-Dixon Line, the national economy was inextricably tied to involuntary servitude and bondage. In fact, in the 1860s, the economic impact of slavery and the material worth of the enslaved population as an asset was greater than the rest of the country's productive capacity, including railroads, manufacturing, and agriculture (Blight 2011).

48. Indigenous groups had lived in the area for thousands of years, but this was formalized according to Western law when Mexican governor Manuel Micheltorena granted the land at the Pauma Rancheria to three native brothers-in-law—José Antonio Serrano, Blas Aguilar, and José Antonio Aguilar—in 1844. This land grant was re-patented to the three men by the US government in 1871 and ultimately designated as the Pauma and Yaima Reservations in 1892 (Hoover 1978: 11).

49. Anthropologist Florence Shipek noted that moving the Indigenous population to reservations brought together a strange political alliance between those who hated California Indians and those who were trying to protect them (Shipek 1977).

50. Beckler insisted that, "The first road on Palomar was over the east end, the one broken through by Joseph Smith" (1958: 8). The Harrison Grade wound up the mountain's west side.

51. The Butterfield stage crossed the southwest from St. Louis to Los Angeles and bypassed the city of San Diego. It ran from Yuma, Arizona, through Vallecito, San Felipe Valley, Warner's Ranch (near the southeastern base of Palomar Mountain), and Oak Grove (Crawford 1995: 45).

52. Although the earliest surveys of the region by the United States Geological Surveyor's (USGS) Office date to the 1850s, these maps provided only general boundary lines of townships and ranges, not specific land tracts held by private individuals. Work done during the 1870s divided the general sections established decades earlier into 40-acre parcels claimed by homesteaders (McHenry 1997: 28).

53. Unknown first name; see Brown and Pallamary 1988.

54. Rose's pre-San Diego days in the US were marked by great turmoil and suffering; while in New Orleans he witnessed a devastating outbreak of yellow fever, his time in San Antonio saw cholera wreak havoc on the town, and on the wagon trail to San Diego he was banished from his initial travel party.

55. It seems fitting that Rose's death certificate listed his occupation as "capitalist" as his tumultuous life had followed the economic ups and downs of the free market (D. Harrison 2004: 206). Rose's many successes (Roseville) were as grandiose and spectacular as his failures (seaweed-stuffed mattresses).

56. Nineteenth-century sailors often used tortoises for fresh meat, and there was a US American whaling camp on nearby Ballast Point at the tip of Point Loma between 1857 and 1873 (May 2001, 1987–1989, 1986).

57. Peter Brueggeman, who edited Asher's account, explained that "turkle" was a nineteenth-century African American word for turtle.

58. Although the arid foothills of Palomar Mountain are full of scrub brush, the top is rife with thick groves of oak, fir, pine, spruce, and cedar, some of

which are nearly 200 feet tall. Pioneers regularly felled mountain trees and sold timber all across the county. In fact, much of the San Luis Rey Mission was constructed out of Palomar Mountain timber (Bailey 2009: 12). During the city of San Diego's lumber shortage in the 1920s, many builders turned to the bountiful California hardwood atop Palomar Mountain. Fred Blum noted that, "Nate was a timber man and chimney builder" (Ryan 1964j: no page numbers).

59. These drought years of 1870–73 followed an even more-pronounced dry spell from 1862–65, known as the Great Drought. Both episodes devastated the local cattle industry and pushed ranchers toward less water-intensive herds. Sheep were far more drought-tolerant than cows, and thus became a far more popular animal to raise (Crawford 1995: 27).

60. Dory Mary Smith's children would have been Harrison's step-great grand-children. East County resident Jim English insisted to me in 2008 that, "I took my daughter to the emergency room about twenty years ago [~1988] and struck up a conversation with a black woman in the waiting area. She told me she was the great granddaughter of Nate Harrison" (Jim English, email to the author, 12 September 2008).

61. Her gravestone is inscribed with her name, the honorific "Mother," and her 1882–1940 lifespan. We have been unsuccessful in our attempts at locating the seven children of Dory Mary Smith or their descendants and are eager to know if their family lore included stories of Harrison.

62. For example, the 1870 San Diego County census recorded fifteen blacks, but only one lived in the city. Likewise, the 1880 San Diego County census listed only three of fifty-five African Americans as being city residents.

63. An additional nuance was that most of San Diego's blacks were from the south, whereas a majority of African Americans in San Francisco were from the north (Fisher 1966: 173). Los Angeles's black community was evenly split between those from the North and South. San Diego's decidedly southern influence, regardless of ethnicity, led William Smythe to label the county as "Californian's deep south" in his comprehensive history of the region (1908: 297). When considering San Diego multiethnic settlement patterns, it is also worth noting that Southern slaves were more experienced with farm labor, which was much more employable in rural San Diego County as opposed to urban areas (Carlton 1974: 9).

64. Anthropologist John P. Harrington featured Juan and Encarnacion Calac in an article entitled "Field-work among the Mission Indians of California" (Harrington 1932). The information in this work drew on the time Chief Calac spent showing Harrington the Rincon Indian Reservation and the surrounding areas, including Harrison's cabin, in June of 1932 (Harrington 1986: volume 3, reel 119, frames 153–55). Harrington's article detailed various Rincon religious beliefs and practices, architectural styles, and tattoo customs (See Winslow 1918).

65. The Bear Valley Township got its name from an 1866 event in which the largest California grizzly bear (*Ursus arctos*) ever captured was taken in the town. Before the killing of this 2,200-pound bear, the town that would become Bear Valley had no official name. Clyde S. James insisted that Harrison had personally witnessed the famous bear, recalling that, "Nate said,

'I seen that ere bear which named de valley-He was as long as here to dar,' point[ing] to a tree about 15 feet away. 'He was a big one!' Nate's scared eyes almost popped out of his head just talking about the bear" (Ryan 1964c: no page numbers). The town of Bear Valley later changed its name to Valley in 1874, to Valley Centre in 1878, and finally to Valley Center in 1887 (McHenry 1997: 9–10).

66. Kentucky-born San Diego resident Thomas Darnall wrote to his brother James on 18 October 1855 that, "There is but one american girl in the place unmarried who is grown, and she can neither read or write" (Crawford 1995: 21). In addition, historian Leland Stanford asserted that "there were less than a dozen white women in San Diego as late as 1866" (Stanford 1978).

67. Robert Carlton noted that, "There had been many blacks in California during the Spanish and Mexican periods, but most had been sufficiently assimilated, by a gradual process of social acceptance and intermarriage, to be able to pass into the 'Spanish' population at the time of the takeover of the area by the United States, and to some extent, before then" (Carlton 1974: 11; also see Weber 1973: 17–18; Beltrán 1946: 200).

68. Don Pedro Alonso O'Crouley, an Irish merchant who frequently visited New Spain during the late eighteenth century, left a detailed account of Spanish racial classifications in his 1774 *A Description of the Kingdom of New Spain by Señor Don Pedro Alonso O'Crouley*. O'Crouley's work included over a dozen different examples of racial mixing, each illustrated with drawings of mother, father, and child. Spanish legal rights were often tied directly to the amount of Spanish blood in one's veins. Furthermore, these rules insisted that time spent in the New World contaminated one's blood, and thus, lowered one's status (Lomnitz 2001; Ruiz de Burton 1992).

69. Californio, which translated from Spanish as "Californian," referred to people of Spanish ancestry born in California while it was under Spanish or Mexican rule. Californio was a new ethnicity. Though it included Spanish, Native American, and African descendants, the identity was selectively used by individuals to elevate themselves socially and attain an elite status above California Indians (Voss 2008).

70. The letter was donated to the project by Peter Brueggeman.

71. The remainder of the census page stated, "Rancho Del Rincon Junio Indians: Indians on this Ranch refuse to give names." This is revealing as to the fractured state of US–California Indian relations at the time.

72. Dona Lavierla, also known as Isabel Place, was from Santa Barbara; her mother was Chumash Indian, and her father was listed in the 1850/52 census as "mulatto, born in the West Indies." A majority of the recorded information about her focused on her life after she split with Harrison in the early-to-mid 1880s. For example, in the mid-to-late 1880s, Lavierla married William Veal of Pala. William owned the store and blacksmith shop at Pala, was the postmaster, and, incidentally, signed Nathan Harrison's water claim in 1892 and voter registration card in 1894. Sometime around 1885 William Veal purchased the entire Pala *asistencia*, greatly upsetting the local tribes. It was Isabel who persuaded him to give the chapel and cemetery back to the church. William Veal was abusive; Isabel and William

separated and filed for divorce in 1891. There was a court record for "Isabel Veal v William Veal, Case No. 5777, judgment entered Sept 9, 1891." Isabel claimed in the pleadings that, "[William] struck and bruised her and on 25 May 1891, hit her three times, blackened her eye and that he drank heavily." Dona Lavierla/Isabel Place's sister, Ramona Place, married Louis Wolf. Ramona (Place) Wolf was likely one of the inspirations for Helen Hunt Jackson's famous 1884 novel, *Ramona*. Jackson stayed with the Wolf family in 1882. Jackson's scathing description of mission life in the early 1880s directly blamed Ramona Wolf's brother-in-law, William Veal, for his brutality, heavy-handed ways, and poor management skills.

73. This could have been in 1886. Herbert Crouch wrote that, "The snow storm of Nov. 21st., 22nd. And 23rd. in 1886 on the Laguna Mts. was the worst I ever experienced on our mountains, and I have been out in a great many" (Crouch 1965: 27). The Laguna Mountains and Temecula were far apart and in different micro-climates, but the 1886 storm did take place around Thanksgiving.

74. Generations of fans hailed him as the "Mexican Robin Hood" (Robin Hood of El Dorado) and noted that he was the inspiration for Johnston McCulley's legendary Zorro character—McCulley created Don Diego de la Vega after reading John Rollin Ridge's 1854 book, *The Life and Adventures of Joaquin Murrieta*—yet his many critics labeled him a murderer, a horse thief, and one of the most wanted men in California.

75. Soon after Joaquin's alleged death, mythical stories began to surface that Murrieta had never been caught and that the celebrated stewed noggin belonged to a rather unfortunate imposter.

76. Murrieta promptly moved to Los Angeles and became a deputy sheriff.

77. Few historical details remain from Harrison's near-drowning in the San Luis Rey River. There was an account from Fred Blum, a friend of Harrison during the early twentieth century, that described a river accident, but it did not specify the year of the incident. Blum recalled that, "Nate was crossing the swollen San Luis Rey river going to the flour mill. Nate swore the horse got dizzy and fell down. Nate had to be fished from the willow tree he was clinging on to. Nate was the one who was dizzy. Too much bottle! Nate liked his drink" (Ryan 1964j: no page numbers).

78. Gift giving is enigmatic in that it can be seen as inspired by generosity, obligation, or opportunism. Anthropologist Marcel Mauss specified the presence of desire and obligation in gift exchange, noting that, "Society always pays itself in the counterfeit coin of its dream" (Bourdieu 1997b: 231). On the one hand, "society paying itself" refers to obligatory reciprocity, the mandatory offerings made by people participating in a gift economy. Giving is required—a nuance that makes the act more of a payment than a gift. Regardless, the exchange is made "in the counterfeit coin of its dream." The gift must maintain the superficial form of pure something-for-nothing generosity and appear as a selfless act of altruism. Although these exchanges are indeed mandatory, they maintain an uncanny resemblance to magnanimity (Mallios 2005b). Mauss's metaphor reveals that "the dream is generosity; the hidden reality is an obligation to give" (Mallios 2006a: 26).

79. Despite the fact that a native gift might not have been recognized by US land customs, it underscores perceived Indigenous land use and identification during the time. According to native rules and norms, it was theirs to give to Harrison.

80. This might explain why Harrison ended up with only 45.55 acres instead of 60.

81. Bartlett's 1931 article on Harrison was printed in *Touring Topics*, the original member magazine of the Automobile Club of Southern California. *Touring Topics* was first published in 1909; its name was changed to *Westways* in the 1930s. It was fitting that a driving magazine would spotlight Harrison as the steep grade that bore his name lured many early twentieth-century car adventurers to Palomar Mountain's precipitous west side.

82. Frank and Louis Salmons purchased Doane's cattle for $5,000 and kept the large herd in Doane Valley for many years.

83. Milton Bailey started a stage line between San Diego and the Bailey resort (Palomar Lodge) in 1912. He drove passengers up the precipitous road for $6.50 and frequently stopped at Harrison's cabin along the way. Most of the photographs of Harrison were taken during the time in which Milton Bailey ran his stage line. Beckler noted that the Bailey resort atop Palomar Mountain was "a favorite vacation spot for all the Southland" (1958: 17). Theodore's daughter, Hodgie Bailey Salmons, recalled that her family did not plan to create the Palomar resort, noting that, "We never intended to have a hotel, but people kept coming up and wanting to stay and eat, so what could we do?" (Beckler 1958: 18).

84. Harrison's cabin was made of stones and a shake roof; it was framed by four wooden posts but was not a log cabin.

85. His other works included a Luiseño tale published in the 1908 *Journal of American Folk-Lore* and multiple papers in the University of California Publications series (Sparkman 1908a).

86. The matter was complicated further when local native Francisco Calac was arrested for Sparkman's murder and then pronounced insane by a San Diego jury. The 14 August 1907, *Los Angeles Herald* explained that, "[Calac] wished the sheriff to bring a paper to be signed whereby [he] would give his permission to be instantly executed. If [Calac] regains his reason he will be tried on the charge of murder." There are no further records regarding this case, suggesting the execution never occurred.

87. Bentley Elmore was in charge of the county road on Palomar Mountain.

88. There were no official records of the tax-delinquent sale or the return deed back to Harrison.

89. The phrase "gone right up into the air" refers to one figuratively exploding with rage.

90. Listed on the 1900 census for the Pala Township as a merchant, Frank Salmons owned the Pala general store, was a prominent land developer, and was active in the tourmaline mining business. Found in gem mines in and around Pala, pink tourmaline was in high demand during the early 1900s because a Chinese empress (Dowager Empress Cixi of the Qing Dynasty) was infatuated with the stone.

91. This assumes that Fred Smith's mother and Dona Lavierla were of similar age to Harrison, in their fifties or sixties, when married to him in the 1880s.

92. The fact that Lee Utt paid Harrison's property taxes might have indirectly given support to the bogus theory that Lysander Utt once owned Harrison and brought him cross-country. As mentioned earlier, Lee and Lysander's biographies were often blended into one in popular accounts, and the established notion that an Utt fronted Harrison's bills might have appeared to the uncritical eye to be consistent with the romanticized tale of what a benevolent former owner would do for his recently emancipated slave.

93. Horses were especially valued during the 19-teens because of their importance in warfare. In World War I alone, eight million horses died (Ulrich 2018).

94. Asher's assertion that Harrison did not want to leave the mountain was echoed in a contemporary newspaper article. A year after his passing, the *Oceanside Blade* reported that Harrison was "heartbroken because the infirmities of age had made it necessary for him to be removed to the hospital where he could have proper care" ("Memorial Fountain" 1921).

95. The most detailed historical accounts, like multiple narratives from Asher and Davis, were noticeably silent about any visitation that Harrison received. The only reference came from Bartlett, who quoted an anonymous rancher as stating, "Some of us would visit him, and he would beg to be taken back, back to Palomar" (Bartlett 1931: 24).

96. Was it just a coincidence that Harrison's father and former owner were both named Ben?

97. Bartlett's phrase "pauper's field" seemed to have been a combination of the traditional terms "potter's field" and "pauper's grave." The former was a biblical reference [Matthew 27: 3–8] to a large area of internments for unknown individuals—"they bought with them the potter's field, to be a burying place for strangers"—and subsequently the indigent; the latter was a single grave for a poor person who could not afford a plot.

98. "Cawn" was a phonetic spelling of "corn."

99. Archaeological excavation of the fireplace uncovered no rabbit bones; in fact, fieldwork unearthed no *Sylvilagus* (the most common local rabbit genus) remains at all.

100. The original land for Palomar Mountain State Park included the homesteads of William Bougher, William Pearson, Solomon Todd, George Doane, and others (Beckler 1958: 40).

101. These projects offered a public service that often involved construction and massive earth-moving. Sponsored by many different New Deal relief associations, public works projects were very common in San Diego County. Despite the conservative politics of the region, local Works Progress Administration (WPA) offices were inundated with requests for work even prior to opening ("1,240,000 WPA Aid" 1935). In fact, "The first of over 1,000 WPA-era projects in San Diego County began in October of 1935 with the construction of a road up Palomar Mountain to facilitate access to the new observatory" (Mallios and Purvis 2006: 18).

102. The CCC, which consisted exclusively of unmarried and unemployed men, built many of the Palomar State Park's roads, campgrounds, and homes during the 1930s and '40s.

103. In the 1920s, world-renowned astronomers from the California Institute of Technology (Caltech) addressed their need for a new site for their observatory as the emerging light pollution from Los Angeles greatly limited their abilities to look deep into the cosmos. Southern California astronomers had visited Palomar Mountain previously when searching for an observatory site in the early 1900s. In fact, according to Abel Davis, "Nate [Harrison] saw the first scientists mount to the top of the mountain in search of a place for a large telescope in 1903. It was rejected then, and the telescope was placed on Mount Wilson [located in the San Gabriel Mountains near Pasadena. Los Angeles County's Mount Wilson would become home to the world's largest aperture telescope in 1917]" (Davis c. 1955: 64). George Ellery Hale received a $6 million Rockefeller grant to investigate potential sites across the globe for an optimal astronomical spot and concluded that the top of Palomar Mountain, just ninety miles southeast of Caltech, would be ideal because of its three hundred clear nights each year, lack of surrounding development, and earthquake-proof granite base (E. Davis 1938: 48; Beckler 1958: 37).

104. Although the first operational astronomical instrument on Palomar Mountain was the 18-inch Schmidt telescope, first used in 1936, far more attention was placed on the construction of the 200-inch Hale telescope. The Hale telescope was housed in a dome 12-stories high, celebrated for being the same size as the Pantheon in Rome and weighing over 1,000 tons ("Palomar Mountain" 1958: 13). At the time, it was the world's largest electrically welded structure (Bailey 2009: 108).

105. The gigantic telescope lens ferried up this specially-designed road was arguably the most valuable piece of glass ever constructed.

106. While the west side of Palomar Mountain remained relatively quiet in the decades after Harrison's passing, the vast attention thrust on the world-famous Caltech observatory brought an assortment of outsiders to the region, the most infamous of which was George Adamski. A Polish immigrant who served in the US Cavalry in 1916, Adamski was an amateur theologian and highly successful winemaker who received a government license to produce alcohol during Prohibition for religious purposes. He moved to Palomar Mountain in 1944, claimed to see multiple alien mother ships in the late '40s, and then allegedly made first contact with Venusian visitors in the 1950s at his Palomar Gardens cafe. Adamski cleverly capitalized on the growing fame of the nearby telescope as the Palomar Mountain Observatory had just been featured on a 3-cent postage stamp in 1948, was on the cover of many leading magazines, and was a major tourist destination. "Professor" Adamski lectured to many public audiences about his purported otherworldly contacts, wrote two bestselling books—*Flying Saucers Have Landed* (1953) and *Inside the Space Ships* (1955)—and perpetuated a series of well-publicized hoaxes, each involving aliens and their spacecrafts. Though widely derided as a con artist, his legend lives on in

modern science fiction as many writers, video game designers, and others often give alien-themed frauds the moniker "Adamski."

107. For example, Escondido resident "Mrs. Stephen Thompson" wrote a letter to the editor of the *Daily Times-Advocate* on 17 August 1972 that declared, "N——r Nate. So this is how history gets changed. Someone decides a word doesn't sound good, so they change it. Uncle Nate, indeed. Quit trying to foist a man born in the 1800s into 1972. He was known all around as N——r Nate. This is what he called himself. He wasn't shackled by this word 'n——r.' Can't you see this man meeting a wagon or car and looking at white people, smiling and saying, 'Hello I'm N——r Nate, the first white man on the mountain.' He laughs, they laugh, then they all start talking and enjoying life and each other."

108. The act of pothunting involves digging for artifacts without any recordation or concern for location.

2

THE MAN, THE MYTH, THE LEGEND

Truth be told, it rarely is. Lies, exaggerations, and biased accounts are seemingly everywhere in modern Western society, and they are often presented overtly as facts. References to this phenomenon are equally commonplace, be it in music, movies, or even high-brow philosophy. When blues legend B.B. King sings, "Everybody lies a little, and some people lie a lot," we collectively bob our head in agreement and ponder the contradiction of our society that purportedly values truth but so seldom experiences it (King 1975).

Falsehoods take many forms and arise from a wide variety of inspirations. They range from fibs to whoppers and include slightly embellished stories and outlandish legends. Our mistruths may be accidental (poor attention to detail), self-inflated (the big brag), warm-heartedly altruistic (delicate white lies), sinister (devious agendas), entertainingly exaggerated (fish stories), etc. Faulty memories, boorish boasts, euphemistic half-truths, petty manipulation, and tall tales are so commonplace in our everyday life that they are incredibly easy to locate, recognize, and explain.[1]

Our perpetuation of falsehoods is even aided by the biology of the human brain. Recent research has shown that while newly learned ideas are initially stored in the hippocampus, when we recall them at a later date the brain transfers them to the cerebral cortex (Miller and Sweatt 2007; Wang and Aamodtjune 2008; LaFee 2008). This reprocessing of memory separates the learned material from the context in which it was first experienced and often results in "source amnesia"; we remember the content but not the context. When the original ideas are true, the consequences are minor; we are just unable to remember how or why we know what we know. However, when the ideas are false, it means that we often still believe them to be true because we no longer can reference the source material that exposes their dubiousness. This phenomenon is especially pronounced when the memory triggers an emotional response because powerful feelings result in memories that are more likely to be retained (Schwabe et al. 2011). Thus, even the structure of our brain can lead us to insist that emotionally charged falsehoods are true and, eventually, to perpetuate them.[2]

A myth is more than just a fib though; it unites individual mistruths with a broader agenda and a deeper message. Myths are societal lies; they are intentional fabrications that serve a bigger purpose. As such, they have an additional layer of intrigue. These time-honored stories deliberately make literal truth secondary for a larger and more permanent audience. Facts, especially those relating to the past, are often mundane; they can strike us as unglamorous, unsettling, and, worst of all, unmemorable. Conversely, romanticized tales of the past are not shackled by details from a previous reality; they can be molded to satiate our desire for the inspirational by forging a modern-day mythology. Paleontologist Stephen Jay Gould captured this dualism, noting that, ". . . myths identify heroes and sacred places while evolutionary stories [scientific histories consisting exclusively of empirical evidence from actual events] provide no palpable, particular thing as a symbol for reverence, worship, or patriotism" (1991: 57). Thus, the inherent mundaneness of the truth can challenge its very survival.

Modern Greek philosopher Nikos Kazantzakis took the exaltation of the myth a step further, completely reversing expected notions of fact and fiction. He asked and answered in his memoir *Report to Greco*, "Is there anything truer than truth? Yes, legend. This gives eternal meaning to ephemeral truth" (1965: 471). Kazantzakis emphasized that truth, while accurate in a given moment, is often adrift of greater significance without an enduring legacy. Today's truth may be tomorrow's fiction and vice versa. Conversely, myths transcend time and are always germane. Once memorable tales replace unmemorable occurrences, there is great difficulty in going back and unlearning the gratifying yarn. Paradoxically, it is tempting to conclude that a gripping fictional account has far more prominence, permanence, and poignancy for many of us than one that simply prioritizes accuracy.

One of the ironies of the rampant distortion in our daily lives is that the process of creating these falsehoods often reveals many truths. I believe that Scottish essayist Thomas Carlyle was only partially accurate in his assertion that, "no lie can live forever" (1837: part 1, book VI, chapter 3). While it is true that historical lies are often ultimately exposed, they can nonetheless transcend time for extended periods when the fabrication continues to change to suit new needs. An engaging mistruth can perpetuate itself in continually evolving forms. However, it is in this fluidity that the alluring fiction's verisimilitude—the superficial and false appearance of truth without being genuinely authentic or accurate—can be unmasked.

The perpetual evolution of a historical lie is frequently its undoing. This is the paradox of an alluring fictional past: the story needs to evolve to stay relevant, but the many past forms of a purportedly singular, static, and "true" narrative can be exposed to reveal the discordance. Intricate analyses of the transformation of a story over time can unveil an historical narrative's actual status as myth, the reason for its evolution, and the agendas, perspectives, and biases of the series of storytellers. These details are some of the many facts in each fiction. Myths obviously create history, but they also explain it. These dual abilities are all the more remarkable when we remember that legendary fictional tales often lack, or even contradict, direct historical evidence.

We are all well aware of how a deliberately skewed rereading and retelling of the past can manufacture an alternative past reality, but are the distinctions between myth, secondhand history, and primary historical sources so vastly different? An overwhelming Western belief in scientism often leads audiences to extend rigorous principles to the humanities without an appreciation of multiple perspectives and storytelling dynamism. Even when handed the same literal text to read, each person experiences a slightly different story based on his or her own perspective and past. Accordingly, when someone reads a text a second time, it too is a slightly different tale because of continuing transformative life events and the experience of previously reading it. As much as literary critics and people over forty are loath to admit, the video gaming experience is similar to the literary experience in that each pass through the art form is different. Static history, static literature, and static art gain a dynamic dimension when engaged by diverse audiences and diachronic perspectives.

When faced with seemingly overwhelming waves of alternative perspectives, far-reaching diversity, and intricate complexities in the past, we often cling to the easier-to-digest concept of a singular history. There is comfort in a bounded explanation of how something occurred—regardless of nuance, complication, or interpretation. Sometimes we yearn to answer endless interpretive queries (of "but why") with the firm conclusion, "It just was." For example, consider baseball slugger Barry Bonds's panic in 2007 when confronted with the chance of his record-breaking baseball being branded with an asterisk because of his much-debated and litigated anabolic steroid use. Fashion designer Marc Ecko purchased Bonds's 756th home-run ball at auction for $752,467.20 and then conducted an internet poll asking fans what he should do with it. He proposed three strikingly different options: 1) mark it with a tarnishing asterisk because of the controversy surrounding Bonds's accomplishment before giving it to the Baseball Hall of Fame, 2) donate it to Cooperstown unmarked, or 3) banish it to space on a rocket. Ecko deliberately gave the general public, not the sport's elite or accepted leaders, the final decision. When informed of the results (respectively 47 percent, 34 percent, and 19 percent), Bonds—desperately holding onto the notion of his singular history, free of public interpretation—defiantly declared, "You cannot give people the freedom, the right to alter history, you can't do it" ("Bonds would opt of Hall over asterisk ball" 2007). Sorry Barry, people alter history with every single story they tell; the past is a fluid construction that is under constant revision. Furthermore, your ball is now branded with an asterisk; but at least it is not in outer space.

People have and commonly execute the right to alter history, and, as you will read, the legend of Nathan Harrison is a striking example. In the life-story of this celebrated San Diego pioneer, the lines between information, misinformation, and myth-information are quite blurry. One of the reasons it is essential to track down every existing historical account of Harrison is that there is so much fiction surrounding this local legend. On numerous occasions, purportedly reliable sources provided historical details that were contradictory with other seemingly indisputable narratives. Only by seeing the full inventory of narratives can we simultaneously experience the saturation of these stories and begin to appreciate meaningful patterns that identify plausibility, embellishment, and invention. Rather than lament the many fictional aspects of his biography that have come to be perpetuated and accepted as fact, it is possible to pinpoint how specific story elements have changed and provide context that helps explain why they evolved in that particular manner. While these insights start with Harrison and his contemporaries, they also include the community that cultivated and continues to propagate his legend.

Archaeologist Laurie Wilkie poignantly observed that, ". . . history is a conglomeration of past voices combining to tell the events of their time as they saw and interpreted them" (2000: xvi). Whereas the previous chapter detailed the histories of Harrison and offered context to identify the more reliable accounts, this chapter attempts to uncover the context for the rampant myth-making that ensued following his death.[3] It does not merely suggest which narrative was most likely; it delves into the reasons that such fictions were created in the first place and why they were so eagerly perpetuated as fact. Instead of embracing an approach that forgives inevitable inaccuracies, it seeks to expose motive. As anthropologist Gananath Obeyesekere stated, "One must probe into the hidden agendas underlying the writing of [historical] . . . texts" because "a text does not exist by itself; it is embodied in a context" (1992: 66; 1990: 130). Myth-busting can be a messy business, one that simultaneously pinpoints liars and the society that avariciously devours and passes on their fictitious creations.

Myths and Legends

Though the words "myth" and "legend" are often used interchangeably, there are important differences, especially for this book. Myth derives from the Greek word *mythos*—a word, speech, or story. It refers primarily to "a traditional story of unknown authorship, ostensibly with a historical basis, but *serving usually to explain some phenomenon of nature, or the customs, institutions, religious rites, etc. of a people*" (Guralnik 1986: 942; italics added). Conversely, the term "legend" comes from the Medieval English term *legende* and is "a story handed down for generations among a people and popularly believed to have a historical basis, although not verifiable" (Guralnik 1986: 806). While there is much overlap in the definitions, the differences are meaningful. Specifically, a myth is designed with the particular agenda to explain something larger about certain cultural norms. Writers of mythology imbue their stories with specific elements of proper societal roles; they plot (Brooks 1984: 35; Mallios and Lennox 2014; Little 2004).[4] This deliberate action injects moral invention into traditional narratives and distinguishes myth from both realistic biography and time-honored legend. Whereas a myth is tied to its moral, the denotation of legend reveals that its core quality is based in having been told and retold for many generations. The process of telling and retelling further substantiates the story. The power of the legend is its duration, not necessarily its societal message, which may have disappeared long ago. When a myth evolves into legend, the story gains permanence but often at the expense of its overt meaning.[5]

Anthropological historical archaeologists have actively examined the interplay between myth-making, public memory, and identity. Paul Shackel has been at the forefront of detailing how past constructions of history result in the production of public memory, which consists of circulating recollections among members of a given community (2001). He and others have noted how dominant stories about the past have less to do with authentic historical events and more about mirroring the concerns, beliefs, and desires of the time period in which they were told (Wilson 1997; Blight 1989; Brandon and Davidson 2005; Flores 2002; Handler and Gable 1997; Horning 2001, 2002; Julia King 2012; Pitcaithley 2001; Slotkin 1998; Yentsch 1988). This trend is not confined to US history. Rosemary Joyce and Ruth Tringham's work at Mayan sites in Honduras (2007) and Natasha Leriou's studies of Mycenaean colonization (2004) demonstrate how "master narratives have a way of infiltrating scholarship in tenacious ways and then never letting go" (Julia King 2012: 176).

This chapter covers many different components of the myth-making process as it pertains to the life of Nathan Harrison. It begins with close scrutiny as to how the stories evolved over time, showcasing regular and periodic transformations and the larger societal factors that influenced many of these changes. Attention then turns to Harrison's personal agency in his identity construction and how it facilitated the growth of his legend. His use of self-deprecating humor, ironic role reversals, and multiple identities was especially successful in creating a lasting persona that was riveting for a wealth of past and present audiences. The many photographic images are also analyzed in terms of how they helped solidify Harrison's legendary status in the region. They are a starting point for deeper discussions about the many late nineteenth- and early twentieth-century visitors to the mountain, the symbolism inherent to the arduous trek to his cabin, and the lasting power of printed pictures. The final part of this chapter on myth-making is a counter-example that focuses on how Harrison's celebrated mountain identity was later lost and forgotten in the city of San Diego. It contrasts his celebrated status in Palomar's rural community with the anonymity and social insignificance Harrison experienced as a solitary stranger in urban San Diego during the last year of his life.

Due to a multiplicity of perspectives, agendas, and biases, singular historical truth can be a bogus concept; but the examination of myth-making gets at a subsequent set of concrete realities that can be highly informative. Although the term "apotheosis" conventionally refers to the elevation of a person to the rank of a deity, I use it loosely to refer to the celebratory transformation of an actual person into myth and legend. It is precisely this process of exaltation—whatever the motives—that is of primary significance here. Examining the apotheosis of Harrison expands the study of his specific history into a broader and more complete analysis of his life, times, and ongoing legacies. Nathan Harrison is the obvious focus of this book, but in the words of poet W. H. Auden, "What he was he was; what he is slated to become depends on us" (Sorenson 2009: 372).

The Myths of Nathan Harrison

In the annals of modern American mythology, George Washington could tell no lie, Paul Bunyan had staggering size, strength, and a sapphire-shaded sidekick, and a far less celebrated Nathan Harrison was seemingly everywhere in the Old West. Whereas young George's cherry-chopping confession and Bunyan's gargantuan stature have been inseparably woven into the very fabric of American lore, Harrison's omnipresence is no less pronounced in Southern California's legendary history. In fact, Harrison can effectively be seen as the Forrest Gump of Wild West San Diego; he is included in nearly every major historical event in the region (Groom 1986). Harrison's legend features many famous firsts, famous encounters, and famous parallels. While remarkably few of these accounts stand up to historical scrutiny, the notion that Harrison participated in so many significant events, met so many celebrated individuals, and lived so many important experiences at the American birth of the Golden State is an alluring idea that has captivated local audiences for over a century.

Even though it is almost certain that he made only one cross-country journey, the stories of Harrison placed him on nearly every possible contemporary mode of transportation and route to California. Once in the Golden State, he was allegedly present at several important Old West moments, including fighting in Frémont's Battalion during the Bear Flag Revolt to help the US acquire California from Mexico, arriving with the Mormon Battalion in San Diego, and driving the first wagon train over Tejon Pass to open the route connecting the Central Valley with Southern California. It is important to note that these events were famous for both what occurred and for what resulted. Frémont personally accepted Mexican surrender at Cahuenga Pass in 1846; his name is synonymous with the start of the early American period in California, especially in the southern region of the state. The Mormon Battalion was equally important in symbolically securing the American Southwest for the US and as the longest infantry march in the nation's history. Likewise, the placement of Harrison on the inaugural wagon over Tejon Pass marked the first regular and reliable land connection between Gold Rush territory in the north with Los Angeles and San Diego in the south; it was essential to California being a singular and unified American state. These three events were instrumental in the creation of a unique US identity for California, one that could be framed as separate from Spanish and Mexican influence and in the context of a major military victory.

Harrison was allegedly present at these key moments in California's early American period as well as at everyday sites that typified the Golden State experience at its inception. He purportedly toiled in the gold mines, at the missions, and on the reservations, intersecting with nearly every different ethnic group in the Old West. Furthermore, there was seemingly no community he failed to win over with diligence, savvy, and humor. In addition, he supposedly faced and barely survived the most notorious and stereotypical foes of the time, including tomahawk-wielding Indians, seceding Confederates, natural threats like grizzly bears, mountain lions, and rattlesnakes, and the most infamous Mexican bandito in the land, Joaquin Murrieta. Each of these figures represented prominent and adversarial symbols of early American nationalism in California as US pioneers in the West actively clashed with the Indigenous population, the natural environment, internal Civil-War era divisions, and long-standing Spanish and Mexican settlers. In purportedly enduring all of these significant obstacles, Harrison's mythical biography served as an empowered tale of US perseverance in the face of long odds. One of the primary reasons that people told and retold Nathan Harrison's story was that it so well bolstered the Anglo-American origin story of the United States in the West.[6]

Harrison's purported military service was important in the myth-making process for multiple reasons. First, battlefield valor is a high-status trait in US society; this attribution would be especially meaningful if Harrison had fought for the United States in the Civil War, the Indian Wars, or the Spanish-American War. African Americans had a long history of defending a nation that denied them their most basic rights as citizens, and heroic black military service was especially effective at exposing American racial hypocrisy. In the words of Ralph Ellison, "How could you treat a Negro as equal in war and then deny him equality during times of peace?" (Ellison 1952: xii–xiii). Second, the military ventures in which Harrison might have participated each dated back to the earliest days of US settlement in the region. Thus, they further bolstered his great antiquity in the area. Third, nineteenth-century military service was often rewarded with land ownership. Consequently, alleged military service by Harrison would help bolster any claim he might have made due to governmental link between military experience and land ownership. Overall, the implication of military service, regardless of historical accuracy, further grew his mythical status as rightful resident and owner of land on Palomar Mountain.

Having great antiquity—being extremely old—served multiple purposes for Harrison and clearly enhanced his legend. During his lifetime, it helped establish his right to live on Palomar Mountain, as US property ownership through homesteading was based on inhabiting and claiming a specific tract of land first. The person who initially occupied and improved the land, as long as a they were a US citizen, had rights to the land over anyone who arrived at a later date. In addition, deep historical ties to the region provided Harrison with an additional layer of security, especially against threats from bigoted or other ill-intentioned newcomers. His oft-repeated claim of being "the *first* white man on the mountain" was a clear statement of primacy. In securing and continually affirming this original settler status, Harrison explicitly answered any queries regarding his justifiable place on the mountain even before they were asked.[7] Regardless of ethnicity, it also placed him in the esteemed cohort with the white founders of the area, including Joseph Smith, Theodore Bailey, Enos Mendenhall, and others. Few individuals would question Smith's claim to the mountain (it was named after him from 1860–1901), Bailey's ties to the region (his lodge at the top of Palomar Mountain was a primary destination and it supplied the stage that traversed the grade), or Mendenhall's economic influence (his lucrative cattle industry sustained the community during certain fiscal downturns); likewise, Harrison had attained a similar status of privileged primacy, which was bastioned in two interrelated ways: 1) by his seniority on the mountain and 2) by his advanced age.

Harrison's great antiquity was also an engaging story, rich in irony and celebration of rustic lifeways. Even though he had endured staggering hardship during enslavement, the Gold Rush, the Old West, and rugged frontier conditions atop Palomar Mountain, Harrison was purportedly a centenarian. His long life was a testimony to the benefits of country life. Rural residents took great pride in a narrative whose primary character eschewed urban existence for mountain life and outlived city dwellers without the comforts of electricity or other technological advances. Accordingly, the trend of Harrison's age being exaggerated during his lifetime was continued well after his passing. In fact, it peaked in the 2000s with the claim that he lived to be 107 years old. The combination of being first on the mountain and surviving to an almost unbelievably old age for the early 1900s intimated that Harrison was a nearly permanent fixture in the region. Primacy and permanence on Palomar Mountain were the cornerstones of his legend.

In order to be a Gump-like cultural figure, however, there needed to be an exaggerated ridiculousness to his ubiquity. The omnipresence must be depicted almost farcically, playing up the comedic irony that any singular character—especially one of such modest means[8]—could intersect so many historic events and celebrated figures. Harrison's purported historical reach, his alleged ability to be everywhere, was so broad that it even extended into one of the most celebrated fictional works of the day. Consider the example of this particular Harrison origin tale related by local author Laura James in 1958:

> [Harrison] was from the state of Mississippi. When a boy of about sixteen, he and a number of other slaves were put up for auction. As he was small of stature (caused, he claimed, because as a child he had been

worked so hard and fed so little) he was not attractive to buyers. They were looking for large strong men to work in the fields. During the excitement of the auction Nate saw a chance to slip away. He dropped into the river, and swam and floated for miles. At last he came to a landing where a side-wheel steamer was taking on fuel. He stole into the fuel bunker. There he stayed for days. He lost track of the number, and when he finally saw a chance to get out, he was almost starved to death. He hid out in the woods all day. When the lights in a nearby farm house went out at night, and he figured everyone would be asleep, he crept up to the house and ate food that had been set out for the dogs. He said that was the best tasting food he had eaten in all his life. (1958: 7)[9]

Clearly, Nathan Harrison's legend grew in a spectacular manner over time, one that inserted him into some of the frontier's most popular stories and blended his biography with well-known characters from American classics (Mallios and Stroud 2006: 72). Mark Twain described nearly the same account for his enslaved African American "Jim" character in *The Adventures of Huckleberry Finn* (1885).[10] Twain's Jim matter-of-factly stated, "I run off," when describing how he fled an impending slave auction, floated down the Mississippi River, and hid in the woods to escape capture (1885: 43). In transcending real and imaginary realms, Harrison simultaneously lived his own mythical life story and periodically occupied other legendary tales as well.[11]

Harrison's unbelievable ubiquity was occasionally coupled with an almost supernatural ability to survive. During the worst recorded rainstorm in San Diego history, Harrison allegedly met his demise—or did he? The spring of 1884 saw a downpour measured in feet instead of inches; over three feet of rain fell in thirty hours! Ever Gump-ian Nathan Harrison was directly and publicly impacted by this most memorable catastrophic event as the local newspaper reported the drowning of the beloved local pioneer in "The Great San Diego Flood." One can argue that if an event was historically significant, a story would place Harrison there, and conversely, if he was at an event, there was a good chance of it being historically significant or at least highly memorable. Harrison's purportedly fatal intersection with the storm of the century was big news, as was the miraculous discovery a month later that he had somehow survived the torrent.

Patterns of Change

Whereas Harrison's exaggerated age, time on Palomar Mountain, and ubiquity in the Old West were constant components of his legend, there were two general patterns of change in the stories told about him. The first adhered to expected models of gradual transformations over time. Archaeologists have long witnessed how style changes slowly, observing artifact frequencies that show the initial rise of a trait, its peak, the diminishment of its popularity, and its ultimate disappearance. This normal distribution often transcends archaeological material culture and can be seen across daily life in everything from dance styles to food recipes to modern-day phone-app downloads. Furthermore, as one style increases in popularity, its predecessor decreases; yet each hip trend will eventually be out of style and replaced by the next emergent trend. The second pattern in the Harrison narratives consisted of a punctuated and immediate change without any gradual build-up; it was a sudden shift from describing one particular aspect of his life to a completely different interpretation of the same biographical element. These new variants on previously established topics seemed to appear out of nowhere and were suddenly accepted as permanent facts.

When archaeologists engage in seriative analyses to trace change over space or time, they often construct seriations to show the results. Studies with many cases (large sample sizes) traditionally use exact-count/percentile frequency seriations, and those with fewer cases often employ presence/absence seriations. The latter is a table of "+"s and "–"s (+ for presence and – for absence) that tracks the appearance of a certain trait being measured at a given time (Mallios et al. 2009; Mallios and Lennox 2014: 60) (Table 2.1). Since things usually change in a normal and gradual manner, the typical graph of a presence/absence seriation table shows a diagonally slanted elliptical trend of "+"s surrounded by "–"s that reveal the slow replacement of one style by another over time. The process for constructing these tables is relatively simple: 1) select mutually exclusive time periods, 2) choose categories of analysis with mutually exclusive traits, and 3) if the trait in question appears during a specific time period, place a "+" in the box; if not, give it a "–".

Table 2.1. Presence/absence seriation model. ("+" denotes the presence of a trait and "–" denotes its absence over time.)

Time/Trait	Form A	Form B	Form C	Form D	Form E	Form F
Period 1	+	+	–	–	–	–
Period 2	–	+	+	–	–	–
Period 3	–	+	+	+	–	–
Period 4	–	–	+	+	+	–
Period 5	–	–	+	+	+	–
Period 6	–	–	–	+	+	+

The seriations created here for the narratives of Nathan Harrison followed these steps. The accounts were divided into five twenty-year intervals: 1910–29, 1930–49, 1950–69, 1970–89, and 1990–2009. The categories were specific descriptions from the accounts of Harrison, like "what terms were used to describe his home," "how was his intelligence described," "how was his alcohol consumption described," etc. The traits within the categories included each different kind of response; these were the story-telling elements of the narratives. For example, for the home-description category, the range of actual elements included "shack," "hut," "crude cabin," "house," and "cabin." Finally, the "+"s and "–"s were placed according to the presence or absence of certain category elements for each time period. If necessary, the columns were reordered to correspond with the order of appearance for each trait. With the seriation created and the pattern of change demonstrated, discussion could then ensue as to why the particular transformation occurred and whether this was part of a broader narrative metamorphosis.

Dwelling Description Seriation

Descriptions of Harrison's Palomar Mountain home underwent regular change over time. As a group, authors of his biographies employed more flattering terms over the decades; what was first called a "shack" was labeled in the interim a "hut" and a "crude cabin" before later being deemed a "house" and a "cabin." While there was some overlap in these descriptions, it is easy to draw temporal lines between the extreme terms. "Shack" and "hut" both literally implied poor construction, and neither term was used in a written description of Harrison's home after 1970. Conversely, the more complimentary terms of "house" and "cabin" never occurred in an account before 1950. Seriation of these terms over time reveals a perfectly gradual and unimodal linguistic evolution (Table 2.2). Although Harrison's cabin had been razed long before most of these authors wrote their accounts, their narratives clearly romanticized the structure as time elapsed. In the minds of Harrison biographers and their resultant audiences, his hillside home grew more elegant with each year.

Purported Intelligence Seriation

Likewise, accounts of Harrison's intellect were undoubtedly more positive over time. Initial narratives underscored his limitations, employing phrases like "lack of education" and "illiterate." Mid-century

Table 2.2. Historical narrative seriation of Harrison dwelling description at twenty-year intervals.

Date	"Shack"	"Hut"	"Crude cabin"	"House"	"Cabin"
1910–29	+	−	−	−	−
1930–49	+	+	+	−	−
1950–69	+	+	+	+	+
1970–89	−	−	−	+	+
1990–2009	−	−	−	−	+

stories used more complimentary terms, like "cultivated" to describe his cognitive abilities. The most recent accounts expressed no reservations in celebrating his mental prowess, calling him "intelligent." All of these terms referred to the same individual, yet the most negative phrase ("no education") was only used before 1949, and the most positive adjective ("intelligent") was only employed after 1950 (Table 2.3). According to the chroniclers of Palomar Mountain history, Harrison's intellect grew by leaps and bounds well after his passing. The Nathan "Nate" Harrison Historical Archaeology Project indirectly contributed to this assessment as many of its material findings suggested that he was savvy, skillful, and multi-talented.

Table 2.3. Historical narrative seriation of Harrison's purported intelligence at twenty-year intervals.

Date	No description	"No education"	"Illiterate"	"Cultivated"	"Intelligent"
1910–29	+	−	−	−	−
1930–49	−	+	+	+	−
1950–69	−	−	+	+	−
1970–89	−	−	+	−	+
1990–2009	−	−	−	−	+

Harrison Freedom Seriation

Stories of how Nathan Harrison gained his freedom also changed in a remarkably regular fashion. The earliest accounts related that Harrison illegally fled from his owner. Interim stories stated that Harrison was emancipated when his owner died and that Harrison's owner granted him liberty. Only in the final narratives was it suggested that Nathan Harrison was able to pay for his freedom. These biographies collectively showcased a transformation in the legality of Harrison's emancipation and the growing role Nathan Harrison himself played in securing independence (Table 2.4). The stories that initially depicted him as a fugitive gave way to passive liberation through the death of his owner, which were subsequently replaced by tales of an active choice of emancipation by his owner. These accounts culminated with Harrison himself buying his independence, the apex of legality and empowered personal agency.[12]

Table 2.4. Historical narrative seriation of Harrison emancipation description at twenty-year intervals.

Date	Harrison ran away	Harrison's owner died	Owner granted freedom	Harrison purchased freedom
1910–29	–	–	–	–
1930–49	+	+	–	–
1950–69	+	+	+	–
1970–89	–	+	–	–
1990–2009	–	+	–	+

Alcohol Use Seriation

It was tempting, but incorrect, to assume that all aspects of Harrison biographies were told in more complimentary terms over the decades. Perhaps the most pronounced example of a seemingly negative trait that was increasingly emphasized over time concerned his consumption of alcoholic beverages. Early stories celebrated Harrison's teetotaling sobriety, interim accounts posited that his consumption was moderate, and only the later narratives suggested drunken binges (Table 2.5). As Harrison's legend grew, his cabin became nicer and his intellect became keener, but his excessive drinking was also more pronounced and, consequently, exalted.

Punctuated Shifts

Some of the changes that occurred in the stories of Harrison happened very suddenly; instead of the gradual transformation or exaggeration of a trait, there was a punctuated shift to an entirely new story element. The most pronounced example of this concerned the identity of

Table 2.5. Condensed historical narrative seriation of Harrison's purported alcohol use at twenty-year intervals.

Date	Sober	Moderate consumption	Stories of drunkenness
1910–29	+	–	–
1930–49	–	+	–
1950–69	–	+	–
1970–89	–	+	+
1990–2009	–	–	+

the slave owner who first brought Harrison to the Old West. Without exception, every account before 1952 identified Nathan Harrison's original owner either as "Mr. Harrison" or left him anonymous. On the contrary, a wealth of sources after 1952 claimed that Lysander Utt was Nathan Harrison's owner and took him west during the Gold Rush. The abrupt narrative switch started with in a single account, Philip S. Rush's May 1952 *Southern California Rancher* article, "The Story of 'N——r Nate.'" This one publication was a highly influential narrative tipping point that significantly altered Harrison's established biography for over a half century (Gladwell 2000). It created a new and highly influential narrative based primarily on Utt owning Harrison and bringing him to Southern California in 1849.

There were multiple clues as to why Rush dubiously claimed Utt was Harrison's original owner. The first was in the text of the narrative itself. Rush spent more time celebrating the Utt family than providing any details of the article's alleged subject matter, Nathan Harrison. This exaltation of all things Utt suggested an ulterior motive. This hunch is verified by the enormous half-page advertisement that ran next to the article, which featured the congressional political campaign for James B. Utt, Lysander Utt's grandson (Figure 2.1). In fact, the *Southern California Rancher* was a frequent vessel for James B. Utt's political propaganda. The April 1952 issue featured a ringing endorsement for Utt, again penned by Philip S. Rush; the June 1952 issue included a story on Utt entitled, "Meet the Top Men"; and the November 1952 issue proclaimed that Utt was "heavily elected" in the recent election. Rush's articles, especially the May 1952 installment, seemed to be a politically driven fabrication that linked the Utt family legacy with the popular tales of Harrison. They built on aspects of the 1952 Utt campaign, which celebrated James and his family's deep ties to the region.

THE STORY OF "NIGGER NATE"

High above the nicely groomed citrus and avocado groves of the Pauma Valley, pretty well up the southwestern slope of old Palomar Mountain, is a neglected rock cairn, which marks the spot where "Nigger Nate" lived for many years. It was erected by his friends after he passed on in 1920; the old darkey had many friends. With the passing of the years, his name has become a legend, but there was a real "Nigger Nate," as the old timers all know, and his name is perpetuated in "Nigger Nate Grade" on Palomar, and "Nigger Nate Springs."

Something over a century ago, there lived at Westfield, Virginia, Lysander Utt and his family—comfortable plantation slave owners, as most everyone except the Negroes and "poor white trash" of Virginia were in those days. Mr. Utt, hearing of the California gold discoveries, headed west in 1849, taking one healthy Negro man slave with him. He went to Independence, Mo., where he outfitted for a trip across the deserts, mountains and plains of the Far West. Weeks were spent on the trail, but after much hardship, Utt and his slave reached the tiny Mexican pueblo of Los Angeles on Christmas Eve, 1849. It was a strange, strange country to the high bred Virginian, but with undaunted courage he proceeded to Auburn where for a time he tried his hand at gold mining.

After indifferent success on the placers of Northern California, he returned to the Southland, first to Anaheim, then to what promised to be a new and great city, Tustin. Two years later, 1874, he established the L. Utt Pioneer Store at Tustin, and it became the trading post and stopping place of travelers and ranchers going from San Diego and San Juan Capistrano to Los Angeles.

When Mr. Utt arrived in Mexican California, little was thought of the fact that he had a Negro slave, but when the Americans took over a few years later, one of the principal points of contention was whether California should be a free or slave state, and the first constitutional convention at Monterey settled the problem for all time—decreeing that unpaid servitude should be prohibited in the new state. So Mr. Utt released his slave man, and Nate wandered away, finally settling for a few years in the Doane valley on Palomar, then called Smith mountain. Then he moved to the west side of the mountain, built a small shack, and lived there until he passed on. He is remembered as a picturesque figure, very friendly and talkative—that is talkative about everything except his own past—a subject which he studiously avoided. He lived largely upon the wild game and herbs of the mountainside, as the Indians had done for centuries before. Near his shack was a good spring of fresh water, and when old Nate would spy a teamster toiling up the difficult trail of the mountain to the small farms and orchards atop Palomar, he would always greet him with a pail of fresh water for his team, and in return the traveler would give him bits of food, or perhaps a nickel or dime, and wave a friendly goodbye, as he urged his team farther up the mountainside.

There was work a plenty in the fields and groves at the foot of the mountain, but Nate was absolutely alergic to labor of any kind. Sometimes he would go to the Doane or Bailey or Mendenhall ranches, maybe even promise to work in the hay fields, but he always "had a misry" about the time work got under way, and needed a shot of "misry medicine"—the stronger the alcoholic content the better. Then he would entertain his friends with stories of all sorts—tales, that is, about everything except himself and his early

life. He gave himself the title "the first white man to live on Palomar," and eked out an existence there for more than a half century.

In the meantime, the Utt family, had begun the development of the Agua Tibia Ranch, a few miles west of Palomar, and had other extensive land holdings in Orange, Ventura and Los Angeles counties. Lysander Utt, who brought "Nigger Nate" to California in 1849, passed on in 1890, his son, C. E. Utt, continuing the store for a time, and developing the ranch properties. To bring this story down to date, James B. Utt, who is now a leading candidate for the United States Congress from the new San Diego-Orange county district, is a grandson of old Lysander Utt, one time master of "Nigger Nate."

CHANGES AT WHITING-MEAD CO.

Glen Miner, general manager of the Whiting-Mead Co., announces a number of promotions amongst the company's personnel. A new position, Supervisor of Branch Stores, is awarded to Rollin Hughes, who has been manager of the National City store. Gordon Myrick succeeds Hughes at National City and Kenneth Hartley, formerly assistant manager at El Cajon, becomes El Cajon manager succeeding Myrick. All have for years been trusted employees of the Whiting-Mead Builders Market.

ENCINITAS COMMUNITY ORCHESTRA

The Encinitas Community Orchestra—otherwise known as The North Shore Symphony Orchestra, has been reorganized under the leadership of the well known San Diego Conductor John Meagur. This organization has arranged to meet every Friday night at 7:30, at the San Dieguito Union High School, Encinitas. They are now preparing for their summer series of concerts. This organization has a present membership of 30 musicians with an auxiliary branch in San Diego of 35 musicians making a group of 65 musicians. If you enjoy playing your instrument, join this adult organization now and prepare with us for our summer concert series. As this organization is under the Adult Night School Program there are no dues. Application to join may be made any Friday night, at the school by applying in person. This organization was founded in 1947, and is under the management of Alfred Williams, Jr. of Encinitas.

CAL POLY AWARDS

Wilbur C. Idler of Alpine was awarded top prize in the poultry egg judging contest at Cal Poly, San Luis Obispo, recently, and in addition was given a special award for the best display in the show. He displayed brown eggs.

Kermit Kliener of Escondido took first place in the 4 oz. white egg contest.

Phil Clark of the Rock Haven Ranch, El Cajon, won second in showmanship judging of Suffolk Yearlings. Allen Hatch of Escondido won second in Ayreshires. Glen Bell of Fullerton and Dick Wetleck of Newport won second and fourth, respectively, in judging Angus steers. Other awards were widely scattered throughout the state.

PIONEERS ATTENTION

The Mountain Pioneers of San Diego county extend an invitation to all pioneers of San Diego county to attend their annual picnic, which will be held on May 25 at Hulburt's grove, two miles north of Descanso. Bring lunch and table service, and enjoy an old time picnic. This annual picnic is a wonderful place to renew old friendships and talk over the days that are no more.

Figure 2.1. An article entitled "The Story of N——r Nate" featuring the Utt family's role in Harrison's arrival in California (*right*) was printed alongside a large advertisement for an Utt descendant's congressional campaign (*left*). (Courtesy of Southern California Rancher Philip S. Rush, May 1952.)

The May 1952 Rush article explicitly concluded, "James B. Utt, who is now a leading candidate for the United States Congress from the new San Diego-Orange County district, is a grandson of old Lysander Utt, one-time master of 'N——r Nate'" (Rush 1952a: 18). Overall, this new Harrison narrative successfully tied the Utt family to one of the most well-known local historical figures (Harrison) and simultaneously portrayed the Utts as dominant (they were allegedly the original owners) and kind (they purportedly granted Harrison his freedom).[13]

James Boyd Utt, who served in eight succeeding Congresses from 1953 to 1970, was an outspoken conservative with an unyielding record on issues of civil rights. In 1964 and 1968, he voted against the Civil Rights Act, and in 1965 he actively opposed the Voting Rights Act. It was not just his voting record, however, that revealed his views against racial equality. In 1963, Utt made national headlines when he declared that, "a large contingent of barefooted Africans might be training in Georgia as part of United Nations exercise to take over the US" (*Orange County [OC] Almanac* 1963). The same year he also alleged that, "African Americans might be training in Cuba to invade the United States."[14] James B. Utt's political career strongly suggested that his use of the Harrison biography in his 1952 campaign was not a tool to empower African Americans. On the contrary, his actions indicated that he embraced, publicized, and even exaggerated the fact that his recent ancestors owned slaves. In fact, his paranoid statements against African Americans and use of the offensive term "barefooted" in the context of describing Africans, pointed to his employing racist tactics. The details of James B. Utt's campaign and political career seemed to indicate that the punctuated shift in Harrison's celebrated biography, facilitated by Rush's 1952 article, was the result of a single individual with a specific agenda. In essence, James Utt seized family ownership of Harrison long after the local legend had passed and used this false claim for political gain.

Although most post-1952 accounts blindly accepted Rush's revisionism, Escondido historian Frances Ryan's diligent pursuit of Harrison's life story during the 1960s led her to question James B. Utt directly. She sent the US Congressman a letter in 1964 asking for details about Harrison. Representative Utt, who served the 35th District of California and maintained offices in Orange, California, as well as Washington, DC, responded to Ryan, although he admitted that he had no firsthand knowledge of either Lysander Utt or Nathan Harrison. Utt emphasized that, "the information I have on Harrison is rather sketchy" yet then reiterated the story of his grandfather and Harrison arriving together in Los Angeles on Christmas Eve of 1849 (Utt 1964). James Utt offered few details on either man from 1849 to 1877, except to note Lysander's successful business ventures and that Harrison "drifted around," "landed at Rincon, . . . socialized with Indians and had a multitude of progeny," and "[had] an easy life . . . with all the Indian squaws waiting on him" (Utt 1964). Not only did the congressman's chronology for Harrison appear to be off, his stereotypical description of Harrison as a "lazy black man"—especially in contrast to Utt's industrious grandfather—smacked of racism.

A second 1964 narrative echoed the Utt tale and attributed additional negative traits to Harrison's character. Frances Ryan interviewed M. J. Beemer, who knew Charles E. ("Ed") Utt, father of James and son of Lysander. Beemer stated that Ed Utt told her:

> A man member of the wagon train to the west in which Lysander Utt was a part from Virginia (Man's name forgotten) extracted a promise from Nate that if he took him along to California where he'd be free—not a slave—that Nate wouldn't leave him, but stay with him. Nate figured that was just another form of slavery from which he was running away, but to get west he made a tentative promise and joined the wagon train west. (Independence, Mo.) Along the way Nate seemed to disappear . . . in order to get away from the promise he made. (Ryan 1964i: no page numbers)

This brief passage mentioned Harrison's promise three times and emphasized that he was not true to his word. It is again fascinating to note that every recorded narrative of Harrison that used Utt as a source of information highlighted Harrison's purported negative personality traits (laziness, dishonesty, etc.), whereas other sources described his affability, resourcefulness, and generosity.

Rush's account was not the only account of the 1950s and '60s to present a fabrication with seemingly sinister undertones. During this time period, Robert C. Fleisher offered a new description of Harrison's understanding of his freedom. Even though numerous other authors established a timeline of Harrison's emancipation and explicit comprehension of the Thirteenth Amendment, Fleisher's narrative offered a tale to the contrary. He wrote:

> If [Harrison] knew there were others on the mountain, he had no association with them because he still felt that he was a slave and would be sent back to Kentucky if found. However, one day he was walking along a trail [and] he came face to face with George Doane, who was another pioneer of Palomar Mountain. Nate fell at his feet and begged him not to send him back to Kentucky. George Doane could not understand what Nate meant but finally it dawned on him that Nate did not know that the Civil War was over and that now he was a free man. (c. 1963: no page numbers)

There were many problems with this uncorroborated account. The most significant of which rested in the fact that Doane did not come to Palomar Mountain until 1881. It seems extremely unlikely that Harrison would go eighteen years without learning about the Emancipation Proclamation. Furthermore, it was well established that Harrison interacted frequently and was well entrenched in the local Palomar Mountain community during the late 1860s and '70s. The details of Fleisher's account undermined its reliability, but an additional question arose: why would such a story that mocked Harrison's intelligence, especially on such a key issue of personal freedom and ethnic identity, first surface in the 1950s?

The Rush and Fleisher examples were two of many changes that occurred during the 1950s. Close attention to broad patterns in story-element seriations showed that this particular decade was unique in how many different traits emerged all at once. For example, in the dwelling description chart, the 1950–69 interval had each of the five distinct story-element options whereas none of the others came close to this diversity. The purported intelligence seriation also evinced maximum variation in the 1950–69 range as it did for the table that tracked how Harrison became independent. The same pattern was seen in separate seriations for his birth state and the identity of Harrison's original owner. Both indicated that the 1950–69 was a period of great change and narrative invention, especially in comparison to the 1910–49 and 1970–2009 intervals.[15] By far, the greatest narrative diversity for nearly every aspect of Harrison's biography occurred in the 1950s and '60s.

There were important parallels between changes to the stories of Nathan Harrison and contemporary sociopolitical transformations in the US. Just as Harrison evolved from an individual of virtually no historical significance[16] into something greater and more mythical, the country witnessed a social upheaval with the Civil Rights Movement. Looking at these changes both microcosmically (e.g., James B. Utt's personal agenda) and macrocosmically (national political movements), as well as examining prominent literary styles of the time, facilitated explanations as to why the accounts of Harrison changed in such dramatic fashion from 1950 to 1969. It enabled the many highly individualized narratives to be viewed in the context of three broad and strikingly different historical periods: Period I) 1910–49, Period II) 1950–69, and Period III) 1970–2009 (present). These time frames also marked Harrison's twentieth-century evolution from person to myth to legend.

During Period I, we observed that the accounts of Harrison's life were highly uniform. They consisted of relatively realistic stories that often depicted his disempowerment in a highly segregated society. These narratives were written at a time when the national sociopolitical landscape was dominated by the landmark US Supreme Court case *Plessy v. Ferguson* (1898) that upheld and legitimized "separate but equal" racial segregation in public.[17] Despite the fact that California state lawmakers had passed legislation requiring "full and equal accommodation," San Diego was highly segregated during the first half of the twentieth century and brutal sundown laws were the norm across the southern half of the state. Civil rights victories were rare and often quickly undone. For example, in 1897, African Americans Edward and Mary Anderson successfully sued the Fisher Opera House in downtown San Diego when they were denied access to elite seats on the playhouse floor, but Superior and State Courts soon thereafter dismissed the case and mandated that the Andersons pay for all legal fees related to the incident. Inequity and disempowerment were the norm during this period, despite misleading labels, such as "separate but equal."

The narratives of Harrison that were written during Period I echoed the hegemonic imbalance of the social landscape. Harrison was depicted as unintelligent, living in squalor, and defined only by his previous enslavement. The stories emphasized that his emancipation was either illegal—as a fugitive slave—or passively attained through the death of his owner. None alleged that he had in any way earned his independence. During a time that was dominated by "separate but equal" precedents, Harrison's accepted biographies seemed to embrace this Jim Crow dualism. They affirmed that he chose to live apart from white San Diego. In opting for self-segregation, the narratives implied that he agreed, or at least acquiesced, to explicit racial separation.

Fictitious details clearly made a significant impact on established Harrison biographies, but the manner in which these accounts were presented went through a marked transition as well. Earlier narratives from Period I (1910–49) were told in a realistic style, albeit one of realistic fiction. Despite the fact that authors of the time might have intended to be writing factual accounts, they were not. Regardless, they seemed to have been influenced by contemporary literary authors who were Realists. Instead of presenting romanticized descriptions designed to exalt the reader, the authors offered more unemotional accounts that were intriguing in their intricate and often ironic nuances instead of unbridled celebration. Literary theorist Maurice Shroder noted that in the genre of Realism, "The novelist plays the role of a God who . . . may be neither malevolent nor benevolent, but who is constantly ironic" (1967: 25). One of the reasons that the early narratives of Harrison were so realistic was that a majority of the authors of these accounts knew him personally. Harrison was not a foreign character in a distant story but a friend or an acquaintance in a shared community.

Since Realism is often punctuated by irony, this expression of the opposite of what was expected was highly prevalent in early narratives of Harrison. Just as one of most famous titles in modern literature was a contradiction—Joseph Conrad's *Lord Jim* was simultaneously formal in using "lord" and quaint with "Jim" (rather than James)—Harrison's standardized introduction of "I'm N——r Nate, the first white man on the mountain" brimmed with obvious ironic opposition in terms of ethnicity. It immediately begged the question: How can he be black and white simultaneously? Furthermore, Harrison's longevity, property ownership following enslavement, and elaborate storytelling about everything except his own antebellum past each defied expectations and presented nuanced yet realistic oddities in a narrative format. I lumped these early Harrison accounts into a "proto-apotheosis" period as they did not yet collectively insist on placing him at historic events in the Old West. On the contrary, these stories presented Harrison not as a hero but as a person, albeit a fascinating individual whose long life included numerous accidents of chance and bizarre contradictions.

The second period of narratives about Harrison (1950–69) seemed to reflect the great social upheaval that gripped the nation. Such political dynamism across the cultural landscape of the United States was paralleled in a broad range of inventive stories that served specific purposes and were often untethered to historical accuracy. When the Supreme Court case of *Brown v. Board of Education* struck down legal segregation in public schools in 1954 and overturned *Plessy*, it had far-ranging social reverberations that undermined core elements of Jim Crow laws. The court defined "separate" as inherently unequal and galvanized the nascent Civil Rights Movement. California was often a test ground for new ideas regarding racial equality as renowned leaders like John F. Kennedy and Dr. Martin Luther King, Jr. used the state's status as neither traditionally northern nor southern to make statements about the social health of the nation from a safe distance (Mallios and Campbell 2015; Mallios 2013).[18]

While there was great invention in the Period II (1950–69) stories of Harrison, these accounts were far from singular or consistent. Some of the tales greatly empowered Harrison; the construction of his home was portrayed in increasingly complimentary terms, his intelligence was lauded, his emancipation narrative featured acceptance and legitimacy, and he was repeatedly linked, for the first time, with the region's most famous people and events.[19] However, other authors created stories to serve different purposes, most notably Rush's 1952 article that invented a new Harrison origin story in the Old West to further the political campaign of vociferous Civil Rights opponent James B. Utt. In fact, just as the National Association for the Advancement of Colored People (NAACP) was successful in petitioning San Diego County to change the name of the road along Palomar Mountain's west grade from "N— —r Nate Grade" to "Nate Harrison Grade," Congressman Utt was elected to his first term. This second era was not marked by unilinear change or progress but instead by creative invention, full of rampant, purposeful, and myth-inspiring exaggeration. Heavy-handed myths were clearly polarizing in content and reception; these hyperbolic tales simultaneously gravitated toward opposite extremes. At the same time that certain new stories celebrated Harrison's intelligence, self-sufficiency, and agency, others portrayed him as dull, passive, and dependent. The accounts that went untold during this time were middle-of-the-road narratives, which although historically realistic, were highly unmemorable.

Numerous factors led to the transformation of Harrison from person to myth during Period II. Sociopolitical turmoil upset traditional norms, be it as monumental as choosing a seat on a segregated city bus in Montgomery, Alabama in 1955, or as peripheral as stories about a lone African American Palomar Mountain pioneer. The writers of Harrison's biographical accounts were no longer exclusively his contemporaries; Harrison had now been dead for more than three decades. Furthermore, the stories took the form of an entirely different literary genre; instead of employing ironic and nuanced Realism, the tales were now Romances, embellished with exaggerated characters and fanciful feats.

In this second period, Romance-inspired narratives included a wealth of sensationalized details about Harrison's westward journey to California, the process of his emancipation, and the wondrous drama of daily life in the Old West. Simplistic caricatures—such as Fleisher's circa 1955 depiction of Nathan Harrison as a dim black man ignorant of his own freedom—replaced nuanced realism. Where irony once flowed, stereotypes now dominated and were augmented with implausible feats (Harrison's ubiquity, antiquity, etc.). The characters that filled these tales were vessels for whichever purposeful mythical message was being relayed.

One of the more fascinating aspects of this period was that there were romanticized accounts that artificially-inflated Harrison's empowerment at the same time that there were embellished tales that were diminishing and downright racist. It was often difficult to determine authorial intent, especially when assessing bigotry, but there was no doubt that at least a dysconcious racism—a lack of thinking about or awareness of racism—permeated many of the stories from this second period (Joyce King 1991). The years 1950–69 were undoubtedly a time of great invention and myth-making in the biographies of Harrison, but what was gained in the moralism of the stories was done at the expense of historical accuracy.

During the final period of 1970–2009—following the end of the US Civil Rights movement—the myth of Harrison became legend. Just as the historical details of the 1910–1949 had been forsaken for the morals inherent in the tales of the 1950s and '60s, these deeper mythical meanings were now lost to the overall phenomenon that Harrison's biography had become a time-honored tradition. Instead of the main point of the accounts being a purportedly culturally constructive comment on black empowerment or a justification for segregation, the primary message of his legend was merely in terms of his great antiquity and primacy in the region. It was precisely at this moment of transformation from myth to legend that Harrison was first called a "pioneer" in print (Madyun and Malone 1981). Above all, this term emphasized his presence at the outset of Palomar Mountain's early American community and completed the century-long apotheosis from person to myth to legend. The lengthy journey of Harrison's posthumous identity is yet another testament to William Faulkner's observation that, "The past is never dead. It's not even past" (1951: act 1, scene 3).

Harrison's Personal Agency in the Myth-Making Process

It was easy to place responsibility for the prevalent mistruths about Harrison on other people, especially white people. While it was true that white authors wrote nearly every contemporaneous and historical account of him, Harrison himself played an active role in shaping his own myth and legend—even during his lifetime. He was well known as one of the finest storytellers in the region; local author Clyde S. James avowed that, "Nate was a great spinner of yarns" (Ryan 1964c: no page numbers). Furthermore, as Palomar Mountain became a tourist attraction in the early 1900s and as Harrison's ability to engage in rigorous ranching work diminished with age, his talent at entertaining visitors became one of his primary vocations. Harrison did not have to deliver water to people venturing up the mountain, nor did he have to regale them with gripping tales of the Old West. Nonetheless, when he did engage visitors, it routinely resulted in reciprocity in the form of food, money, and an expanding amicable social network. These goods and relationships were highly beneficial and, at times, essential to Harrison's prosperity atop a rugged mountain in a region and time period rife with volatile race relations.

Testimonies of Harrison's skilled storytelling abilities abounded. While he preferred not to speak of his pre-Palomar days, Harrison entertainingly recounted numerous adventures of daily life on the mountain to visitors. As Robert C. Fleisher recalled:

> Nate would tell one of his tales and he had many. He would tell about the large number of horses he had on the range and the great herds of cattle and sheep he was feeding for market. There were tales of mountain lions preying on his stock and numerous encounters he had had with rustlers. (c. 1963: no page numbers)

In offering engaging narratives of his slow-changing rustic surroundings, Harrison drew his audience into the lore of Southern California's Wild West. Harrison was a throwback to the region's early-American birth, and his yarns simultaneously entertained and reified the US origin story for San Diego County. Harrison delighted in portraying himself as a walking anachronism; in fact, he would playfully depict himself as independent of time. As John Davidson observed in 1916, "In 1886 [Harrison] said he was 86 years old and still claims to be 86 years old" (1937: 2). Harrison's stories were so enticing—yet still light-hearted and playful—that it was as if he had frozen time on Palomar Mountain and then somehow momentarily thawed it for visitors to see.

Storytelling was a time-honored art form integral to African American culture, history, and heritage. Oral traditions were especially important tools in promoting and perpetuating cultural legacies in the face of oppression; they were essential in a society that forbid slaves from learning to read or write.[20] As author and literary critic John Edgar Wideman noted, ". . . talk functions in African American communities . . . as a means of having fun, getting serious, establishing credibility and consensus, securing identity, negotiating survival, keeping hope alive, suffering and celebrating the power language bestows" (Hurston 2001: xx). Anthologies of African American storytelling, like Linda Goss and Marian E. Barnes's 1989 *Talk That Talk*, have compiled a wide array of slave stories that include animal tales, ghost stories, freedom parables, sermons, and outlandish yarns. Harrison employed many well-known African American storytelling types, plots, and devices into his tales.[21] For example, Harrison's joking style often employed inversion humor, which reversed relationships—especially ones that reflected social inequity—to create comedy in the face of racial prejudice. Labeling himself as white—e.g., "the first white man on the mountain"—

was a prime example of his satirical comedic inversions, which were a time-honored staple of African American storytellers.[22]

Famed author Zora Neal Hurston collected African American folk-lore from many different regions and compiled them in the book, *Every Tongue Got to Confess*. Hurston, a former student of anthropologist Franz Boas, was both a skilled writer of fiction and a rigorous folklorist. Though there were hundreds of tales in her book, many contained the common theme of racial struggle. Hurston's collected stories often employed ironic humor, specifically momentary reversals and rigid dualism, to drive home poignant messages of ethnic inequality (Hurston 1935). For example, one of the tales she collected from Arthur Hopkins related the following details:

> Once there was a Negro. Every day he went under the hill to pray. So one day a white man went to see what he was doing. He was praying for God to kill all the white people; so the white man threw a brick on his head. The Negro said, "Lord, can't you tell a white man from a Negro?" (Hurston 2001: 172)

This story addressed white oppression of blacks and black resentment and despair but then provided a humorous ending in which the protagonist misinterpreted an action as divine and falsely attributed typically white obliviousness to the Almighty. The tale included certain stereotypes—including the dimwitted black man and the malicious white man—yet it also ironically suggested that the divine somehow had flawed human perceptions. In essence, a human being accused an all-powerful god of being fallible, like his creation. All of these factors contributed to a tale of despair with an undertone of comedy; the genuine despondency of the situation was lightened with the comically incorrect divine attribution, which although false, could seem true in such a disempowered scenario.[23]

One of the keys to effective storytelling was in knowing one's audience and tailoring a narrative to fit the listeners. Although it was difficult to link many of Harrison's exact tales with those who heard the yarns, there were a few details in the secondary historical accounts that offered insight. For example, close scrutiny of the many sources indicated that saved his most hyperbolic stories for children. There were only two references to Harrison directly telling visitors that he arrived in California by boat, and both of those fantastic tales were recounted to young listeners: Allan Kelly as a seven-year old and Chris Forbes as a child (Kelly 1978; Day and Melvin 1981). Though his actual trip by covered wagon across the nation was likely rife with challenges, Harrison added swashbuckling sea-faring adventure to his arrival story when addressing youthful audiences. Furthermore, the tales about Harrison allegedly escaping a slave auction by floating downriver was also first told to Max Peters Rodriguezés when he was ten years old (Day 1981b).

Even though some aspects of Harrison's stories were fluid and tailored to his different visitors, there was one major consistency in his accounts: he talked only about his time as a free person. Harrison steadfastly refused to discuss his time in bondage, including his Kentucky origins and his early days mining for gold in California. According to the many firsthand narratives, Harrison offered autobiographical details only from his 1860s' stay at Mission San Gabriel onward. These accounts intimated that Harrison stylized his personal narrative as beginning with emancipation; according to these stories, his slave origins did not even exist. He seemed to embody what historian W. Fitzhugh Brundage called "the propensity . . . to suppress as well as recall portions of the past" (2000: 6) and what historian Jennifer Jensen Wallach labeled a "historical reality . . . composed of both lying and truth telling, remembering, forgetting, and perhaps reinventing" (2008: 145).

Harrison's storytelling, an essential part of his identity, was adaptive and carefully nuanced. Anthropologist Paulla Ebron emphasized that African American storytelling was a social activity and that the performance helped to "create a narrative of identity and community which conspire[d] to forge a recognition" (1998: 97). Her use of the word "conspire" implied a secretive scheme with an intended negative result. Harrison's stories drew on deep cultural traditions but were also careful adaptations for his particular situation. His performed narratives were not confrontational, heavy-handed, or alienating. In fact, he focused primarily on entertainment and forging social bonds with his almost exclusively non-African-American guests. While these actions were clearly not undertaken to achieve some sort of sinister detriment for others, they were still deliberate and might not have been fully appreciated by those in attendance. He regaled others, and in the process won their acceptance and gratitude, both of which were extremely valuable for someone who occupied such a vulnerable state because of his ethnicity and the identity politics of the region.

Harrison put on a well-choreographed act for his visitors. At the core of this performance was humorous self-deprecation. He actively made fun of himself, which seemed to comfort his traditionally white audiences; his cheery demeanor revealed no palpable resentment about his enslaved past, likely easing any symptoms of white guilt in his visitors. Harrison put on old clothes, spoke with a thick Southern accent that emphasized subservient antebellum ancestry, and played the fool. The first phrase out of his mouth was a racial slur that self-mocked.

This African American introduced himself and started each performance with the memorable alliteration, "I'm N——r Nate";[24] and he repeatedly delivered this line with a joyful smile. Harrison then capped his comic opening with the ironic follow-up, "the first white man on the mountain." Specifically, he followed the skin-color self-slur with a proclamation that he was white, a deliberate contradiction drenched in humor. Sometimes he took the joke in a different, yet still ironically impossible, direction, proclaiming, "I'se de fust white man on dis here mountain, but I's stayed so long I'se turned black" (Ryan 1964c: no page numbers). Whatever the particular humorous variant, Harrison set the tone of the visit, and guests routinely found it funny, nonthreatening, and engagingly distorted. Furthermore, his physical presence was also welcoming. His diminutive statue—Harrison was only 5' 3" tall, which was short for men even by nineteenth century standards—and his advanced age added to the kind and safe persona he projected (Bielicki and Welon 1982; Meredith 1983).

Harrison's humor was a social lubricant that facilitated positive relationships with many visitors. There was a direct link between the efforts he made to be disarmingly funny and the comfort his audience felt. The ease he created in his guests led to widespread praise of his personality. These visitors—be they tourists, neighbors, or others—often made the connection between Harrison's joking demeanor and his popularity. Clyde S. James summarized that Harrison had a "great sense of humor [and was] liked by all" (Ryan 1964c: no page numbers).

Minstrelsy

Harrison's performance was neither unique nor out-of-place in late nineteenth-century America. It paralleled a prominent entertainment genre known as the minstrel show or minstrelsy, which included a variety of humorous skits and musical numbers that actively mocked the African American experience. Poet, activist, lawyer, and NAACP leader James Weldon Johnson explained that minstrel shows "fixed the tradition of the Negro as only an irresponsible, happy-go-lucky, wide-grinning, loud-laughing, shuffling, banjo-playing, singing, dancing, sort of being" (Loewen 2005: 39). While these performances in the 1830s initially featured white actors in black-face makeup, later groups also included black actors. By mid-century, the minstrel shows, which openly mocked African Americans as stupid, lazy, and gullible, were one of the nation's most prominent and popular art forms. They peaked during the years of 1890–1920; historian Joseph Boskin noted that, "By the turn of the [twentieth] century, practically every city, town, and rural community had amateur minstrel groups" (Loewen 2005: 39). For many white audiences, this derisive portrayal was their lone view of what they thought was black culture. Although whites often perceived the portrayed behavior as authentic, blacks who participated in these performances knew the difference. Zora Neal Hurston quoted one former minstrelsy performer as stating that, "I'll set something outside the door of my mind for him [the white man] to play with and handle. He can read my writing but he sho' can't read my mind. I'll put this play toy in his hand, and he will seize it and go away" (Hale 1998: 17). Harrison's buffoonish minstrelsy was consistent with contemporary performances and often met the distorted expectations of his white visitors.

Minstrelsy had a profound influence on late nineteenth- and early twentieth-century America. It regularly rewrote popular white narratives for African American identity. One of the most glaring examples involved the Uncle Tom character from abolitionist Harriet Beecher Stowe's 1852 novel, *Uncle Tom's Cabin*. In the book, Tom was *not* a weak, subservient, or sniveling character; he was a smart, honorable, and heroic Christ figure. Accordingly, Stowe ended her novel with the unambiguous proclamation, "Think of your freedom every time you see Uncle Tom's Cabin. And let it be a memorial to put you all in mind to follow his steps, and be as honest and Christian as he was" (1852: 434). Minstrel shows, however, co-opted this figure and transformed him into a spineless sell-out with an absurd loyalty to his white owner (Railton 2007). It is an almost incomprehensible irony that in a matter of a few decades Stowe's influential text and title character would go from being credited by President Lincoln for inspiring widespread public support to free the slaves to a highly offensive racial epithet that portrayed black men as quivering toadies undeserving of emancipation (Sachsman, Rushing, and Morris 2007: 8).

There were intriguing ephemeral links between Nathan Harrison and Harriet Beecher Stowe. Stowe modeled her main character from *Uncle Tom's Cabin* on Josiah Henson, who, like Harrison, was once a Kentucky slave.[25] Furthermore, Stowe was a close friend with Helen Hunt Jackson, Harrison's one-time sister-in-law and the author of *Ramona*. *Ramona* attempted to push a similar progressive agenda for Indian rights that Stowe achieved for African American rights and included the subtitle "A Story of the White Man's Injustice to the Indian." Most obviously, numerous historical accounts referred to Harrison as "Uncle Nate" and his dwelling as "Uncle Nate's Cabin." Historian Michele Wallace holistically insisted that use of the moniker "Uncle" with any African American name implied that the person being described was a "white-identified, elderly, and cowardly bootlicker" (2000: 145). While it is tempting to ascribe all "uncle" monikers as derisive and racist, one must remember that it was occasionally a term of endearment for older community members regardless of ethnicity. For example, Theodore Bailey was often called "Uncle Theo" by many locals, including Ed Davis. Nevertheless, use of the false honorific "Uncle" was also a common ploy to avoid offering respect to aged African Americans. White individuals often went to great lengths to not use the "Mr." or "Mrs." attribution for African American elders and disempowered them with diminishing pseudo-family terms. Loewen noted that, "Aunt Jemima Syrup and Uncle Ben's Rice linger as vestiges of this practice" (2005: 277). It is fascinating to note that authors of secondary Nathan Harrison narratives stopped referring to him as "Uncle Nate" beginning in 1970 yet never ceased using the "N——r Nate" moniker. Whereas "Uncle Nate" was a slur that white people learned to avoid after the Civil Rights Movement, the self-ascribed nickname "N——r Nate" presented a complex paradox that was integral to Harrison's enduring legend.

Despite the fact that racial tensions were very prevalent during his life, much of Harrison's humor centered on issues of ethnicity. It was precisely because he so effectively performed his minstrel show and made his audience so much at ease that he was able to broach such volatile topics of the times. The act he performed for visitors allowed him to engage with certain taboo topics that few other ethnic minorities would dare address publicly.

Harrison's oft-repeated proclamation had an obvious comedic irony. The concepts of contrast and distortion are two of the most essential aspects of humor across many cultures, and Harrison captured both in his assertion (Basso 1979). Contrast involves a switching of roles, and distortion consists of exaggerating a trait. In this case, Harrison successfully employed both of these concepts, comically labeling himself as a white man, which was even more pronounced by the natural darkness of his skin combined with exposure to mountain elements (sun, wind, dust, etc.). His audience customarily met his ironic introduction with hearty laughs. Harrison's joke was successful in injecting humor into the situation, a key survival strategy for enslaved and recently emancipated African Americans in US history.

Not all freed blacks in the region performed Harrison's minstrel show and employed humor to comfort their white neighbors and visitors. A striking counter-example involved the biography of John Ballard, a contemporary resident of nearby Malibu, California. Ballard, also a former Kentucky slave who came to the Old West in the mid-nineteenth century, settled in Los Angeles in the 1860s. He and his wife joined a small but growing black community that founded LA's African Methodist Episcopal Church in 1869. Ballard and his second wife later moved fifty miles west to a valley in the Santa Monica Mountains, where they acquired 320 acres under the federal Homestead Act. Although it was difficult to be certain as to why the Ballard family left Los Angeles, contemporary histories intimated that it was likely as a response to growing segregationist policies developed in response to LA's soaring immigrant population (Rindge 1898). The Ballards' time in the mountains was short lived, however, as in the late 1800s, their cabin was deliberately burned in an effort to chase them from their land. Contemporary Malibu landowner Frederick Rindge described in his 1898 book, *Happy Days in Southern California*, that his neighbors—"men with white faces and black hearts"—mistreated Ballard; Rindge detailed that before Ballard left the area he "put up a sign over the ruins of his cabin which read: 'This was the work of the devil'" (1898: 136–37). Ballard died in 1905, but the mountain of his former homestead was already named after him. It was known as "N— —rhead Mountain" until the 1960s and "Negrohead Mountain" until 2009, when Los Angeles County leaders approved a resolution to change it to "Ballard Mountain" (Pool 2010: AA3).

There were many obvious historical parallels between Ballard and Harrison; both were former slaves from Kentucky who came to Southern California and homesteaded mountain property. Both of their names would be affixed to local landscapes for years after their passing, but inseparable from the N— —r epithet. However, there were two key differences. First, none of the historical records indicated that Ballard engaged in minstrelsy to curry favor with his neighbors and visitors; on the contrary, there were no accounts suggesting that Ballard was prone to comedic antics or subservient behavior.[26] Second, malevolent locals used arson to drive the Ballards off their property. The extensive similarities between the background biographies of Ballard and Harrison and the striking differences in their fates might have rested in how Harrison used self-deprecating humor to win over the local community. The minstrel show, no matter how banal, might have enabled Harrison to avoid provoking neighbors who otherwise might have become uneasy with a land-owning former slave in the region.

Harrison used self-effacing humor to disguise his empowerment and lived for nearly a half-century on Palomar Mountain. John Ballard refused to downplay his material and civil gains and was forced to leave the Santa Monica Mountains after less than a decade. Both men had been emancipated, but whereas Harrison regularly downplayed his independence for white audiences and disguised it through minstrelsy, Ballard apparently refused to temper his freedom. He acted free and paid the price. Even to this day, Harrison is a local legend, and Ballard is virtually unknown.

It does not seem to be a coincidence that highly successful African American hotelier Albert Robinson of nearby Julian also adeptly employed occasional minstrelsy in his dealings with visitors.[27] James Jasper noted in his memoirs that, "When questioned as to the secret of his success in the hotel business, Albert would reply, 'I was raised in the South, Sah, I knows white folks and how to treat 'em'" (c. 1934: 172). The juxtaposition of "the South" with the affectation "Sah," was a direct allusion to the deferential acting that was integral to minstrelsy. Both Robinson and Harrison were enslaved African Americans from the South, traveled to California with their owners, had similar lifespans (circa 1845–1915 and circa 1833–1920), temporarily lost their properties for failure to pay taxes only to reclaim them later, and ultimately succeeded in establishing long-standing legacies as pioneers (D. Lewis 2008: 48–49). Robinson and Harrison also seemed to share certain skills in navigating Old West race politics with delicacy, duality, and diligence. Both were physically unimposing as well, with Harrison listed as 5' 3" and Robinson at 5' 6".

Harrison was able to attain status and security in a time marked by great losses for many African Americans, especially in terms of the gains made immediately following the Civil War. Black social advances of the Reconstruction Era were immediately followed by a time of stricter segregation and increased violence across the nation; in fact, lynchings reached their apex during this 1890–1920 period (Loewen 2005: 7). Historian James W. Loewen called this time "the Great Retreat" and "the nadir of race relations" (2005: 33–34). In fact, due to the many civil rights losses during this time, Loewen declared that, "in about 1890, the South, or rather the white neo-Confederate South, finally won the Civil War" (2005: 33–34). The post-slavery era of the late 1800s and early 1900s was an especially treacherous time for African American males. During this time, black people who had gained great popularity were often on the precipice of virulent white retaliation. For example, at the same time that Harrison was charming visiting San Diegans with his blend of humor, anachronistic musings, and rustic living, boxing champion Jack Johnson, an African American, was imprisoned for his romantic ties with white women. His specific felony was for violating the Mann Act in 1913 by transporting women across state lines for immoral purposes. Johnson loved to flaunt his fame and fortune, brazenly driving racecars through the streets of New York City, ignoring miscegenation laws, and taunting law officials. The decade before his arrest and conviction witnessed the unprecedented rise of this controversial African American star. In 1908, Johnson, the world's first black heavyweight title holder, infuriated white audiences by taking the boxing crown from (white) Australian Tommy Burns by knockout. When Johnson defeated former champion James Jeffries, proclaimed by Anglo audiences as "the great white hope," anti-black riots erupted across the nation in 1910.

Nathan Harrison and Jack Johnson were contemporaneous American black men, but they chose markedly different ways to express their identity. Harrison emphasized his nonthreatening characteristics to white audiences, be it in the form of tattered clothing, obsequious behavior, or self-labeling as "N——r Nate." He self-segregated far from the heart of white San Diego, acted ignorant, inferior, and dependent, and made no demands for change, either personally or societally. Johnson beat people up for a living (most of them were white), was the toughest man in the world, publicly pursued romantic relations with white women, and flaunted his self-professed invulnerability to law enforcement.

Harrison's particular minstrelsy was a symbolically loaded performance of subservience to whites that promoted the "N——r Nate" identity. While this manufactured persona was disempowered, the act fostered important social relationships for Harrison as did his storytelling, charm, and humor. With attention to issues of individual agency and social identity, it was possible to see how Harrison engaged in a racial discourse to legitimize his place in colonial contexts, especially in the process of defining himself in opposition to others (Fanon 1968; Said 1978, 1993; Bhaba 1994; Plane 2010). Harrison adroitly manipulated white expectations of his identity as a former slave from the Antebellum South into an important role in the community (Raibmon 2005; R. Hill 1998; Deloria 1998). He used preconceived notions of a savage mountain lifestyle, the toll of slavery, and exotic authenticity to his own ends—security and permanence. His agency was relational and could be fully appreciated only in context (Schumann 2017: 103). This was more than a commercial ploy; it was a way of continually recrafting his identity within the cultural parameters of a highly racialized Southern California.

It is difficult to find evidence of how Harrison felt about performing minstrelsy. He was clearly skilled at this act and thoroughly convincing to mountain visitors; it is crucial to note that there were no accounts accusing him of presenting a false identity or playing a disingenuous role. Likewise, no narratives suggested that this false front or dual identity took a toll on Harrison. With little direct evidence, broader parallels can offer insight. For example, Ralph Ellison's acclaimed 1965 novel *Invisible Man* focused on African American identity in the early twentieth century.[28] It included a series of symbolic characters, many of whom seemed to have a tie to Harrison's life. Ellison's grandfather character, who represented African Americans enduring Reconstruction losses, implored the main character with these deathbed words: "Live with your head in the lion's mouth. I want you to overcome 'em with yeses, undermine 'em with grins, agree 'em to death and destruction; let 'em swallow you till they vomit or bust wide open" (Ellison 1952: 16). This passage detailed strategic political goals of minstrelsy and emphasized the priority of this agenda over any duress the act might inflict on the actor.

Of all the historical, recorded dialog that Harrison allegedly uttered, jokes that mocked ethnicity in some fashion were by far the most frequent. In fact, nearly all of Harrison's recorded jokes were about racial identity and group affiliation.[29] His introduction—"I'm N——r Nate, the first white man on the mountain"—topped the list of direct Harrison quotes, having been included in seventeen different historical accounts. The second most commonly attributed quote also involved comical ethnic inversions, an ironic reversal of racialized roles that was intended to make people laugh. Described in four different historical accounts, this particular story involved the first time Harrison met George Doane's bride Irene Hayes and her African American servant Amy, also known as Cubby. Ed Davis detailed the encounter, stating:

> As George [Doane] drove up the west grade with his team and spring wagon heavily loaded with people and baggage, he stopped to let grizzled old Nate water his horses, which were dripping wet and puffing hard. George said, "Well Nate, I've brought you a wife." Nate turned around after giving the team all the water they would drink, looked the group [including Irene Hayes, who was white, and her African American servant Amy] over carefully, and finally said, "Which one, George?" (1938: 21A)

Doane, thrilled to show off his new and notably young bride, fell victim to his good friend's sly joke. Harrison's implication that both women could be his wife was a keen and racially-tinged reversal of many contemporary marital laws; at the time, it was illegal in California for blacks and whites to intermarry. His well-delivered punchline intimated that Doane's introduction of "I've brought you a wife" was somehow vague when bigoted laws, conventions, and traditions clearly dispelled any ambiguity. Harrison's quick wit and humorous ability to reverse ethnic expectations of the time were on display with this introduction to Amy. It is important to remember that boxing champ Jack Johnson was imprisoned for his romantic ties with white women in approximately the same year that Harrison made this joke. Whereas Johnson's career and reputation were ruined through flaunting his affection for white women, Harrison could jokingly do the same thing and elicit laughter. The key differences were that Johnson was serious and that he humiliated white boxers—and by extension many white sports fans—for a living whereas Harrison was kidding and humiliating only himself for white audiences.

Harrison seemed particularly comfortable making jokes about skin color as well. In addition to his oft-repeated introduction that comically referenced his simultaneous blackness and whiteness, he had no problem mocking nuances in skin complexion. For example, W. C. Fink explained that, "one time [Harrison] was asked if the Winery man would mistake him for an Indian. [Harrison] replied, 'not 'less I fades considerable'" (c. 1931: no page numbers). Harrison again took a most serious issue of the day (racial identity tied to skin color) and minimized it by suggesting that it could easily change (by exposure). There was an additional irony in that "fading" typically happened in the sun, but extensive time in the sun led to even darker skin.[30]

How could we be sure that Harrison's deferential act was indeed a contrived performance? With so many quoted phrases in a highly stylized Southern slave vernacular, perhaps Harrison did not know any other way to speak. Could it be that this language was not an act? Was his minstrel shtick, in fact, his only means of communicating and interacting? Did he constantly speak in deferential phrases like, "Lord bless you Massa Louis for remembering Uncle Nate."[31]

There were no definitive answers to these elusive queries, but many subtle clues existed in the documents. For example, Eloise Perkins noted that, ". . . although [Harrison] sometimes acted like conversations were going over his head, he was sharp as a tack and very little escaped him" (1971: 3). Furthermore, there was a difference in language and abilities attributed to Harrison based on with whom he dealt—friends or tourists. This was best evinced when close Harrison friend and Palomar neighbor Robert Asher documented a conversation between the two that provided substantive evidence of the language Harrison used when he was not performing for visitors. Asher detailed a particular encounter between the two on a damp night when Robert was returning to Palomar from a trip to Escondido. As Asher struggled to light a fire, Harrison came to the rescue. The exact recorded dialog was as follows:

Harrison: Having trouble getting the fire started?

Asher: Yes, everything is so damp.

Harrison: And you don't know how to start a fire when things are wet?

Asher: That's right.

Harrison: Well, you see those white sage bushes over there with some dead flower stalks sticking up? You get some of those and you can start your fire easy. Not now, you can try it some other time. Better come into the house [Harrison's cabin] where it is dry.

Asher: Thank you, but I don't want to impose on you.

Harrison: You won't be a bit of trouble. You can make your tea on my fire, and I have an extra bed. (Asher c. 1938: no page numbers)

The difference in language between Harrison's frequently quoted and highly phoneticized minstrelsy and this passage was striking. He spoke without affectation; there was not a single word performed in a stylized vernacular, nor any instance of elided consonants or vowels. Harrison employed complete sentences and provided insight in a direct and unapologetic manner. He did not mock himself; in fact, he was the expert in this matter and was willing to share his knowledge. At this moment, Harrison was not performing for an audience. On the contrary, he was helping out a friend in need and offering instructions for the future. This was Nathan Harrison when the tourists and their cameras were away. He was kind, insightful, and most of all, nobody's fool, which was a striking contrast to his oft-performed minstrel act.

Asher would conduct an extended interview with Harrison circa 1910–15. He recorded over two pages of details from Harrison's time on the mountain; most of the description focused on his livestock, how to protect them from predators, and the strange travelers that chanced by his cabin. None of these accounts contained any self-deprecation, nor were they spoken with a Southern slave vernacular. The tales were informative, clear, and thorough. Though the interview was not his usual minstrel-act performance, Asher did note that for the photograph, Harrison ". . . put on dilapidated overalls . . . [in fact,] he had probably dug up the most ragged pair of overalls he could find in the scrap heap" (c. 1938: no page numbers) (Figure 2.2). This duality emphasized Harrison's different audiences, even in the same interview. The photograph would likely be seen by his usual touristic audience and necessitated the exaggerated minstrel show, whereas the interview was a factual account by his friend, the reclusive mountain historian.

Harrison alternated between his core self and a fabricated self-deprecating persona that acted as a symbolic mask—often dubbed "the

Figure 2.2. Robert Asher emphasized that in this circa 1910–15 photograph, Nathan Harrison deliberately changed into his most tattered clothing moments before it was taken. Note the tears in both his shirt and pants. (Courtesy of the Nathan "Nate" Harrison Historical Archaeology Project, Kirby Collection.)

darkey act," or in this case, "N — —r Nate" — for interactions in which public acceptance was necessary (Hale 1998: 17). He was not unique in his use of a split identity to navigate the dynamic realities of postbellum life for African Americans. Noted American sociologist and civil rights activist W. E. B. Du Bois wrote extensively of the psychological masks that many late nineteenth- and early twentieth-century African Americans had to wear. Du Bois asserted that blacks lived in double realities that rendered them legally free yet socially diminished. His seminal work detailed black struggles for freedom in the 1900s, insisting that African Americans' split identity resulted from the "sense of always looking at one's self through the eyes of others, of measuring one's soul by the tape of a world that looks on in amused contempt and pity"; these eyes were far from neutral and took the form of the "white supremacist gaze" (Du Bois 1903: 3, 8). Consequently, blacks were mired in "a double life, with double thoughts, double duties, and double social classes, [which] must give rise to double words and double ideas" (Du Bois 1903: 143). Harrison regularly navigated this "double consciousness" through various tattered and deferential masks; he had extensive experience dressing and acting the role of a former slave for white audiences when they ventured up the mountain. This versatility was essential to his longevity and prosperity in San Diego County and on Palomar Mountain.[32]

Some of Harrison's dualities were subtle and had to be teased out of the historical literature and photographs; other aspects of his split life were obvious. His double identities were clearly evinced in the names used in the personal letters found in his cabin. Whereas he was exclusively called "Inez" by his relatives and those of Spanish, Mexican, and Indian descent, he was commonly known as "N — —r Nate" by white visitors and neighbors.[33] Without exception, Harrison seemed to have reserved his confirmation name for his inner Catholic circle and left his public name to white audiences.

Catholics were highly persecuted in nineteenth-century America. The growth of hatred toward non-Protestant religions during the Second Great Awakening of the mid-1800s was often targeted at large numbers of Catholic immigrants across the US. During this time, Protestant evangelicalism, fueled by populist revivals, regularly demonized other religions. The tactics were highly successful as Protestant church membership surged. Harrison's affiliation with Catholics, including most Mexicans and missionized Indians, was dangerous in late nineteenth-century Southern California, especially in frontier regions that were quickly being evangelized.

Harrison's oft-repeated emphasis on being the first non-Indian on the mountain should not be equated with him distancing himself from the Indian community; it was merely a semantic tool used to emphasize his primacy in the area. Harrison was profoundly close to the Indigenous community, marrying at least two different Native women, living in the heart of a large Luiseño cultural area on land gifted to him by local tribes, and interacting regularly with people from many different groups. As Max Peters Rodriguezés, a direct descendant of multiple Luiseño chiefs, noted, "Nate was a friend of the Indians and the Indians were friends of Nate's, so much so that he was adopted into their tribes to the extent that he could take part in their ceremonial dances. He was present at all the fiestas" (Day 1981b: no page numbers). He also asserted that Harrison "spoke Indian fluently" (Day 1981b: no page numbers).

The dichotomy of Harrison's double life became especially pronounced at his memorial service. Near soap-opera-level drama and intrigue erupted when Ed Davis's eulogy touched on the subject of whether Harrison had been married. Davis insisted publicly that Harrison had many opportunities to wed and "settle down as a 'squaw man,'" but chose not to, opting instead to "walk his own way and . . . never marry" (Asher c. 1938: no page numbers). Yet when Davis finished this sentence, many in the crowd, including Robert Asher and Louis Salmons, knew otherwise. Asher was poised to refute Davis's claim but instead stayed silent on Harrison's multiple marriages. He explained why, stating:

> When Davis said that Nate had never married I was standing right beside Bentley Elmore. Possibly my mouth was all set to say something. . . . However that may be, no words passed my lips—Louis Salmons was looking me full in the eyes with a peculiar expression on his face which said as plain as could be: "Bob, you keep your mouth shut!" You can just bet that Bob [Robert Asher, speaking of himself in the third person] did keep his mouth shut, for the time being at any rate. (Asher c. 1938: no page numbers)

Well beyond the memorial service, the debate continued about whether Nathan Harrison had been married. Differing opinions often clustered along ethnic lines, with white writers (e.g., Ed Davis, Harry P. Jones, etc.) affirming Harrison's eternal bachelorhood, and Indigenous interviewees (e.g., Chris Forbes, Max Peters Rodriguezés, etc.) asserting Harrison's multiple unions with Indigenous women (Asher c. 1938: no page numbers; Hastings 1960a: 8; Day and Melvin 1981: no page numbers; Day 1981b: no page numbers).[34] Furthermore, Harrison likely perpetuated this duality. His public persona as a robust mountain man was inherently unmarried and untethered, but his Indigenous and Mexican communities—and only a few of his closest white friends (Asher)—knew of his married past and the meaningful family connections in his life.[35] This life of Inez Harrison included two wives, a stepson, and a step-granddaughter. Harrison's double consciousness was remarkably pronounced in performance, language, and even in the names he used; this split enabled him to navigate delicate racial politics of the time, but it also came at a price that likely required constant performance and masking of certain realities. Harrison was a former slave and a family member of local Indigenous communities, but at a time when the national narrative of slavery was being rewritten through Uncle Tom shows, centennial celebrations and world fairs, and the propagandist Old West myth of the vanishing Indian, he adroitly bounced between white and non-white worlds (Railton 2007; Dorsey 2007).

The Photographs of Nathan Harrison

An undeniable part of Harrison's legacy is the numerous photographs taken of him by visitors to his Palomar property (Figure 2.3). We have compiled thirty-one different images, but it is likely that more exist.

Figure 2.3. Nathan Harrison sits on his patio in the early 1900s. (Courtesy of the Nathan "Nate" Harrison Historical Archaeology Project, Kirby Collection.)

Although it is difficult to be exact, Harrison was likely the most photographed San Diegan of the late nineteenth and early twentieth centuries. This is a remarkable feat considering he lived so far from the
urban center of the city in which most of the region's cameras were located. Harrison was photographed far more than any other local legend
who lived in San Diego, including famed Kansas lawman Wyatt Earp
(1848–1929), who arrived in booming San Diego in the 1880s; celebrated
American booster Alonzo Horton (1813–1909), who laid claim to the
title of father of the city of San Diego; and many others. Somehow, this
non-wealthy, non-white, non-San Diegan would become the region's
first photographic sensation.

Harrison's popularity incidentally coincided with the emergence of
the camera as a widely obtainable item. His later years on the mountain
were concurrent with the transformation in photography from bulky,
fragile, and inflexible equipment to mail-in point-and-shoot cameras. In
fact, the Kodak company's first slogan in the late nineteenth and early
twentieth centuries was "You press the button, we do the rest," which
emphasized the freedom and simplicity of this new photographic process (Gustavson 2011). The point-and-shoot era emphasized freedom
and spontaneity for amateur photographers no longer bound by cum-
bersome and expensive equipment. However, deep investigations of
the life and times of Harrison revealed many complexities regarding
identity maintenance, strategic staging, and myth-making.

Photography and photographs have long been a cornerstone of substantiating historical existence and constructing knowledge about the
past. In their most basic form, old pictures froze a moment in time.
Roland Barthes asserted that, "Every photograph is a certificate of presence" (1981: 87). The picture verified that what the photographer saw
within the camera frame existed, and that the subjects and imagery captured by film were indeed real—or perhaps, mostly real or real enough.
As a building block of the substantiated past, these images often actively facilitated the narrative process. Acclaimed visual artist Susan
Sontag emphasized that, "Photography is an instrument for knowing
things" (1977: 92). This knowledge could take any form, ranging from
literal to symbolic, ironic to expected, cryptic to straightforward.

The many historical photographs of Nathan Harrison offered scholars and students of the past numerous opportunities for insight. As will
be discussed in the archaeology chapter, there were multiple material
one-to-one correspondences between items in the historical images—
the cabin itself, smoking pipes, watch fob, suspender clips, boots, etc.—
and the features and artifacts excavated at the site (Noël Hume 1979:
92–93; Deetz 1993: 150–51). A potentially deeper discussion, however,

can come from appreciating the social, historical, and cultural processes that created the opportunity for these photographs to be taken in
the first place (Mallios and Purvis 2006; Mallios and Byczkiewicz 2008;
Mallios 2016). As historians James Davidson and Mark Lytle noted,
"Any series of photographs . . . must be analyzed in the same way a
written narrative is. We can appreciate the full import of the photographs only by establishing their historical context" (2000: 189). The
pictures of Harrison were an instrumental part of his life and legend;
they warranted significant scrutiny as one attempts to answer the primary questions, "What do the pictures show?" and "Why are there so
many?" In thinking about multifarious explanations to these queries, a
wealth of additional enigmatic questions arose as well, including:

- Who ventured up to Harrison's property to take his photograph?
- Why were people traveling to see Harrison in the first place?
- Why did they take his photograph?
- Did Harrison exercise any control about how he wanted to be
  seen and photographed; specifically, what did Harrison wear for
  the photographs and with what did he pose?
- What was the backdrop for the photos?

The factors that contributed to Harrison's prominent presence in
front of a camera were intertwined with key aspects of his identity,
community, and the overall mountain landscape in which he lived. The
pictures were powerful symbols. Furthermore, the photographic process was rife with symbolic behavior. Appreciating the context, meanings, and ramifications of both process and product were essential to
gaining a greater understanding of Harrison's life and legend.

Overall, the pictures were remarkably consistent. They depicted Harrison with a white beard past his chin, standing at his mountain property in the 1900s and '10s, fully clad in multiple layers of well-worn
clothing, accompanied by one or more of his seemingly favorite objects
(wide-brimmed hat, pipe, watch, walking stick, or dog), and looking
directly at the camera with neither smile nor frown (Figure 2.4). In each
case, Harrison was one of the primary focal points of the image, usually
as the center of the image. The set of images can be broadly divided
into three basic themes: 1) Harrison as the primary subject of the image; 2) Harrison posing with other people (visitors to his property); and
3) Harrison posing in front of domestic spaces, in which his living space
is also part of the subject matter.[36]

Nathan Harrison deliberately created a particular mood for his mountain visitors. By all accounts, he was an engaging, pleasant, and memo-

Figure 2.4. This picture from 1912 captured many of the most common elements of historical Harrison imagery: he stood alone on the mountain, wore a large hat, leaned on his walking stick, carried a watch and pipe in his pockets, and squinted into the sun as his photograph was taken. (Escondido Historical Society. Public domain.)

rable individual who charmed the many guests that traversed Palomar Mountain. He affably disarmed outsiders with humor, welcoming them up the precipitous road with water, good cheer, and an entertaining tale. Part of his charisma was grounded in his nonthreatening behavior. Harrison was a small man and regularly played up his subservient qualities. Many visitors quoted his nonplussed, self-deprecating, and overly acquiescent speech, giving him significant local fame. Historian James Loewen put this behavior in broader context, noting:

> Often the one African American in town becomes a celebrity, in a perverse sort of way. Everyone "knows" that person, including their harmless eccentricities. Piety is good, as is always having cookies ready for neighboring children or going by a nickname . . . African Americans who played this part well became genuinely liked by whites. (2005: 290)

Whereas most Westerners don their best garb to welcome honored guests, Harrison put on his worst; both acts involved dressing up— but in Harrison's case it was literally dressing down—and playing a part. His role involved donning tattered clothes, speaking in a fractured lingo, and acting the role of a deferential former slave. In a time of severely strained race relations across the United States and in California as well, Harrison had perfected his performance of the Antebellum South high up Palomar Mountain.

In the late nineteenth century, San Diego County was home to thousands of individuals who had fought in the Civil War (Palmer 2006). Harrison's act simultaneously welcomed supporters of both the Union and Confederacy. Progressives and abolitionists in favor of African American emancipation could clearly celebrate Harrison's monumental accomplishments of surviving slavery and persevering in the Old West, his acquisition of land, and his central role in a multi-racial community. Conservatives who romanticized the Antebellum South witnessed a purportedly still-subservient black man that seemingly clung to many pre-war traditions. In this overt deference, he could hardly be perceived in an aggressive manner as pushing for change or equality.

What was depicted in the images of Harrison is as important as what was not included. Only one of the historical photos shows Harrison with his rifle, and it is off to his side, nearly hidden by its natural camouflage with the wooden platform.[37] Harrison owned at least one firearm—the historical accounts and archaeological evidence made it overwhelmingly clear—but he virtually never posed with the rifle for a photograph. This seems to be a choice that was consistent with the identity he crafted for outsiders, the central quality being Harrison's nonthreatening character.[38] Furthermore, although Harrison often left the mountain, none of the photographs showed him apart from his Palomar property. It remains unclear exactly why this was the case. Was it Harrison's choice? Or perhaps the photographer's? It is reasonable to assume that Harrison seemed to know that his presence on the remote hillside was charming while his activities in the city could be lumped in with growing racist fears in San Diego of minority intrusion. In the city, he may have been, in the words of anthropologist Mary Douglas, "matter out of place" (1966: 35). Harrison self-segregated, choosing to live alone and apart, which perfectly paralleled "separate but equal" precepts that ruled the land. All of the images emphasized his separateness from mainstream San Diego and his contentment with this division. In addition, he was never photographed on one of his many horses,[39] which would imply mobility, in addition to wealth. Again, this seemed to be intentional as many accounts mentioned Harrison actively riding horses and raising them as one of his most important vendible commodities. Clearly, part of Harrison's lure to white San Diegans was his stasis, both in terms of his historical anachronism (staying put in time) and his implied sedentary life on the remote mountain (staying put in place). People came to the mountain to see and photograph a certain character, and Harrison gave them what they wanted. As was often the case with tourism, visitors tend to seek out experiences that reaffirm their hopes and expectations; Harrison helped make that possible.

Harrison's property, and in a way Harrison himself, was a touristic destination for many San Diegans. He provided a glimpse of the exotic other, representing a safe version of the Antebellum South that individuals with ties to the North and South could both embrace. His neighbors, the Baileys, ran a stage that took visitors up the mountain; it celebrated the natural beauty of Palomar Mountain at many stops but was focused on history during the visit with Harrison. In a time of world fairs and expositions that paraded the different races at which white audiences could gawk with "imperialist nostalgia," Harrison satisfied that voyeurism, and the photograph was a touristic keepsake (Bokovoy 2005: 123). The souvenir was cultural capital for those who had made the arduous trip and they could boast to their friends of completing the perilous challenge; it was also a multivalent symbol that verified the contemporary social order of liberated yet segregated African Americans in the West.

Palomar Mountain was part of a surge of Southern California destination tourism during the 1890–1940 period that celebrated the natural terrain and emphasized US conquest of the West (Camp 2013). Historian Marguerite S. Shaffer insisted that many white tourists from across the nation took Manifest Destiny to an extreme during their trips, extolling blind patriotism in the belief that the US had acquired the West through a preordained divine intervention (2001). During this time, millions of visitors flocked to western resort destinations, like Los Angeles's Mount Lowe Resort and Railway, and Palomar Mountain's Bailey Resort. Collectively, these resorts packaged an experience that united American nationalism and Western expansionism, simultaneously highlighting the natural terrain yet insisting that its wildness had been tamed (Camp 2013: 82). Although rustic, they were safe and manufactured vacation destinations—a revisionist phenomenon that anthropologist Renato Rosaldo first identified as "imperialist nostalgia"—that followed the colonial process of first decimating Indigenous peoples and destroying natural landscapes and then expressing an "innocent yearning" for these same native groups and environs (1989: 107).

Various anthropologists have studied tourism cross-culturally and noted how the touristic process follows the well-established form of a rite of passage, marked sequentially by separation, seclusion, and reaggregation. Arnold van Gennep developed the classic analytical frameworks of rites of passage, Victor Turner expanded the model with the concept of "communitas" (the sense of community, camaraderie, and common experience established for groups through rites of passage), and Nelson Graburn created a model of tourism as a secular ritual (van Gennep 1961; Turner 1969; Graburn 1977). Graburn drew on the work of van Gennep and Turner to outline a transformative process for the tourist that included exiting a familiar world, entering "another kind of moral state in which mental, expressive, and cultural needs come to the fore," and then returning to their previous regular lives as transformed individuals (Graburn 1983: 11). He emphasized that scholars need not insist on analytical boundaries between formal religious pilgrimages and local touristic ventures, writing:

> Tourism, even of the recreational sort—sun, sea, sex, and sport—is a ritual expression—individual or societal—of deeply held values about health, freedom, nature, and self-improvement, a re-creation ritual which parallels pilgrimages and other rituals in more traditional, pervasively religious societies. (Graburn 1983: 15)

Even today, any trek up the steep road on the west side of Palomar Mountain results in a pronounced separation from daily life in San Diego, Escondido, and the many other surrounding cities. Even with modern technology, the narrow single lane, hairpin turns, absence of guardrails, and boulders of all sizes that sporadically appear in the midst of the road dramatically restrict one's movement and slowly strip away connection to the hustle and bustle of everyday life. A wealth of changes marks the journey to the top of the mountain. The vegetation transforms with the elevation; orange groves give way to desolate chaparral and then oak trees appear at the 4,000-foot level. By the time one arrives at the former Harrison spring, there is a distinct feeling of seclusion bolstered by natural solitude, breathtaking views of the valley below, and extended visibility to the ocean (thirty miles away) and to the foreign nation of Mexico (seventy-five miles away). This wilderness-based seclusion is most pronounced when cloud cover completely seals Pauma Valley below the mountain. Standing on the west face of the mountain, one completely loses any view of the cities below; Palomar Mountain and its few residents appear to float in the clouds (a threshold between the land the sky), completely secluded from the nation's eighth-largest city (Figure 2.5).

When tourists trekked up Palomar Mountain to see Harrison over a century ago, they entered a beautiful, contradictory space of nature; it was a wonderland that was rife with incongruities. It truly was the liminal state that Victor Turner would famously describe as "betwixt and between" and clearly separated from the norms of everyday life (1969: 95). If visits to Palomar Mountain were a new rite of passage for

Figure 2.5. A digital elevation model (DEV) of Palomar Mountain's west side highlighting Nate Harrison Grade and the Harrison cabin (expanded in size for reference). (Courtesy of the Nathan "Nate" Harrison Historical Archaeology Project.)

urban whites, then Harrison acted as a guide in that process. He seemed to transcend time, an anachronistic symbol of the Antebellum South. Turner noted that liminal performances often included inversed representations of society; this may explain why Harrison's ever-present irony and anachronistic charm were so well received by his white audiences (1992: 57). Harrison's home was a liminal space in which typical social mores and cultural expectations were suspended or inverted. As a result, a black man and white women could be photographed close to each other, even touching perhaps, and happy; this collegiality would likely not have been possible elsewhere during this time (Figure 2.6). Turner saw these sorts of rituals as dialectical performances in which social narratives were produced, deconstructed, and then reconstituted (Bruner 1986). He believed strongly that these moments were "in and out of time" and a contest between traditional societal roles and "a communion of equal individuals" (Bruner 1986: 3–32).

Figure 2.6. In this photograph from 1910, four white women pose with Nathan Harrison, who apparently was the recipient of a bouquet of flowers from his adoring visitors. (Escondido Historical Society. Public domain.)

The end of the touristic experience, like every rite of passage, included reaggregation; it was the return of the individual to mainstream society and culture. Whereas rites of passage marked individual growth in a ceremonial process, the touristic path could also tap into personal gains through a temporary break with seemingly inescapable societal norms. Photographs of the touristic process could be seen as light-hearted mementoes or as something more powerful and important, like proof of a fantastic journey that served as cultural capital. Turner and Turner offered insight to the relief tourists experience in such a rite of passage, stating:

> [A] tourist is a half pilgrim, if a pilgrim is a half tourist. Even when people bury themselves in anonymous crowds on beaches, they are seeking an almost sacred, often symbolic, mode of communitas, generally un-

available to them in the structured life of the office, the shop floor, or the mine. Even when intellectuals, Thoreau-like, seek the wilderness in personal solitude, they are seeking the material multiplicity of nature, a life source. (Turner and Turner 1978: 20)

Were the touristic trips up to the Harrison cabin pilgrimages? There were many structural similarities. Turner and Turner wrote that, "Pilgrimage provides a carefully structured, highly valued route to a liminal world where the ideal is felt to be real, where the tainted social persona may be cleansed and renewed" (Turner and Turner 1978: 30). However, the ideal was in the eye of the beholder, in this case the traveler. Some tourists likely wanted to escape the pressures of a modern and constantly evolving society, which included a surge in the rights of ethnic minorities. Their ideal was an anachronistic realm of black subservience; and Harrison played that role successfully. For others, the ideal was racial equality and they traveled up the mountain to escape the widespread bigotry of early 1900s San Diego. Harrison could represent liberty, freedom, and a future of equality to these visitors. He was a multivalent symbol with a finely honed survival streak.

The photograph also served as proof of the journey itself. The trip up the mountain was undeniably arduous. A photograph substantiated that one had indeed conquered the road. Just as modern travelers snap endless photos of themselves in front of or on the Eiffel Tower in Paris to prove to their friends that they achieved the exotic goal of making it to France, past San Diegans had their picture taken with Harrison to verify their successful ascent up the treacherous west side of Palomar Mountain. So steep was the grade that one traveler told Palomar historian Catherine M. Wood that, "St. Gothard's Pass [the famed mountain pass through the Swiss Alps known for its daunting path] has nothing on this except the snow" (1937: no page numbers). The rugged physical landscape was an inseparable part of Harrison's life and legend. It provided the separation necessary to both comfort white San Diegans with his presence and the challenge to lure them to this personally and geographically exotic destination.

Very few of the photographs have an explicit attribution that specified who took the image. Nonetheless, it was likely that two of Harrison's closest friends, Robert Asher and Ed Davis, were the photographers. Asher owned a 5" x 7" plate camera and sold many of his mountain photographs for profit. Likewise, Davis was also an avid photographer who specialized in taking images of Native Americans, the natural environment, and presumably, Nathan Harrison. Whereas Asher was dedicated to studying and recording the natural and historical environment of Palomar Mountain, Davis was a celebrated adventurer/photographer whose avocational forays into ethnography and archaeology took him all over the American Southwest and northern Mexico. One obvious reason for the preponderance of historical pictures of Harrison was likely his frequent interaction and friendship with skilled camera operators Asher and Davis.

Edward Harvey Davis was a complex individual. A native of Brooklyn, New York who came to San Diego in 1885 in the hope of surviving kidney disease, he made numerous successful real estate deals on Southern California land and ultimately settled on hundreds of acres on Mesa Grande, near Palomar Mountain (Martinez and Wyaco 1988: 88). Davis was a prideful maverick with abundant resourcefulness and a taste for danger; he developed close relations with the local Indigenous population and embarked on a lengthy and lucrative second career collecting native objects, recording stories, and photographing all aspects of daily life. It was George Gustav Heye, the person behind the large-scale amassing of Indigenous photographs and artifacts that would become the photographic collection at the Smithsonian Institution's National Museum of the American Indian, who hired Davis to take photos of American Indians in California, Arizona, and northern Mexico (Martinez 1998: 40). Davis's work would become one of the largest collections of Indigenous photographs ever taken.

Defenders of Davis's legacy point to his accomplishments and relationships. They celebrate the fact that Kumeyaay Indians bestowed him with the title of "honorary chief" in 1907 (Russell and Quinn, n.d.: 21–30). In addition, Davis succeeded in taking some of the only existing photographs of tribes who were difficult to find (Martinez and Wyaco 1998: 90). Furthermore, by the end of his life, Davis adamantly proclaimed equality between Indigenous and non-Indigenous peoples (Davis, n.d.: box 3, folder 29).

Davis detractors have ample material from which to draw as well. As an independent collector, he demanded a steep price for his images, manipulated his subjects for various photo shoots—he not only dressed up as an Indian, he also dressed Indians to pose them—and collected highly sensitive materials, including cremated burials, in a stealth manner. Davis was decidedly anti-intellectual; in fact, he deliberately stereotyped and exaggerated Indigenous barbarity in published articles as a means to tantalize and titillate white audiences (Gonzales 2014). In addition, Davis often propagated the myth of the "disappearing Indian," avowing that Indigenous people were soon to be extinct, and he was fixated on the amount of "pure blood" each native person had (Gonzales 2014; Coleman 2012). These flawed colonial narratives undermined native rights and facilitated rampant theft of Indigenous territories and goods. Though Davis's good intentions toward and close relations with various Indigenous populations were well documented, the results of his life's work—the photographs and artifacts—reflect complex issues of native identity and ownership in the modern age.

It is not a coincidence that a majority of the National Museum of the American Indian's 100,000 pictures were taken between 1870 and 1930, approximately the same period Davis was photographing Harrison and many local Native Americans. Substantial study of these sorts of Indigenous photographs, especially the ca. 40,000 taken by Edward S. Curtis, revealed important power dynamics between white photographers and their native subjects. Scholarly discussions of this subject have often focused on white guilt in the context of attempting to preserve cultures destroyed by US American expansion, annihilation, and imperialism (Martinez 1998; Momaday, Horse Capture, and Makepeace, 2005; Lawlor and Curtis 2005; Gulbrandsen 2010). Likewise, the Harrison photos likely brought together notions of salvaging the disappearing past (Harrison's antebellum life, which was resuscitated through his minstrelsy) and collective white culpability for the sins of slavery.

Poet and cultural critic David Levi Strauss emphasized that, "People use photographs to construct identities, investing them with 'believability'" (2005: 74). When looking at the many photographs of Harrison, one cannot help but wonder if some of these images were staged as well. Just as Davis, Curtis, and others were derided for manipulating Indigenous images before and after the click of the shutter, we must ask whether Davis created these scenes with Nathan Harrison. Did Davis choreograph the image? Furthermore, did Harrison also contribute to this performance? Were photographers and their audiences more interested in an image of a quaint little black man with a walking stick performing minstrelsy than a picture of an armed former slave atop an easily defensible high ground? Imagine how differently Harrison would have been received if he met visitors with a rifle in hand and was photographed dozens of times atop an imposing white stallion and with a loaded firearm at his side. Consider the different narratives, legacies, and legends that would have likely resulted.

Human staging for touristic purposes was extremely prevalent in the late nineteenth and early twentieth centuries. World fairs, often organized on themes of industrialization and other purported Western achievements, regularly featured human exhibitions. For example, the 1889 Parisian World's Fair included a "Negro Village," the World Columbian Exposition of 1893 in Chicago displayed a "human park," and a *Mbuti* pygmy from the Congo named Ota Benga was put on display as a human exhibit at the Bronx Zoo in the early 1900s (Hinsley and Wilcox 2015). The exhibited peoples were presented as racial stereotypes and often placed in mock villages. There was nothing subtle about the power relationships on display; the fairs celebrated Columbus, Manifest Destiny, and other overt symbols of Indigenous annihilation and then put various native groups on display for white audiences to ogle. White superiority and native primitiveness were unified concepts that these global festivals of progress displayed, perpetuated, and championed (Martinez 1998: 32). There were important parallels between these world fairs and the fabricated scene visitors to the mountain witnessed at the Harrison cabin. In both cases, white tourists made the trek aboard the latest advances in technology, arrived at a rustic setting, and watched an exotic Other in a transplanted traditional home. In addition, like zoos, the visitors were able to have this thrilling experience without jeopardizing their own safety. However, rather than being a centerpiece in an urban zoo, Harrison managed to display himself—with at least some agency and his status as a free person—on an out-of-the-way mountain "museum" of his own creation.

It is essential not to overlook the possibility of Harrison's agency in staging the scene for these photographs. Indigenous peoples or ethnic minorities of the past should not be automatically described in historical contexts as powerless victims. Although these groups often bore the brunt of colonial and imperial encounters, they were not always disempowered, and more importantly, their actions did not inevitably reflect a disenfranchised state. There was no doubt that Harrison could have easily avoided nearly every camera on the mountain. The particular spot of his cabin and the path that every traveler had to take to visit his homestead ensured that Harrison had hours to decide whether to engage with visitors, what to wear for the encounter, what objects to bring along as accessories, and how to present himself for the cameras. I believe that Harrison strategically participated in these encounters in part because he recognized how the results of the photographic process helped to solidify his claim and permanence on the mountain.

There is an important dichotomy between Harrison as the most photographed late nineteenth/early twentieth-century San Diegan and the most photographed American of the 1800s. Though most people would guess President Abraham Lincoln, the honor belonged to Frederick Douglass. An African American and former slave, Douglass posed for 160 separate photographs. Douglass was a fiery orator, writer, and publisher, a leader in the abolitionist movement, and a lover of photography; he called it the "great democratic art" and both lectured and wrote extensively on the subject (Stauffer, Trodd, and Bernier 2015).

Douglass's staggering number of portraits was not accidental; he deliberately wanted to project a new image for emancipated African Americans, one that embodied and radiated dignity, strength, and determination. Douglass insisted on formal dress—black coat, vest, stiff collar, and bow tie—and often posed with his fists clenched, projecting power and dissatisfaction. Douglass anticipated the power of photographs in popular culture and deliberately sought to replace past images of disenfranchised and passive African Americans with powerful new symbols. He wrote that, "Poets, prophets, and reformers are all picture makers— and this ability is the secret of their power and of their achievements" (Douglass 1861: 455). In actively producing a new African American identity, Douglass waged an ethnic war of perception with photographs during the nineteenth century. As Maurice O. Wallace and Shawn Michelle Smith noted, "The photograph became a key site through which a new identity could be produced and promulgated" (2012: 5; Gates 1990; Shaw 2006; Willis 2007).

Harrison likely waged a parallel battle but with his customary self-effacing style. He used photography to construct and craft identity, but it was a deliberately anachronistic image that facilitated his very survival.[40] Harrison's struggle was not a broader political movement; it was a day-to-day challenge for enduring the highly bigoted Old West. As such, he would not pose in his finest clothing or a defiant glare. Nonetheless, he did manage to produce a multitude of images that cemented his role as rural Southern California pioneer at the end of the nineteenth century and catalyzed his status as local legend by the end of the twentieth century. Consequently, the overall scene that Harrison regularly projected for the camera was antithetical to Douglass's; Harrison was deliberately disheveled, nonthreatening, and seemingly content.[41]

The Permanence of Nathan Harrison

The many myths and images of Harrison, be they about his age, ubiquity, primacy, longevity on the mountain, all coalesced to establish his inseparability from Palomar Mountain. By the end of his life, he was commonly hailed as a pioneer and as San Diego's first permanent African American (Madyun and Malone 1981; Carlton 1977: 50). With the growth of his legend came additional acceptance and celebration. Exalted status, communality, and permanence were all deeply intertwined and self-perpetuating as entertaining stories of his legend only furthered his elevated status.[42]

Permanence is a complicated concept. Harrison successfully occupied Palomar Mountain for at least four decades, and more importantly, was an essential part of the community. As San Diego County's first African American homesteader, he owned land, which was a measure of status and accomplishment in a time dominated by the white control of property. Permanence also implies the final resting place of the individual, and although Harrison was not buried on Palomar Mountain, he was still interred in San Diego. In addition, those outside of the immediate area associated him with Palomar; in fact, for much of white San Diego, Nathan Harrison was the mountain's primary attraction.

Harrison was not the first black person in San Diego, as has often been falsely attributed (Lerner 2017). When Spanish conquistador Hernando Cortés invaded the Aztec Empire in 1519, he had many black slaves as part of his crew, many of whom had descendants that intermarried and assimilated into Mexican-Era California. For example, at the Presidio in 1790, forty-five of ninety occupants were of African or mixed African descent (Carrico et al. 2004: II–1). Furthermore, the initial US African American documented in San Diego was John Brown, a sailor who jumped ship and deserted the *O'Cain* in 1804 (Smythe 1908: 92). In addition, African American Richard Freeman was widely known as San Diego's unofficial postmaster in the late 1840s (Carrico et al. 2004: II–1). However, Harrison was arguably the first fully accepted person of African descent to live in San Diego (Madyun and Malone 1981).

Myth-Making and Myth-Breaking

Myths augment real people, actions, and events, but they are also contingent on being separate from authentic factors that detract from the proper societal roles and intended moral invention facilitated by the myth-making process. When the truth gets in the way of a good myth, it is quickly abandoned. One of the most insightful ways to examine a myth is to examine what happens when mythicized individuals break with their legend. Audiences choose to remember them solely in terms of the myth and refuse to include non-mythical characteristics into their narratives. Heroes remain heroic and mountain-men remain on the mountain. Multiple Palomar pioneers broke with their myths, and their actions were almost entirely ignored and forgotten.

Just a few years after Harrison died, the mountain community had a large monument placed in his honor on the grade, and yet his grave in the city of San Diego was unmarked (Mallios and Caterino 2006, 2007b). This opposition was neither subtle nor accidental. Celebrated on the mountain and forgotten in the city, Harrison's life and legacy were intrinsically tied to the natural bounty and rigors of Palomar, and his ultimate demise in a sterile urban area was anathema to his mythical story.

In 1972, more than fifty years after Harrison's death, local historian and activist Ed Diaz successfully led the effort to acquire and place a gravestone for the unmarked grave that held Harrison's corporeal remains. Diaz remarked that, "I was astonished to find that the great pioneer and friend of humanity has no marker (let alone a headstone) on his grave" (J. Stone 1972). He rallied numerous members of the local community, including Phil Hoadley of the Pyramid Granite Company, who agreed to furnish the slant marker at cost (Figure 2.7). A small ceremony on 28 July 1972 was the culmination of substantial research, fundraising, and community engagement by Diaz and his colleagues. Without the efforts of Ed Diaz, Harrison's final resting place would likely still be unknown and unmarked.

Diaz's choice of epitaph—"Born a slave; died a pioneer"—was poignant. In starting with the phrase "born a slave," Diaz emphasized that

Figure 2.7. The choice of this kind of gravestone for Harrison, who died in 1920, was especially appropriate considering that slant markers peaked in popularity in San Diego during the late 1910s and early 1920s. (Courtesy of the Nathan "Nate" Harrison Historical Archaeology Project.)

Harrison's origins in slavery resulted in his being born socially dead (Patterson 1985). To end the epitaph with "died a pioneer" celebrated the arduous path he had forged and the high social status he had attained. The label of pioneer attributed specialized and select primacy in a new region that required ingenuity and perseverance. The attainment of pioneer status was equated with being foundational in a new community. Harrison's trek was from a socially dead state to one in which he was part of the creation of a new community and a burgeoning social network.

The dichotomy between Harrison's permanence on the mountain—further cemented by the placement of the memorial cairn—and his ephemerality in the city of San Diego was striking. The comfort and ease with which he seemed to manage life for decades at Palomar was in direct contrast to his disempowered final year in the hospital and his unceremonious and anonymous internment. Nearly all of the characteristics that were celebrated by visitors to his cabin were likely greatly diminished in the hospital. Off the mountain, an elderly and infirmed Harrison was clearly out of his element, and, as a result, was far from legendary.

So, what happens when a person betrays his persona, or when the legend acts in a less than legendary manner? For ordinary people, character inconsistencies abound; hypocrisy is mundane. However, for individuals that transcend a given community and become part of a larger ritual process, there are greater consequences. Exalted people who betray societal expectations often fall from greater heights and experience broader and more brutal ramifications (Sahlins 1985, 1995; Obeyesekere 1992; Mallios 2006b). In Harrison's case, this meant a final year and death that was solitary, anonymous, and ignored. Atop Palomar, Harrison—even in life—was a near mythical figure. He was the essential element in a ritual process that many white San Diegans engaged. His failed health, however, removed him from the exotic landscape, stole his age-defying virility, and placed him in the heart of the city as a dependent. Harrison inadvertently broke the ritual process. Consequently, those same city-dwelling San Diegans who marveled at his mastery of the mountain let him die alone and penniless.[43]

Harrison friend George Doane was another Palomar pioneer who attained near legendary status and experienced a similar late-in-life break with his famed biography. Doane was almost as well-known as Harrison and had similar exaggerated elements to his persona that fueled his fame. Furthermore, historical archives contained eighteen different photographs of Doane. Like Harrison, he was a celebrated pioneer, maintained a distinctive physical appearance, and had a close friend (Robert Asher) with a camera. Nearly all Palomar Mountain biographies included a chapter on Doane that highlighted his distinctive facial hair, overly romantic yet lovelorn plight, and ill-fated marriage to a teenager who was less than a third of his age. The stories were derisive yet light-hearted, mocking the gruff mountain man as a diamond in the rough. For example, Thekla James Young of Valley Center related witnessing that, "Colonel and Will James went up to buy cattle of George Doane. He was churning butter in an old-fashioned churn. [He] Caught his beard in the churn [and] Wiped [the] butter off beard and put [the butter] back into churn. [As a result, I] Lost appetite for butter" (Ryan 1964d: no page numbers). Historical narratives never portrayed Doane holistically negatively, nor was he deemed dangerous or criminal in any manner. Celebration of his life and legacy continued through the decades and were later perpetuated by various popular George Doane beard-growing contests on the mountain in the 1980s (B. Litchfield 1982b: 90). He is still often exalted as a hyper-masculine hero for Palomar's rugged terrain. All contemporary secondary accounts of George Doane ended with his departure from Palomar Mountain. There was typically a one-sentence conclusion, which mentioned that George and Irene Doane divorced soon after moving to Imperial Valley. George Doane's post-mountain reality, however, was far from a simple story.

In 1918, four years after his divorce, George Doane was arrested by San Diego Police Detective O. A. McCollum for raping a twelve-year-old girl named Frances Anstey (Brueggeman 2018: no page numbers). During the preliminary hearing on 8 August, lurid details surfaced regarding Doane's alleged criminal behavior; he purportedly induced the girl into a private room he rented from her parents, locked the door, showed her lewd photographs, and sexually assaulted her. The judge set the bail at $3,000 and insisted that it be raised to an even larger amount if Doane attempted to free himself by paying that sum. Before the case could go to trial, Doane bought off the Anstey family. He paid them $1,500 cash in addition to transferring substantial property holdings to forego the case. The Ansteys took the money and land, dropped the charges, and immediately moved to New Jersey. Without a witness, the police were forced to let Doane go. George fled the area, promptly moving with his son to Argentina.[44]

Quaint and romanticized stories of Doane's frustrations with finding love on Palomar Mountain abounded in the annals of local history, yet these tales take on a sinister tone when confronted with the fact that he was an alleged pedophile and rapist. With this added historical context, Doane's teenage-bride tale no longer appeared charming, but instead highly disturbing. The Doane rape case was well publicized in San Diego, Escondido, and on Palomar Mountain. Palomar historian Peter Brueggeman succinctly declared, "Everyone absolutely knew about it" (2018: no page numbers). Nevertheless, none of the local histories ever mentioned it. Like Nathan Harrison, there was an accepted biographical storyline that reified expected norms for Doane. His exaggerated characteristics—waist length beard, seemingly tragic inability to find a mate, decision to wed a young teenager—were celebrated as part of the Old West lore of Palomar Mountain. In the context of contemporary urban San Diego, however, some of these same traits were overtly deviant and tied directly to criminal behavior. George Doane's legend stopped the moment he left the mountain community, as did Nathan Harrison's. Furthermore, when the historical records presented a narrative for Doane that was at odds with his accepted myth, these stories were quickly lost and forgotten. The tales of George Doane were retold in partial truth, including what people wanted to hear and omitting the darker realities. It is these revisionist tales that have become local legend.

The apotheosis of Nathan Harrison is far from over. He has been dead only for one hundred years. Changes in storytelling, myths, and legends are ongoing and a continual process of the cultural experience. One need look no further than Christopher Columbus to see how dominant narratives can change over a century. In 1892, the famed "discoverer of the Americas" was hailed as one of the world's greatest heroes and feted across the planet in a slew of celebrations. On the contrary, only one hundred years later in 1992, Columbus was condemned as a global pariah; he was the face of Indigenous genocide, the slave trade, and European imperialism. The 500-year anniversary of his inaugural New World expedition was marked by rampant protests instead of the acclaim that adorned the previous centennials. It is becoming increasingly clear that few historical legacies are impenetrable to the scrutiny of time, which often results in a devolution from legend to myth to fallible mortal.

The enduring yet constantly evolving myths of Nathan Harrison are intriguing and engaging puzzles. They simultaneously hold clues about exact events of the past and subsequent attitudes, behaviors, and agendas. Like so many legends, they contain trace elements of actual occurrences. These mythical stories are just as revealing about future generations that continue to tell and twist the tales. The narratives that people pass on speak volumes about their priorities and politics. While the content of individual memories may seem capricious, odd, or counterproductive, collective memories of a community galvanize the group and form a broader pattern that can reveal important themes over time.

When a story such as Harrison's evolves into myth and legend, it becomes one of the prominent narratives that defines us as a group. It is part of our collective social fabric, grounded in, but not limited to, our history, morality, and tradition. In this narrative cycle of life, our ancestors are the legends we tell. As such, these legends are intractable pieces of ourselves. Despite the inseparable nature of legend in our identity, these tales are still malleable symbols that can change over time. They can be used to mean many different things and interpreted in highly varied manners. As stories grow further from the original historical accounts and are subject to greater modern-day fabrication, there is a literal and figurative way to ground these untamed myths. We can do so by searching the soil, trowel in hand, for hidden archaeological treasure; clues abound in the delightful everyday detritus of the past.

Notes

1. In a delightful parallel, both author Franklin Pierce Adams and comedian Robert Benchley are credited with originating the quote, "Nothing is more responsible for the good old days than a bad memory."
2. Furthermore, researchers at MIT recently concluded that on Twitter false stories travel significantly faster and farther than the truth (Vosoughi, Roy, and Aral 2018).
3. Together, these chapters uncover what historical archaeologists Mark Warner and Margaret Purser called "nexus points between past and present . . . between myths and reality" (Warner and Purser 2017: xiii).
4. The word "plot" has an important double meaning, referring to both the central action of a story and an intentional and often secret scheme. Authors engage in the two facets of the word simultaneously, creating a narrative around a core set of events and facilitating a deeper message for audiences to ponder and debate. Interpretation of authorial plotting often takes on a disconcerting life of its own, leading Joseph Conrad's Marlow character in *Lord Jim* to conclude, "Frankly, it is not my words that I mistrust but your minds" (Conrad 1899: 225).
5. My distinction between myth and legend also takes into account a spatial aspect that derives from their origin as different varieties of religious narratives. Myths were traditionally set in times before customary conditions were established, and as such, verifiability was irrelevant. Legends were set in well-established surroundings, and were seen as far more accurate in that they contained the same information as other contemporary written records. For this reason, while myths were about faith (whether sacred truths or secular concepts), legends were about history.
6. Harrison's inclusion in seminal US origin myths emphasized his Anglo-American affiliation, as opposed to a strictly African American ethnicity. Furthermore, it was often in direct contrast to his real-world inclusion in the Indigenous Luiseño community.
7. Due to the arrival of the railroad, San Diego's population dramatically increased from 2,500 to 20,000 during the 1885–90 period. Since Harrison was

clearly in San Diego County before 1885, he preceded the arrival of nearly 90 percent of the people in the region. Harrison's verbal introduction was a savvy statement that underscored his relative antiquity in the area, especially compared to the many newcomers that were flooding San Diego.

8. Gump's inherent limitation was his lack of intelligence; Harrison's was being born an African American slave in the nineteenth-century United States.

9. James's tale is clearly fictitious—Harrison was not from Mississippi, there was no corroboration of him escaping enslavement at auction, etc.—but it was difficult to discern if she believed the veracity of this account or was merely passing on an overtly plagiarized fiction designed to mock gullible audiences. Of note was the fact that James did not affirm the truth of this narrative; she started it with the phrase, "Nate told them . . . ," perhaps deliberately foreshadowing the entertaining myth, its richly ironic ending (dog food ends up being delicious), and the inclusion of Harrison in an American classic. Max Peters Rodriguezés related a similar tale in a 1964 interview. He called it Harrison's "most memorable story," intimating that it privileged style over substance (Ryan 1964h: no page numbers).

10. Harrison and Mark Twain's Jim character shared other characteristics, in addition to ethnicity and enslavement. For example, both were celebrated for their keen storytelling abilities (Twain 1885: 6). Ernest Hemingway's declaration that, "All American writing comes out of *Huck Finn*," apparently alluded to both fiction and purported works of nonfiction, like James's account, as well (Hemingway 1935).

11. It is also worth noting that Laura James wrote her seemingly Huck-Finn-inspired tale of Nathan Harrison only four years (1958) after the Doubleday Publishing Company had brought out *The Adventures of Huckleberry Finn* as a Doubleday Classic (1954). This act caused the novel to be recirculated with great regularity, and the iconographic image of Huck, Jim, and the raft was common in its promotion, appearing on paperback covers and posters (Stroud 2005: 31). The raft scene was not only an immediately recognizable story image, it was also where main character Huck Finn engaged in a poignant dialogue regarding the morality of slavery. He concluded, despite contrary lessons from his preacher, that human enslavement was wrong, even if it meant damnation. After denouncing slavery, Huck declared, "All right, then, I'll go to hell" (Twain 1885: 237; Bush 2007: 40). Clearly, this raft story was rife with racial symbolism and ramifications for US audiences at the start of the Civil Rights Movement.

12. Despite this gradual trend, the persistence of the narrative throughout the decades that Nathan Harrison became free once his owner died suggested the likely veracity of this detail.

13. In fact, the exaltation of the Lysander Utt verged on biblical hagiography as Rush insisted that Utt and Harrison arrived together at their destination on Christmas Eve; one might wonder if there was no room at the inn for the legendary travelers.

14. Elizabeth Archaumbault, the great-granddaughter of Lysander Utt recalled that James was "an ultra-conservative right-wing Republican," although his sister Louise was "a liberal New-Age Californian" (Wilken-Robertson 2008: no page numbers).

15. It is possible to quantify the different periods in terms of degree of invention by calculating an average index of similarity per time period. This process tallies the total number of narrative elements seen in a given time period and divides it by the total number of elements for the entire study. The scores range from 0 to 1, with 0 reflecting no variation and 1 denoting 100 percent variation (every possible element occurs). The 1950–69 time period had a 0.50 index of similarity average; none of the other periods was over 0.36 (Lennox 2008: 108).

16. For example, William Smythe did not mention Harrison in his extensive 1908 *History of San Diego*.

17. Though the *Plessy* decision occurred in 1896, it served to codify Post-Reconstruction segregation processes that were already underway in 1870s and signed into law during the 1880s and '90s (Franklin 1997: 127; Hale 1998: 23).

18. San Diego witnessed a few Civil Rights victories in the 1930s and '40s, including the Lemon Grove Incident—Lemon Grove Grammar School principal Jerome T. Green barred seventy-five children of Mexican descent from entering his institution on 5 January 1931, leading to the first successful US legal challenge to school segregation—and Dr. Jack Johnson Kimbrough's antidiscrimination sit-ins (Mallios 2012: 158). Nevertheless, the region was still highly segregated and derisively known as "the Mississippi of the West" for its overt bigotry and segregation (Mallios and Campbell 2015: 380).

19. Julia King explained that mythical origin tales were fluid and highly dependent on the contemporary contexts in which they were told. She noted that, "Founding stories, the need to tell them, the frequency of their telling, and the purposes for which they are told all change as circumstances change. Some eras appear to have had a greater need for these stories; in others founding settlements and the stories told about them seem to have been almost forgotten" (2012: 108).

20. Joyce Middleton noted that, "Oral memory [was] highly valued in an oral culture but ignored and devalued in a highly literate one" (1993: 64). Likewise, Lawrence Levine explained that African Americans "lived in a world of sound; a world in which the spoken, chanted, sung or shouted word was the primary form of communication" (1977: 157). So important were spoken stories and accurate memories in a realm without the written word for confirmation and longevity that African Americans told and retold folk tales celebrating individuals with total recall (B. Robinson 1989: 213).

21. His recurrent tales of Palomar Mountain animals—Harrison acquaintance Fred Blum insisted that when Harrison entertained visitors with yarns, "they were mostly tales of encounters with wild animals"—paralleled the prominent use of animal allegory in slave tales drawn from African mythology (Ryan 1964j: no page numbers; Goss and Barnes 1989: 21–112).

22. Furthermore, Harrison's status as an elderly male also paralleled African storytelling traditions in which the role of tale teller was almost exclusively filled by senior males in the community (Goss and Barnes 1989: 11).

23. There were many other ironies in this tale as well; it also showcased the danger of language—treacherous eavesdroppers, spies, and tattlers were seemingly everywhere in the Antebellum South—yet was a spoken tale in

itself. The brief narrative skillfully united oral storytelling with a simultaneous message on the danger of speaking.

24. Lerone Bennett, Jr., Senior Editor at *Ebony* Magazine, detailed the four-
hundred-year linguistic evolution of self-employed ethnic terms for African
Americans in his 1967 article, "What's In a Name?" He traced the nonlin-
ear and highly circuitous path of language as the terms "negro," "Negro,"
"black," "colored," "African American," "Afro-American" went in and out
of style. Bennett pinpointed that during the early 1900s, there was a general
increase in the use of the "Negro" (with a capital "N") and a drop in the
terms "black," "colored," and "Afro-American." Although some scholars
of this time period celebrated the term "Negro," later activists would lam-
bast the term for being a product of slavery and one without geographic or
cultural specificity. Bennett's analysis helps to establish that Harrison could
have used the phrase, "I'm Negro Nate," if his intent was not to self-depre-
cate and still be alliterative.

25. In fact, many editions of Stowe's acclaimed book have used William Aiken
Walker's painting, "The Old Cotton Picker," for its cover. Walker's central
figure in the late nineteenth-century painting—an elderly African American male with grey hair, a beard, and layers of tattered clothing—could
easily be mistaken for Nathan Harrison.

26. Mary and Adrian Praetzellis noted in their study of African Americans in
Northern California that it was essential for black families to come to terms
with "accepting racial barriers [and] never overstepping the limits of their
place within the order established by the racist social structure" (1992: 109).

27. The Robinson Hotel was one of the first African American owned and operated businesses in San Diego County. Albert Robinson, a former slave who
had migrated to Julian with his owner, and Margaret Tull Robinson started
their Julian business operations with the Robinson Restaurant and Bakery
in 1887. The success of this venture led them to open a hotel a decade later.
The Robinson Hotel, which has been in business for over a century, is the
oldest continuously operated hotel in Southern California.

28. Ellison stated explicitly in the introduction to his text, "So my task was one
of revealing the human universals hidden within the plight of one who was
both black and American" (1952: xviii).

29. Harrison's jokes enabled him to inverse power relationships and "deaden
the pangs of a sense of inferiority" (Oster 1990: 550).

30. Former Kentucky slave A. E. Fred Coleman, the African American who first
found gold in Julian and started a Southern California gold rush in 1869,
also employed self-mocking skin-color jokes in his minstrel act with white
audiences. James Jasper wrote that, "In 1873 a stranger rode into Julian in
quest of a friend and the first man he happened to meet was Fred Coleman of whom he enquired if he happened to know a man by the name of
William Bunton. 'Yes, sah,' answered Fred, 'I sho knows Mistah Bunton.
Why, when I fus came to Boulder Creek me an him was all the white men
here.' The stranger eyed Fred a moment, then remarked, 'Brother, you must
have been on the desert lately.' 'Yes, sah,' answered Fred, 'I sho been on dat
desert chasen dat los' Pegleg Mine yarn. Dat's where I got dis tan'" (Jasper
c. 1934: 168). This passage united many common characteristics with Har-

rison, including ironically claiming to be one of the first white men in the area, making a joke that his dark African American skin was the result of excessive sun exposure, and using broken English to amplify the comedy of his minstrelsy. Coleman and Harrison also shared a long life in rural San Diego County, a formidable role in the local community, and a hallowed place in the regional lore.

31. This quote came from one of Asher's histories, and occurred as Louis Salmons brought Harrison a bottle of alcohol for Christmas (Asher c. 1938: no page numbers). The attributed language is especially obsequious, employing "Massa" (stylized version of "Master,") clearly building on the legacy of white owners for black slaves, and self-identifying with a pusillanimous "Uncle Nate" parallel to derisive "Uncle Tom" monikers.

32. While Du Bois identified the kind of split existence that Harrison endured through this double consciousness, it was another prominent African American intellectual who captured Harrison's socioeconomic approach to success. Booker T. Washington wrote *The Negro Problem* in 1903, which focused on how blacks had to work (labor) without being worked (exploited in servitude). Washington stated that, ". . . being worked meant degradation, while working means civilization; that all forms of labor are honorable, and all forms of idleness disgraceful. It has been necessary for [the black person] to learn that all races that have got upon their feet have done so largely by laying an economic foundation, and, in general, by beginning in a proper cultivation and ownership of the soil" (Washington 1903: 9). Washington visited San Diego in support of his book in January of 1903. At the time, Washington was the most well-known and influential black leader in the US; accordingly, his San Diego appearance was marked by sold-out crowds. In fact, his initial show at the Isis Theatre to an all-white audience had to turn away over one thousand people because it had already exceeded the venue's capacity; and his later show at the YMCA to an all-black audience was equally well attended. Over 15 percent of San Diego's total population attended one of Washington's two talks. In his public appearances, Washington strongly advocated for economic progress through employment opportunities but avoided applying political pressure against segregationist impediments (Dorsey 2007). In the coming years, Washington would be celebrated for his perseverance but chastised for being overly submissive and slow to push for change; he was often derided as an "Uncle Tom" (Bauerlein 2004–05). Washington died in 1915, but his focus on economics over politics would be a polarizing issue for civil rights advocates for decades. There were many aspects to Washington's approach that Harrison seemed to embody. Harrison owned land on multiple occasions, had a diverse skill set that led to frequent employment, but rarely insisted— at least overtly and to white audiences—on equality, progress, or change. Both were "accommodationists" (Bauerlein 2004–05).

33. Max Peters Rodriguezés insisted that, "Indians called Nate 'Inez'" (Ryan 1964h: no page numbers).

34. These matters were likely complicated by white failures to acknowledge native marriages, and the fact that polygamy occasionally occurred in Luiseño society (Sparkman 1908b: 214).

35. Yet even Asher was unaware that Fred Smith was Harrison's stepson until after Harrison passed. It is worth emphasizing that Harrison's seemingly closest white friend, Robert Asher, never met either of his wives, stepson, or step-granddaughter.

36. This pattern of characteristics was so standardized that it could be seen as a photographic grammar for Harrison.

37. I believe this image is the exception that proves the rule.

38. Harrison's lack of a firearm in the photographs was conspicuous because so many other contemporary Palomar Mountain residents were repeatedly depicted with their rifles. Numerous photographs showcased white Palomar men with their rifles, including ranchers Jim Frazier, George Doane, Clark Cleaver, and Leonidas Robert Hayes. Firearms were seemingly everywhere in the Old West and exceedingly common in many contemporaneous pictures, except in the case of Harrison. White settlers were often photographed armed, as were, interestingly enough, Native Americans. Contemporaneous photographs of gun-toting Indigenous people were very common; in fact, Richard W. Hill, Sr., concluded that, "the image of the [Indian] warrior is the most pervasive stereotype of Natives" (1998: 155). Portraying the Indigenous population as armed and dangerous clearly stoked Old West fears and duplicitously offered justification for the continued cultural annihilation of California Indians by early US Americans. I believe that Harrison and his photographer friends avoided persuasive meta-messages in their portraits of him by insisting that he appear unarmed.

39. Historical accounts indicated that Harrison rode a white horse. This also might have been too empowering of a symbol for widespread dissemination in the late nineteenth and early twentieth centuries as in contemporary stories white horses were typically ridden by heroes and god-like figures as they triumphed over evil. Furthermore, since slave owners often forbid slaves from having horses, these animals became symbolic representations of empowerment and freedom (Dorson 1954). In fact, Lawrence Levine noted an extended series of taboos involving African American slaves and white animals; he noted that they were punished for whipping white horses, had to "address their light-skinned animals with respect," and were forbidden from wearing white clothes, drinking white liquids, eating white food, or owning white animals (Levine 1977: 310–11). In his 24 November 1981 letter to landowner Richard Day, journalist Robert Melvin wrote, "... I'd give my right arm, yours too, for a picture of Nate on that famous white horse. Somebody must have one" (Melvin 1981e: no page numbers). I believe that this conclusion was undermined by the fact that Harrison deliberately chose not to be photographed with the horse because it would betray his finely-honed survival strategy of seeming stationary, static, and most of all, nonthreatening.

40. There was irony in how Harrison used photography—"an emblem of human progress"—as a tool for strategic anachronism (Wexler 2012: 23). It was especially contrary in relation to how Frederick Douglass viewed photography as a prophecy for positive change (Wexler 2012: 25).

41. Despite the clear differences, there was one important parallel: both men were highly consistent in their images over time. Douglass's images from

the 1840s to '80s were stunningly similar with nearly identical poses, facial expressions, clothing, etc.; and Harrison's 1890s–1910s photographs were equally homogenous in terms of the same factors (Wexler 2012: 36). The stasis in their images strongly suggested that both men went to great lengths to control the staging of their photographical depiction. Former slave Sojourner Truth, also an often-photographed African American, experienced a different relationship with her images. The famed women's rights advocate and abolitionist had little control over her early realistic pictures but played a major role in crafting the scene for her self-proclaimed "favorite image," an 1864 carte de visite (a thick paper card that was often sold and collected) that highlighted her "genteel and domestic femininity" through flowers, knitting, and Quaker garb (Rohrbach 2012: 89). Though the images of Truth initially varied greatly over time, she ultimately seized control of the photographic process and retooled it to advance her causes (Rohrbach 2012: 91). Clearly, the camera lens was dynamic hegemonic device, leading anthropologists Jeffrey Schonberg and Philippe Bourgois to conclude that, "There will always be an impossible, contradictory tension in photography—between exploiting versus giving voice; manipulating versus denouncing injustice, stigmatizing versus dignifying, objectifying versus humanizing" (Schonberg and Bourgois 2002: 389).

42. Famed black historian Arthur Schomburg proclaimed in his 1925 essay "The Negro Digs Up His Past," that, "The American Negro must remake his past in order to make his future" (Schomburg 1925: 671). While the primary meaning of this powerful quote was that the rediscovery of black history would help restore what slavery had stolen, it also sheds light on the political process of reconstructing ethnic history in volatile environs. Harrison continually remade his past—omitting many things and manipulating others—to construct a viable life for himself in the Old West.

43. For the interpretation that Harrison was abandoned because of the break with his mythical identity to be viable, it would help to have an historical example of a similar individual facing parallel hardships but without an exaggerated mountain persona that was buried in a marked grave. Interestingly, that person existed. African American William H. Lodine, the personal servant of Captain Matthew Sherman, came to California in the 1870s and was first listed in a San Diego registry in the 1880s. After Sherman's passing, Lodine became a preacher and one of the best-known mission workers in San Diego. Like Harrison, Lodine grew ill at an advanced age and ended up in the San Diego City Hospital ("Negro Pioneer is Removed to Hospital" 1909: 10); like Harrison, Lodine passed away in the hospital; like Harrison, Lodine was buried in Mount Hope Cemetery; but unlike Harrison, Lodine was placed in a marked grave (Carrico et al. 2004: II–38).

44. George died in 1929 in San Jose, California. He was placed in an unmarked grave in Santa Clara Cemetery's potter's field.

3

Digging for Answers

As archaeologists, we start in the ground. In fact, we begin with the dirt itself. Every archaeological site has a physical reality in the earth. Archaeological dimensions of space, time, and form provide an analytical framework for scientific study of the material past. The artifacts we find occupy a specific location; they were produced, used, and discarded at an exact time; and they have measurable shape and size. Theoretically, every archaeologist will find the same items in the same places that date to the same times at a given site. This is the science of archaeology; the ability to repeat techniques under like circumstances and measure tangible results. The past is everywhere awaiting discovery. Archaeologists do not create the debris from previous human activities; we merely uncover it.

When it comes to determining the meaning of the artifacts and the significance of the past behavior, however, archaeology is highly humanistic. Interpretations from different sites vary greatly. Even more telling, explanations from the same excavation by different archaeologists occasionally exhibit marked distinctions. Heated debates in the field regularly involve rival interpretations of the same artifact assemblage. Despite the singular reality of artifacts in the ground, there are unlimited potential explanations as to their significance.

In historical archaeology, scientific discoveries can undo contradictions and solve mysteries. When fieldwork intersects with acclaimed narratives of past behaviors—e.g., Nevada archaeologists saw no material remains of cannibalism by the nineteenth-century Donner Party (Hardesty 1997; Dixon, Schablitsky, and Novak 2011) while *Jamestown Rediscovery* archaeologists found unmistakable evidence that colonists from the early 1600s had indeed murdered, butchered, and consumed a young woman (Horn et al. 2013)—historical archaeology is often front-page news. Archaeology often has the final say, in terms of the most accurate interpretation, on difficult-to-understand past behaviors. It can also reorient mainstream history as exhumed artifacts frequently tell a story independent of wealthy, white, male perspectives that dominate so many historical documents. Though the sherds are typically partial and the interpretations are often expressed only as probabilities, they can be pieced together to redress some of the most pervasive, oppressive, and sinister historical mistruths.

Nathan Harrison's biography is rife with contradictions that only archaeology can mediate. For example, separate polarizing historical records called Harrison a drunk and a teetotaler, a hermit and a socialite, a shepherd and a man who never tended sheep. An overall abundance of alcohol bottles, a mixed deposit containing a perfume bottle, a rouge tin, and various children's toys, and a wealth of sheep shears and sheep remains clearly weighed in favor of historical accounts that portrayed Harrison as a man who at least occasionally consumed alcoholic beverages, entertained visitors, and cared for sheep. Archaeological evidence is especially useful in debunking blanket assertions—e.g., Harrison *never* drank, *never* engaged others, *never* raised livestock, etc. Without inter-or intra-site comparisons, however, it is far more difficult to address nuanced assessments reflecting how much he drank, how many visitors he entertained, or how well he cared for his animals.

Rather than frame the discipline as only a source of answers, I believe archaeology is also especially well-suited in finding new questions to ask. For example, the historical records repeatedly established Harrison's illiteracy through various censuses, an "X" for his signature on multiple governmental documents, and many secondhand narratives. The archaeological recovery of multiple writing instruments strongly suggests that Harrison, at least by the end of his life, was literate. These items inspire additional queries about what types of activities Harrison might have kept hidden from visitors and why. It is important for historical archaeologists to use standardized typologies based on function to organize their artifact assemblage, but equally essential to then let go of these traditional categories in pursuit of more nuanced and contextualized insights.

The archaeological process offers an opportunity to be intellectually provoked by a separate set of materials. The site's total artifact assemblage is both specific to Harrison and general to frontier life in the Old West. Objects Harrison used on a daily basis reflected the deeper societal and technological issues confronting the US at the time, like Reconstruction, impending Prohibition, national advertising campaigns, rampant fraud, the transcontinental railroad, the standardization of time zones, and, of course, ethnic turmoil. Just as Harrison's legend became incorporated into so many different iconic stories of frontier life, the bits and pieces of his everyday life reflected ideas that were a product of the nation at this time in its history.

This chapter uses the results of years of fieldwork to solve historical contradictions, bust prominent myths in Harrison's legendary biography, offer new perspectives on his life and times, and raise important new questions about the past. It includes traditional analyses but also occasionally expands to consider diverse implications. The goal is to synthesize multiple viable interpretations that saturate the audience with plausible narratives, allowing readers to move about freely in the totality of Harrison's life stories.[1] Nevertheless, the chapter starts small with an archaeobiography of Nathan Harrison. This term is relatively new and refers to archaeological and historical studies focused on a specific individual (Clark 1996; Clark and Wilkie 2007; Ziegenbein 2013). Even though scale and scope are eternally relative in the social sciences, it is still a shock for many archaeologists and enthusiasts to see a project so seemingly fixated on a single person.

Personhood, or each individual's socially situated identity, is created within limitations of given communities, and, as a result, can be studied to provide important insights into responses to broad and far-reaching communal behaviors (Clark and Wilkie 2007: 5–6). Of great significance is the interaction between social pressures and individual responses. Furthermore, identity is dynamic; it is an ever-changing mix of experience, agency, and external influences (Gunderman 2010: 2). Though this chapter begins simply with a single historical individual and the material remains at his homestead, the archaeobiography quickly grows in complexity due to manipulations of identity and the interplay of seemingly isolated people and their communities over time. Intricate issues of group affiliation, evolving identities, and power dynamics force archaeologists to go beyond linking an individual's life history with simple ethnic markers, isolated calculations of status, or other singular measures (Orser 2007). When interpreting individual artifacts and assemblage-wide patterns, it was necessary to think broadly of the many social, cultural, economic, and political factors at play and simultaneously consider the specific historical context of his situation.

The connections between an individual's biography and the stories behind an artifact found at that person's home are often enigmatic and tangential. Furthermore, material culture studies regarding the function, history, archaeological context, regional pattern, and potential links to culture, class, and ethnicity can pull researchers in numerous different directions. Rather than see these seemingly endless historical twists and turns as frustrating or tedious, they can offer important context for critical insights that transcend individual theories and solitary perspectives. Archaeologists have come to have deep appreciation for the fact that "artifacts have their own social histories" (Kopytoff 1986: 68).

Nowhere was this more evident than in a small medicinal vial found on one of the first days of excavation in June of 2004. This tiny vessel took researchers on a wild journey through different archaeological interpretive models, each of which provided insight but none of which provided an answer on its own that told enough of the complete story. Only 3½" tall and less than 1" in diameter, the tiny clear glass bottle in question dated to the early 1900s and was embossed with the letters "MURINE EYE REMEDY CHICAGO USA" (Figure 3.1). A contemporary advertisement from the Murine Eye Remedy Company stated that this product had the ability to provide "reliable relief for all eyes that need care."[2] At face value, this item seemed consistent with the needs of Nathan Harrison as he lived in a bright, dry, and dusty environment. Furthermore, one of the grainy historical photographs seemed to depict him, then in his eighties, with cataracts in one or both of his eyes. Characteristic of this medical condition, the coloring of his iris and pupil appeared to be a foggy blur instead of distinctly separate areas. According to the National Eye Institute, factors that have been scientifically proven to increase cataract frequency include age, smoking, and prolonged exposure to sunlight. Harrison lived for much of his lengthy life on an exposed mountaintop with intense sunlight, never wore sunglasses (as far as the historical photographs and archaeological artifacts indicated), and was a life-long smoker. Clearly, numerous factors seemed to underscore the link between Harrison's life and the need for an eye tonic.

The Murine bottle was one of thirty-seven late nineteenth- and early twentieth-century medicinal bottles recovered from the Harrison site. In fact, over a quarter of the site's entire glass assemblage consisted

Figure 3.1. This early twentieth-century Murine Eye Remedy bottle has a remarkably rich background story. (Courtesy of the Nathan "Nate" Harrison Historical Archaeology Project.)

of medicinal bottles. Other examples included a Pinex Cough Syrup bottle, a Pluto Water bottle, and an Optimus Mentholated Syrup bottle. What these tonics might have lacked in actual health-curing abilities, they made up for with hyperbolic promotion. For example, contemporary Pinex advertisements promised that once a consumer "starts using Pinex he forgets about the cough medicine that mother used to make." Pluto Water contained strong natural laxatives, like sodium sulfate and magnesium sulfate; associated ads insisted that, "When Nature Won't, PLUTO Will."[3] Optimus' Mentholated Syrup contained eucalyptus, hoarhound [mint], honey, and tar; its advertising campaign claimed the elixir combatted "bronchial afflictions which might result in Consumption."

During the Gilded Age of the late nineteenth century, most US Americans still relied on folk remedies to cure their ailments. For example, in the 1880s, San Diego County storekeeper Luman H. Gaskill kept an extensive ledger of folk-medicine remedies that included cures for toothache, diarrhea, cough, canker sore, fresh wounds, piles, sore throat, earache, rattlesnake bite, habitual drunkenness, tobacco antidote, fever, and ague (Crawford 1995: 60–61). "Heroic medicine," which featured a variety bloodletting, shocking, purging (especially through laxatives, enemas, and other medicines that induced sweating, vomiting, and the expulsion of toxins), was the norm for Western medicine during the eighteenth and nineteenth centuries (Cassedy 1991; Agnew 2010). Furthermore, doctors were scarce in the Old West; in 1889, there were only twenty-six physicians in a region with over 35,000 people (Davy, Price, and Davis 1890). The lack of doctors, especially in rural contexts, further pushed those dealing with ailments to self-medicate.

Patent medicines, those that could be purchased without a prescription (like Murine), surged in popularity during the late nineteenth and early twentieth centuries. Katherine Collins completed a comparative study on medicinal bottles at archaeological sites in the Old West and found that the Nathan Harrison site yielded the least relative amount of prescription medicine bottles and the greatest amount of patent medicine bottles (2013). These figures would be even more extreme if one counted alcohol as form of patent medication. In addition, the ratio of patent to prescription medicine in turn-of-the-century Southern California seemed to follow status lines, with wealthier individuals privileging prescription medicines, and poorer people resorting to patent medicines. While some scholars have noted that self-medication was most common in rural areas and among lower socioeconomic classes, others have noted that African Americans historically favored tonics and patented remedies over those prescribed by physicians (Mullins

1999: 50).[4] There is debate as to why. One interpretation suggests these choices were acts of resistance to the dominant white culture, while another posits a cultural link with African healthcare practices that used herbs and water-based tonics (Mullins 1999: 51; Genovese 1972: 228). The field of archaeology often witnesses interpretive disputes between scholars who identify status (socioeconomic class) as the primary motivation for past actions and others who point to cultural traditions (ancestral lifeways) as the catalyst.

This class vs. culture interpretive debate was a minor footnote compared to the metaphorical skeletons lurking in Murine's closet. Perhaps no company in the late nineteenth-century US was more emblematic of Gilded-Age fraud and quackery than Chicago's Murine Eye Remedy Company. Although Murine did operate out of Illinois in the late 1800s, as the bottle stated, its elixir did little to refresh, cleanse, or strengthen overexposed eyes.[5] The Murine hoax was elaborate. Brothers James B. and George W. McFatrich started the crooked venture and, in true Dickensian fashion, got symbolically fat and rich off of their Mc-company.[6] The McFatrich brothers not only pushed a dubious product, they also created a phony medical institution as a backdrop for their scam, the "Northern Illinois College of Ophthalmology and Otology." According to a skillfully assembled and highly deceitful brochure, the college offered seven degrees and conferred diplomas that were "framed handsomely 28 x 28 inches." It was all a ruse. The classroom pictures were staged in the local Masonic Temple, the classes did not exist, and the diplomas were just another way to bilk people out of money. The Murine Company excelled at false advertising and hyperbole for its fake college and worthless product. The Company's ads frequently proclaimed that the McFatrich brothers strove "to give an ailing public an eye lotion that will further the interests of humanity." Their eye-remedy product, which secretly consisted of water, borax, and berberine (ammonium salt), had no therapeutic qualities.[7] In fact, borax is often corrosive to the eye. Furthermore, the ingredients could be collectively purchased for less than five cents a gallon, yet were sold by Murine for $1/ounce, a staggering mark-up of 256,000 percent!

Murine was not alone in this sort of entrepreneurial deception and trickery. Even the name "patent medicine" was a misnomer as it implied that these items had received a patent issued through the United State Patent Office, which was seldom the case (Agnew 2010).[8] In truth, patent medicines were often discovered to be ineffective and even harmful. In the contemporary words of Samuel Adams, they ranged from being useless to "a dose of poison" (1912: 48). The negative effects of the products were exacerbated by the fact that many patent medicines contained addictive ingredients, including narcotics, which were not disclosed on the packaging. The prevalence of these items was bolstered by incessant promotion.[9] Patent medicine manufacturers were relentless in their outreach, inundating the public with advertising through magazines, the sides of buildings, traveling shows, paid local professionals, radio shows, and millions of printed pamphlets and almanacs (Ryzewski 2007: 15).

While there was no way of knowing whether the dubious Murine Eye Remedy elixir duped Harrison, research revealed that Harrison had encountered snake-oil salesmen in Southern California. Harrison told Robert Asher a story of one particular visitor to Palomar Mountain who had attempted to sell him on a railroad scam. Asher quoted Harrison as stating:

> A fellow from San Francisco came here from Julian hunting a railroad [looking for opportunities to build a railroad line]. He wanted a place to sleep. [Andres] Scott had fed him and given him a paper [packet] of crackers. He had one extra coat, and that was all he had to sleep on. I gave him two blankets. He snored like sixty. In the morning, I told him I would show him how to find a railroad and I gave him some coffee. I sent him to Pala. He was well educated. He said, "Do you believe in dreams?" I said no. He had dreamed of a fortune coming from the ground. He had letters [of intent] and papers [authorized support]. I was glad to get shed of him. I didn't want that sort of a fellow around. Didn't want my throat cut. (c. 1938: no page numbers)[10]

Harrison was guarded in his interaction and his responses, even refusing to take the bait of gilded prose ("do you believe in dreams?"). He behaved in a way that balanced hospitable behavior with a self-preserving streak.

The Murine Company is still in the business of tonics. It now specializes in ear wax removal products. In fact, this self-proclaimed "wellness" company has a different origin story on its current website, with no mention of the notorious McFatrich brothers. According to Murine officials, the product got its start in the late nineteenth century after it successfully healed a man's eye after being cut by the tail of a horse.

The many disparate stories behind this singular Murine bottle, one of over 50,000 artifacts found at the Harrison site, emphasize the importance of an inclusive interpretive approach that allows for different narratives. Furthermore, these stories need not be reconciled as strictly corroborative or conflicting. In this particular example, highly divergent issues of self-medication, aging, physical duress, fraud, self-preservation, and many others were brought together to offer insight into Nathan Harrison's individual life and greater societal concerns of the time period. Although one can only wonder how the Murine bottle ended up on Harrison's patio, its presence readily tied to some of the most prominent aspects of life in the Old West.

Questions

Different types of questions govern each archaeological dig. Research queries guide the excavation strategy and expand the analytical fruits of the endeavor from what was found to what was found out (Hurst-Thomas 1989). Deep questions involving the meaning of the unearthed artifacts and the context in which they are found are relevant only after certain practical worries are put to rest. At the outset of the project I juggled crafting an intricate research design of questions with a more fundamental anxiety about the site itself. Given that the original cabin was knocked down by the Civilian Conservation Corps (CCC) in the 1930s, razed by a tractor in the 1960s, and pot-hunted in the 1990s, I wondered if we would even be able find it.[11]

The Nathan "Nate" Harrison Historical Archaeology project began with three sets of research questions (Mallios et al. 2005). The first focused primarily on the site and its primary resident. This initial set of queries started with the core question: "Is this Nathan Harrison's homestead?" The second set of research questions attempted to situate our findings in broader context, focusing on comparison, both in terms of historical activities and regional contexts. The final set of research questions delved into deeper issues of meaning and evolved with the ongoing historical and anthropological aspects of the project. These queries emerged with a more complete understanding of Harrison's biography and subsequent apotheosis, a more nuanced appreciation of his multiple identities with different communities, and attention to individual agency in the context of the many visitors to his property. These questions dealt with issues of how he constructed, maintained, and used his identity.

Project Background

Once our work began on Palomar Mountain, the primary goal was to locate the site.[12] There were four corresponding clues as to where to look: 1) the standing 1923/24 granite cairn at the entrance to the property that memorialized Harrison and his spring, 2) oral histories passed down through a series of landowners that placed the Harrison cabin on a rise past the property entrance on the left (north) but before the current guest house on the right (south), 3) various landmarks in the historical photographs, maps, and records that indicated his cabin faced west on a slope with Boucher Hill in the background, and 4) a small L-shaped pile of rocks near the areas highlighted by the other clues. When we started fieldwork, there were no artifacts poking out of the ground, no brightly-colored crop marks suggesting the presence of a buried trash pit, and no major indentations in the ground suggesting previous living spaces. In fact, the above-ground clues of past behavior that archaeologists so treasure—called "palimpsests"—were virtually nowhere to be found. On the contrary, the most likely site area was home to waist-high weeds, poison oak, and rattlesnakes (Figure 3.2).

At the outset, we established a datum off-site, a point from which we could base all of our measurements that would never be in danger of being excavated, moved, lost, or impacted. It was arbitrarily labeled as 10,000' North/10,000' East/10,000' Z (elevation above sea level) to ensure that only northing, easting, and positive elevations would be used on our field maps. The datum and true cardinal directions guided us in establishing a grid of 5.0' squares across the potential site area.[13] We excavated each 5.0' square by natural layers, following the contour of the land and the composition of the soil, as opposed to creating arbitrarily flat layers.[14] If no changes in soil color, texture, or inclusion were seen

Figure 3.2. A photograph of the general site area in 2004 before excavations commenced. (Courtesy of the Nathan "Nate" Harrison Historical Archaeology Project)

after 0.25' (3"), a new layer was assigned to the dirt just in case there were meaningful soil differences that were not apparent to the eye.[15] Subsoil on the mountain was a gritty tan sand, markedly different from the brown sandy loam layers that were deposited and impacted during the last few centuries of occupation. This sterile matrix is the natural stopping point for historical archaeologists on our excavations as it predates historical activity in the region.

My initial fears of not finding anything were immediately allayed when the first square units in which we dug produced hundreds of historical artifacts and began to expose the foundation of the Harrison cabin. The units in the cabin averaged 2.0' in depth, and the adjacent patio region were an additional 0.5' deeper. Thorough excavation of the structure area revealed the complete stone foundation of the dwelling. The artifact-rich area that included the patio and an additional region stretched over 40.0' to the west and 20.0' to the south. Although the site produced tens of thousands of artifacts in and around the cabin foundation and western patio area, shovel test-pits—2.5' by 2.5' units at 20.0' on-grid intervals suggested that the primary site did not extend far beyond the immediate 30.0' by 60.0' area.

Despite my obvious love for discussing projects in separate terms of space, time, and form, I fully acknowledge that these archaeological dimensions often intermingle and are rarely entirely distinct entities (Mallios 1999, 2000, 2014).[16] Regardless, I still prefer to present archaeological findings at least initially along these three classic dimensional divisions as organizing principles. Though initially presented as separate, later discussions will engage interwoven nuances of archaeological form across space-time. I start here with space because the collective historical accounts emphasized that Nathan Harrison told his own stories with an emphasis on place, and in particular Palomar Mountain, instead of time. His spatial histories grounded the narratives in the palpable and still-existing landscape, as opposed to temporal histories that traditionally represent the past as vanished or at least receding in significance (Glassie 2010: 79).

Space

I believe that all detailed discussions of space at the Harrison site must start with Palomar Mountain itself, the highest peak in San Diego and Imperial Counties, the primary watershed for the San Luis Rey Valley and Lake Henshaw, and a plentiful mix of timbered ridges, evergreen valleys, and flowing meadows (E. Davis 1938: ii). Moisture-rich ocean winds dump fifty to sixty inches of rain and sixty inches of snow a year on the crest, making it the wettest spot in the San Diego region ("Palomar Mountain" 1958: 11). A rich wildlife of mountain lions, bobcats, gray fox, mule deer, gray tree squirrels, turkey vultures, ravens, hawks, jays, chickadees, woodpeckers, and towhees scamper among the incense cedar, fir pine, and oak trees and the buttercups, azaleas, blue lupine, tiger lilies, larkspur, and poison oak. In years past, the mountain was also home to grizzly, black, and brown bears.

Indigenous Peoples

Palomar Mountain's Indigenous California Indian population has occupied the area for thousands of years.[17] Long before interaction with Europeans, Native American groups established seasonal villages on the mountain, actively hunting game (deer, jackrabbits, rabbits, ducks, wood rat, fish, etc.) and gathering acorns and a wide variety of plants (greens, fruits, and berries) and seeds (pine, grass, etc.) during the summer and fall months (Heizer 1978; Spier 1923; Carrico 1987; Horr 1974; White and Fitt 1998; Lightfoot and Parrish 2009). Many of these settlements were in ecotones—a region of transition between two biological communities—and allowed them to reap the ample resources of both oak and pine forests (Shackley 1980). Natives lived on the mountain in the summer and fall and would then spend winter and spring months along the coast. Perhaps the most pronounced reflection of their lengthy occupation throughout the mountain territory is in the numerous deep and well-worn bedrock mortars and associated metates that decorate the local landscape. The deep mortar holes typically range from 8–12" deep and 6–7" across; most large rocks have a few dozen, but many have over fifty (Wood 1937: no page numbers). In fact, there is one at the apex of Palomar Mountain with hundreds. These acorn-grinding mortar holes and grain-processing slicks cover many of the region's large granite boulders; they are most common along valley drainages that include nearby water, many boulders, and numerous oak trees with acorns.[18] These areas were both food-processing areas and social centers. The acorns were ground and the meal (*we'wish*) was leeched to remove the tannic acid. Indigenous women primarily congregated at these spots, toiling and enjoying the scenic views of the valleys below. Local natives also used portable mortars, which allowed them to take their grinding tools directly to the nuts and ultimately transport crushed acorn flour as opposed to heavy baskets of acorns. Sparkman observed:

> So there are two kinds of mortars, the permanent ones of the large rocks, and others made from loose boulders, which, being portable, may be used where there are no large rocks near, or when, on account of bad weather, it is necessary to do that grinding under shelter. (1908b: 207)

Acorn was the staple food of the Luiseño Indians, as was the case for many California native groups. The flour was made into a variety of food products, including tortillas and mush (Sparkman 1908b; Wood 1937; Wilken-Robertson 2018; Shackley 2004). The black acorn, or Kellogg's Oak (*Quercus californica*) was the most prized of the acorn varieties, notable for its sweet flavor. It grew above the 3,000' elevation mark. Red oak (*Quercus agrifola*) was the second most desired variety for food products, and it flourished below the 3,000' elevation horizon. Harrison's homestead varied in elevation from 2,800–4,200' (with his cabin being situated 3,686' above sea level) and included both Kellogg and red oak acorns in great quantity (N. Litchfield 1982: 97). Overall, archaeologists have recorded dozens of Indigenous sites on Palomar Mountain, including temporary camps and gathering stations as well as expansive milling areas, that indicate Indigenous occupation of the region for thousands of years.

Sparkman was quick to emphasize that Luiseño occupation on Palomar Mountain was far from arbitrary or haphazard; he wrote:

> Each band had its allotted district, in which it had the right to gather food and hunt. . . . The land of each band seems to have been sometimes again subdivided among the different families of which the band was composed; at least the part of the land which was valuable for certain food products was thus subdivided. (1908b: 190)

These distinctions seemed so important to Sparkman that he specified in his glossary of place-names the different terms for the acorn-gathering encampment on Palomar for Pauma Indians ("Wavam"), Pala Indians ("Shoau"), and Yapicha Indians ("Shautushma") (1908b: 190). Likewise, Ed Davis emphasized that a wide variety of tribes frequented Palomar Mountain, including, "Yipeche, La Joya, Potrero, Rincon, Pauma, Pala, Pechanga, Aguanga, Puerta La Cruz, and Puerta Noria" (1938: 1).

Important details have been recorded by Sparkman and others that offer a glimpse into the lives of the native people of the area. The Indigenous inhabitants called themselves "Payómkawichum"—which meant "people" or "people of the west"—and knew the region as "Wavamai." Some of the original place names have been passed down for generations. There is a spot near Boucher Lookout known as "T'ai" and another in the vicinity of the Bailey Lodge is called "Paisvi." "Pauma," originally the primary Indigenous village in the area, is at the foot of the mountain. It was once home to numerous well-built conical houses. Davis and other white settlers often called them "wikiups," although the local Indigenous populations referred to them as "'ewaa" or "ke-chakechumat." These structures had a core of pine poles covered with brush as well as a variety of semisubterranean sweat houses that were central to ceremonial and medicinal rituals. Those houses found higher up Palomar Mountain were similar in form with a central ridge pole, but they tended to use bark as a covering instead of brush. In fact, archaeologists noted that two of these cedar bark huts were still standing as late as 1955. Other prominent forms of Indigenous material culture included clay jars (for keeping water cool and storing seeds), bows and arrows, coiled woven basketry, fishing and carrying nets, and throwing sticks.

Palomar's Indigenous peoples—today's Luiseño—speak a dialect of Shoshonean. It is a subfamily of languages shared by tribes in Idaho, Oregon, Utah, New Mexico, and coastal California from Malibu in the north to Carlsbad in the south. They are the most southwesterly Shoshonean speakers in the US. This nuance, along with the fact that Shoshonean is a subset of the Uto-Aztecan language family, has led many anthropologists and archaeologists to suggest that they migrated to the region from the east (Kroeber 1976).

Not only were there many distinct Indigenous groups in and around Palomar Mountain, the area was also a nexus of multiple native bands. The region was not home to just Luiseño people; there were Cupeño to the east, Kumeyaay to the south, and Cahuilla to the north (Phillips 1990: 7). This diversity and the overall local Indigenous ability to remain relatively culturally intact through the missionization process are key factors that resulted in San Diego County having more federally recognized tribes than any other county in the United States (Lightfoot 2005).

Contact with Europeans, Mexicans, and US Americans

European, Mexican, and US American land titles to Palomar Mountain—the Western law of the land—are often completely irrelevant to local Indians with deep ancestral ties to the region. Nevertheless, a chain of title helps to situate Western conceptions of land ownership and how they have changed over the last 250 years. Upon arrival in the region, Franciscan missionaries named the local river "Rio San Luis Rey de Francis" (River St. Louis King of France) as a gift from the Spanish crown to their homeland European allies to the east. Accordingly, they initially called the local Indigenous population near the river, "San Luiseño," although the label was soon after shortened to "Luiseño" (Kroeber 1976). In one of the stranger naming ironies, the exact Western term of "Luiseño Indians" drew its origins from a Spanish gift to the French king and an Italian explorer's geographic misidentification of Indigenous Americans as inhabitants of the Asian country of India.

Even though the Spanish claimed the land in and around Palomar Mountain, very few Europeans ventured anywhere near it for many years. Local historian George Taye noted that Juan Baptista de Anza (1774–76) "passed some twenty miles to the northeast [of Palomar Mountain] . . . and did not stop," and "[Gaspar de] Portolá, [Junípero] Serra, and [Juan] Crespí and other Spanish settlers passed up and down along the coast some twenty miles to the west, but did not visit the Palomar regions" (c. 1940: 2). Even after Indigenous laborers hauled pine and fir timbers from Palomar Mountain and constructed Mission San Luis Rey in 1798, the area still went unexplored by the Spanish, except for chasing down native runaways and pursuing new converts (Taye c. 1940: 2). In 1816, when the Spaniards established an *asistencia* (or outpost) at Pala—named after the Luiseño word "paala," meaning "water" (Hyde 1971: 226, 236)—the Europeans finally began to inhabit the Palomar Mountain area. Father Antonio Peyri, a Franciscan missionary who worked at Mission San Luis Rey from 1798 to 1832, played a prominent role in proselytizing the local Indigenous population. Many current Luiseño follow the religious tradition of native ancestors who were converted by Father Peyri; others either maintain their earlier exclusively Indigenous beliefs or have amalgamated the two practices. The Luiseño population plummeted during the proselytization process due to European diseases, disruption of Indigenous life ways, and outright Spanish and then Mexican hostility.

Relations between the Luiseño and Mexicans continued to deteriorate during the first half of the nineteenth century. In fact, sustained conflict between the two groups was part of the larger Mexican-American War. Even though Mexican Alta California Governor Jose Figueroa granted three pueblos to the Luiseño in 1833, his successor Pío Pico routinely failed to honor Indian land grants and even made one of the aforementioned pueblos his personal ranch. Furthermore, Figueroa's decision to secularize the missions in 1834 resulted in the closure of both the San Luis Rey Mission and the Pala Asistencia. Another local consequence of the Mexican government making land grants to private citizens was that the land just to the south of Palomar Mountain, especially what was then known as San Jose Valley, received far more attention than the mountain itself. For example, Silvestre de la Portilla, brother of San Luis Rey Mission property administrator Captain Pablo de la Portilla, petitioned for the mission lands in 1834 and was refused by Governor Figueroa. However, his request was approved by Figueroa's successor, Governor Nicholas Gutierrez, in 1836. Governor Juan B. Alvarado granted this same land to Jose Antonio Pico in 1840. Neither Portilla nor Pico seemed to have used the land extensively, leaving it open for US American J. J. Warner to petition for it in 1844. California's Mexican legislative assembly approved the grant in 1845. The following year Warner successfully applied for a second grant that included Palomar Mountain as well (J. Hill 1927: 35–38, 104–54).

Western intrusion onto native lands was met with a variety of responses, from abandonment to open warfare. Settler-Indian relations remained tense and complex throughout the middle of the nineteenth century. For example, Luiseño/Californio bloodshed erupted in 1846 when Pauma Indians killed eleven Californios in retaliation for the theft of horses used in the Mexican-American Battle of San Pasqual. The Mexican military would avenge those deaths with the Temecula Massacre when Californios and Cahuilla Indians killed approximately three dozen Luiseño.

Though Mexican and US American settlers considered Palomar Mountain to be part of the Warner Ranch in 1846, the Indigenous population saw the region as its ancestral and current home. Natives drove Warner off his land in 1851, leading to a period in which Palomar Mountain had virtually no permanent residents. Furthermore, foreclosure resulted in Warner losing all of his San Jose Valley/Palomar Mountain land by 1861 (J. Hill 1927: 35–38, 104–54). During the Early [US] American Period, the Indigenous population continued to use the land seasonally for hunting and processing acorns, and various outlaws had learned that the mountain's many hidden meadows were perfect hiding spots to stash stolen livestock before moving their ill-gotten goods to Mexico.

The mid-to-late 1870s were an especially volatile time for relations between various Luiseño tribal members and US settlers in San Luis Rey Valley at the base of Palomar Mountain. Elected Indigenous leader Manuel Olegario Calac led the native defense of Indian lands, regularly confronting white settlers who unlawfully attempted to seize additional acres. Anglo-American settlers were wary yet impressed with him; US Indian agent John G. Ames reported to Congress in 1874 that, "[Manuel Olegario Calac] is intelligent, above average, peacefully disposed toward whites, capable of controlling his Indians . . . and is at the same time an enthusiastic defender of his people and disposed to take advanced grounds on questions of their rights" (Crawford 1995: 38). Although the imminence of warfare between the Luiseño and white settlers waned in the mid-1870s when Calac met with President Grant in Washington, DC and secured over 52,000 acres in San Diego County for various Indigenous groups, the summer of 1877 witnessed another dramatic rise in tensions (Crawford 1995: 38). However, just as full-scale warfare was about to erupt, Calac died. Many Luiseño felt certain that he had been poisoned although the official autopsy indicated that he died of natural causes.

The Harrison Homestead

Luiseño settlements continued in and around Palomar throughout contact with Spanish, Mexican, and US American settlers. In fact, Sparkman mapped a variety of Luiseño winter villages, summer villages, temporary camps, and Indigenous trails on Palomar Mountain (True, Meighan, and Crew 1974: 130). One of the trails passed in close proximity to the Harrison cabin and led to the Pauma summer camp known as To-ko-ma, which was just north of Harrison's tract (Figure 3.3). Archaeologists recorded this large site and its plentiful bedrock outcroppings with mortars and milling stones during survey work in the 1950s (True, Meighan, and Crew 1974: 130). They noted that local informants recalled this area as a prime location for gathering acorns and gooseberries (True, Meighan, and Crew 1974: 130).

The Luiseño gift of Palomar Mountain land to Harrison was even more remarkable when one recalled how fiercely the Indigenous population guarded its territories. Sparkman wrote, "Each band seems to have guarded its allotted territory with the greatest jealousy, and more quarrels are said to have arisen over trespassing than from all other causes combined" (1908b: 190). Therefore, it was incorrect to assume automatically that the Luiseño either gave Harrison a tract they did not want or use, or that they did not cherish their individual territories in general.[19]

Close examination of the exact placement of the Harrison cabin on Palomar Mountain provided ample evidence that this decision to settle there was meaningful and strategic. Harrison had a dual claim on the land. The local Indigenous population gave him the tract, and he homesteaded the property with the US government. Harrison adroitly secured permission from the two primary stakeholders in the immediate vicinity; he also had close family ties to numerous Mexican ranchers in the region, the one-time resident owners. There were no local stakeholders from whom Harrison did not obtain permission, consent, or at

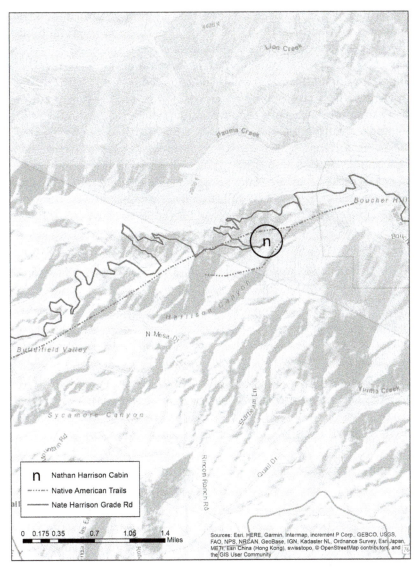

Figure 3.3. Harrison strategically built his cabin next to a set of Luiseño trails and near the most prominent Palomar Mountain road. (Courtesy of the Nathan "Nate" Harrison Historical Archaeology Project.)

least some sort of buy-in for his presence there. Harrison built his cabin near an active native trail that led to seasonal acorn-harvest activity areas and was close to the mountain road used by white pioneers. The structure was near his spring—one of his sources of income and sustenance—but was still behind a steep bend and well cloaked if one was not intimately familiar with the terrain. Interestingly, his cabin was not on a particularly flat area; this did not seem to be an important criterion. There were two other far more level choices down the hill on the same property. However, neither of these was at the intersection of two different trade routes while still being secluded.

The Harrison cabin occupied an easily defended high ground but also had ample backroads for abandonment and escape should an oncoming force prove too daunting. In fact, the many lookout points along the Nate Harrison Grade bore striking resemblance in plan-view to various colonial fort bastions (Figure 3.4). These projections jutted out at an angle from the curtain wall of a fortification, enabling the additional flanks to protect the primary wall and other bastions. Whereas his cabin was concealed in a nook at the edge of his property, Harrison's multiple lookout points on Palomar Mountain enabled him to see virtually all activity below him on the surrounding hills and valleys. Asher recalled:

> One of Nate's spots was "Billygoat Point" which was about a mile below Nate's well and some hundred feet south of the road. This point commanded an extensive view of the whole mountainside, stretching from Pauma Canyon on the northwest to Nate's own canyon to the southeast. I have seen him perched there for an hour or two at a time while he was waiting for me to get abreast of the point as I toiled up the grade afoot. (c. 1938: no page numbers)

The architectural concept of being able to see all potential threats at once is called a panopticon (*pan*, "all" and *opticon*, "observe"). Developed in 1785 by social theorist Jeremy Bentham to enable prison architects to create a structure in which a warden could watch every incarcerated

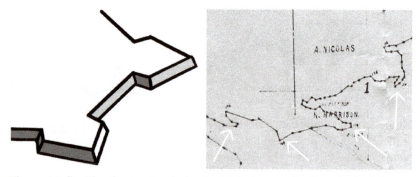

Figure 3.4a/b. The classic, elevated colonial fort-corner bastions in the left image are echoed in the natural terrain of Nate Harrison Grade (*right*, in the 1896 Sickler survey map), which made Harrison's home easily defensible against oncoming threats. (Courtesy of the Nathan "Nate" Harrison Historical Archaeology Project, Kirby Collection.)

inmate from a single locus without the prisoners being aware they were being monitored, it was popularized in academic circles by Michel Foucault (1975). Harrison, a former slave living in a region regularly hostile to non-whites and rife with Old West lawlessness, homesteaded a tract that enabled him to create a strategic safe place, one that could see all, allow selective interaction, facilitate a formidable defense or quick retreat, maintain close proximity to Indigenous allies, and empower him in a virtually invisible manner. Simply put, he could see without being seen. Harrison experienced spatial hierarchical power atop Billygoat Point, as he could—in a single moment—see all visitors ascending the treacherous grade for miles and hours in advance.

The Harrison Cabin

In contrast to the seemingly complex consideration he gave to the defensive potential of his property, Harrison's personal dwelling bore a more modest resemblance to a simply constructed slave quarters from the Antebellum South. Though separated some three thousand miles from the heart of the Confederacy, constructed well after the end of the Civil War, and assembled by a free man, Harrison's cabin high up on the west side of Palomar Mountain was square in plan, small in inner dimensions, made of local materials, and emphasized outer space over inner. It could easily be confused with many others built by enslaved Africans and African Americans south of the Mason-Dixon Line. The fact that Harrison constructed this antiquated form, regardless of his emancipated status, was likely a strong testament to the power of culture, memory, and identity. He could have created a much larger structure or fashioned a house with entirely different dimensions; instead he built his home in a form that he knew best. Ed Davis emphasized that, "A log house was the ordinary style of architecture in the mountain," but Harrison chose to construct and inhabit an entirely different kind of cabin (1938: 25).

Though initial archaeological survey of the area identified little more than a few stones in a semicircular arc, complete excavation of the site revealed that the structure's free-stone granite boulder foundation was a near-perfect square in plan. The four corners were right angles, the four interior walls were 11.0′ in length, and the two diagonals were each 14.1′. The doorway and chimney were centrally located on opposite west/east ends of the structure, and both were constructed into and as part of the stone foundation. Historical photographs indicated that four wooden corner posts helped support the large granite stones chinked with mud and the split shake roof. They also highlight the extended patio to the immediate west of the structure. The stone walls of the cabin were each individually standing units. Nonetheless, these were not cold joints that reflected separate and independent construction sequences. On the contrary, Harrison constructed the walls of his cabin all at once, as the stones were remarkably similar in size, orientation, and assembly pattern; the dimensions of the cabin formed an almost perfect square, and the chimney and door sill were integrated parts of the east and west wall, respectively. These factors, when taken together, strongly suggest a deliberate and carefully engineered design for the structure. Though many photographs of the Harrison cabin exist (Figure 3.5), many of them do not, at first glance, reveal the intentionality and precision of its construction.

Archaeological investigations confirmed that the original cabin floor was dirt. Excavators encountered subsoil at a horizontal level at the base of the large cornerstones, and a small layer of flat ashy soil covered the dirt floor next to the rock chimney base. Although there was bioturbation (animal disturbance) at the site and later mechanical disturbances by a subsequent landowner, *in situ* artifacts also corroborated the dirt-floor interpretation. Also of significance was that the floor in the Harrison cabin was not flush with the patio or the doorsill; it was sunken by a full step (1.0′). There was a large flat granite rock that

Figure 3.5a/b/c/d. Historical photographs captured all four sides of the Harrison cabin (*clockwise from top left*: west, east, north, south). (Escondido Historical Society. Public domain.)

served as a threshold under the doorway, but this stone rested above smaller stones in fill that gave way to the natural subsoil. As a result, the flat floor of Harrison's home was a foot lower than the earth outside of the cabin. Simply put, the cabin had a sunken dirt floor with no sub-floor pits (Samford 2007) (Figure 3.6).

Figure 3.6a/b. The square cabin foundation in the top image on the left included no subfloor pits; the living surface was 1.0′ below the base of the doorway (*bottom image*). (Courtesy of the Nathan "Nate" Harrison Historical Archaeology Project.)

Excavators recovered relatively few artifacts in the cabin compared to the rich deposits in the patio area. These material finds emphasized that different kinds of activities occurred in distinct areas of the site, with the outer area just to the west of the structure being a locus for refuse. This artifact discrepancy was especially pronounced in terms of items related to food preparation, consumption, disposal, and storage. The only artifact type found in large quantities inside of the cabin was nails, which formed part of a larger pattern of architectural debris in and around the cabin. While nails, both machine-cut and modern wire, were found in abundance at the primary residence, there were other singular items that, despite their relative scarcity, had direct ties to the architecture function of the abode. For example, a skeleton key was uncovered less than two feet from where the front door was once located.

Excavators found different kinds and amounts of historical artifacts in three distinct areas in and around the cabin: 1) the dwelling interior, 2) the enclosed patio adjacent and to the immediate west of the front door, and 3) the extended area farther to the south and west (Figure 3.7). Although materials from each of the three areas cross-mended with each other—implying they were all filled or impacted at the same time—there were nevertheless important and distinct spatial differences at the site. In general, the cabin had very few artifacts except for architectural debris, the enclosed patio featured glass and ceramics, and the extended area was rife with faunal material and meat cans. The cabin's small interior space seemed to have been reserved primarily for sleeping and was a private and less social area.[20] The enclosed patio reflected active food processing, and the extended area beyond resembled a dumping area for trash. It was not a refuse pit as there was no evidence of digging a specific hole for the debris. On the contrary, Harrison, who owned many animals on his property through the years, likely left food scraps out and practiced broadcast refuse as a way to offer supplemental food to his dogs and livestock.

Matthew Tennyson conducted a survey of historical photographs, standing structures, and archaeological site records of the region and pinpointed the distinctiveness of this particular dwelling (2007). Simply put, no other historical building in the region looked like the Harrison cabin in terms of shape, materials, or construction. Traditional Native American structures were conical huts, and oval and rectangular thatch houses; these were later augmented with adobe and wooden buildings that were rectangular in plan (Tennyson 2007). Spanish and Mexican structures, like many of the later Indigenous buildings, were adobes with rectilinear floor plans (McAlester and McAlester 1984). Likewise, the many Anglo-American pioneer homes in the region were

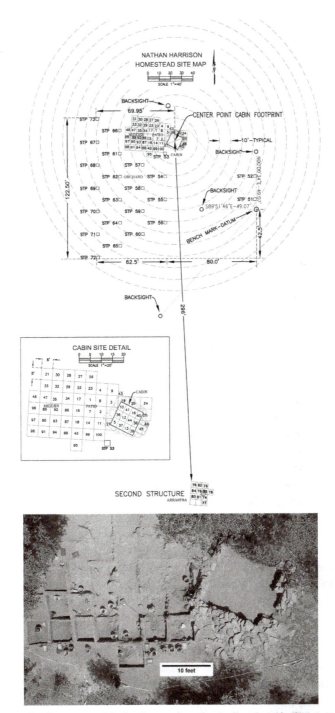

Figure 3.7a/b. Site map with the five archaeologically identified activity areas (cabin, patio, midden, orchard, and arrastra) and a close-up aerial photograph of the cabin, patio, and midden areas. (Courtesy of the Nathan "Nate" Harrison Historical Archaeology Project.)

rectangular cabins; some consisted of horizontal logs and others had wood siding. Even the other African American structures in early San Diego County resembled these Anglo pioneer homes in terms of wood construction, finished floors, and rectilinear floor plans (Mallios et al. 2008). The Harrison cabin was also especially distinct from widespread white Southern California building conventions that evolved through separate Victorian, Ranch, and Craftsman styles during the twentieth century (McAlester and McAlester 1984).

Harrison's Palomar home was clearly an exception to established and dominant house forms of the region. Vernacular or folk architecture has been the subject of much study and debate among scholars but usually centers on the concept of informal construction, as opposed to formal building (Upton and Vlach 1986). Dynamic cultural traditions and local adaptations are often highlighted instead of strict architectural blueprints. This fluidity across space, time, and form is distinctive and led architectural historian Dell Upton to opine that, "vernacular architecture is regional architecture" (1982: 95). This seems to be particularly true for Harrison, but somehow his vernacular home was from another region and even another time. Many aspects of his cabin made it seem that it was specifically vernacular to the Antebellum South and not to the Old West in which it was built. The key to understanding this apparent contradiction was remembering that vernacular architecture referred to the informality of the building process, not just the resultant structure (Glassie 2000). Vernacular architecture drew on past traditions and experiences but also specialized in adaptability.[21] It was this unofficial and adaptive style that made the Harrison cabin both out of place and appropriate on Palomar Mountain.

A brief background of early colonial architecture in what would become the United States helped to contextualize this paradoxical statement. In the 1600s, many English colonists lived in the same house as their indentured servants and then later their African slaves (Bell 2005). It was not until the 1700s that a spatial reorganization occurred. As a result of growing rural estates, Anglo settlers began subdividing plantation land and setting up separate areas that were designated as quarters for field slaves. These quarters were often simple wooden structures or cabins. For example, John W. Blassingame, who studied autobiographies from former enslaved African Americans, noted, ". . . they reported that they lived in crudely built one-room cabins with dirt floors and too many cracks in them to permit much comfort during the winter months" (1972: 6).

The work of John Michael Vlach provided a detailed analysis of slave structures from Southern plantations. His book, *Back of the Big House:*

The Architecture of Plantation Slavery, drew on hundreds of photographs and drawings from the federal Historic American Buildings Survey (HABS) and interviews from the Federal Writer's Project (FWP) with former slaves and their relatives (1993). Vlach observed that many of the structures in his study were built by slaves apart from the main house and without direct supervision from owners and overseers, meaning that slaves were often creating their own spaces.[22] Vlach also cited multiple ethnographic accounts by former slaves confirming that slave structures were typically square, had few or no windows, and typically included a single stone fireplace for cooking. One of Vlach's primary sources was Frederick Law Olmsted, who in 1862 wrote *The Cotton Kingdom: A Traveler's Observations on Cotton and Slavery in the American Slave States*. Olmsted, like Blassingame, detailed that slave cabins were small, generally 10–12 square feet, with no additional openings besides doors (1862: 161).

A cabin is a specific kind of house. The word "cabin" is an Irish term describing a small one-room house, but the exact size of "small" is of significant importance to this discussion. Most Anglo-American cabins during this time period were rectangular in plan. However, those that were square were traditionally 16' to a side, matching the width of a single-bay medieval house.[23] The Harrison cabin was significantly smaller, with walls measuring only 11'. While Harrison's home was dwarfed by typical Anglo houses, it was right at the norm for African American structures.

This link between square structures and slave quarters is coarse, with as many contrasts as there were similarities. For instance, there were many historical buildings that were square and not associated with slaves, and many slave quarters that were not square in plan. Some slave quarters were nearly identical to structures occupied by non-slaves, especially log cabins occupied by poor white individuals (Glassie 1963; Horning 2002: 134). There was also great variability in slave quarters across the Antebellum South and little uniformity between structures found in Kentucky, Virginia, or Louisiana during the eighteenth and nineteenth centuries.[24] Likewise, many historical properties contained buildings with a variety of different functions (e.g., kitchens, smokehouses, outbuildings, barns, etc.), each of which was often tailored to its specific function. Nonetheless, descriptions of rural lowland antebellum slave cabins in Kentucky, Harrison's state of origin, also detailed the prevalent use of single-room stand-alone cabins made of local materials (Talbott, n.d.). For example, Lowell H. Harrison and James C. Klotter noted in *A New History of Kentucky* that, "slaves on a small farm probably lived in a cabin, with one room . . . stoves were rare, most of the cooking was done at the hearth or outdoors in hot weather" (1997: 170).

Contemporaneous Palomar Mountain locals were well aware of the similarities between Harrison's cabin and slave quarters, calling his dwelling "a darkey's shack" and emphasizing that "anyone from Dixie would recognize it as such" (Bostic c. 1964: no page numbers; Bartlett 1931: 24). These unambiguous phrases directly tied the form of the Harrison home to building traditions employed by enslaved African Americans in the South. Harrison seemed to have made the decision to recreate a living quarters from his past, no matter how directly it might have tied to his previous enslavement.

There were a few architectural nuances at the Harrison cabin that strayed from the Southern norm and seemed to reflect regional adaptation. For example, he built out of natural stone, in this case large granite boulders and cobbles. The stones were uncut, the mortar was local sediment, and the floor was dirt. Construction of this dwelling was a one-person endeavor that was both inexpensive and quick. In addition, similar free-standing cobble structures with dirt floors, though not square in plan, were prevalent in mining camps in regions to the north and east (Figure 3.8).[25] Furthermore, Harrison's sunken floor likely

Figure 3.8. Though the Lost Horse Mine cabin resembled the Nathan Harrison site structure in terms of materials and construction, it was different in plan form and flooring level. (Courtesy of Ginger Shoulders.)

served a functional purpose as lowered floors often reduced drafty gusts in high-wind areas.[26] Harrison might have learned this technique from the Indigenous population who had long since figured out that dug-in houses used the insulation of the earth to retain heat.[27]

Another deviation from typical slave quarters in Harrison's cabin was that it had its entrance and chimney at the structure's gable ends. An overwhelming majority of one-room square slave quarters from the Antebellum South had the primary door on an eave end (at a right angle and on adjacent walls). Harrison's door placement was likely an adaptation to the local environment dictated by the slope of the terrain onto which he built his home. Building a level home on a hill required that the core axis of the structure be perpendicular to the slope instead of parallel; in this way, far less of a slope had to be compensated for in the flooring. Once this decision had been made, it was a logical extension to have the door at the gable end because an entrance at either the north or south side would have had a dramatically different elevation than the east or west end.

Harrison's cabin was unique in Southern California, but many nearby houses were equally distinctive. For example, Palomar Mountain's Harry Burch constructed a cabin with neither doors nor windows. There was a small vent in the corner of the roof that he used to enter and exit the structure. Ed Davis explained that, "Being a sailor, climbing and lowering himself in the hold of a ship became natural to [Burch]" (1938: 28). George Doane's Palomar cabin did not stand out from others—it was a traditional rectangular log cabin—but what was distinctive was Doane's habit of repeatedly moving the cabin from place to place on his property, one log at a time.

These quirky examples were an important reminder when analyzing the architecture of the Harrison cabin to balance broad cultural patterns and immediate environmental factors with individual idiosyncrasies. Architectural historian Dell Upton warned those who study the past to avoid "positivistic models . . . [that] reduce ethnicity to a list of traits and practices that can be isolated from later contaminants" (1996: 3). Instead, it was essential to examine Nathan Harrison's cabin in a multicultural setting "as a synthesis of imposed and adopted characteristics that is forged through contact and conflict" (Upton 1996: 4). Upton emphasized that individuals of the past who built and lived in historical structures made choices, played roles, invented traditions, and commodified their identities (1996: 5). He urged scholars to move away from interpretations that exclusively highlighted collective patterns and toward appreciations of individual selves and singularities. Upton concluded that, "Landscapes of experience are more numerous

and more important than the architecture of memory . . . [and] experience permits choice" (1986: 10–11).

Upton's warning regarding linear extensions of cultural patterns was
pertinent to the evaluation of the Harrison cabin. While the structure
obviously bore striking resemblance to slave quarters from the Antebellum South and strayed far from architectural norms of the Old
West, this did not mean Harrison was following this cultural tradition
unknowingly or without careful consideration of his contemporary
surroundings. Harrison's minstrelsy repeatedly resulted in him deliberately presenting dilapidated and subservient displays (clothing, language, behavior, etc.) in order to diminish any threat that his existence
as a free, popular, and land-owning African American male might project to traditional white audiences. Harrison might have simply built
what he knew from his childhood, but perhaps this particular construction was another deliberate decision in order to appear unassuming
and accepting of the existing social order.[28]

Having the opportunity and ability to recognize these sorts of individualized nuances in the archaeological record was especially important when studying the physical remains of the cabin. While most of
the large cobbles that formed the foundation and walls of the Harrison
residence were indistinct in quality, there was one rock outside of the
collapse of the cabin chimney of particular interest (Figure 3.9). It was
a flat granite stone measuring 1.9' in length and 1.0' in width and likely
broken in half. The center of the stone had been ground down to form
a circular hole 4.0" in diameter, indicating that it had once been a portable metate or grinding stone. Whereas Harrison might have used this
former Indigenous acorn processing tool as just another cobble in his
cabin, it is noteworthy that the Luiseño regularly tied great symbolic
value to these stones and their primary users. They often broke a portable metate in half to mark the passing of a tribal member. Considering
Harrison's close and continued ties with the local Luiseño community,
their decision to give the land to him, and their continued use of the
territory, the inclusion of this ceremonial item in or near his home likely
held additional significance. Could it have been tied to the passing of
someone close to him, perhaps even one of his Indigenous wives? It
might also have been placed at the cabin site by Indigenous inhabitants
in Harrison's honor after his passing.

The Harrison cabin was one of the most important singular expressions of his identity. He built it himself and could have constructed
a home of many different forms, styles, and functions. However, the
meaning behind the structure can be interpreted in multiple ways. According to universal laws of comfort and convenience, the cabin satis-

Figure 3.9a/b. These images show the *in situ* location of the broken granite metate, half near the southern wall debris and a close-up of the cobble's central hole. (Courtesy of the Nathan "Nate" Harrison Historical Archaeology Project.)

fied basic human necessities. Since Harrison seemed to bring the design of a slave quarters from the Antebellum South, it was easy to argue that it was part of his mental template, the analytical starting point for structuralist thought. Nevertheless, even this blueprint was highly intricate as the cabin was his own adaptation of African American as well as Anglo-American ideas from a place in Kentucky where the old English square plan was used by black people, enslaved and free, and poor white individuals as well. In addition, Harrison adapted to the Southern California mountain environment by using a variety of local materials and techniques borrowed from native groups and Mexican settlers. Power relationships—a key tenet of Marxism and agency theories—undoubtedly influenced the building of the Harrison cabin in terms of strategic location. Furthermore, Harrison's potential architectural minstrelsy—presenting visitors with a quaint, unassuming, and nonthreatening "throwback" home—reflected one of many strategic individual decisions that he made when designing and building the structure. Overall, the cabin was a blend of all things Nathan Harrison, reflecting choices regarding his most intrinsic universal human needs, his modest economic means, his most idiosyncratic individualized tastes, and even the consequences of his own unique and particular history. He carried cultural norms and traditions with him and reinvented them with every decision he made, experience he lived, and role he played.

The Harrison Arrastra

Some narratives claimed that Harrison's homestead had a second dwelling, similar in unmortared stone construction but located southward and downhill from his primary home. One story insisted that it housed a close friend; another maintained it was a storage facility for Harrison's secret stash of gold. Both referred to a flat area hundreds of feet south of the primary cabin. However, an account from Asher suggested Harrison used that particular spot for mining purposes. Asher stated:

> I have seen the old arrastra on the flat south of Nate's cabin. An arrastra is an animal-motivated contrivance for reducing mineral ores to powder. It is the supposition that the mill was erected to treat gold ores presumably found in the vicinity, but the hillside canyons around Nate's cabin have been thoroughly prospected and the mystery still remains unsolved. (c. 1938: no page numbers)

An arrastra was a primitive mill designed to grind ore in the search for precious metals. Powered by a person riding or leading a horse in a circle, the arrastra's beast of burden dragged a large stone in a circle that crushed the ore. Although their designs varied greatly, arrastras usually included a central vertical post affixed to a horizontal bar whose ends were tethered to the animal and the large stone respectively. The word "arrastra" derived from the Spanish phrase "dragging along the ground." Arrastras were common on remote mines; they had been introduced to the New World by the Spanish during colonization and continued through Mexican periods in California.

One of the unexpected benefits of a devastating fire that burned much of the former Harrison homestead in 2007 was that it offered archaeologists a glimpse of the surrounding landscape without plant cover.[29] This stark and unobscured view of the natural terrain exposed remnants of an eight-foot rock wall 300' south of the Harrison cabin. The stones were large cobbles, nearly identical to the shape, size, and stacking formation as the rocks that formed the foundation and walls of the Harrison cabin. Furthermore, a large, heavily rusted metal can from the early twentieth century was found next to the rocks. This wall seemed to share many spatial, temporal, and formal similarities with the primary Harrison dwelling.

Excavation of units in the vicinity of Structure II produced some surprises. First, the wall was more of a semicircle in plan than a line or a right angle. Second, it appeared to be a border that separated the flat area to the west from the steep ravine to the east, as opposed to a foundation for a complete structure. Third, there was a small circular feature in the projected center of the semicircle of rocks, strongly suggesting that these two features were contemporaneous (Figure 3.10). The small circular feature had two distinct layers and resembled a larger posthole (a hole dug to place a post) and a smaller central postmold (the remains of the post originally placed in the hole). The postmold was full of charred clay and angled to the southwest, suggesting that the original post had burned and been knocked over or dragged off to the side.

The architectural remains found in the 20' by 20' excavation area narrowed probable interpretations regarding the primary purpose of the structure. The rock wall was not part of a rectangular building and did not appear to be designed or bastioned to support any kind of overhead roof. In fact, there was no evidence that this stack of stones did anything more than establish a boundary for an activity area. Furthermore, the circular pattern of the stacked rocks and the central posthole and postmold strongly suggested this space was designed to radiate about a centralized point. Additionally, this part of the local landscape was a natural saddle or ridge pass, which was a flat area with rounded sides ideal for containing livestock. These factors, combined with a light domestic artifact scatter—there were a handful of nineteenth century artifacts (buttons, nails, and pottery sherds)—intimated that this was a work area. Overall, the archaeological remains clearly privileged the arrastra interpretation as these traditional dragging areas were circular,

Figure 3.10a/b. Sketch of a historical arrastra (*top*) and the archaeological remains of Structure II at the Nathan Harrison site (*bottom*). (Courtesy of the Nathan "Nate" Harrison Historical Archaeology Project.)

centered about a singular post, confined (bounded) yet open-air (no roof). The other interpretations of, 1) a hiding place for his precious metals, and 2) a hang-out spot for a friend, might have had tangential ties to the primary purpose of the area. Specifically, the ore being processed could have led visitors to believe Harrison had found and stashed some gold in the immediate vicinity, and that Harrison might have had an acquaintance supervise the arrastra.

Additional support for the arrastra interpretation came from the chemistry of the soil itself. Simply put, dirt is full of highly informative microscopic remnants of the past. Soil-chemistry tests, once reserved solely for farmers in search of clues for how to maximize their yield, have quickly become a standard part of most archaeologists' analytical toolkits.[30] Elevated readings—well above the background average—of phosphorous, potassium, calcium, magnesium, and various other elements in the soil have been shown at many historical sites across the globe to be the result of distinct past activities (Keeler 1978; Pogue 1988; Knudson et al. 2004). They can pinpoint occupation areas, disposal practices, and specific behaviors (Lambert 1997). Since phosphorous is present naturally in animal tissues and waste, archaeological soils with readings that spike for this element often reflect past animal pens and barns, privies, and trash pits; they also have been associated with the disposal of chamber pot night soils.[31] In addition, people of the past who practiced broadcast refuse—regularly scattering their garbage across the yard for consumption by their animals as opposed to placing it neatly in confined trash pits—created a ring of phosphorous-rich debris around dwellings. Likewise, since wood ash was rife with potassium, high potassium readings reflected the dumping of hearth ash.[32] In addition, calcium—a primary component of bone and hard tissue in animals—regularly reflected the presence of trash pits, middens, and broadcast refuse. Although most soil is not directly datable, the intersection of a datable artifact found in a layer of soil with elevated levels of one of these distinctive chemical elements can link a distinct time period with a specific activity.

Soil-chemistry tests were undertaken for every excavated layer at the Harrison site, and these analyses produced readings for twenty-four different elements. For the sake of this discussion, these elements were grouped into three clusters. Group I consisted of elements that were identified in detectable amounts and diagnostically specific to only some areas of the site. Phosphorus (P), calcium (Ca), and strontium (Sr) were present in relatively large quantities and formed a spatially distinct pattern of being concentrated in some areas and diluted in others. Group II included the elements iron (Fe), barium (Ba), and zinc (Zn). Although these elements were easily detected in the chemical analysis, they were present in every sample in uniform amounts. For the most part, iron, barium, and zinc are consistent and ever-present in the Palomar Mountain soil and are not likely reflective of human activity. Group III consisted of elements that went virtually undetected (less than 100ppm throughout or present in less than 50 percent of the samples). It included cadmium (Cd), palladium (Pd), silver (Ag), molybdenum (Mo), niobium (Nb), rubidium (Rb), Bismuth (Bi), selenium (Se), lead (Pb), tungsten (W), copper (Cu), nickel (Ni), cobalt (Co), potassium (K), chlorine (Cl), sulfur (S), magnesium (Mg), and arsenic (As). Only Group I provided differential readings that could be used to distinguish different activity areas of the site.[33]

The Harrison site maintained extremely high phosphorous levels — more than double the off-site control readings — in two general areas: 1) the primary refuse area just west of the patio, and 2) inside the cabin in a layer associated with a perfectly horizontal ash lens that marked the original cabin floor. Elevated calcium and strontium levels further validated the western area beyond the enclosed patio as a trash midden. In fact, the three elements of phosphorus, calcium, and strontium were highly interdependent at the site,[34] revealing a specific chemical signature of intense human and livestock activity.

The soil chemistry readings from Structure II were also insightful. The units in and around the structure had moderately elevated phosphorus levels, supporting the animal enclosure interpretation. In fact, the high phosphorus levels and low artifact densities were consistent with expectations for an area primarily used by animals although constructed and tended to by humans. Furthermore, the central feature likely originally serving as a post for the arrastra had two layers with different soil-chemistry signatures. The posthole, or hole dug to hold the post, reflected construction of the arrastra and likely pre-dated heavy animal use of the area. It had a relatively low phosphorus reading. The postmold, or remains of the deteriorated post itself, seemingly revealed the end of the structure's use. It maintained a high phosphorus reading, reflecting the recent use of the area. This particular example showcased the value of soil chemistry analyses as the remaining artifacts and architecture provided rather limited evidence. The phosphorus readings were an important additional line of evidence bolstering the arrastra interpretation.

In addition to the two major excavation areas involving 1) the primary cabin, patio, and midden and 2) the secondary animal structure (arrastra), a series of shovel test pits were also dug across the north section of the original property to investigate Harrison's use of the land. These units were a quarter of the size of traditional excavation areas, measuring 2.5' by 2.5' and being placed at 20' intervals along five different transects. The test pits identified boundaries for the trash midden at the southwest edge of the cabin's patio area and suggested the probable area for Harrison's historically documented grove of fruit trees. Multiple test pits in the area just to the south of the primary structure contained few artifacts and low chemical signatures specific to animal tissue and waste but multiple fruit pits. In addition, a pear tree likely dating to Harrison's time on the mountain sprung back to life after the Poomacha Fire in 2007. Although the tree had been heavily damaged by the flames, the catastrophic event also led to sizeable new growth and a fresh crop of pears (Figure 3.11).[35]

An additional soil-based line of evidence emphasized how the distinct areas of the site were used and impacted differently by its inhabitants. Tests in granulometry measured the size, weight, and density of the soil particles at the site. Comparisons from samples taken off-site, in the cabin fill, the patio debris, the trash dump, the second structure, and the orchard indicated great variety in the physics of the dirt between the

Figure 3.11a/b. This historical pear tree, which sprang back to life following a recent massive fire that burned much of the west side of Palomar Mountain, proved to be nearly as resourceful as Harrison himself. (Courtesy of the Nathan "Nate" Harrison Historical Archaeology Project.)

different areas. Simply put, some areas endured events of great energy (like human activity or natural water movement), and others seemed minimally impacted and did not vary from off-site samples. For example, the bulk density of the soil from the orchard was nearly one and a half times higher than the samples from the cabin's interior, and even the measures from the posthole and postmold in the arrastra were noticeably different. While these results are preliminary and more work is being undertaken to isolate granulometric signatures from various activities and areas of the site, these early readings further support the idea that Harrison used distinct parts of his property in different ways.

Overall, spatial insights from our excavations drew on multiple lines of evidence, including architectural elements, artifacts, buried soil stains, chemical residues, physical properties, and geological patterns. Each of the identified activity areas—cabin, patio, midden, arrastra, and orchard—were distinctive in their unique combination of archaeological factors. Clearly, the abundance of artifacts was not the only measure of past inhabitation as other archaeological nuances also reflected specific historical activities.

Time

Discussions of time dominate historical archaeology as the purported antiquity of every artifact found at the site is one of the first and most direct analytical springboards to the past. There are multiple ways to determine chronology for a site; some focus on the range of occupation, some isolate the latest date for the assemblage, and others seek measures of central tendency that average dates across the different datable finds and isolate a midpoint for the occupation. The analysis presented here employs each and observes their similarities and differences.

Of the 51,359 artifacts that student excavators found at the Harrison site, nearly one hundred different datable artifact types are represented. Historical archaeologists have conducted extensive research establishing clearly delineated production and use date-ranges for many groups of artifacts. For example, studies of various ceramic kilns have pinpointed when certain distinctive types of pottery were made, and the same can be said analogously for a wealth of other artifact types, including glass bottles, ammunition, cans, and even nails. Furthermore, some items were tied to specific patents or technologies that were not in existence until a given date. These items, like dated coins, offer a chronological range starting with the specific date on the object itself. All of the datable items found at a site can be graphed together from earliest to latest and the overlap of these individual chronologies can provide a date-range intersection that offers the period of occupation for the site. Since there are so many artifacts with long use ranges, an important task for the archaeologist is to find clues that narrow the occupation period when possible.

Date-range intersections for a site are bounded by two key dates: 1) the artifact with the latest start-of-production date, and 2) the artifact with the earliest end-of-production date. The first date is relativity easy to grasp. The latest start-of-production specifies the last possible moment when it is certain that someone was at the site. For example, a coin dated to 1916 uncovered archaeologically indicates that that particular item was placed at the site in 1916 or later. A coin from the year 1916 could not have been used at a site in 1915. Although the site might have been continuously occupied for decades earlier, it does not change the fact that this coin did not exist before 1916 and could not have been used before then. Even though the site would not likely be abandoned at the exact production date of that latest artifact (in this case, 1916), the lack of items with later production dates intimates that the site was not occupied for much longer. When scouring an entire artifact assemblage for more recent artifacts to mark the end of occupation, it is the item with the absolute latest start-of-production date that marks the end of the minimal chronological range for the whole site. This item often forms the site's *terminus post quem* (TPQ), a term from Latin that refers to "limit after which." Sites can be ordered by their TPQ or their absolute latest certain date of occupation.

On the contrary, the steps used to determine the *start* date of the minimal chronological range for the site often confuses people. In this case, it is the earliest end-of-production date that pinpoints the moment in time in which the artifact was no longer made and used. Assuming these items have a relatively short lifespan once production has ceased, this date provides the latest possible start date for the site. For example, if a certain type of button or ceramic was no longer made after 1865 and that button or ceramic was uncovered at the site, then it is presumed that inhabitants were at the site by at least 1865; the start date would not be after 1865. This can serve as the site's *terminus ante quem* (TAQ), which translates to "limit before which."

The items used in the explanation above were not arbitrary examples; artifacts from the Harrison site indicated that it was occupied from 1865 to 1916. Every datable artifact fit, at least in part, into that minimal time-span (Figure 3.12).[36] Two different dated coins from 1916—a Buffalo nickel and a Liberty dime—provided the end date. Clearly, these coins could not have been used before they were minted in 1916. The start date also came from two sources: 1) a four-hole sunken panel shell button that was no longer produced after 1865, and 2) an Ironstone pitcher

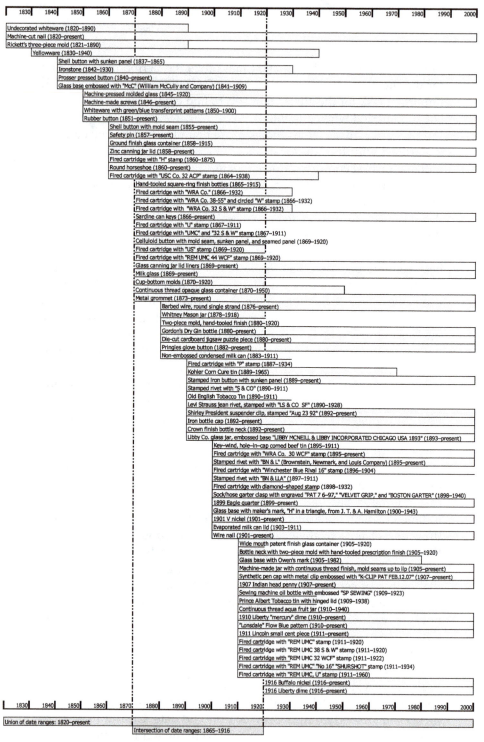

Figure 3.12. The cumulative Nathan Harrison site artifact date-range intersection situated the occupation from 1865 to 1916. (Courtesy of the Nathan "Nate" Harrison Historical Archaeology Project.)

with a William Adams, Tunstall England, Royal Arms Mark that was only made from 1850–65. These early end dates provided the start date for the minimal date-range intersection.

One inherent limitation of using artifact date-range intersections as the basis for a site's chronology is that it does not take into account the quantity of each artifact type. A lone and potentially anomalous specimen carries as much influence in determining the exact occupation span as an artifact that is discovered by the thousands. In order to balance quality and quantity, archaeologists developed measures of central tendency that could weight the different date ranges on the basis of how many of each type were uncovered. Accordingly, they calculated the midpoint of each artifact type, multiplied it by the quantity of the item found, and then averaged the results for all of the datable finds. Although this technique was developed initially for historical ceramics on East Coast sites, it can be extended to any datable artifact type, as long as it is understood that the shorter the date range for each item, the more accurate the resultant mean date (Binford 1962; South 1977; Monroe and Mallios 2004; Mallios 2005a).

Using the same dates for the artifact types with discrete ranges, the site maintained a mean date of 1895, well within the established 1865–1916 timeframe (Mallios 2009). The slightly-later-than-median central date likely reflected two factors. First, the later debris at the site seemed to outnumber the earlier debris. This suggested that Harrison was more sedentary later in life than in his earlier days on the mountain, an observation echoed in the historical records and narratives. Second, almost all mean dates highlight the later part of established date ranges for the simple fact that time moves forward. The inherent potential for error stems from the reality that initial production dates are easy to verify, while end production dates are often vague estimations as to when an item was no longer in circulation. The wealth of information about certain patents and inventions dwarfs the lack of documentation about products becoming obsolete and parent companies going out of business.

In an ideal archaeological situation, the site would be layered, with strata of debris that contained gradually earlier material the deeper one dug. Due to subsequent terracing with a tractor by one of the landowners in and around the cabin, much of the Harrison site did not have vertical spatial integrity. In fact, we found that artifacts from the top layers routinely fit together with items from the bottom layers. Furthermore, artifacts from the cabin were part of the same vessels as sherds from the patio and midden. Had the site never been contaminated by tractors and pothunters, these "crossmends" would have indicated all of this material was deposited at the same time. Considering the later earth-moving activities at the site, it was clear all of these artifacts were redeposited in a singular event, an earth-moving episode that erased much of the original archaeological context.

Despite the clear disturbances at the site, the materials still seemed to represent a single 1865–1916 occupation as opposed to shorter occupations separated by periods with no one at the site. Close inspection of all of the datable artifact types uncovered at the site revealed a smooth and gradual transition of types from the 1860s through the 1910s, with no blocky gaps in the graph at any given year or decade. Simply put, the artifacts strongly suggested a consistent and constant occupation at the site with growing intensity over time.

Form

Many of the over 50,000 artifacts unearthed at the site corresponded precisely with possessions showcased in photographs of Harrison. For example, there was a direct match between historical pictures and a rubber tobacco-pipe mouthpiece, wooden tobacco-pipe bowl, metal "Presidential" suspender clips, and a 9" leather boot (Figure 3.13). There were

Figure 3.13. The Harrison site produced many matches between historical photographs and excavated artifacts. (Courtesy of the Nathan "Nate" Harrison Historical Archaeology Project.)

many near matches as well, like a nickel watch fob (chain) that was similar but not identical to the ones captured in the old pictures.

Some of the more fascinating individual artifacts were those that helped contextualize details from the historical records. For example, excavators found a tiny lens (1/2" in diameter) that likely fell off a camera after one of the many pictures of Harrison was taken. It consisted of a glass interior and a ridged nickel edge. This lens perfectly matched those found on Eastman Kodak "Brownie" cameras, the first inexpensive and portable equipment for photography. Kodak made the Brownie out of a wood-covered box with black cardboard; both were wrapped with fake leather and nickel fittings. The Brownie changed modern photography as it was cheap ($1), simple to use (hold waist-high, aim, and turn the switch to shoot), easy to prep (film could be rolled in daylight), and even more straightforward to develop (Kodak processed the pictures for its customers). These factors made this camera extremely popular; in 1900 alone, Eastman Kodak Company sold more than 250,000 Brownie cameras (Gustavson 2011).

Nearly every bucketful of dirt at the site offered a mixture of intriguing artifacts, each of which had its own production history and distinct use in Harrison's life. On a single afternoon of digging in June of 2006, students working in different areas of the cabin uncovered within minutes of each other a plastic comb for personal grooming, a metal file for sharpening tools, and a small glass sherd from a thermometer. The comb was celluloid, the first plastic of the 1800s, and was a cheap and mass-produced imitation of the expensive and fashionable tortoise shell combs of the late nineteenth century.[37] The foot-long iron file and its double-cut teeth were nearly identical to twenty-first-century tools serving the same sharpening purpose. The fragmented mercury-in-glass thermometer tube registered temperature gradients for assessing the weather, personal health, and cooking practices. These three artifacts presumably reflected Harrison's everyday concerns regarding his appearance, ability to work efficiently, and the temperature—not too different from many of our own primary interests—yet could be purchased in the 1897 *Sears Roebuck & Co. Catalogue* for 15 cents (the comb), 17 cents (the file), and 20 cents (the thermometer) respectively.[38] While they cross-cut different spheres of his life—personal, industrial, household—these items were found within a few feet of each other, mixed in with the fallen debris of his cabin.

Although there is no consensus in historical archaeology as to standardizing functional artifact-classification systems, most projects employ a technique that focuses on generalized past behavioral spheres and activities. Archaeologists enter artifacts into their computerized catalogs on an individual basis, but also usually group them into a series of categories that can be broken down into smaller subcategories. For example, in the work discussed here the major heading of "Domestic" includes "Consumer Items," "Kitchen Items," and "Household Goods"; "Personal" contains "Garments," "Individualized Goods," and "Coinage"; "Architecture" subsumes "Building Materials" and "Hardware; and "Work" covers "Tools," "Machinery," "Munitions," "Livery Items," and many others. Each subcategory contains a long list of individual mini artifact classes as well (e.g., "Consumer Items" contains "Bottles," "Jars," "Tin cans," etc.).

There is an inherent paradox to cataloging a site's artifacts. On the one hand, it is best to have mutually exclusive categories to avoid items being double counted; on the other, singular items were often used for different purposes and in distinct activities. For example, was an alcohol bottle reflective of food, medicine, or socializing? There is no easy answer, nor does there need to be. An inclusive approach can allow for multiple interpretations and does not insist on mutually exclusive frameworks while still appreciating the cumulative power of archaeological research. It starts with standardized frameworks when possible in order to facilitate meaningful inter-site comparisons (alcohol is initially counted as a "consumer item") but uses these systems only as the beginning of the interpretive process.

The link between individual artifact and meaning is as precarious as the tie between assemblage pattern and identity. The field of historical archaeology is rife with impassioned debates regarding the practice of identifying specialized artifacts as markers of ethnic identity or using artifact scales of value to assign socioeconomic terms. As the following pages show, singular measures often fail to appreciate the fluidity of individual identity, the dynamism of group membership, or the complexity of wealth. Assemblage-wide patterns that are measured through multiple lines of material evidence with careful attention to historical and archaeological context can help to broaden reductionist practices (Lightfoot, Martinez, and Schiff, 1998: 201).

Traditional activity spheres are important for site comparisons even if some information is lost in the process of creating categories that inherently reduce variation or do not allow for multiple uses of a single item. Though there were individual exceptions, an overwhelming percentage of the artifacts found at the Nathan Harrison site fit easily into the aforementioned broad categories of domestic, personal, work, architectural, and other.[39] Furthermore, the relative number of items in each of these groupings could be compared to other sites across space and time.

Domestic Goods

Domestic goods dominated the Harrison site assemblage. Within this pattern, however, were telling imbalances. For example, the site's containers were predominantly metal cans, glass bottles, and jelly jars; there were few ceramic vessels and minimal utensils. The bottles were extensive; a wide majority were for beverages, and many of those were specifically designed to hold alcohol. Sauce bottles were almost nonexistent at the site. The jelly jars, used for preserving and storing various fruit and vegetable mixes, were distinctive in that many were part of the same matching set. Conversely, Harrison's cutlery, plates, and cups were a disjointed set of unmatched forms.

Cans

An overwhelming majority of the hundreds of metal meat and seafood cans uncovered at the site were located in the primary dumping area of the property, just to the southwest of the hillside cabin (Figure 3.14). The distinctive form of these containers revealed the contents of the cans. For example, oblong cans were primarily reserved for seafood,

Figure 3.14. Student archaeologists meticulously excavate in the midden area of the site, which contained an extensive variety of meat and tobacco cans, animal bones, and other remains. (Courtesy of the Nathan "Nate" Harrison Historical Archaeology Project.)

and tapered rectangular cans usually contained corned beef. Lid types were also especially insightful as removable lids and pry lids typically held dry goods like coffee, baking powder, and tobacco; key-wind tins were reserved for meat and seafood; and puncture marks reflected liquid contents. In many instances, excavators recovered the can, lid, and opening apparatus together. For example, over a dozen sardine-can keys were uncovered with the metal lid coiled tightly around them, some still partially attached to the original tins.

Can-production technology changed regularly over time so that nuances on individual tins, especially in terms of how they were sealed, often detailed a specific decade in which the containers were produced. Though artisans in the Middle Ages developed the earliest tin-plated cans, commercial canning did not become widespread until the early nineteenth century in Western Europe and grew out of colonial and military necessity.[40] Despite various advances, can-making was slow and can-failure was common. It was not until the late nineteenth and early twentieth centuries that sanitary cans with an airtight seal were perfected. Can makers first developed a rubber gasket, then a rubber and gum-sealing compound, and finally a double seam with an enamel to prevent chemical reactions between the food and the metal. Fortunately for archaeologists, each of these techniques resulted in a distinctly different and easily datable can seam and lid.

The most commonly found metal container at the site was the sardine can. Sardines were not an individual species of fish but a general term for all small, young, silvery, oily-fleshed fish whose heads, tails and innards had been removed prior to canning. Most were commonly stored in oil, water, tomato, or mustard sauces. Sardine cans were typically packaged with a key made out of a distinctive long metal wire that served to wind up the lid of the can. Primarily a European industry until the early twentieth century, large-scale sardine-canning did not take hold in the US until 1875 and did not have a West Coast presence before 1889 (Jarvis 1988). Furthermore, California sardine companies quickly turned their attention to far more lucrative tuna fishing in the early 1900s (Ueber and MacCall 1992). However, the start of World War I (1914) had an immediate impact on domestic fishing industries as war-ravaged European nations were unable to keep sardine production centers running, and the US government offered financial incentives for American canneries to increase sardine production for soldiers fighting overseas (Jarvis 1988). By the middle 1910s, the federal government had become the largest buyer of California sardines.[41]

During the early decades of the California sardine industry, three coastal locales dominated production: Monterey, San Pedro (in Los Angeles), and San Diego. Since sardine fishing was more regionally focused and did not require extended voyages, the catch was tied to local environmental factors[42] and distinct technologies used by different immigrant fishermen.[43] The result was that the sardine cans came in different sizes based on the type of pack: there were one-pound cans, half-pound cans, and regular (packed in cottonseed oil) and fancy (packed in olive oil) quarter-pound cans. Regardless of size, sardines were still a cheap, protein-rich food option for working-class Americans; one-pounders sold for only 10 cents.[44] Most California sardine cans were one-pounders, and this type made up over 97 percent of Monterey's pack (Ueber and MacCall 1992). Likewise, San Pedro produced a mere 7 percent of their pack in quarter-pound cans (Ueber and MacCall 1992). These figures made it most probable that Harrison's sardine cans—of which 95 percent were quarter oils—came from San Diego, which strongly suggested they were produced during the 1900s and especially the 1910s. Thus, although Harrison's diet included sardines produced and packaged in San Diego, his plentiful seafood meals were a reflection of globalizing markets, massive military conflicts of the time, regional environmental factors, and local production nuances.

Excavators also unearthed over a dozen tapered corned beef tins in the primary refuse area of the site. The lids on these vessels contained hole-in-cap closures (one end of the tin had a centered pinhole vent to allow steam to escape; once cooled, a circular lid was soldered into place above the vent), and the walls were crimped as opposed to hand-soldered. Furthermore, many cans showed evidence of a scored strip below the lid that was rolled away with a metal key (Snodgrass 2004). These two factors—the hole-in-cap lid and the key-wind strip—dated these corned beef tins between 1895 and 1911. Though beef consumption was a sign of wealth and aristocracy in Europe and reserved for consumption by hoi polloi only during major holidays, in the US corned beef was cheap and widely distributed in the late 1800s and early 1900s (Mac Con Iomaire and Gallagher 2011).

Many of the metal cans recovered from the site were seemingly tied to Harrison's historically documented culinary skills. Excavators found multiple lids to baking powder tins, including one from the KC Baking Powder Company and another from the Royal Baking Powder Company. These companies were at the epicenter of the "Baking Powder wars" of the late nineteenth and early twentieth centuries (Morrison 1907). During this time, rival baking powder producers attacked one another in negative advertisement campaigns portraying others' products as unsafe (Reisert 2018). Traditionalists like the KC Baking Powder Company and Royal Baking Powder Company insisted on using cream of tartar in their products; they were outraged over the rise of upstart companies using aluminum phosphate and even lobbied Congress for a law banning the chemical on the grounds it was allegedly poisonous, dangerous to the stomach, and a cause of malarial outbreaks (Morrison 1907). None of these claims were true. Furthermore, the Royal Baking Powder Company's ire at its rivals seemed to have more to do with the fact that it controlled the industry's cream of tartar supply than any genuine public health concerns (Reisert 2018). Excavators also recovered an assortment of condensed and evaporated milk cans from the Harrison site; the condensed milk cans were identifiable by their hole-in-cap closures, crimped side seams, and lack of lid embossing (1883–1911), and the evaporated milk cans had hole-in-top or vent-hole cans sealed with a spot of lead and crimped side seams (1903–11).

Jars

Though the Harrison site was typified by mismatching vessels, one type of container was found in consistent forms and patterns across the site and especially in the main patio area: canning jars. Excavators found at least eight jelly jars, including one fully intact vessel still capped with an iron lid. These short jars were less than 4" tall and 3" in diameter and maintained a consistent pattern of fine vertical lines repeated in close formation around the sides of the vessels. Jars like these appeared in the 1898 *Sears Roebuck & Co. Catalogue* and were primarily used for food storage. The prevalence of canning jars at the site corroborated local Fred Axe's observation that during this time: "Everyone . . . canned foods" (email from Fred Axe to author, 21 February 2005). Archaeologist Bonnie J. Clark commented on the general all-or-nothing approach to canning at rural sites, noting that, "The knowledge and investment involved in canning typically means you do not dabble in canning; you either do it or not" (Clark 2005: 446). The site's artifacts suggested that, when it came to canning, Harrison was an active participant in the labor-intensive endeavor.

Bottles

Glass bottles dominated the artifact assemblage at the Harrison site, with sherds from 140 different vessels strewn across the site but most prominently in the main patio area just to the west of the cabin. The production process of many of these bottles left tell-tale clues on the vessels. For example, far-reaching seams revealing that they were machine made, and certain Owens marks on the bottle base indicated an early twentieth-century production. As a whole the bottles dated from

1880–1920, although most seemed to cluster toward the first two decades of the 1900s. Only a few of the bottles were embossed with the name of the manufacturer or contents of the vessel. Most of those were alcohol products.

The alcohol bottles found at the site had little in common with each other; they were of different distilled spirits and originated in a wide variety of countries. For example, the Gordon's Dry Gin bottle (1880–1920) came from England, a Schlesinger & Bender brandy bottle (1890–1915) was produced in San Francisco, a McBrayer Bourbon bottle foil was from Kentucky, and the unique eight-sided Schutzen Strasse Number 9 German liquor bottle (1876–1920) was from Berlin, Germany.[45] These embossed alcohol bottles were mismatched but likely a subset of a much larger liquor assemblage that included many unmarked vessels.

Of the many dozens of bottles recovered from the Harrison site, the contents of only one were undeniably not consumed by occupants of the site. Excavators uncovered a complete Welch's Grape Juice bottle in the northwestern corner of the patio; the bottle was fully intact, included an affixed metal cap, and contained a white powdery residue that was clearly the remnants of the sugary grape juice that slowly leaked out of the bottle during its time in the ground (Figure 3.15). The machine-made bottle has an Owens mark and the glass was slightly iridescent, indicating that it dated between 1904 and 1920.

Figure 3.15. Since the lid was still affixed to the Welch's Grape Juice bottle (*right*) and the interior contained extensive sugar crystals, it was easy to tell that the beverage within had never been consumed. (Courtesy of the Nathan "Nate" Harrison Historical Archaeology Project.)

Welch's Grape Juice was more than a simple sugary beverage at the turn of the twentieth century; it was a key symbol and tool in the prohibitionist strategy that would succeed in 1920. Dr. Thomas B. Welch, founder of Welch's Grape Juice, began producing the beverage in 1869 as a nonalcoholic alternative to wine used in church for Communion (Fucini and Fucini 1985). Welch, a teetotaling dentist and former ministry student from Vineland, New Jersey,[46] was adamantly opposed to intoxicating beverages and outraged that devout individuals such as himself were forced to imbibe every Sunday. As a result, he came up with a fermentation-interrupting technique that involved boiling bottles of grape juice, thereby killing the yeast with heat (Hallett and Hallett 1997). Welch was further infuriated when church elders rejected his new creation, "Dr. Welch's Unfermented Wine," as a nonalcoholic substitute for sacramental rituals (Fucini and Fucini 1985). He channeled this frustration into a temperance crusade; Welch appointed himself guardian and prosecutor of Vineland's dry law and also championed crusades against neighboring towns until they buckled to prohibitionist pressures (Hallett and Hallett 1997). Welch's son Charles, also a dentist, was the one responsible for the highly successful commercialization of his father's beverage; he removed the name "wine" from the product, gave out free samples at the 1893 Columbian Exposition in Chicago to millions of world's fair visitors, and spearheaded an extensive national advertising campaign in prominent magazines (Fucini and Fucini 1985). Early twentieth-century ads for Welch's Grape Juice combined two prominent contemporary marketing themes, temperance and healing elixirs. They tapped into rising prohibitionist sentiments and simultaneously assured consumers that the beverage cured pneumonia, typhoid fever, and tuberculosis. Though Thomas Welch died over a decade before Prohibition was enacted on a national level, his beverage contributed to the successful temperance movement, and his family reaped highly lucrative results stemming from the 1919 passage of the Eighteenth Amendment.

At first glance, the historical records clearly seemed to indicate that Harrison would have been diametrically opposed to Thomas Welch's prohibitionist crusade. Numerous accounts emphasized Harrison's regular consumption and enjoyment of alcoholic beverages. Furthermore, a collective look at historically verified goods brought to the Harrison cabin underscored that visitors routinely brought him alcohol. It was worth noting, however, that Nathan Harrison's son-in-law, Fred Smith, resided in a temperance colony during the 1870s and '80s. Westminster inhabitants even refused to grow grapes during the last quarter of the nineteenth century for fear they would be used in wine production.

Perhaps Smith was a teetotaler who was encouraging Harrison to try nonalcoholic beverages, especially considering the impending restrictions of Prohibition.[47]

Ceramics

Amongst the thousands of metal can fragments and glass sherds were pieces of only fourteen ceramic vessels (Figure 3.16). For a field like historical archaeology whose practitioners have privileged ceramic analyses for much of its existence, the Harrison site is enigmatic. Ceramics seemed to be of minimal priority to occupants and visitors to the Harrison cabin; even his many pipes—of which over a dozen were found—were made of rubber, not ceramic. In total, excavators recovered pieces of a large pitcher, a common bowl, a cooking bowl, an ornate plate, a delicate tea cup, a miniature toy teacup, a creamer, and multiple sturdy coffee mugs and saucers. These mismatched vessels collectively dated

Figure 3.16. The ceramic assemblage, a traditional favorite of historical archaeologists, was minimal at the Harrison site—shown in its entirety here—and represented only about one-thousandth of the collection. (Courtesy of the Nathan "Nate" Harrison Historical Archaeology Project.)

from 1865–1910, and all but one were found strewn across the cabin, patio, and refuse area. Collectively, these ceramics were durable and cheap, especially in comparison to contemporaneous trend-setting porcelains. This minimalist assemblage seemed to reflect a lone primary inhabitant with occasional visitors.

The large undecorated pitcher was distinctive for three reasons. First, at 9" tall and 5" in diameter, it was the largest ceramic vessel found at the site. Second, it was the only pitcher and the lone form for communal consumption as opposed to an individualized serving. Third, it was the only ceramic vessel found predominantly inside of the cabin, suggesting specialized use. This plain Ironstone pitcher[48] had a maker's mark on its base belonging to William Adams of Tunstall, England,[49] under the royal arms mark;[50] this particular stamp had a limited length of use, dating from 1850–65.

The site also contained fragments of two transferware ceramics, a Flow Blue plate and a nonmatching teacup. Transferware, also an affordable and popular English alternative to expensive Chinese porcelain, was produced through a technique that involved applying intricately decorated paper patterns (stencils) to unfired ceramics (blanks), which were then glazed and fired to create the desired pattern. "Flow Blue" was a blue and white pattern named after the blurring or "flowing" of the cobalt blue glaze during the firing process. The particular Flow Blue vessel found at the Harrison site was a small plate, known as a butter pat; the pattern was the Ridgway Company's "Lonsdale," which dated to circa 1910. Both the form (small butter pat) and style (floral) were outdated when Harrison used the vessel, as bigger butter plates became the norm in the early 1900s and floral patterns had been replaced by Japanese and Art Nouveau designs. The second transferware vessel was a delicate teacup with a pattern of brown leaves and green flowers.

Most of the remaining ceramics from the site were related to beverage consumption. They consisted of a whiteware creamer with the Homer Laughlin China Co. backstamp, five Hotelware vessels (three mugs and two saucers, none of which matched), and an unidentifiable mug, teacup, and toy teacup. The Homer Laughlin China Co. mark was highly symbolic—an American eagle on top of a British lion (1875–1904)—and it reflected the US company's ambitious desire to compete with dominant English pottery producers of the late 1800s and early 1900s. While American brothers Homer and Shakespeare Laughlin sought to best their elite European competition, producers of Hotelware went after an untapped market, that of the mass-produced, cheap, durable, and easily cleaned institutional ceramic. Tailored for hotels, restaurants, hospitals, ships, trains, schools, and the military due to the pottery's highly vitreous surfaces and dearth of decorations or creases, these vessels were the pinnacle of functionality in both production (standardized and streamlined one-piece manufacturing process) and use.

The overall ceramic assemblage was mismatched, highly utilitarian, cheap, and slightly outdated. Archaeologists have been able to determine the cost of an assemblage by comparing what was commonly available at the time commercially with what was recovered through excavation. In locating prices in catalogs for certain wares and placing them on a price scale versus all other ceramics in the catalogs, they can quantify the economic value of the assemblage and compare it to other sites for status measures. George Miller developed the first of the economic indices for historical ceramics, and Susan Henry expanded Miller's work to include values for pottery from the late nineteenth and early twentieth centuries (Miller 1980; Henry 1987). Henry's values ranged from 1.0 (least inexpensive) to 4.0 (most expensive), and the Harrison assemblage fell decidedly toward the cheapest measures possible with a score of 1.50.

The Harrison ceramics were typified by four factors: 1) relatively few vessels, 2) mismatched vessels, 3) a variety of forms, and 4) dominated by tea ware. The ironstone pitcher was clearly an item of value for Nathan Harrison; it was spatially distinct and tied directly to his primary means of social and economic engagement with visitors—water production, delivery, and consumption. Nevertheless, the overwhelming majority of the ceramics made up an oddly mixed tea assemblage. In Chapter Two, I invoked an *Alice in Wonderland* metaphor when describing the rite of passage of visiting Palomar Mountain and the liminality one experienced in meeting Nathan Harrison in all of his titillating social reversals. Perhaps Lewis Carroll's famed tale had far more literal interpretive relevance for Harrison's ceramic assemblage. Multiple historical photographs depicted Harrison having picnics with guests of all ages. Like the Mad Hatter, perhaps Harrison hosted a slightly disheveled yet enduring tea party for his guests who trekked up the precipitous mountain (instead of down the rabbit hole).[51]

Utensils

Eating and serving utensils found at the Harrison site mirrored the ceramic assemblage. Few were found—three forks, five spoons, two cork screws, and two can openers—and those that were uncovered were wildly mismatched in terms of form, design, and material. Some were ornate and silver-plated, and others were entirely undecorated and uncoated metal. In fact, the fanciest of the bunch were *not* products from the famed Rogers Brothers Company, the premiere silver-plated ware producer of the nineteenth century. Instead, they were imitations. The 1898 *Sears Roebuck & Co. Catalogue* contained the following warning for consumers: "Do not be deceived by allowing any dealer to sell you any other Rogers' goods, claiming that they are the same or as good. These goods are all stamped 'Rogers Bros. 1847' and no goods without that stamp are genuine." Like the ceramics, even the seemingly ornate utensils often had a backstory that revealed them to be off-brands, outdated, derivative, or in some other way less valuable.

Faunal Remains

Animal bones were extremely prevalent at the Harrison site; in fact, excavators uncovered 10,472 faunal remains—nearly a fifth of the entire assemblage—during the first seven archaeological field seasons. These artifacts included the remains of domestic sheep (*Ovis aries*), pig (*Sus*), cow (*Bos taurus*), mule deer (*Odocoilus hemionus*), chicken (*Gallus gallus*), dog (*Canis*), bobcat (*Lynx linx*), and an assortment of rodents including squirrel, rat, and chipmunk. Kristin Tennesen detailed how these bones contained a wealth of unique insight into the diet of those residing at and visiting the Harrison site (2010). Four criteria in particular were instrumental in assessing dominant food preparation and consumption practices. These were: 1) the quantity of each animal species represented in the faunal assemblage, 2) the presence of butchering marks on the bones, 3) the number of each identifiable body-part element per species, and 4) the age of the animal at its time of death. The exact quantity of each species helped to establish which animals had more dietary significance to Harrison. Identification of butchering marks ensured that slaughtered animals were not accidentally combined with the remains of scavengers that died at the site but were never eaten by humans. The ratio of skeletal parts could be insightful when attempting to identify possible factors reflecting status and ethnicity as bone-element frequency could indicate meal choice and quality. Whereas high-quality elements, like long bones, were rich in animal flesh; low-quality elements had little meat but could be used in stews to add fat and flavor. Furthermore, Mexican cooking traditions used crania (cow, sheep, and pig) far more frequently than Anglo-American recipes (Clark 2005: 445). Patterns in faunal assemblages regarding the age of death for particular animals suggested additional priorities for site inhabitants beyond immediate feeding. For example, collections that featured herd animals slaughtered at an advanced age, beyond breeding years, revealed that certain animals were only eaten once they were no longer used to increase the size of the herd.

The patterns in the faunal assemblage from the Harrison site were not subtle; furthermore, they showed daily life activities beyond eating. Sheep bones dominated the collection (Figure 3.17). There were remains from at least fifteen different sheep, which was over seven times more than any other species. Furthermore, there were ample butchering marks—from hatchets, knives, and saws—on dozens of sheep bones; it was clear that these animals did not die of natural causes and were slaughtered for consumption. The archaeological evidence revealed that a majority of the sheep were slaughtered over the age of 3½, suggesting a deliberate and strategic delay until wool diminishment occurred.[52] Furthermore, equal representation of wholesale versus non-wholesale cuts of meat suggested that all parts of the sheep were being processed or used at the site.[53] This intimated that the animal was butchered on site as opposed to being slaughtered elsewhere with only certain cuts being brought back to the Harrison cabin. All of these factors pointed to the prominence of sheep in Harrison's diet as well as its potential role as part of a cottage industry that included the production of wool and related sheepskin commodities.

Figure 3.17. Sheep remains, like the mandible (lower jaw) here, underneath a Prince Albert tobacco can, dominated the faunal assemblage. (Courtesy of the Nathan "Nate" Harrison Historical Archaeology Project.)

Apart from the sheep, no other animal species exhibited the same pattern of dietary prominence and specialized cultivation in the artifact assemblage. The site included bones from at least four different cows, but most were young cattle under the age of four. This strongly suggested that Harrison did not keep, breed, butcher, or trade cattle. Even though there was relatively equal body-part representation, the few specimens and young average age of death, indicated that the beef present at the site was likely brought to the cabin after it had been slaughtered. Likewise, the minimal number of pig (2), deer (1), and chicken (1) specimens, although butchered at an advanced age and of equal body-part representation, suggested that these animals played only a small role in Harrison's diet. Nonetheless, every butchered animal present in the archaeological assemblage showed equal body-part representation. At other sites, this lack of exclusively high-quality elements has been correlated with lower status (Brandon 2009). In addition, the dog (1), bobcat (1), and rodents did not show signs of butchering and were likely pets and scavengers in and around the Harrison refuse area to the southwest of the cabin patio.

While it was tempting to identify the low-quality elements with lower status, a broader investigation of faunal material at archaeological sites across San Diego showed that the augmentation of low-quality domesticated elements with wild fauna was common in rural areas of the county, regardless of wealth (Droessler 2015: 177). Most non-urban sites from this time period also had evidence of diverse on-site butchering, with a variety of cut marks (Droessler 2015: 177). The Harrison site followed this pattern with extensive examples of chop, saw, and knife butchering marks on the site's faunal remains (Tennesen 2010: 39). A final factor that linked the Harrison site with typical rural sites was the general dearth of faunal material; overall, urban sites have many more faunal remains and a much higher percentage in their assemblages (Christenson 1996a: 326).

Many of the particular animal species found at the Nathan Harrison site were greatly impacted by cultural, economic, and environmental factors of late nineteenth-century rural San Diego County. California's cattle boom of the 1850s and '60s was devastated not only by draught but also a pronounced shift from ranching to agriculture and the overall economic downturn (Burcham 1982: 129). The region's sheep population swelled in the 1870s and '80s with the sharp rise in wool prices and the ability of Southern Californians—thanks to the moderate climate—to shear their flocks twice a year (Towne and Wentworth 1946). Even the first line of the region's most iconic book, Helen Hunt Jackson's 1884 *Ramona*, proclaimed, "IT was sheep-shearing time in Southern California. . . ." However, reductions in grazing areas due to expansions in agriculture and plummeting wool prices curtailed the sheep industry by 1890. Although Spanish and Mexican ranchers had long used pigs for home consumption, attention turned to pork production in Anglo-American communities at the end of the nineteenth century (Szuter 1991). While pigs required little land—which was of significant importance with expanding agriculture—pork products were high in fat, did not dry well, and spoiled quickly without refrigeration; as a result, hog raising as a local industry failed to take hold for any lengthy duration (Szuter 1991). In addition, San Diego County's poultry production grew during the last quarter of the 1800s but did not become a lucrative business until the 1910s (Christenson 1996b: B-33; Simons 1980).

Overall, the domestic goods found at the site shed numerous insights into Harrison's daily life. The many items tied to contemporary foodways revealed a diverse diet that included ample protein (canned meat and seafood and domesticated fauna, especially sheep), and wild fauna (deer), carbohydrates (baked goods), and sugars (fruits). Furthermore, Harrison clearly augmented consumption of his ample water supply with regular alcoholic beverages. The goods brought to the hillside homestead varied greatly in origin; some were produced locally, and others came from across the globe. In general, the site's material culture that tied to domestic life was highly mismatched. Archaeologist Mark Walker interpreted this sort of evidence at multiple nineteenth- and early twentieth-century sites in Butte County, California, as the result of a transient population (2017: 103–5).[54] However, it has been well established that Harrison was not transient at this site, in fact, just the opposite was true. He was a fixture on the property for decades. However, the artifacts at the site likely reflected the temporary nature of his visitors who brought these goods to the site. The many tourists who flocked to Palomar Mountain during the late nineteenth and early twentieth centuries were highly transient, visiting for mere hours before continuing up the grade. Individual guests brought Harrison goods as gifts and often left items behind, but obviously it was unlikely that these items would match the materials associated with the next set of visitors.

Personal Goods

There is great overlap between items that archaeologists consider "domestic" and "personal," even though these categories were designed to be exclusive. Regardless of semantic debates regarding domesticity and personhood, the latter traditionally consists of clothing, jewelry, items related to grooming and health, social drugs, currency, writing materials, game pieces, and other miscellaneous goods. They focus less on foodways and more on individual and non-consumptive activities.

The Harrison site teemed with remains from his wardrobe. Although none of the fabric survived the test of time, archaeologists uncovered hundreds of clothing fasteners in the form of buttons, rivets, snaps, and clips. Many of the fasteners were nondescript and utilitarian, but some were highly specialized, intricately marked by their producers, and ornate. As a group, the large quantity of clothing-related artifacts underscored Harrison's lengthy occupation at the site, the importance of rugged outerwear in the mountain environment, and certain nuances of exchange between visitors and the site's primary inhabitant.

Buttons

The Harrison site assemblage included 223 buttons, greatly outnumbering traditionally artifact-rich categories from historical sites, like pottery and pipestems. These tiny circular pierced items varied in material and included specimens of wood, bone, composition, shell, porcelain, and metal (Figure 3.18). Although buttons began as early as the sixth century AD, based on dating across the globe, they surged in popularity during the late 1800s due to contemporary fashion trends and mechanization that facilitated mass production (Peacock 2009: 7). These factors led to great changes in button material culture during the late nineteenth and early twentieth centuries; traditional handmade wood, shell, and bone specimens were quickly replaced by molded composition, porcelain, and plastic forms (Hughes 1981: xxii). Whereas some of the buttons, like those made of cloth, had long production ranges, many were made only for a few decades at a time, meaning that they were especially helpful in pinpointing the exact chronology of the Harrison site. For example, one of the two bone buttons in the assemblage had four holes and a lethe (a circular depression in the center), which dated it between 1800 and 1865.[55] Furthermore, an aluminum button found at the site was embossed with a particular "USA" logo, revealing that it had first been sown onto Krieger, Frankel Company Incorporated Marine Corps/Army pants, which were primarily in use from 28 July 1914 through 11 November 1918.

Each of the button types at the Harrison site had numerous informative intricacies, a cross-section of which is discussed here. Nearly all of the wooden buttons were found inside of the cabin, likely resulting from the fact that these soft items deteriorated rapidly when exposed to

Figure 3.18. The massive collection of buttons at the site was one of the biggest surprises of the assemblage. (Courtesy of the Nathan "Nate" Harrison Historical Archaeology Project.)

exterior elements, especially water. The bone buttons, due to their utilitarian design and lack of carving and inlays, likely fastened underwear. Half of the site's twelve composition buttons, made from wood shavings, glue, powdered metal, shellac, and any other leftover materials on the factory floor, were produced in early twentieth-century whistle molds—with two holes in back and one in front—that were designed to save thread. Furthermore, even though freshwater shells from the Mississippi River accounted for half of the shell-button market in the 1890s, many of the forty-nine shell buttons from the Harrison site appear to be made from Southern California abalone, clam, and California mussel due to the color, size, and flakiness of the specimens. Porcelain buttons, of which there were twenty-six from the site, were made of hard-paste kaolinite fired so hot that the resultant rock-hard specimens regularly outlasted the clothes they adorned.[56] Nineteenth-century metal button production reflected international political tensions; when the US Congress declared war against England (the War of 1812), the US demand for military uniforms—with strong metal buttons to keep them properly affixed—surged just as trade was cut off with one of the world's primary metal button producers (the British). As a result, entrepreneurial American button makers, like Connecticut's Aaron Benedict, "bought up every brass pot, pan and kettle he could find, established a rolling mill outside of Waterbury and began making buttons" (Pearsall 1997).

When analyzing the button assemblage along classic archaeological dimensions, a clear pattern emerged. In terms of different uses of space at the site, archaeologists found historical buttons in every area, but the southwestern corner of the cabin contained the most. This area seemed to be an area of special significance with many one-of-a-kind items for Harrison; it also contained a majority of the ironstone pitcher, a skeleton key, picture-frame glass, and a sharpened pencil lead. Temporally, individual specimens dated the site to 1865–1914. This range was further bolstered by the lack of brass buttons, which stopped being widely produced in the 1860s.[57] The site's buttons themselves provided an independent chronology corroborated by entirely separate and highly diverse lines of evidence, including ceramics, headstamps on fired rifle cartridges, and historical censuses.

The inauspicious button has been the center of much debate in historical archaeology, especially at sites with a tie to African American heritage. Depending on context, they have been interpreted as items with a symbolic link to African culture, counters for economic transactions, salvageable goods that could be reused, components of a religious cache, or conspicuous ornamentation (Wilkie 2000: 155–57). Furthermore, the mismatched nature of the buttons—especially wood, bone, and composition—found at the Harrison site, likely reflected the site's visitors. Items of clothing were standard offerings made by tourists and friends alike.

Rivets

Excavators also uncovered nearly one hundred rivets, which were metal fasteners designed to increase the resilience of work clothes, especially denim jean pants and overalls. In the mid-nineteenth century, tailor Jacob Davis invented the first jean rivets after a laborer's wife asked Davis if he could make her husband's pants more durable. This request gave Davis the idea to place metal rivets at the highest parts of strain on the pants. Davis partnered on this endeavor with Levi Strauss, a dry goods merchant who sold Davis the cloth that he tailored. On 9 August 1872, Davis successfully submitted his "Improvement in fastening pocket-openings" invention to the US Patent and Trademark Office. Although most of the Harrison site's unearthed rivets were unmarked, illegible, or completely corroded by rust, a handful retained manufacture markings, such as "L.S. & CO SF" (Levi Strauss and Company, San Francisco: 1890–1928), "B.N. & L. L.A." (Brownstein, Newmark, and Louis Company in Los Angeles: 1897–1911), "C G & CO" (C. G. Hussey & Company in Pittsburgh: 1848–1930), and "Cones' Boss" (C. B. Cones & Son Manufacturing Company: 1879–1930).

Other Fasteners

Not all of the clothing fasteners were utilitarian; in fact, some were ornate. This included a set of suspender clips and a garter for hosiery (Figure 3.19). Excavators uncovered numerous suspender parts, including four complete clips stamped with the word "PRESIDENT" on the front and back of each. The 1902 *Sears Roebuck & Co. Catalogue* sold these stylish amenities for $5.40/dozen and emphasized they were "high-grade" and "fancy" materials. Furthermore, the catalog insisted that, "Every pair [was] warranted to wear to the entire satisfaction of the purchaser." Multiple historical photographs of Harrison depicted him wearing overalls with suspender clips; a few of the images were perfect matches with the presidential clips.

Figure 3.19. The Harrison site assemblage included numerous remains from President-brand suspenders (*top center*), two nickel-plated sock garters (*left center*), other cheaper suspenders (*right*), and even fragments from two safety pins (*bottom left*). (Courtesy of the Nathan "Nate" Harrison Historical Archaeology Project.)

Perhaps most ornate of all the clothing items found at the site were two gilded nickel garter clasps used for hosiery; they had a loop for attaching a button, as well as a hinged clasp on the top of the loop. Engraved on both sides with "BOSTON GARTER," "VELVET GRIP," and multiple nineteenth-century patent dates, these "non-rustable" clasps were designed to attach socks to a calf-garter or knee-length undergarments (O. Stone 1930). A Velvet Grip advertisement from the 1910s emphasized that hose supporters were used by both sexes and people of all ages; they continued to be popular through the 1940s (O. Stone 1930). Boston Garter made clasps from 1898 to 1940, but this particular style was made only from 1905 to 1915.

Footwear

These elegant clothing fasteners were mixed in with numerous everyday utilitarian items. Although it was easy to fall into the trap of assigning low-status artifacts to Harrison and any and all high-status goods to his visitors, the artifact assemblage revealed that this would be a faulty assumption. In fact, the blend of high-value items among the numerous ordinary goods was seen throughout nearly every artifact type. Whereas individual ownership of certain items at the site was debatable, the intact shoes excavated at the site clearly demonstrated ownership by two different individuals. Excavators uncovered two nearly complete shoes, but they were of markedly different sizes. The first measured 9" in length and was complete, including its iron shank, except for the front upper portion and the tongue. Close examination of many of the historical photographs of Harrison reveals that this shoe was strikingly similar to the footwear worn by Harrison during his time on the mountain. In addition, the smallness of the shoe corresponded with Harrison's diminutive stature in the old photos and his recorded height of 5' 3" on the 1894 voting registration form. On the contrary, the second nearly complete shoe was 12" long. Obviously, it was highly likely that someone other than Harrison wore this footwear. Perhaps it belonged to Cubby, the Doane's short-term servant, whose feet were purportedly exactly a foot in length.

Jewelry

The jewelry found at the site had a direct tie to the local Indigenous population. For example, excavators uncovered a small iron cross and a green-stone pendant (Figure 3.20). The cross, though highly deteriorated, measured nearly an inch in length and was likely worn on a

Figure 3.20. The green-stone pendant and iron cross likely reflected Harrison's connections with the local Indigenous population. (Courtesy of the Nathan "Nate" Harrison Historical Archaeology Project.)

cord as a pendant. This artifact was the only explicit material link to the historical accounts of Rincon chief Juan Sotelo Calac and his wife Encarnacion baptizing Harrison, and of Harrison's occasional attendance of mass at Pala (Day and Melvin 1981: no page numbers). Excavators also unearthed a small (1.5" long and 0.4" in diameter) pierced cylindrical stone pendant. Made of a local garnet-baring green stone, this type of pendant was commonly used by the Luiseño for ornamentation on clothing or as necklace jewelry. Neither piece of hanging jewelry found at the site was ever mentioned in the secondary narratives or evident in any photographs. Nevertheless, they seemed to reflect Harrison's close affiliation with nearby Indigenous communities.

Projectile Points

There was an important contradiction in the Indigenous artifacts found at the site. Few items were found, but those recovered seemed to be more than everyday materials. As discussed earlier, the only portable metate found during survey and excavations was the halved stone that was found in close association with the cabin. In addition, apart from two complete projectile points, excavators did not unearth any chipped stone or other debitage from arrowhead production. One of the projectile points recovered was a basalt Cottonwood triangular point with serrated edges and a concave base. The other was a quartz crystal Poway serrated point. Both of these styles of points have typically been associated with the Luiseño and other nearby Indigenous groups before and after contact (Moratto 1984: 154). The Cottonwood point had no fractures, which suggested that it had never been fired. The Poway point had been reworked, indicating that it had likely been fractured by use and then retooled for additional use. Archaeologists at other artifact-rich sites across the country have identified patterns suggesting that unbroken and reworked projectile points were gifts, whereas broken points were deemed to be the result of hunting or combat (Blanton, Deitrick, and Bartels 2001: 5). Likewise, the distinctiveness and condition of the projectile points found in and around the Harrison cabin hinted at special significance, perhaps ceremonial, symbolic, and gift-based (Mallios 2006a).

Time-Related Artifacts

The photographs of Harrison regularly depicted him wearing a watch fob affixed to his shirt or jacket but never captured the timepiece itself. Not only did excavators find one of his watch chains, they also uncovered a polished metal watch case (Figure 3.21). While it was tempting to define the watch and fob as jewelry exclusively because of their promi-

Figure 3.21. Time-related artifacts abounded at the site as student excavators found (*clockwise from top*): five alarm-clock gears, two watch fobs, a watch case, a central watch component, an alarm-clock key, an alarm-clock backplate, and even a hand from the alarm clock. (Courtesy of the Nathan "Nate" Harrison Historical Archaeology Project.)

nence in the Harrison photographs, the watch backplate and fob were found in close proximity to the back of an alarm clock, numerous clock gears, and timepiece hands as well. These components were part of a small mechanical wind-up bedside alarm clock that became popular in the 1870s; archaeologists even unearthed the key that wound the clock. Advertisements for these clocks from the turn of the twentieth century emphasized that they were not cheap—they often cost $2.50—and were sold primarily by jewelers. A 24 September 1910 advertisement in *The Saturday Evening Post* by the Western Clock Company celebrated the virtues of a "Big Ben" alarm clock—which was identical in form to the one found at the Harrison site—assuring that, "If [the alarm clock] is oiled every other year there is no telling how long [it] will last." While we will never know if Harrison regularly oiled his clock, it is worth noting that excavators also uncovered a large fragment of a "Sperm Sewing Machine Oil" bottle. Sperm whale oil, due to its light and fine texture, was commonly used as a lubricant for fine machinery, including watches, clocks, sewing machines, and firearms (Fessenden 1909).

The prominence of time-related artifacts at the Harrison site was intriguing, considering one might justifiably wonder why a person living alone on a remote mountain would need or want to have constant knowledge of the exact time of day. Even though much attention in recent archaeology has been on the individual motivations of specific people, the analysis of broader historical and cultural patterns can also be highly informative. In this case, the fob, watch, and alarm clock fragments from the site seemed to parallel changes in attitudes regarding the importance of time in the late nineteenth century (Mallios and Stroud 2006). It was at this moment in history (18 November 1883) when American time zones were standardized, an act that was both highly practical and symbolic. Rigid control of time facilitated the coordination of railroad scheduling and worked with the telegraph to unite society in immediacy (Kern 1983). Simultaneously, symbols of time became significant symbols of status, connection, and sophistication. Paul Mullins singled out clocks in particular as items that drew great consumer interest among African Americans because of their symbolic link with modernization and high status, and Lawrence Levine saw them as deliberate symbolic refutations of ethnic stereotypes depicting African Americans as tardy and lazy (Mullins 1999: 188; Levine 1977: 331).[58]

It is difficult to know what the watch meant to Harrison, and the explanations need not be singular or exclusive. Was Harrison fixated on knowing the time at all moments; was he joining in a cultural performance that cherished material trappings of a time-obsessed society;

was he asserting his equality through possessing this sort of high-status item; was he making an ironic statement pairing an ornate watch with his most tattered clothes; or was it something else? Whatever the motivation, even though the historical records intimated that Harrison was rarely required to be any specific place at any particular time, he was almost never photographed without his trusty timepiece.

Cosmetics and Salves

Three small, flat, cylindrical tins surfaced during excavations at the site (Figure 3.22). The first appeared to be an unlabeled brass cosmetic tin containing white makeup, although chemical tests have yet to confirm that identification. Often called a rouge tin, these sorts of containers and the commercial cosmetics they held—like light-colored powders, bases, and waxes—grew in popularity during the late nineteenth century (Angelogou 1970). In addition, excavators found two similarly shaped iron canisters at the site; both were intact, sealed, and rusted shut. One had remnants of a bottom label with writing, although over half of the script was missing. A tireless student was able to track down the identity of this item on the basis of the text; it turned out to be a tin of "Kohler's One Night Corn Cure," and the script was instructions on how to apply the salve to aching feet.[59] The Kohler Medicine Company, founded in 1889, specialized in foot salves and cough syrup and was especially prominent during the 1890s and early 1900s. During this time, the "One Night Corn Cure" sold for 10 cents a jar. This salve was one of many self-medicating products (Murine, Pluto, etc.) that Harrison amassed and likely used.

Tobacco Products and Paraphernalia

Tobacco use clearly occupied a prominent role in Harrison's life. The old photographs repeatedly depicted him with a smoking pipe in hand or pocket. Multiple historical accounts mentioned his fondness for tobacco—Ed Davis insisted that Harrison's "inseparable companion" was "a short-stemmed black pipe"; and Laura James reported that his pipe "was so strong [and caked with tobacco] that all he had to do was put a coal in it and he could have a good smoke" (Davis 1938: 11; James 1958: 8). In addition, friend Max Peters Rodriguezés noted that, "Everyone who came up [Palomar Mountain] brought Nate a few cans of tobacco" (Day 1981b: no page numbers). He also explained how Harrison was adept at getting the most out of limited resources, noting that, "Indians brought [Harrison] tobacco, which he chewed, then dried, and

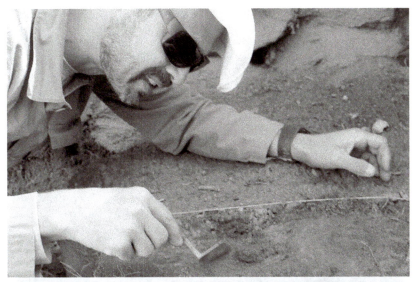

Figure 3.22a/b. Excavators unearthed three small sealed tins at the site: the first contained a sticky white residue, the second remains sealed, and the label on the third revealed that it was a foot salve. (Courtesy of the Nathan "Nate" Harrison Historical Archaeology Project.)

[then] smoked" (Day 1981b: no page numbers). Accordingly, archaeologists uncovered extensive tobacco products at the site, including over a dozen pipestems, two pipe bowls, multiple silver-plated metal bands that secured the pipes and bowls together, various pipe lids and wind covers, multiple metal snaps that sealed tobacco pouches, and many distinctively shaped tobacco cans. These items took many forms and

ranged in price from cheap and utilitarian to expensive and ornate (Figure 3.23).

The pipestems were intentionally detachable from the bowl and commonly known as mouthpieces, bits, or mounts. Most were made of rubber, but a few were bone. In 1844, Charles Goodyear patented "hard rubber"; he combined heated rubber and sulfur to form highly durable vulcanite, also called ebonite. Even though Goodyear was not a pipe maker—he produced materials for larger markets and was the namesake for the famous Goodyear Tire and Rubber Company—his hard rubber quickly became the most popular material for pipestems, a position it still holds in today's pipe market. In fact, multiple pipestems from the Harrison site contained incised lettering proudly proclaiming

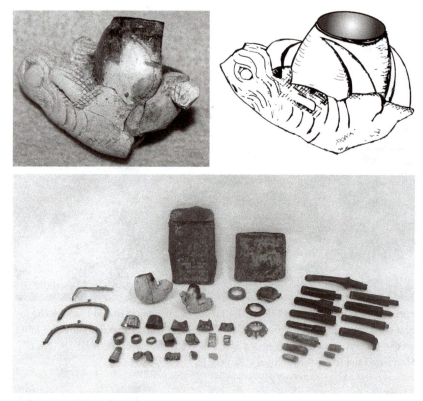

Figure 3.23a/b/c. The tobacco-material culture from the Nathan Harrison site included fragments of a Meerschaum pipe (the pieces of the Meerschaum vessel are top left and a sketch of the reconstructed pipe is right), as well as (*clockwise from left*) tobacco pouch snaps, pipe bowls, tobacco cans, pipestems, pipe-bowl wind covers, and pipe bands. (Courtesy of the Nathan "Nate" Harrison Historical Archaeology Project.)

the materials to be "Pure Rubber" or "Solid Rubber." The Wilhelm C. Demuth Company was the largest pipe import, wholesale, and manufacturing business in the United States during the late nineteenth and early twentieth centuries. Demuth pipes were widely available during Harrison's time in Southern California.[60]

The Harrison site contained two markedly different pipe bowls. One was a utilitarian undecorated wooden pipe bowl made of polished apple wood or rosewood; identical bowls were sold in the 1897 *Sears Roebuck & Co. Catalogue* for less than a nickel. The other was an ornate and exotic pipe bowl, known as an "Eagle's Claw Meerschaum Tobacco Pipe."[61] This intricately decorated vessel depicted an eagle claw (the pipestem) holding an egg (the pipe bowl); two of the talons that gripped the bowl were carved as a raised relief, while the other two that held the front and back of the bowl extended from the base piece. Meerschaum products were made from the mineral sepiolite, which started white, but turned darker shades of yellow, tan, orange, red, and brown as the porous pipe absorbed moisture and tobacco tar into the permeable stone. Soft enough to be carved but hard enough to be polished, Meerschaum was native to few countries; the most famous source for the stone was in western Turkey. As a result of the limited supply and time-intensive decorative process, this pipe was a symbol of high status during the nineteenth century. Many pipe makers that specialized in Meerschaum vessels—and consequently, many Meerschaum pipe smokers—were of Jewish descent and emigrated from Eastern Europe, like Harrison friend Louis Rose. This artifact could be a remnant of their bond.

Excavators at the site unearthed over a dozen tobacco tins, distinctive in their flat shape. In fact, students found multiple examples of two of the most popular and identifiable tobacco cans of the early twentieth century, the hinged-lid Prince Albert tin and the curved-cut Old English Tobacco tin. Even though numerous different tobacco products were sold in these particular vessels, they quickly became known as "Prince Alberts" after the leading brand. In fact, these cans gained much fame in popular American culture during the early twentieth century. The joke—"Do you have Prince Albert in a can? Well, let him out!"—was commonly told. Since each of the archaeologically recovered vessels had hinged lids with no front notches, these items dated from 1909–38.

Currency

Even though Harrison was quoted as insisting he be paid only in gold and wanted nothing to do with traditional currency, excavators found six contemporaneous coins at the site, totaling 47 cents (James 1958: 7). These included an 1899 Barber quarter, a 1901 Liberty Head nickel, a 1907 Indian Head small cent (penny), a 1911 Lincoln small cent, a 1916 Buffalo Head nickel, and a 1916 Liberty Head dime. Each of these mismatched coins—none had the same denomination and symbol—had an intriguing history regarding the evolution of design, the changing composition of the currency, various coin-design contests, and the politics of American symbology. Nonetheless, it was difficult to determine whether these issues meant anything to Harrison. In fact, the only coin with a possible documented tie to Harrison was the 1911 Lincoln penny. This particular one-cent was designed by Victor D. Brenner, distributed from 1909–58, and often called the "coin of freedom" and "the emancipation coin" (Yeoman 1989: 87). Until 1909, no American president had ever before appeared on a coin made for regular circulation (Bowers 1979: 243). This penny became the most popular coin ever produced as most people thought it was a special edition as opposed to regular circulation (Schwarz 1980: 242).[62] The potential link between the Lincoln penny and Harrison came from Palomar Mountain old-timer W.C. Fink, who stated (as mentioned earlier), "At the time the Lincoln pennies were minted, I gave [Harrison] a bright penny and told him what Lincoln done for the slaves: he said, 'I know about Abe Lincoln. I had my freedom long before that'" (John Davidson 1937: 2).

Writing Implements

Whereas certain small finds, like the 1911 penny, seemed to have a direct tie to historical accounts and served to bastion the truth of the narratives, other artifacts hinted at activities rarely addressed or even dismissed in contemporaneous stories. For example, the presence of multiple writing implements—a sharpened graphite pencil lead, a pen cap and clip, and multiple eraser components—undermined the repeated assertions of Harrison's illiteracy (Figure 3.24). A lone piece of sharpened graphite would not necessarily have led to conclusions of literacy for Harrison as graphite was commonly used by shepherds across the world to mark their flocks. However, when coupled with the others, it formed part of a larger pattern that suggested writing was a relatively common occurrence at the cabin. While it is possible that Harrison only acquired these writing tools and the ability to write in the final years of his life, the preponderance of these writing artifacts across the site hinted at alternative interpretations. Could Harrison, in fact, have been concealing his literacy to certain visitors?

Figure 3.24. The Nathan Harrison site contained multiple materials associated with writing, including a sharpened graphite pencil lead, a pen cap and clip, and multiple eraser components. (Courtesy of the Nathan "Nate" Harrison Historical Archaeology Project.)

Industrial Goods

The site's artifact assemblage included many items typically associated with industrial or nondomestic work activities. Most of these tied directly to the life of a rancher, an archaeological signature identified in 1962 by Bernard "Bunny" Fontana and his colleagues at historic Johnny Ward's Ranch in Arizona. At the Harrison site, there were multiple tools, including an assortment of files, whetstones, and shears. Many of these items were professional grade. For example, the shears were made by Burgon & Ball, a British tool producer started in 1730 that the *Sears Roebuck & Co. Catalogue* celebrated as a top brand used by industrial sheep shearers. Likewise, the sharpening implements—the files and whetstones (or oil stones) were both high quality and showed extensive use. While these items, unlike the sheep shears, were difficult to assign to any singular task, they were part of the standard toolkit for a nineteenth-century rancher.

Many local nineteenth-century shepherds had ties to California's hide-tanning industry. It was tempting to link Harrison to tanning for three reasons. First, he had previously worked for Louis Rose, who owned the only tannery in San Diego County. Second, Harrison maintained close relations with the local Luiseño, who were skilled hide processors, using the tannic acid found in the bark of oak trees that were abundant on his property.[63] Furthermore, there was a picture of Harrison sitting in front of his cabin next to a table with what seemed to be a stack of hides (Figure 3.25). In fact, the cover of this book has a photograph of Harrison in front of his cabin with a sheepskin hanging from the front door just behind his right elbow. Regardless of these factors, there was simply no soil-chemistry or artifact-based evidence of hide-tanning at the site.[64] Tanning was an elaborate process that used specific tools and products, none of which were found.[65] Overall, the archaeological remains provided evidence of Harrison rearing, shearing, and processing sheep, but the intricate tanning process remained elusive. It seems more likely that he merely skinned the animals and took these skins to others to tan the hides.

Horse-related items were abundant at the site, verifying the significant role of these animals in Harrison's Palomar Mountain life. These artifacts included a wide variety of horseshoes, horseshoe nails, spurs, and numerous saddle and bridle buckles and rings (Figure 3.26). With

Figure 3.25. This undated photograph of Harrison on his patio showcases him sitting next to a stack of something likely related to industrial activities, but, are the items empty flattened wool bags, blankets, tanned hides, or untanned skins? Furthermore, are they the same items pictured on the Harrison patio table in Figure 0.2? (Courtesy of the Nathan "Nate" Harrison Historical Archaeology Project, Kirby Collection.)

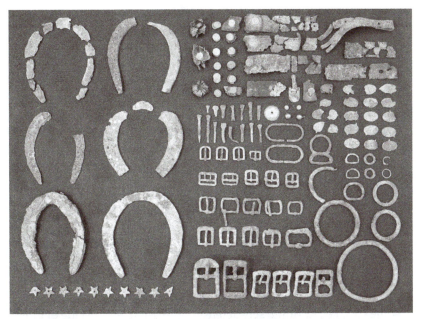

Figure 3.26. The Harrison site assemblage included fragments from six horseshoes, fifteen horseshoe nails, ten spur rowels, and dozens of saddle and bridle buckles and rings. (Courtesy of the Nathan "Nate" Harrison Historical Archaeology Project.)

dozens of each of these types of items, horse care clearly played a major role in Harrison's daily activities (Fontana et al. 1962). Despite the high quantity of horse-related artifacts, nearly all were utilitarian. The spurs were of the "O.K. model working man" type; the rowels were filed down to avoid scarring the horse's flanks, in stark contrast to spiky-roweled Mexican spurs (Forbis 1973: 25).[66] Custom-made spurs became the norm in the West in the 1880s, intimating that the rowels found at the Harrison site were most likely either cheap or outdated. Likewise, the horseshoes were of the everyday "Plain Jane" style, showed heavy use, and were handmade by a blacksmith—they had asymmetrically spaced nail holes along the outer edge of the fullering—even though horseshoe-making machines had become widespread during the late 1800s (Morris 1988: 27–31).

As previously mentioned, Harrison witnessed the transition between horses and early automobiles as primary transportation modes for his visitors during his time on the mountain. Many of the artifacts from the site seemed directly attributable to Harrison's role in the burgeoning tourism industry on Palomar. For example, excavators found multiple highly deteriorated automobile tire inner tubes from the 1910s buried in Harrison's patio. These items contained a highly distinctive natural rubber chemical signature that was verified by scientists from Goodyear. Though historical records emphasized that Harrison had no love for automobiles, he nevertheless seemed to stash strategic supplies for car drivers coming up the mountain. Harrison clearly had no personal need for these items, but they would be of immeasurable value to a visitor who was attempting to trek up the mountain with a flat tire. Harrison's property was analogous to the modern-day gas station as it had fuel (water for horses and car radiators) and supplies (spare tires, fresh fruit, etc.).

Firearms

Excavators found 201 spent rifle cartridges at the site (Figure 3.27). These artifacts, which are also commonly described as fired shell casings from small arms, contained a wealth of information. For example, they had a direct tie to the activity in which they were used (shooting of some sort, i.e., hunting, self-defense, aggression, etc.). Made of brass, they were also remarkably durable. Furthermore, many of these cartridges had distinctive headstamps, which revealed their manufacturer and date of production. In addition, the size of the casings often tied directly to the type of weapon used to fire it. Spatial attributes were also revealing as the wealth of cartridges in and around the Harrison patio and the dearth of bullets clearly indicated that shots were being fired from the patio and not at it. Simply stated, Harrison's patio marked the location of the person firing the weapon, not the target.

Before embarking on detailed analyses of these spectacular artifacts, however, it must not be overlooked that it was illegal during the nineteenth century for Harrison to even own a rifle in the first place. According to California state law in 1854: "the sale of firearms or munitions to California Indians or to persons known to associate with Indians" was prohibited (Assembly Bill 80, Section 1, Chapter 12). Nathan Harrison, who married multiple Indigenous women, was baptized by a Luiseño chief, and an active participant in many native ceremonies, would not legally be able to own a firearm until the law was repealed in 1913. In general, it is rare when one of the site's most prevalent items is contraband.

Of the fired shell casings at the site; each was sorted according to caliber. Nearly two-thirds of the recovered cartridges were .22s, indicating that the most commonly used weapon at the site was a firearm capable of firing bullets of that particular caliber. Furthermore, every

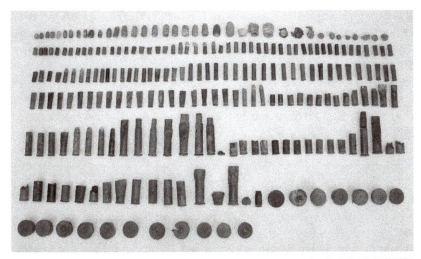

Figure 3.27a/b. Of the assemblage's 201 fired rifle cartridges (*top*), over 50 percent were rim-fired .22s (like the close-up on the bottom image), evinced by the strike mark on the rim of the cartridge. (Courtesy of the Nathan "Nate" Harrison Historical Archaeology Project.)

.22 casing found on site was rim-fired, which refers to a specific style of bullet that is still used today and primarily found in smaller calibers. Rim-fire bullets were unique in that unlike other bullets whose firing pin ignited the primer by hitting it in the center of the round, rim-fire round primers were ignited by being struck on the outer rim. The .22 was commonly found with this style of primer. Another archaeological clue on the recovered casings was the manufacturer's stamp on the rim of the fired shells. The .22 calibers from the Harrison site were almost all stamped with "H," "P," or "U," each of which dated to rim-fire production years of 1885 to 1911.[67]

On the basis of the caliber, rim-fire style, and headstamp date ranges, it was possible to narrow down the make and model of the rifle that was most likely used at the Harrison site in the late 1800s and early 1900s. However, like many issues with Harrison histories, there was ample debate. The most popular rim-fire .22 of the time was the Winchester Repeater Model 1873, the famed "Gun That Won the West."[68] Winchester was a leading name in firearms in the late nineteenth century, and its Model 1873 was one of the only rifles of the time that could fire .22 rounds. Other prominent contemporaneous rifles, such as the 1866 "Henry" Repeater, exclusively fired .44 rounds.[69] While the idea of Harrison arming himself with the same weapon associated with celebrated American icons Billy the Kid (Henry McCarty) and Buffalo Bill (William Cody) was enticing, the Winchester Model 1873 was only compatible with rim-fire .22 caliber cartridges after 1884 and in limited numbers (19,000 total).[70] To confuse matters further, Chris Forbes insisted that Harrison's rifle was a "muzzle loader," which was at odds with both the Winchester Model 1873 interpretation and the abundant archaeological evidence (Day and Melvin 1981: no page numbers).

The .22 rifle was a versatile and useful weapon. It was powerful enough to take down an array of large animals (bear, deer, mountain lion, bobcat, etc.) but also appropriate for small game (raccoons, squirrels, birds, etc.). Commonly referred to as a "varmint rifle" or a "survival rifle," it was a favorite for pioneers, ranchers, and other outdoorsmen. Historical accounts indicated that Harrison took measures to keep rodents out of his food stores, and archaeological excavations revealed extensive rodent disturbance at the site. Nonetheless, despite being loaded with a small caliber bullet, this weapon was highly effective; ammunition specialists F. C. Barnes and W. T. Woodward avowed:

> The .22 Short can be deceiving, because it looks small and relatively harmless. When fired from a rifle, it can penetrate two inches of soft pine board and has an extreme range of almost one full mile. It can seriously

wound or kill a person right up to the limits if its range—be careful!
(Barnes and Woodard 2016)

The associated artifacts, the highly homogenous casing assemblage, the photograph of Harrison with his rifle at the spring, and a variety of historical and contemporaneous accounts made it overwhelmingly likely that Harrison was personally responsible for the most commonly found casings (.22s) at the site. Accordingly, visitor activity (hunting, recreational shooting, etc.) probably resulted in the less common and higher caliber shells.

The fired rifle cartridges at the site were especially useful for site chronology. The large quantity and distinct date ranges of production for each individual headstamp enabled similar chronological analyses to be undertaken that were previously developed for historical ball clay pipestems on pre-Civil War sites east of the Mississippi River (J. C. Harrington 1954; Binford 1962; Heighton and Deagan 1971; Deetz 1987; Mallios 2005a). Accordingly, the site's traditional date-range intersections could be augmented with a cartridge mean date (1897) and a cartridge histogram that graphed counts of datable headstamps per decade. The resultant histogram was unimodal and offered another material line of evidence of the occupation length at the site (1860–1930).

In January 2009, Dr. John W. Bond of the Forensic Research Centre at the University of Leicester was invited to examine a number of spent cartridges recovered from the Harrison excavation site. The intention of this examination was to establish whether any fingerprints had survived on the shell casings in the form of corrosion of the casings. Dr. Bond, a forensic scientist who often aided the police with criminal investigations, had developed an innovative technique of finding nearly invisible fingerprints and was intrigued to see if his methods would work on materials more than a century old. His stunning discoveries started with the fact that when a person's finger comes into contact with a surface, secretions of sweat are deposited, leaving an impression known as a latent fingerprint. For identification purposes, these prints are highly significant because every individual's fingerprints are unique, and they do not change during a person's lifetime (G. L. Thomas 1978; McCartney 2006). The challenge, however, is that latent fingerprints are almost always invisible to the naked eye because of their translucence.

The key to Dr. Bond's analysis was two-fold: 1) he recognized that the natural salt in finger sweat inevitably corroded the metal cartridges loaded into the weapon (when done barehanded), and 2) he developed a novel technique to make this corrosion more visible. It was aided by the fact that the firing of these weapons occurs at an extremely high temperature that often preserves the latent fingerprint—the print's oil corrosion is cauterized by the heat of gunpowder reaction. As a result, Dr. Bond was able to employ aggressive techniques to make the prints visible and could be less concerned about contamination from later post-firing fingerprints, like those from grubby archaeologists. He vigorously scrubbed the rifle casings in warm water with a few drops of commercial detergent, and then, like Dr. Frankenstein, used electricity to bring the fingerprints to life. Dr. Bond ran an electric current through the metal casings and coated them with a conducting powder (Bond 2008a, 2008b, 2008c). The tiny spherical beads of the powder coagulated at the spots where the metal casing had been corroded by the fingerprint. They formed a cast of the original fingerprint!

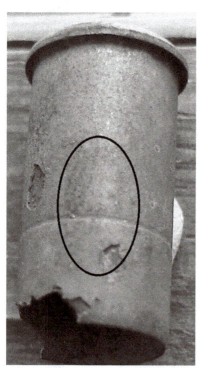

Figure 3.28. Look closely at the fired rifle cartridge from the Harrison site that Dr. Bond tested, and you can see a faint thumbprint in the superimposed black circle. (Courtesy of the Nathan "Nate" Harrison Historical Archaeology Project.)

We sent Dr. Bond fifty fired brass shell casings in the hopes of finding fingerprint deposit corrosion. Only one, a 0.38 caliber casing, produced a partial fingerprint (Figure 3.28).[71] On the basis of the headstamp, the cartridge was produced between 1911 and 1920. Even though the casing in question was severely corroded and partial, once Dr. Bond performed his techniques, the fingerprint appeared as three dark parallel ridgelines bounded by multiple less-distinct lines. Dr. Bond performed many additional scientific tests to confirm the discovery, including analysis via scanning electron microscopy (SEM), energy dispersive x-ray analysis (EDX) and x-ray photoelectron spectroscopy (XPS).

Dr. Bond's discovery of a fingerprint more than one hundred years old on a fired cartridge from the Harrison site was spectacular in isolating such a delicate trace of the distant past with a direct tie to Harrison. It also underscored the remarkable breadth of information that can come from a single artifact. A lone unearthed item was subjected to a wide variety of scientific, historical, and humanistic studies, none of which had to be presented as corroborative. On the contrary, the wide mix of analyses offered a wealth of informed perspectives on one of the site's historically unseen yet archaeologically ever-present artifacts. Clearly, spacious and inclusive thought was not restricted to broad theoretical considerations; it even seeped into the microanalyses of a single item.

Answers

Artifacts serve as powerfully insightful conduits to the past. Material possessions reflect, embody, and communicate an enormous range of cultural values, individual actions, and time-honored beliefs (Perkins 1991: 509). Though often discarded, trampled, and buried, they reflect a complex system of information. Whereas answers to the who, what, where, and when of the Harrison site were relatively straightforward and echoed throughout the many lines of artifactual evidence, ascertaining the how and why of the site required delving deeper into the contextualized meaning of the assemblage. Archaeological interpretations regarding Harrison's values, motivations, and decision-making processes were difficult to ascertain, tenuous, and debatable. Rather than pit cultural patterns, consumer choice, regional distinctiveness, and other interpretations against each other as singular and exclusive understandings of Nathan Harrison's life and legend, I looked at them all in the historical context of his Palomar Mountain home and how he negotiated his identity among the different groups in the region. Each of the different schools of anthropological thought contributed to my appreciation of the past, but no single theory inherently negated the others.

Space, Time, and Form

Archaeological excavation produced clear answers to the project's two initial research questions. The extensive architectural and artifactual remains confirmed that this was Harrison's cabin. Furthermore, spatial nuances identified five distinct site areas. The small cabin had fewer artifacts, but many of the items discovered from within seemed to hold special significance in terms of being complete, unique, or ornate. The cabin's extended patio to the west was clearly a high-intensity activity area; it contained the remains of many food-processing tasks, especially faunal remains. The area to the south and west of the patio was likely the primary trash dump; it teemed with cans, bottles, and other containers. An extended area to the south was his orchard and garden. In addition, Harrison had an arrastra ore-grinding station 300′ south of his primary residence.

Temporal insights for the site were equally definitive. The date-range intersection of the artifacts recovered from the site produced a minimum occupation of 1865–1916. The end date maintained remarkable precision with Harrison's known day of departure, 21 October 1919. Furthermore, there was no evidence of a pre- or post-Harrison occupation at the cabin site. The archaeologically verified start date of 1865 for the site addressed a question with which the primary historical records and secondary narratives so mightily struggled. Harrison first occupied the site well after some of the more celebrated claims placed him on the mountain (1848), but before he had legally claimed the water (1892) or homesteaded it (1893). Perhaps, there was less disagreement between the records and narratives than at first perceived, especially if close attention was paid to the issues of occupation and residence. The governmental agreement of homesteading was tied to permanent residence, whereas Harrison was affiliated with groups of Mexican and Indigenous ranchers and other native groups that followed a long tradition of seasonal occupations. Harrison might have been the first non-Indigenous person on Palomar Mountain as he often claimed—although not in those words—but his presence was likely part of seasonally tending to flocks of sheep on the move. This idea was supported by Harrison's presence on two different 1880 censuses that were miles apart. Viewed inclusively, the archaeological evidence allowed for initial visits and seasonal occupations during the 1860s and '70s—even before Joseph Smith—but a more full-time and permanent residence starting in the 1880s that was cemented by his water claim and homestead certificate in the 1890s.

Many of the artifacts found at the site had exact parallel forms in the historical photographs and contemporary narratives of Harrison. The numerous one-to-one correspondences included smoking pipes, footwear, clothing fasteners, and architectural hardware. Other near matches were time pieces and accessories, extensive sheep remains, alcohol bottles, and baking materials. Overall, there was no doubt as to the answer of the project's initial research question. This site was incontrovertibly the Harrison homestead.

One of the more intriguing questions about Harrison concerned how he made a living. Since the historical records and contemporary accounts offered such great disparity as to this issue for Harrison—was he idle or active?—the archaeology offered crucial evidence. Archaeology did not answer how hard he worked, but it did address the great diversity of working tasks in which he was engaged. The site's artifacts not only provided definitive evidence of Harrison's daily industrial activities, but they shed light on the elusive issue of whether any of these tasks went beyond mere subsistence and provided him with a surplus for use by others. Since contemporaneous households usually were not entirely self-sufficient, this surplus was often key to survival by providing people like Harrison with items of value to exchange. In fact, he engaged in various forms of cottage-industry labor that were beyond his immediate need. Arguably, his surplus was integral to his social identity on the mountain as a productive community member.

Multiple lines of archaeological evidence, including artifacts, features, soil-chemistry analyses, etc., were essential in evaluating and ultimately corroborating many of Harrison's historically-referenced industrial activities. He raised a wide variety of livestock, especially sheep and horses, and participated in the burgeoning tourist industry on Palomar Mountain during the early twentieth century. Each of the activities seemed to produce a surplus, especially when considered with all of the available historical evidence.[72] For example, the ample sheep remains showed a proclivity toward deliberately butchering animals after optimal wool sheering had occurred, an interpretation bastioned by historical photographs of wool bags, multiple pairs of sheers, and contemporary accounts of a deep family tie to shepherding (i.e., stepson Fred "Sheep" Smith). Likewise, an extensive assortment of horse hardware, including shoes, buckles, rings, and spurs, when united with Asher's testimony of how the sale of a horse to Nathan Hargrave enabled Harrison to reclaim his homestead and the later account of Harrison's horses roaming the mountain after his passing, offered strong support to the notion that Harrison kept more horses than he needed and used these animals as key items of wealth.

Regional Context

It was important to place the Harrison assemblage in regional context so that individual interpretations about wealth, industry, identity, etc., were not absolute statements without some sort of comparative insight. Drawing on decades of research, archaeologist Stephen Van Wormer was able to identify major status and geographic patterns among archaeological sites in the Old West (1996). He employed four distinct quantificational measures in his analyses: 1) percentage of the total assemblage that were consumer items, 2) percentage of the total assemblage that were kitchen items, 3) ceramic index value, and 4) percentage of the glass assemblage that were beverage bottles. Using these calculations, he deduced three different clusters: 1) Middle to Upper Middle Class Urban Sites, 2) Small Town Working Class Sites, and 3) Rural Sites. Middle to Upper Middle Class Urban Sites had high percentages of consumer items, high ceramic indices, and high bottle frequencies, but Small Town Working Class Sites had equal amounts of kitchen and consumer items, low ceramic indices, and high bottle frequencies. Van Wormer saw Rural Sites as different from the two previous types, with elevated kitchen items, moderate consumer items, low ceramic indices, and lesser beverage bottle frequencies. Van Wormer deliberately avoided labeling all rural sites as low status because he believed that Southern California's rural inhabitants—regardless of status—used their economic wealth to reinvest in their ranches instead of purchasing luxury items.

Due to its remote location, one would have expected the Harrison site to be classified as a Rural Site. However, this was not the case. The Harrison assemblage was decidedly split and did not correspond well with the model. The high overall percentage of consumer items (25.2 percent) was far greater than the norm for Rural Sites, but not quite as high as Middle to Upper Middle Class Urban Sites. The overall kitchen assemblage percentage (29.3 percent) fit both the Small Town Working Class Sites and Rural Sites ranges, as did the low ceramic index of 1.5. However, the extremely high beverage bottle percentage (51.4 percent) exceeded the limits of even Middle to Upper Middle Class Urban Sites. It was especially different from traditional rural sites, which averaged less than 30 percent beverage bottles.

The Harrison site would have fit the Rural Sites model if it were not for the decided influx of alcohol bottles and meat cans. The alcohol bottles inflated the beverage bottle percentages, and the meat cans boosted the consumer item counts. According to the historical accounts, these two particular types of items directly reflected the surge of visitors to the site and their regular offerings of canned food, alcohol, and clothing.[73] Many sources verified the repeated gifts of alcohol, but Heath detailed that the standard offering also included clothing. She wrote:

> Rt. Rev. Bishop H. B. Restarick . . . was a staunch friend of Mr. Harrison, always in his trips to the mountain remembering him with provisions and clothing. Hundreds of others also remembered him the same way, including the Mendenhalls, Baileys and other permanent residents of the mountain. (J. H. Heath 1919: 8)

These goods were delivered for multiple reasons. They reflected his important social role in multiple local communities, they served as reciprocity for his customary gift of water to all visitors, and they resulted from the elevated status he had achieved toward the end of his life as a revered elder. These complexities transcended simple labels of rich or poor and enabled Harrison to embody qualities of both; it was in this way that he could simultaneously be described by his peers as "poor like everyone else" and "always pretty well supplied" (Day and Melvin 1981: no page numbers; Hastings 1959a: no page numbers).

The Tourism Industry

Instead of lamenting that the Harrison assemblage did not fit the Van Wormer classification or dismissing pattern analyses for being rigid and overly normative, the discrepancy can be an opportunity to delve for deeper insights (King 2012: 183–84). The Harrison results underscored a key distinction about the site in terms of how and why it did not follow contemporary norms of consumer behavior. Whereas other historical archaeologists have linked anomalous site patterns with factors related to class or ethnicity, the Harrison site assemblage seemed to correspond with a particular activity (Praetzellis, Praetzellis, and Brown 1988). Specifically, many of the goods Harrison acquired—especially those that strayed from the Van Wormer model—were given to him by the extensive visitors to his property.

The overall artifact assemblage from the Harrison site had a baseline that matched with traditional ranching sites (Fontana et al. 1962; Van Wormer 1996). However, this baseline was then augmented with materials directly related to the burgeoning tourist industry on Palomar Mountain. Harrison's hospitality-driven activities were not subtle. Accordingly, there were three lines of archaeological evidence that directly tied aspects of the material assemblage from the Harrison site to tourism.

First, there were isolated finds most probably linked to visitors, like the camera lens, the automobile tire inner tubes, and a variety of items seemingly tied to women and children (rouge tin, perfume bottle, marbles, puzzle piece, etc.). Second, the site's assemblage consisted largely of canned meat, alcohol bottles, clothing fasteners, and tobacco products, few of which seemed to match or reflect a singular source. Whereas previous measures of industry emphasized goods of a common form, the spoils of Harrison's touristic endeavors seemed to have been distinctively mismatched because of the inherent variety of visitors. In fact, the well-represented artifacts that formed matching sets—horse- and sheep-related material culture, jelly jars, and fired rifle cartridges—were the ones tied most directly to traditional ranching activities. Conversely, the mismatched goods, including widely variable status indicators and seemingly arbitrary items of prestige, were far more personal and directly reflective of the constant influx of new and different guests. Third, a majority of the artifacts from the site dated to the last twenty years of occupation, precisely the time in which visitation and traffic up the mountain surged. Historical records indicated Harrison was highly mobile in his early years on the mountain, especially before 1900, working on a variety of projects that took him all over Southern California. In his later years—Harrison would have been 68–87 years old between 1900 and 1919—he seemed to be much more sedentary and focused on entertaining visitors.

Harrison's participation in local tourism provided for him beyond his basic ranching activities. Furthermore, his success in this endeavor was not just the result of living in the right place at the right time. There was far more to his economic viability than just luck, opportunism, or resourcefulness. Harrison's survival, subsistence, and industries comprised a complex social system that relied on many individuals. It paralleled what anthropologist Maria Franklin identified as an "active collaboration . . . that demonstrated self-sufficiency, creativity, and careful strategizing" (2001: 103). Interdependence was key, but so was skillful negotiation of the volatile social climate. Harrison's strategic actions were complex, but they started with the alluring character he created and perfected for visitors. In fact, Harrison's life on Palomar Mountain was contingent on the success of "N——r Nate."

Notes

1. This book ultimately undermines many myths of Harrison, weakening support for the ideas that he was a centenarian, was seemingly everywhere in California history, etc. Ironically, it simultaneously adds to his legend in that the very act of archaeology implies legitimacy. If my team digs the site, then I have decided—before the first scrape of the trowel—that Harrison's story is worth telling and is more important than others whom I chose not to pursue archaeologically. Instead of the archaeology assessing the importance of the story on the basis of what is found, the dig itself immediately and inherently privileges the story of Harrison.

2. Fittingly, this Murine Eye Remedy quote was from an advertisement in the 1855 book, *Homestead on the Hillside* (Holmes 1855).

3. Pluto was the Roman god of the underworld, and the water company invoked his name because this elixir originated so deep underground in the mineral-rich waters of the French Lick Springs in Indiana.

4. Historian Lawrence Levine quoted an ex-slave from Kentucky as explaining that, "There were not doctors back then. If you got sick, you would dig a hole and dig up roots and fix your own medicine . . . they had remedies for nearly everything at that time" (1977: 64).

5. In the early 1900s, this particular company and its dubious product drew the ire of the American Medical Association (AMA), which published a detailed exposé on Murine's extensive fraudulent activities (1908). The AMA battled rampant health frauds during this time, publishing nine volumes of articles to expose the many contemporary scams. Murine would face repeated investigations by various watchdog groups through the 1940s.

6. This might be an exaggeration as no pictures remain to verify their literal or metaphorical obesity and their business predated the series of late twentieth-century "Mc"-companies that deviously capitalized on the unsuspecting public. Nonetheless, one could easily confuse the nonfictional founders of this venture with Mark Twain's fictional Colonel Beriah Sellers character in *The Gilded Age: A Tale of Today* ([1873] 1969). Whereas the McFatrich brothers promoted a product for "Weak Eyes, Inflamed Eyes, Tired Eyes, Strained Eyes, Children's Eyes, Itching Eyes, Blurring Eyes, Red Eyes," Col. Sellers marketed "Infallible, Imperial, Oriental Optic Liniment, and Salvation for Sore Eyes." The McFatrichs and Sellers were each unscrupulous and quick to privilege individual profit over public health.

7. In addition, when the American Medical Association tested the elixir for its chemical composition, it found little consistency between the contents of each bottle.

8. Furthermore, patent-medicine manufacturers found ways to circumvent a wide variety of legislation aimed directly at the effectiveness of their dubious products, like the 1906 Pure Food and Drug Act, the Sherley Amendment of 1913, and the 1914 Harrison Narcotic Act (Fike 1987).

9. In a country teeming with dubiously qualified physicians self-touting their prowess, cures were often more about marketing and slick sales pitches than ingredients or services. Nowhere was this more apparent than San Diego in the summer of 1882 when a con-artist named Mrs. Lou Patterson, claiming to have spiritual powers to cure women of unnatural growths in their genitalia, scammed numerous wealthy locals. For the price of $75, the self-proclaimed "Doctor" miraculously executed bloodless operations and then provided her patients with their now-removed tumors in a bottle (Crawford 1995: 34–36). Although arrested, tried, and convicted for "obtaining money under false pretenses"—the contents of the bottles turned out to be cooked pig and chicken livers—the Los Angeles Superior Court dismissed the case on the grounds that it "had no jurisdiction over matters supernatural" (Crawford 1995: 34–36).

10. This passage was yet another poignant instance in which Harrison completely shed his minstrelsy when with close friends and not surrounded by tourists. He did not speak in a fractured dialect, was not overly subservient, and acted strategically as opposed to acquiescently.

11. Reporter David Ross left no ambiguity as to whether landowner Richard Day had dug at the historic site on his property, writing that, "Instead of gold, the pile consists of items of everyday living: a spoon, a knife, a planer, the leg of a cast-iron stove, a horse bit, a spike, a hay hook, a length of barbed wire. . . . [T]here was more: a sardine can with a key, a broken whiskey bottle . . . a lead canning lid, a mother of pearl button, a 12-gauge shotgun shell and a rifle shell made by Remington" (1998: part IV).

12. One of the first steps of an archaeological project—even one that is explicitly historical—is to send the local Native American community notification of the proposed work. Although Harrison was not of Indigenous descent and previous surveys of the land had identified no prehistoric sites in the immediate vicinity of the spot where we were most likely to find remains of the cabin, it is best practice to reach out to native groups in an effort to promote collaboration and transparency in research. None of this was required as the work was to be undertaken on private property. Regardless, in the spring of 2004, I sent notification of our proposed data recovery program for the Nathan Harrison site to the State of California's Native American Heritage Commission (NAHC) and to every federally recognized tribe in San Diego County.

13. We dug in feet, not meters, because Harrison and his contemporaries used English Standard measuring systems in their daily lives.

14. The steep slope of the terrain, past and present, would make digging flat levels especially counterintuitive when attempting to uncover historical living surfaces.

15. I chose the 3" interval in an attempt to find archaeological common ground with excavations at prehistoric sites that are commonly dug in 10cm levels (See Lightfoot 1995).

16. For example, Einstein's Theory of Special-Relativity insisted that even though space and time are individually relative, space-time is an absolute entity (Einstein 1905; Greene 2004: 62).

17. Much of what gets repeated about Palomar Mountain's Indigenous culture in popular literature, historical narratives, and archaeological reports draws directly on Philip Sparkman's ethnography (1908b). Another valuable although truncated resource is a dictionary of Luiseño grammar through the letter "C," which was published in Italy in 1926. Authored by Pablo Tac, a Luiseño boy whom San Luis Rey Mission Father Antonio Peyri took to Rome in 1832, this text was never completed as Tac died at nineteen while still working on the project (Hudson 1964: 40–41). It was mistakenly attributed to "Padre Jac" instead of "Pablo Tac" and published in Italy in 1926 in the L'Archiginnasio, Bulletino della Biblioteca, Communiale di Bologna.

18. Ed Davis noted that the bedrock mortars were also used to grind the seeds of white sage, chia, and manzanita, as well as plum and cherry pits, which were all used in a porridge (1938: 4).

19. Even though most Indigenous settlements were near freshwater, the Luiseño were careful not to be too close. Sparkman reported that these natives maintained deep-seated fears of two malevolent water spirits: Yuyungviwut and Pavawut (1908b: 221). The Luiseño believed that Yuyungviwut

kidnapped women away to his distant water home and Pavawut inhabited specific springs and ponds and was infuriated by human encroachment. Sparkman explained that, "For this reason many [Luiseño] will not put their houses near springs, as they are afraid to incur the anger of [Pavawut] by doing so. It is said sometimes to drag them under the water, people who bathe near its haunts, and to drown them" (1908a: 35).

20. Archaeologist Merrick Posnansky emphasized that typical West African dwellings have parallel uses of space, using exterior areas for activities other than sleeping and storage. He wrote that, "Virtually universal [in historical West Africa] is the practice of using [interior] rooms largely for sleeping, storage, and occasionally for shrines but not for cooking, eating, or craft activities. . . This extramural use of space is possibly the most important and pervasive aspect of West African life, and there is no reason to suppose that it was very much different in the past." (Posnansky 1999: 28). Similar patterns are found in archaeologically excavated African American yards (Heath and Bennett 2000).

21. This fluidity led archaeologist Stephen Van Wormer to conclude that, "Folk building forms constituted summaries of problems already solved" (2014: 99; see also Hubka 1986: 428–30).

22. Rhys Isaac collectively labeled this technique "slave opportunism" and emphasized the active role enslaved African Americans had in defining far more of their territorial domains than their owners ever imagined (1982: 53).

23. Henry Glassie's seminal work on vernacular architecture, *Folk Housing in Middle Virginia*, identified the square as the primary geometric entity of all Virginia homes (1975: 21). Although he identified English ancestral influences on square forms and past Scottish and Irish rectangular-house trends, Glassie showed how Anglo-American home builders subsequently transformed the square into a rectangle, reflecting their architectural choice, norm, and competence (Glassie 1963, 1968). Anglo-American builders might have started with the square, but unlike the Harrison cabin, they rarely finished with a singular, square, one-room house. Likewise, many early slave quarters in the Chesapeake were rectangular in plan; the move to square forms seemed to have emerged over time and only in certain areas as later oral histories, archaeological excavations, and standing structures pointed to the trend of the single square-in-plan quarters (Samford 1996: 93–94).

24. For example, shotgun houses, which were a type of especially distinctive African American architectural structure consisting of multiple rooms in a long thin line, had complex historical and cultural connections to West Africa, Haiti, and the American South (Vlach 1986). There were even multiple examples of shotgun houses in San Diego, the Clauder House and the Hudgins Houses; both were built and inhabited by African Americans.

25. In analyzing the architectural remains of the town of Hodges in Imperial County (immediately to the east of San Diego County), archaeologist Stephen Van Wormer found rock-walled dwellings to be a common form for late nineteenth-century and early twentieth-century Mexican miners. He emphasized that the occupants made their homes out of locally available materials, built the structures themselves, and drew on a Mexican cultural building tradition from the Southwest; they employed folk traditions but

also emphasized efficiency and adaptability (Van Wormer 2014). However, these one-room structures were rectangular in plan, not square.

26. Local archaeologist Therese Muranaka noted that, "Harrison built a subterranean house for warmth. The area was remarkable for being out of the wind. We were about 10 degrees warmer up there than up on the road." (Therese Muranaka, email to author, 13 November 2002).

27. Support for this attribution comes from the work of author Willa Cather, who was especially adept at portraying frontier life in the US. In her 1927 novel *Death Comes for the Archbishop*, Cather indirectly described the architecture of a native house in the Southwest when discussing a dinner between two of her characters, a Bishop and a local native named Jacinto. She wrote, "The Bishop bent his head under the low doorway and stepped down; the floor of the room was a long step below the door-sill—the Indian way of preventing drafts" (Cather 1927: 121).

28. It could even be argued that Harrison's decision to build a house form straying so far from white norms was an act of resistance. However, this interpretation would drastically differ with the substantive historical, anthropological, and archaeological evidence indicating Harrison actively avoided overt expressions that undermined the established social hierarchy.

29. The Poomacha fire burned from 21 October–3 November 2007; it merged with two other major fires and consumed over 200,000 acres, including much of Palomar Mountain's west side.

30. There are many ways to run soil-chemistry tests. For this project, x-ray fluorescence (XRF) was used (Mallios et al. 2008; Tennesen 2010).

31. In past centuries, people often slept with a chamber pot under their bed, used as a receptacle for human waste during the night. In the morning, one of the first things people usually did was take their chamber pot outside and dispose of the previous night's waste.

32. Magnesium is a product of intensive burning, and thus, is often associated archaeologically with the hearth-dumping activities.

33. Whereas Group II had the potential to offer insight into natural resources that could have been tapped by the site's inhabitant(s), Group III could reveal whether an activity with a specific chemical signature likely occurred at all.

34. A series of regression analyses between phosphorus, calcium, and strontium levels quantified and substantiated their interdependence. The r-squared value between phosphorus and calcium was 0.89667; the r-squared value between phosphorus and strontium was 0.84615; and the r-squared value between strontium and calcium was 0.93748. All of these values are statistically significant.

35. Multiple historical accounts detailed Harrison's fruit trees and their continued growth beyond his time on the mountain. Ed Davis stated that, "without any attention whatsoever, many trees still survive and continue to bear fruit" (1982: 6); and Robert Asher wrote in the 1930s that, "There is not much left of Nate's cabin now. . . . Around the site of the house a number of grape vines and fruit trees are still alive and vigorous" (c. 1938: no page numbers).

36. Though historical accounts made it clear that Harrison lived at the site until 1919, there was no archaeological artifact exclusively produced after 1916 found at the site.
37. High-status tortoise-shell combs figured prominently in O. Henry's famed short story, "The Gift of the Magi" (1905).
38. Adjusting for inflation, these items would cost $4.23, $4.79, $5.63 today.
39. These categories derive from the seminal work of Stanley South and the important regional considerations of Stephen Van Wormer (South 1977; Van Wormer 1996). Van Wormer started with South's functional artifact classification that was developed on antebellum sites in the Mid-Atlantic region and altered it to be more specifically tailored to postbellum Southern California sites.
40. The canning industry owed much of its innovation to Napoleon Bonaparte. During the end of the eighteenth century, French forces lost more casualties in Russia from malnutrition and starvation than from enemy fire. As a result, in 1795 Napoleon offered a 12,000-franc reward to anyone who could develop a reliable method of food preservation. Nicolas Appert, an obscure confectioner, brewer, and baker, won the prize by developing a method of preserving food in bottles. He packed foods in glass bottles, corked them, and submerged them in boiling water, unknowingly sterilizing the vessels and impeding bacterial growth. Napoleon personally presented the reward to Appert.
41. Ironically, the end of the war (1918) left the US government with far more sardines than it could pay the canneries for, which led to the near failure of the entire West Coast sardine industry (Ueber and MacCall 1992).
42. Larger fish were far more common in the colder waters of Northern California, and smaller fish were the norm for warmer currents in and around Southern California (Ueber and MacCall 1992).
43. Japanese, Portuguese, and Italian fishermen in California often used different kinds of nets when fishing for sardines. These included lampara nets (Japanese), semi-purse (Portuguese), and purse seine (Italian); each of which was tailored to a different kind of haul (Ueber and MacCall 1992).
44. Ten cents is $2.12 in today's economy.
45. This bottle contained kummel, a 76-proof German liqueur that is sweet, colorless, and flavored with caraway seed, cumin, and fennel; it is often called the "funky caraway liqueur."
46. Vineland was named for its many grape vineyards. In fact, Welch was often paid for his services with bushels of fruit (Fucini and Fucini 1985).
47. While San Diego was dry during Prohibition (1919–33), its effect was minimal because Mexico stayed wet and the border was open.
48. Ironstone was a semi-vitrified type of Whiteware created by adding china stone to harden the paste (Majewski and O'Brian 1987).
49. The Adams family had a long tradition of pottery in the Staffordshire region of England, tracing back to the 1650s. The potteries were handed down to family members through the years. William was a highly popular hereditary name for the Adams family, leading to a number of backstamps with the name "William Adams" or "W. Adams."

50. Although the royal arms mark was used exclusively by companies that had been given a royal warrant for services by England's royal family, various unscrupulous potters—not the Adams family—illegally copied the royal arms on their products with slight alterations.

51. Tea wares and tea services played a significant social role in nineteenth-century everyday life in the US, but Harrison seemed to have put his own ironic stamp on the ritual (Spencer-Wood and Heberling 1987).

52. Sheep used for meat were traditionally slaughtered at two to three years of age, whereas sheep used for wool would only be butchered after wool diminishment occurred, which was at approximately six years of age (Landon 1996).

53. Though it varies by species, sheep wholesale cuts included the bones of the shoulder, front legs, lumbar and thoracic vertebrae, and upper back legs, while the head, neck, lower back legs, and feet were non-wholesale cuts (Szuter 1991).

54. It was not just the mismatched nature of the Harrison assemblage that mirrored the transient labor sites that Walker analyzed. It was also the extensive meat, fish, milk, and tobacco cans, minimal utensils and ceramics, and extensive liquor. The key difference is that Harrison augmented his diet with extensive fresh meat—Walker conversely described the transient diet as "monotonous"—and engaged in various cottage industries (horse and sheep raising) (M. Walker 2017: 103).

55. This button was similar in form to "Type 20" in Stanley South's "Analysis of the Buttons from Brunswick Town and Fort Fisher" (1964: 123).

56. Porcelain buttons of the mid-to-late nineteenth century were often called "china," "prosser," or "agate" buttons.

57. The dearth of brass buttons at the Harrison site can serve as a *terminus ante quem*. Since brass buttons were exceedingly common on most pre-1860 sites, the absence of these items hints at a post-1860 occupation.

58. Booker T. Washington mocked this practice of contemporary African Americans insisting on purchasing clocks and other time pieces for status-related reasons. He wrote in his autobiography that most of the clocks he encountered "were so worthless that they did not keep the correct time—and if they had, in nine cases out of ten there would have been no one in the family who could have told the time of day" (1986: 113).

59. It stated: "DIRECTIONS APPLY AT NIGHT TO THE CORN, BIND WITH A PIECE OF LINEN TO KEEP IN PLACE REPEAT 2 OR 3 NIGHTS, IF NECESSARY, THEN SOAK FOOT IN WARM WATER AND REMOVE THE CORN."

60. A recent visit to the "Racine & Laramie Tobacconist" in Old Town San Diego, which was opened in 1868, revealed numerous Demuth products for sale, including a prominently displayed package of a dozen Demuth pipestems from the early 1900s in the original packaging. Many of these pipe bits were identical to the ones discovered at the Harrison site.

61. This form is also commonly named the "Cock and Egg pipe" and the "Large Eagle Talon pipe."

62. This sentiment was partly due to the fact that Brenner, known as a die cutter and coin and medal designer, was initially commissioned to design a

plaque and medal in Lincoln's honor but insisted instead on a coin to commemorate 1909 as the 100-year anniversary of Lincoln's 1809 birth (Schwarz 1980: 243).

63. Tannic acid was a natural byproduct of the acorn mush process (Lightfoot and Parrish 2009: 30). To make an acorn edible, the nut was cracked and ground down, and then the bitterness was leached out with water. This leaching process divided acorn flour from a residue of water infused with tannic acid. The flour was then used in a variety of dietary forms (mush, tortillas, etc.), and the infused water was used to tan hides. In addition, some Indigenous tanners cooked the bark, soaked the skin in the solution, and then worked it with a wooden chisel (Cline 1984: 48–49; Lapham 2005: 10–11).

64. Analogous Old West archaeological sites with evidence of hide production have revealed a clear pattern of faunal-element counts and frequencies for given species and chemical residues that was not seen at the Nathan Harrison site (Conrad et al. 2015).

65. The tanning process created strong unpleasant odors and would most likely have been undertaken at quite a distance from one's home. In addition, tanning vats in most Mexican and US American contexts were deep pits in the ground lined with bricks or stone. Tanning solutions were made by pouring water through crushed oak bark, which released the bark's tannic acid. The hides were soaked in this solution for nearly half a year before being washed, softened with grease and tallow, and hung to dry. The hanging process was also involved, necessitating large structures over which to drape the hides. Archaeologists found no evidence of any of this process, although excavations were focused on areas in and around the cabin.

66. A rowel is the spiked revolving disk at the end of a spur.

67. The "H," "P," and "U" were all from US companies absorbed by the Remington Arms Company by the 1920s.

68. This phrase was part of Winchester's marketing campaign.

69. Firearm expert Arthur Pirkle noted that, "The vast majority of M1866 rifles and carbines were produced in .44 Henry Rimfire caliber only" (1994: 32). In addition, the successor to the Model 1866 and Model 1873—the Model 1876—was never built with the capacity to fire .22 rounds (Pirkle 1994).

70. Winchester's Model 1873 .22 Rimfire Rifle was America's first .22 caliber repeating rifle; it had a twenty-year production run from 1884–1904 ("Model 1873," n.d.).

71. While it was likely that Harrison owned the rim-fire .22 rifle, the same could not necessarily be said for the weapon that fired this .38 because of how few .38s there were in the assemblage.

72. On the basis of archaeology alone, it was difficult to distinguish between sustenance and surplus. For instance, there was evidence that Harrison cultivated an orchard, hunted and processed wild fauna, and was a skilled cook, but the artifacts and other relevant information did not offer overwhelming proof of excessive production. This versatility in subsistence strategies was highly characteristic of rural frontier life (Van Wormer 1996). On the one hand, a tree that Harrison grew is still alive, there was ample

evidence of canning jars, and one of the historical photographs even contained a sign in the background advertising the on-site sale of avocados and apples for 22 cents per crate. Likewise, there was historical and archaeological evidence of Harrison hunting and cooking. On the other hand, the artifacts did not overwhelmingly indicate these activities were necessarily anything more than individual sustenance as opposed to the backbone of a cottage industry.

73. Van Wormer did not have a calculation for personal items in this classification of site types. Nonetheless, I believe the large number of buttons at the Harrison site would make it much higher than other similar sites. Just as the canned food and alcohol that visitors brought were a poor fit with the Van Wormer model, I would expect the inflated percentage of personal items—due primarily to buttons—to make the site an outlier.

 # Conclusion

For over a century, the accepted story of Nathan Harrison was that he was a charming yet anachronistic fool. Virtually every historical and modern account presented Harrison as "N— —r Nate," the backward former slave whose heartwarming kindness and memorable sense of humor was matched only by his simplicity. Ironically, even though contradictory details of his pre-Palomar Mountain life (1832–80) were hotly debated, the narratives were in complete agreement when describing his behavior as his homestead transitioned gradually from a ranch to a destination for tourists (1880–1919). Few accounts suggested that there was anything more to "N— —r Nate" than what he offered to the public, and none mentioned that he might be putting on an act for visitors.

On the contrary, the intertwined historical, anthropological, and archaeological analyses presented here indicate that Harrison was neither a relic nor a simpleton. He acted strategically in order to ensure his survival in a most hostile environment for non-whites. Harrison lived an intricate double life, performed an elaborate minstrel act for visitors, and initiated a sequence of gift giving that both elicited reciprocity and forged essential social bonds. His nuanced blend of deference, adaptation, and manipulation allowed him to be successful where many of his contemporaries had failed. These actions, though unrecognized for what they were, also led to his celebrated permanence on Palomar Mountain and his legendary status in San Diego history.

Successful minstrelsy required a convincing self-deprecating performance. The act had to cloak one's inner identity and present an outward portrait that conformed to the expectations held by dominant others (Sapirstein 2012: 170–71; Dunbar 1896). It entailed skilled duplicity because at the heart of this deception was a secret double life. A minstrel's hidden identity was the unseen yet authentic reality that surfaced only once the primary audience was gone. In fact, the performer had to be so convincing that the audience could not even suspect the possibility of an alternate identity. Success could be attained only if the minstrelsy was accepted as authentic.

An Historical Archaeology of Minstrelsy

Clues of Harrison's well-disguised minstrelsy were hidden amongst the historical narratives, modern myths, and archaeological artifacts. At first glance, these different sources were largely consistent; they did not evoke a question of whether Harrison's behavior was a performance. However, a closer and more careful examination of the evidence across a variety of contexts revealed something more complex and intriguing. It uncovered Harrison's dual identities and pinpointed many aspects of his covert double life that were cloaked to in order ensure that he never be seen as brash, allied with non-whites, or threatening.

Nathan Harrison's hidden identity had an entirely separate name. Known only to his Native American and Mexican friends and family, "Inez" Harrison was an active member of the Indigenous community, who spoke the native language, intermarried with multiple Luiseño women, and socialized with tribal leaders on a weekly basis. Baptized Catholic by the local Rincon chief and given the confirmation name "Inez" by his native godparents, he presumably wore both the archaeologically recovered iron cross and Indigenous pendant but kept them concealed from white visitors and photographers. Furthermore, Inez Harrison allowed unfettered native access to his land, which itself was a gift from the local Luiseño. The Harrison site's only other Indigenous material culture—two unfired projectile points and a ritualistically-halved portable metate—seemed highly symbolic. Each seemed linked to amicable intercultural gift giving and relationships of alliance and affinity.

Though subsequent oral histories by Indigenous friends related Harrison's deep ties to the native community, none of the prominent white Palomar Mountain historians recorded any details of his bonds with the Indigenous population, except for repeated titillating passages regarding his interethnic romantic life. Harrison seemed to intentionally and consistently keep his ties to the Indigenous community muted. Anglo-Luiseño relations were volatile during the late nineteenth century and regularly erupted in violent conflict. It was risky to live in the white world and celebrate one's close relationships with the Indigenous population. In a time when ranchers were routinely photographed with their guns, Harrison regularly opted to place his rifle out of the camera's picture frame. Despite hundreds of fired rifle cartridges covering his patio, Harrison repeatedly created a deliberate portrait of himself unarmed. Self-armament was anathema to his minstrel act and had to be concealed.

Likewise, Harrison's archaeologically-suggested literacy had no place in the identity he presented to white visitors. Illiteracy and ignorance were common components of historical minstrelsy as the ability to write was often seen as a threat to those who sought to keep African Americans disempowered. Feigning illiteracy might have been a crucial survival technique for Harrison when making important civil strides, like registering to vote, claiming water, and owning land. The pen is mightier than the sword, but Harrison strategically chose to keep both a secret by keeping them out of virtually every picture and government document. It is fascinating to note that Harrison admitted his literacy only to the 1920 census taker when he was off the mountain, at the hospital, and no longer performing minstrelsy.

The persona Harrison created for tourists drew on well-established minstrelsy but was infused with aspects of his own rugged pioneer identity and deep-seated African American traditions. He dressed and played the fool, wearing tattered rags adorned with ironic status symbols and speaking in self-deprecating riddles that both excited and disarmed his unsuspecting audience. At the same time, he established himself as a leading authority on mountain history, culture, and environs and thrived as an acclaimed storyteller. He crafted distinct tales for different audiences yet maintained a consistent façade that reified expectations. Whether it be a trusty dog by his side (see Figures 0.2 and 2.2),[1] a handkerchief to wipe his brow, or layers of dust-covered clothes, Harrison mixed in rustic symbols of determination, grit, and perseverance with the standard minstrelsy caricature.

Harrison's seemingly deliberate act of projecting an anachronistic image of subservience was the opposite of an important social change that contemporaneous African Americans were experiencing across the nation. Archaeologist Paul Mullins has written extensively on how poor blacks at the end of the nineteenth century were pulled into a world of conspicuous consumption and ornamental display. He noted that they yearned to be materially affluent because "consumption was an African American sociopolitical statement of civil aspirations, material desires, and resistance to monolithic racist caricatures" (Mullins 1999: 18). Mass-produced goods became a cultural primer for American normalcy that resulted in even the humblest black homes displaying luxurious items (Harvey 1990; M. Praetzellis and A. Praetzellis 1992; Mullins et al. 2011). Due to race-based price gouging, humiliating treatment, and other manifestations of white supremacy, African Americans had access to only part of the vast consumer markets of the time period (Mullins 1999: 42). Despite being forced to fit into a system that placed them as inferior, black consumers resisted and found alternatives. The *Sears Roebuck & Co. Catalogue*, *Montgomery Ward Catalog*, and other mail-order ventures allowed African Americans to obtain and show off items of status without having to endure racist abuse at the local store (Mullins 1999: 188).

On the contrary, Harrison was exceptionally careful with any brash literal or figurative statements regarding his aspirations, desires, or resistance. He mocked material affluence by pairing ornate "Presidential" suspender clips, an ostentatious Meerschaum pipe, and a gilded pocket watch with his most tattered jeans, sometimes layered one atop the other. He built a home virtually identical to slave quarters from the Antebellum South, clearly projecting that upward mobility was neither a priority nor a reality. Most saliently, Harrison did not resist monolithic racist caricatures; he actively performed them! Harrison's well-honed survival strategy involved careful handling of his audience's attention and focus, especially at a time when the growth of rampant racist ideologies and consumerism were so volatile.[2] He manipulated racist stereotypes and constructed multiple African American identities "to navigate a landscape of racism and violence" (Wilkie 2000: 4). Concerns over safety were omnipresent for Nathan Harrison; as historian James W. Loewen noted, "These lone African Americans had better be liked by all, because if one person doesn't, even if one person merely doesn't know who they are, they may be in danger" (2005: 290).

Nathan Harrison's identity was complex, dynamic, and under constant reconstruction (Pauketat and Loren 2005: 22). It included an inner sense of self overlaid by a public persona that he projected for certain audiences. Harrison controlled their fluidity, making thousands of intricate decisions about who he was and how he wanted to be perceived. At the same time, others also played an active role in shaping his identity, both during and following his lifetime. One of the more interesting examples of this fluidity concerned how Harrison spoke of George and Irene Doane's African American servant. Even though contemporaneous Palomar locals referred to her as "Amy N——r," Harrison did not use that racial epithet for her. Every recorded account insisted that he instead called her "Cubby," suggesting that Harrison's use of "n——r" was exclusively reserved for self-deprecation and not a default term for African Americans.

The myth-making chapter of this book detailed how others experienced Harrison's outward identity. One of the most difficult facets of identity to investigate, however, was Harrison's inner sense(s) of self. Although perhaps impossible to deduce, a number of clues hinted that there were reasons for certain decisions. For example, he made it a priority to forge relationships with every group in his immediate vicinity but still chose to live alone high up a desolate mountain. As such, his existence on Palomar Mountain embodied a landscape of both independence and dependence (Hutchins-Keim 2018). He escaped his former white oppressors by occupying one of the most secure homesteads in the state yet then participated in a lucrative minstrel act aimed almost exclusively at white audiences. He owned valuable water rights but chose to share them freely with every visitor. Harrison seemingly cloaked every act of separation and resistance with an offer of inclusion and community. I believe that nuanced mediation of these contradictions was the key to his success.

Gift Exchange, Obligatory Reciprocity, and Social Capital

Harrison's earliest historically verified jobs in San Diego County were profit-oriented. These ranching chores differed significantly in type and scope from his later touristic exchanges, which were dominated by debt-oriented gift giving. Anthropologists, starting with seminal scholar Marcel Mauss, have long established gift exchange as far more than the transfer of two something-for-nothing gifts (Mauss 1990, Lévi-Strauss 1969, Sahlins 1972, Gregory 1982, Mallios 2006a). They noted that the mutual exchange of gifts prioritized people over goods, relationships over the value of the items, and debt over profit. In essence, the identities of the goods being given back and forth were almost irrelevant when compared to the fact that amicable relationships were being forged. This process regularly transformed strangers into perpetually and permanently bonded groups of people. A comprehensive inventory of the historical records contained far more examples of Harrison-initiated gift exchanges (something-for-nothing transactions) than sales or trades (something-for-something transactions), indicating that this type of exchange was significant (Mallios 2006a).

Harrison's interactions with visitors almost always began at his spring. Weary travelers trekked up the precipitous mountain, and Harrison offered them water. Harrison legally owned the water and could have simply sold it to visitors, but instead, he chose to engage with them in an entirely different manner. He gave it to them for free and asked for nothing in return. Harrison's maneuver was risky. Visitors could take advantage of his generosity, and he would receive nothing. There were few other contemporary examples of individuals giving away one of their most valuable resources.

Despite the uncertainty of reciprocity, Harrison repeatedly and routinely started the cycle of gift exchange with his offer of water. Water was central to Harrison's existence on the mountain, evinced in his filing a water claim even before he officially homesteaded the property. In obliging his visitors, Harrison immediately placed them in his debt.

Gifts warrant return gifts, but they also transform relationships. The initial act of seeming magnanimity ensured that recipients would be on their best behavior because they had been obliged by unsolicited generosity. Anthropologist Pierre Bourdieu insisted that the recipient of the initial gift recipient was "expected to show his gratitude towards his benefactor or at least show regard for him, go easy on him, pull his punches, lest he be accused of ingratitude and stand condemned" (1997a: 199). Harrison's opening gift transformed what could have been a competitive and adversarial interaction into an opportunity for community building. As a former slave constantly living in disempowered and dangerous environs, Harrison knew firsthand that chances to build alliances were rare and could be life-saving. Gift exchange inherently facilitated peaceful relationships. On the contrary, commodity-based sale or trade, in which goals of maximizing profit at the expense of others were placed above social bonds, did not offer an opportunity for the same type of security (Sahlins 1972: 169).

Since gift exchange was dependent on interpersonal relationships, it was much more social than traditional trade and other forms of commodity exchange. It was noteworthy that many of the items found at the site represented social as well as functional activities. Eating, drinking alcohol, and smoking could be isolated acts, but they were often undertaken in social situations that facilitated interpersonal bonds. For example, historical accounts repeatedly detailed Harrison cooking for others, sharing spirits with friends, and offering generously of his tobacco. Although he lived in relative seclusion, Harrison frequently participated in social activities with visitors and local residents that further bonded them as a community.

Social capital is a form of wealth in which the communal interpersonal networks greatly outweigh the accumulation of material goods (economic capital) (Bourdieu 1986). Harrison frequently operated in a gift-based system that downplayed the acquisition of finer things but celebrated interpersonal connections. It was these relationships that established, secured, and maintained his role in the local community. The story of local mountain residents pressuring unscrupulous Nathan Hargrave to give Harrison back the deed to his property was a powerful example of the importance of these communal bonds.[3] It was not an exaggeration to state that these relationships saved his home. Folklorist Henry Glassie's observation that "community is a matter of action" was evinced in the overt manners that Harrison's Palomar Mountain neighbors repeatedly sprung to his aid (2016: 22).

When considering Harrison's simultaneous accrual of social status and conspicuous use of self-deprecating minstrelsy, it was imperative to recognize that a person could acquire significant social capital within specific communities *without* undermining existing hierarchies of race, class, or gender (Purser 2017: 9). Exalted status, when carefully earned and continually negotiated, need not be seen as a threat to the established social order, even if gained by traditionally disempowered individuals. Harrison's decision to perform minstrelsy kept him safe, as did his use of gift exchange to secure a place in the many local communities. The exceptionality of this craftiness was in how he executed these acts with such deference. The minstrel act came off as genuine subservience, and the gift offerings seemed unnecessary and overly generous, but both actions resulted in important gains.

Harrison avoided conflict by being deferential and generous and carefully accumulated allies through the gifting of goods. In fact, this gifting of goods brought in more gains—in terms of social capital—than selling did. This astute combination of survival skills—conflict avoidance and social engagement—was summarized by Harrison friend Max Peters Rodriguezés, who stated that, "Nate made it a rule to walk away from trouble. Nate never knew a stranger" (Ryan 1964h: no page numbers). Harrison developed this finely-honed survival strategy through decades of turmoil in bondage and chaos. By the time he was performing minstrelsy on Palomar Mountain, Harrison was well versed in this act and an expert in surviving racial hostility through building relationships.

Harrison's often-proclaimed title as "San Diego's first permanent African American" was the culmination of many facets of his minstrelsy (Madyun and Malone 1981; Carlton 1977: 50). While drawing heavily on his acceptance by the surrounding communities, it was also predicated on extensive years in the region—both in terms of an early arrival and an extraordinarily long life span that was twice the norm (Larsen et al. 1995). Creative storytelling by Harrison and his contemporaries extended both of these chronologies, as did his keen survival skills. Independence also seemed to be a key factor in his permanence, as Harrison freely chose to settle Palomar Mountain and stay there for nearly half a century. In fact, this freedom—but never a brash expression of being too free—was an essential part of his most prominent narratives.

In summary, when appreciated in historical and cultural context, it becomes clear that Harrison created the "N——r Nate" persona as his mask and minstrel for visitors. He skillfully navigated dangerous identity politics of the time, performing an act that assuaged any white fears that he was too smart, too ambitious, too well-armed, too well-connected in the mountain community, or too Indian. Harrison put "N——r Nate" on display for tourists, but kept him separate from his life as Inez Harrison. These carefully executed strategies were undertaken out of necessity and resulted from many years in ethnic strife, be it in bondage or under constant duress. Ironically, "N——r Nate" enabled Inez Harrison to live free, love women of mixed ancestry, vote, and own land; it was one of his primary tools in surviving a world controlled by whites.

There was an important irony in interpreting Harrison's act as minstrelsy. The more successful he was at this performance, the less likely others—including modern readers—would perceive that it was indeed an act. In my mind, there were three reasons that no one till now identified his behavior as minstrelsy. First, Harrison was especially convincing in his performance. Second, visitors wanted to see his deferential behavior and were eager to believe it. Third, the believability of Harrison's act had life-or-death consequences. Had Harrison flaunted his gains as a former slave in San Diego, he might have been burned off his property as John Ballard had been in nearby Malibu. Instead, Harrison did not push his independence and freedom on white San Diego, convincingly playing the role of former slave by living apart, invoking self-deprecating humor, and not shying away from Uncle Tom references or attributions. Harrison's acceptance of this public disempowerment and his ever-present/ever-pleasant mask was yet another fable of the Reconstruction, one that was propagated across the South and in the Old West as well.

Moving Forward and Spreading the Word

In early June of 2017, Black Mountain Middle School—located in the city of San Diego—produced and distributed a yearbook to more than one thousand students that included the word "N——r" on its cover.[4] The theme of the annual was "Looking for Adventure," and the yearbook staff used an early 1900s United States Geological Survey (USGS) topographic map of the local terrain as the backdrop. Since the school was in the general vicinity of Palomar Mountain, the map included the label "N——r Nate Grade," as that was the official name of the road until 1955. Public outrage erupted over the racial epithet on the yearbooks; even *Time* magazine covered the controversy (Warth 2007: B-10). The Black Mountain Middle School principal insisted the error was inadvertent and responded by having her staff collect the books, scratch the word off each cover, and then redistribute the annuals as quickly as possible.

I contacted the principal and volunteered education materials and services in an attempt to help the school teach its community about local history, but I was never taken up on the offer. The school's response was to bury the issue instead of using it as a teachable moment for history, ethnic identity, and cultural sensitivity. At the time, multiple James Baldwin quotes ran through my mind, namely: "The past is all that makes the present coherent" and "[Americans] are in effect still trapped in a history which they do not understand and until they understand it, they cannot be released from it" (1955: 4; 1962: 1). Despite the fact that excavations at the Harrison site had again received substantial media coverage just weeks earlier in April and May of 2017—including multiple newspaper, television, and online stories—the yearbook controversy disappointingly revealed to me the difficulty of reaching San Diego County residents with Harrison's story.

There are conflicting challenges when attempting to bring the Nathan "Nate" Harrison Historical Archaeology Project to the public. I have found that most people have never heard of Harrison; of those that have, much of what they know is often untrue. While the current legacy of Harrison might be more fiction than fact, legacies can be changed. Specifically, we can change them. Our project was designed to engage local communities with relevant, insightful, and carefully contextualized histories. Despite occasional setbacks, we have begun to accomplish this through widespread dissemination of our research. Our strategy for the future includes formal educational curricula, a museum experience, and public engagement at the Palomar Mountain site.[5] The stories to be told are not just of Harrison, but of the struggle for survival that many different groups in nineteenth-century California engaged in and the lasting impacts these struggles have on society today.

Nathan Harrison and his homestead were among the first tourism destinations for the region. I believe that historical archaeology has great potential to help return this place to being a focal point for visitation. A recent surge of scholarship and practical application into the issues of tourism and archaeology have resulted in the creation of sustainable meeting grounds in which sites are simultaneously protected and visited, preserved, and celebrated (C. Walker and Carr 2013; Castañeda and Matthews 2013). Rather than portray tourism and archaeology as adversaries, it is possible to celebrate history in an instructional manner that is equally engaging to visitors (Hughes, Little, and Ballantyne 2013). In fact, the very process of creating archaeological interpretations at every site is part of an inevitable touristic experience that involves using buried material culture as a basis for a narrative to be shared with others (Joyce 2013).

The current American racial vitriol of the early twenty-first century has made it clear that Harrison's life story, rife with issues of agency, identity, and community-based empowerment, is equally relevant to current social commentary as it is to US history. Examining how Harrison gained acceptance as San Diego's first permanent African American ties directly to modern race debates about whether social acceptance is predicated on acquiescence, permission, and assimilation. As black people assess on a daily basis the ramifications of presenting themselves as holistically nonthreatening to white authority figures—whether it be deciding how to wear a hoodie, how to act when engaged by a police officer, etc.—we all must consider how Harrison navigated parallel issues a century and a half earlier. What are the consequences of minority groups brashly expressing independence in the period immediately following significant societal gains, be they post-Emancipation former slaves in the 1880s or post-Obama-presidency black youths in the 2020s?

In pursuing social transformations, activists throughout history have been confronted with the question of how hard to push the empowered for change. Brash or reserved? Nonviolent or violent? Grateful for the opportunity to discuss alternatives or defiant until concessions are made? San Diego's modern racial tensions, especially during the Civil Rights Movement, witnessed two African Americans employ decidedly different strategies. Leon L. Williams was the consummate politician. Not only was he San Diego's first African American city councilman and county supervisor, he never lost an election (Carrier 2015). He chose to change the system from within, priding himself on knowing when it was strategic to compromise and how to leverage for long-term gains. Conversely, Harold Brown was a defiant activist; he founded the local Congress for Racial Equality (CORE) chapter, was arrested on multiple occasions for his lawful protests, and endured horrendous treatment by whites for his actions. His firsthand accounts of having feces hurled at him during protests are particularly unforgettable. I am fortunate to have spent time with both Williams and Brown during research on other books, but their life stories are equally poignant for this project. They have strikingly different personalities, came from different parts of the country before settling in San Diego, and have remarkably different skill sets. Nevertheless, Williams and Brown both succeeded in exposing, addressing, and transforming various forms of bigotry in San Diego County over the past seventy years.

Traditional histories have often downplayed the significance of nonwhites in the making of America. Nathan Harrison was exceptional, and the stories of his life are important and should be told. Furthermore, African American history is integral to American history; it is neither separate nor secondary. In addition, the Old West is not peripheral to US history, nor is San Diego tangential to California's past. In fact, Harrison had direct ties to some of the most important institutions and times in US history and his strategic navigation of treacherous environs was nothing short of extraordinary.

I have given more than one hundred public talks on the Nathan "Nate" Harrison Historical Archaeology Project but will never forget the first. It was in the fall of 2004, only a few months after our trowels first hit the ground at the site. Even though the lecture came early on in the life of this dig, I was still able to present extensive evidence regarding our initial finds (~4,000 artifacts) that clearly linked the cabin remains to Harrison. After my presentation, I took questions, most of which were requests for additional information, but the last one was a statement. A tall, clean-cut, white-haired, fair-skinned man in his sixties raised his hand patiently and politely and then declared, "Good lecture and all, but the stuff you found couldn't be Nate's. It's too nice."

Being new to San Diego but not to public archaeology, I responded carefully, "Interesting point, but let me make sure I understand you. Despite how the artifacts lined up in terms of the same space, the same time period, and the same items in the old pictures, you're still not convinced?"

"Nope," he said, ". . . way too fancy for Nate. And another thing, even though you won't say it, he was 'N— —r Nate.' He called himself that, so he must have liked the name."

It was immediately obvious that I had been unsuccessful in my attempts at convincing this man of an historical interpretation different from his own through the empirical rigors of archaeology alone. In the decade and a half since that presentation, however, I have seen how balancing this sort of singular scientific approach with additional perspectives steeped in studies of history, culture, literature, photography, identity, etc. can facilitate broader and deeper understandings of the past. This inundation of all available evidence and theories has not led to consensus among my audiences, but that was never my goal. It has, however, generated engaged discussions and thoughtful debate, and I have heard far fewer inflexible assertions.

A Final Thought

This book marks the first time I have published the phrase "orthogonal historical archaeology," a concept that I have been developing for years across a variety of projects. It is a theory that endeavors to go beyond singular thought and individual scholastic agendas. I also hope it helps people develop insight, empathy, and integration in their hearts and minds. John Steinbeck once expressed his frustrations over critics reducing his works with singular explanations. He faced mutually oppositional critiques for *The Grapes of Wrath*; some reviewers lambasted him for fomenting a Marxist revolution between the classes, and others condemned his realistic prose as anti-immigrant, derisive, and unflattering of impoverished workers (Steinbeck 1992). Exceedingly annoyed at reviewers who went to great lengths to pigeonhole him with a specific literary agenda and then condemn him for that particular scholarly intention, Steinbeck chastised the critics by explaining that his book—and in fact, all of his writing—served a far larger motivation. He unabashedly declared, "My whole work drive had been aimed at making people understand each other" (Steinbeck 1990: 38).

In a time when so many people seem to be polarized due to seemingly opposing core beliefs, I yearn for more nuanced discussions that can facilitate better communication and understanding. Reductionist debates force opposing groups to entrench themselves in their position rather than seek out contextualized common experiences. I believe orthogonal thought is an opportunity for this kind of mutual understanding, even in today's climate of great political, intellectual, and social disagreement. The resultant saturation of stories on a singular topic—like Nathan Harrison's life and legend—allows individual audience members to witness alternative perspectives, appreciate broader issues of context, and identify which accounts resonate most personally with their own conceptions of morality and reality. It honors each of our own experiential truths but acknowledges how many of us there are. We can simultaneously hold to our narrative yet still know it is subjective; and we can make space for others when they do the same. Then, in uncharged political moments, we can reassess in light of all of the available evidence. Orthogonality enables a fluidity of thought that transcends rigid categories of past and present, truth and fiction, liberal and conservative, humanist and scientist, and many others. Italo Calvino hinted at this approach long ago, stating that, "to stay still in time I must move with time, to become objective I must remain subjective" (1969: 109).

When interpreting nuances of a human story, there is no such thing as a singular truth. Thus, an orthogonal perspective invites one to intentionally take in all available relevant information for the purpose of drawing the most informed, contextualized, and dynamic conclusions.

May this book inspire you to play with these ideas and see for yourself if they do, indeed, lend themselves to greater understanding.

Notes

1. Dogs were important symbols of loyalty in an untamed landscape. Harrison and his hillside homestead were no exception; his dogs were omnipresent in photographs, oral histories, and even archaeology—as evinced in multiple dog teeth unearthed at the site. In order to identify the dogs in the photographs, we assigned names to each of the pooches in the images. Fred Blum revealed that one of Harrison's dogs was named "Bill Dukes," but—in a touch of revisionist poetic justice—one of my former students labeled the other one "Lysander Mutt" (Ryan 1964j: no page numbers).
2. This calculating performance shared many qualities with the Trickster, a common character in black folklore who regularly undermined the racism of whites (Martin 2017).
3. The transaction with Nathan Hargrave showcased the uses of both social and economic capital. It was Harrison's extensive social capital with the local community, which resulted in their immediate action against Hargrave. However, since Hargrave had legally acquired Harrison's property at auction and since Hargrave was an outsider who had already proved to be an unworthy ally, only economic capital could be used to pay him off. It took the transfer of one of Harrison's vendible commodities—a horse—to complete the deal.
4. Black Mountain was not named after Nathan Harrison.
5. Aware that museums are facing challenges nationwide—over the last fifteen years, museum attendance in the US has been declining, and for many institutions, the funding situation has become precarious (Holm 2018)—our museum must be sustainable and part of a larger heritage management strategy for the site (Hodder 1999, 2000).

🌿 Epilogue

August 1897, early evening

Nathan Inez Harrison slowly rises from a crouched position as the horse-drawn wagon of wide-eyed visitors finally passes the massive ancient oak trees marking the edge of his hillside homestead. Though his 65-year-old knees pop and tingle as he stands, the salve he applied earlier that morning has eased his nagging foot pains. The arriving travelers are not part of his native Luiseño Indian family from the base of the mountain, nor are they alpine neighbors with whom he has regularly partnered as a rancher. They are strangers from the city; the women clad in long dresses and ribbon-festooned hats, and the men in crisp suits and bowlers. Harrison looks down at his tattered clothes and a wry grin slides across his face. He reflects on how little in common he has with these tourists. But that's the point of their trip, isn't it? To witness a different world and a different time. And what better way to commemorate this unforgettable journey up the mountain than with a photograph of this mythical man who inexplicably survived the Wild West. Although he has been watching these visitors for hours as they navigated the grade, this is the first glimpse the dusty-but-dapper travelers have had of the mountain's most legendary resident. The women whisper among themselves and giggle bashfully at his rather shocking, but not at all surprising appearance. He reckons these guests perceive him as somewhat exotic, and he gives them what they want and what they expect. With a twinkle in his eye, a pitcher of cool mountain-spring water in his hand, and an irresistibly welcoming smile, Harrison shuffles over to his parched guests and proclaims, "I'm N——r Nate, the first white man on the mountain."

 References

"1,240,000 WPA Aid." 1935. *San Diego Union*, 1 October, Section 1, 2.

Adams, Samuel Hopkins. 1912. *The Great American Fraud: Articles on the Nostrum Evil and Quackery*. Chicago: American Medical Association.

Agnew, Jeremy. 2010. *Medicine in the Old West, A History: 1850–1900*. Jefferson, NC: MacFarland and Company.

American Medical Association. 1908. *Nostrums and Quackery*. Chicago: American Medical Association.

Angelogou, Maggie. 1970. *A History of Makeup*. London: Studio Vista Ltd.

Armstrong, Douglas. 2011. "Excavating Inspiration: Archaeology at the Harriet Tubman Home, Auburn, New York." In *The Materiality of Freedom: Archaeologies of Postemancipation Life*, ed. Jodi A. Barnes, 263–76. Columbia: University of South Carolina Press.

Asher, Robert. [1938.] "Manuscripts of Robert Asher." Unpublished manuscripts, California State Parks Collection.

Bailey, Brad. 2009. *Palomar Mountain*. Charleston: Arcadia Press.

Baldwin, James. 1955. *Notes of a Native Son*. New York: Beacon Press.

———. 1962. "A Letter to My Nephew." *The Progressive*, 1 January.

Barnes, Frank C., and W. Todd Woodard. 2016. *Cartridges of the World: A Complete and Illustrated Reference for More Than 1500 Cartridges*. Zephyr Cove: Krause Publications.

Barthes, Roland. 1981. *Camera Lucida: Reflections on Photography*. New York: Hill and Wang.

Bartlett, Virginia Stivers. 1931. "Uncle Nate of Palomar." *Touring Topics* October: 22–25.

Barth, Fredrick. 1969. "Introduction." In *Ethnic Groups and Boundaries*, ed. Fredrick Barth, 9–38. Boston: Little, Brown and Company.

Basso, Keith H. 1979. *Portraits of "the Whiteman": Linguistic Play and Cultural Symbols among the Western Apache*. Cambridge, UK: Cambridge University Press.

Bauerlein, Mark. 2004–05. "Booker T. Washington and W. E. B. Du Bois: The Origins of a Bitter Intellectual Battle." *The Journal of Blacks in Higher Education* 46(Winter): 106–14.

Beaudry, Mary C. 1996. "Reinventing Historical Archaeology." In *Historical Archaeology and the Study of American Culture*, ed. Bernard L. Herman and Lu Ann De Cunzo, 473–97. Winterthur: Henry Francis du Pont Winterthur Museum.

———. 2006. *Findings: The Material Culture of Needlework and Sewing*. New Haven: Yale University Press.

Bean, Walton E. 1973. *California: An Interpretive History*. New York: McGraw-Hill.

Beasley, Delilah L. 1919. *The Negro Trail Blazers of California*. Los Angeles: Times Mirror Printing and Binding House.

Becker, Carl. 1935. *Everyman His Own Historian*. New York: F.S. Crofts.

Beckler, Marion F. 1958. *Palomar Mountain Past and Present*. United States of America: Self-published.

Bell, Alison. 2005. "White Ethnogenesis and Gradual Capitalism: Perspectives from Colonial Archaeological Sites in the Chesapeake." *American Anthropologist* 107(3): 446–60.

———. 2008. "On the Politics and Possibilities for Operationalizing Vindicationist Archaeologies." *Historical Archaeology* 42(2): 138–46.

Beltrán, Gonzalo Aguirre. 1946. *La Población Negra de México, 1519–1810*. México City: Ediciones Fuente Cultural.

Bennett, Lerone, Jr. 1967. "What's In a Name?" *Ebony* 23(November): 46–54.

Bevil, Alexander D. c. 1995. "San Diego Biographies: Nathan Harrison (1823–1920)." Retrieved 21 May 2002 from http://www.sandiegohistory.org/bio/harrison/Harrison.htm.

Bhaba, Homi K. 1994. *The Location of Culture*. London: Routledge.

Bielicki, Tadeusz, and Zygmunt Welon. 1982. "Growth Data as Indicators of Social Inequality: The Case of Poland." *Yearbook of Physical Anthropology* 25: 153–67.

Binford, Lewis. 1962. "A New Method of Calculating Dates from Kaolin Pipe Stem Samples." *Southeastern Archaeological Conference Newsletter* 9(1): 19–21.

Bintliff, John. 2011. "The Death of Archaeological Theory?" In *The Death of Archaeological Theory?*, ed. John Bintliff and Mark Pearce, 7–22. Oxford, UK: Oxbow.

Blanton, Dennis B., Veronica Deitrick, and Kara Bartels. 2001. "Brief and True Report of Projectile Points from Jamestown Rediscovery as of December 1998." *The Journal of the Jamestown Rediscovery Center* 1: 5–9.

Blassingame, John W. 1972. *The Slave Community: Plantation Life in the Antebellum South*. Oxford, UK: Oxford University Press.

Blight, David. 1989. "'For Something beyond the Battlefield': Frederick Douglass and the Struggle for the Memory of the Civil War." *Journal of American History* 75(4): 1156–78.

———. 2011. *American Oracle: The Civil War in the Civil Rights Era*. Cambridge, MA: Harvard University Press.

Bokovoy, Matthew F. 2005. *The San Diego World's Fairs and Southwestern Memory, 1880–1940*. Albuquerque: University of New Mexico Press.

Bond, John W. 2008a. "Visualization of Latent Fingerprint Corrosion of Metallic Surfaces." *Journal of Forensic Sciences* 53: 812–22.

———. 2008b. "The Thermodynamics of Latent Fingerprint Corrosion of Metal Elements and Alloys." *Journal of Forensic Sciences* 53: 1344–52.

———. 2008c. "On the Electrical Characteristics of Latent Finger Mark Corrosion of Brass." *Journal of Physics D: Applied Physics* 41(12): 1–10.

"Bonds would opt of Hall over asterisk ball." 2007. *Reuters*, 1 November.

Bostic, Dennis. c. 1964. "Nathan Harrison Early Settler." Unpublished article, San Diego Historical Society Collection.

Bourdieu, Pierre. 1986. "The Forms of Capital." In *Handbook of Theory and Research for the Sociology of Education*, ed. John Richardson, 241–58. Westport: Greenwood.

———. 1997a. "Selections from the Logic of Practice." In *The Logic of the Gift: Toward an Ethic of Generosity*, ed. Alan D. Schrift, 190–230. London: Routledge.

———. 1997b. "Marginalia—Some Additional Notes on The Gift." In *The Logic of the Gift: Toward an Ethic of Generosity*, ed. Alan D. Schrift, 231–44. London: Routledge.

Bowers, David Q. 1979. *The History of United States Coinage: As Illustrated by the Garrett Collection*. Los Angeles: Bowers and Ruddy Galleries, Inc.

Brandon, Jamie C. 2009. "A North American Perspective on Race and Class in Historical Archaeology." In *International Handbook of Historical Archaeology*, ed. Teresita Majewski and David Gaimster, 3–16. New York: Springer Science and Business Media, LLC.

Brandon, Jamie C., and James M. Davidson. 2005. "The Landscape of Van Winkle's Mill: Identity, Myth, and Modernity in the Ozark Upland South." *Historical Archaeology* 39(3): 113–31.

Brew, John. O. 1946. "The Use and Abuse of Taxonomy." In *Peabody Museum Papers*. Vol. 21: *The Archaeology of Alkali Ridge, Southern Utah*, 44–66. Cambridge, MA: Harvard University Press.

Brodie, Natalie Jane. 2013. "The San Diego River: An Archaeological, Historical, and Applied Anthropological Perspective." Master's thesis, San Diego State University.

Brooks, Peter. 1984. *Reading for the Plot*. New York: Alfred A. Knopf.

Brown, Curtis M., and Michael J. Pallamary. 1988. *History of San Diego Land Surveying Experiences*. San Diego: Self-published.

Brueggeman, Peter. 2018. "George Edwin Doane of Palomar Mountain." Palomar Mountain History. Retrieved 15 January 2018 from http://www.peter brueggeman.com/palomarhistory/doane.pdf.

Brundage, W. Fitzhugh. 2000. *Where These Memories Grow: History, Memory, and Southern Identity*. Chapel Hill: University of North Carolina Press.

Bruner, Edward M. 1986. "Introduction." In *The Anthropology of Experience*, ed. Victor W. Turner and Edward M. Bruner, 3–32. Champaign: University of Illinois Press.

Bryson, Jamie. 1962. "Old-timers Recall Negro who Found Freedom in Life on Palomar Slopes." *The San Diego Union-Tribune*.

Burcham, L. T. 1982. *California Range Land: An Historico-Ecological Study of the Range Resource of California*. Center for Archaeological Research at Davis, Publication #7. Davis: University of California, Davis.

Bush, Harold K., Jr. 2007. *Mark Twain and the Spiritual Crisis of His Age*. Tuscaloosa: University of Alabama Press.

Calvino, Italo. 1969. *t zero*. New York: Alfred A. Knopf.

———. 1981. *If on a Winter's Night a Traveler*. New York: Alfred A. Knopf.

Camp, Stacey Lynn. 2013. "From Nuisance to Nostalgia: The Historical Archaeology of Nature Tourism." *Historical Archaeology* 47(3): 81–96.

Cannon, Aubrey. 1989. "The Historical Dimension in Mortuary Expressions of Status and Sentiment." *Current Anthropology* 30(4): 437–58.

Carlton, Robert Lloyd. 1974. "Blacks in San Diego County: A Social Profile, 1850–1880." *Journal of San Diego History* 21(4): 7–20.

———. 1977. "Blacks in San Diego County, 1850–1900." Master's thesis, San Diego State University.

Carlyle, Thomas. 1837. *The French Revolution: A History*. London: Chapman & Hall.

Carrico, Richard L. 1987. *Strangers in a Stolen Land: American Indians in San Diego 1850–1880*. Newcastle: Sierra Oaks Publishing Company.

Carrico, Richard L., Stacey Jordan, Jose Bodipo-Memba, and Stacie Wilson. 2004. "Center City Development Corporation Downtown San Diego African-American Heritage Study." Unpublished report. San Diego: Mooney & Associates.

Carrier, Lynne. 2015. *Together We Can Do More*. San Diego: Montezuma Publishing.

Cassedy, James H. 1991. *Medicine in America: A Short History*. Baltimore: The Johns Hopkins University Press.

Cassidy, Frederic Gomes. 1985. *Dictionary of American Regional English: P-Sk*. Cambridge, MA: Belknap Press of Harvard University Press.

Castañeda, Quetzil E., and Jennifer P. Matthews. 2013. "Archaeology Meccas of Tourism: Exploration, Protection, and Exploitation." In *Tourism and Archaeology: Sustainable Meeting Grounds*, ed. Cameron Walker and Neil Carr, 37–64. Walnut Creek: Left Coast Press.

Cather, Willa. 1927. *Death Comes for the Archbishop*. New York: Alfred A. Knopf.

Chamberlain, Newell D. 1936. *The Call of Gold: True Tales on the Gold Road to Yosemite*. Mariposa: Gazette Press.

Chargaff, Erwin. 1977. *Voices in the Labyrinth: Nature, Man and Science*. New York: The Seabury Press.

Chase, J. Smeaton. 1913. *California Coast Trails: A Horseback Ride from Mexico to Oregon in 1911*. Boston: Houghton Mifflin Company.

"Chino Ranch, San Bernardino County, California." 1889. CA Genealogy. Retrieved 29 August 2018 from www.californiagenealogy.org/sanbernardino/chino_ranch.htm.

Chiu, Ping. 1967. *Chinese Labor in California, 1850–1880: An Economic Study*. Madison: State Historical Society of Wisconsin.

Christenson, Lynne E. 1996a. "Economic Analysis of Bone from Selected Historic Sites." *Proceedings of the Society for California Archaeology* 9: 324–29.

———. 1996b. "Lard Busts, Piglet Reindeer, and Other Delights: Faunal Analysis in Downtown San Diego." Unpublished report. San Diego: South Coastal Information Center.

Clark, Bonnie J. 1996. "Amache Ochinee Prowers: The Archeobiography of Cheyenne Woman." Master's thesis, University of Colorado.

———. 2005. "Lived Ethnicity: Archaeology and Identity in Mexicano America." *World Archaeology* 37(3): 440–52.

Clark, Bonnie J., and Laurie A. Wilkie. 2007. "The Prism of Self: Gender and Personhood." In *Identity and Subsistence: Gender Strategies for Archaeology*, ed. Sarah M. Nelson, 1–32. Lanham: Alta Mira Press.

Cleland, Robert Glass. 1922. *A History of California: The American Period*. New York: MacMillan Company.

Cline, Lora L. 1984. *Just Before Sunset*. San Diego: Sunbelt Publications, Inc.

Cloke, Kenneth, and Joan Goldsmith. 2000. *Resolving Conflicts at Work: A Complete Guide for Everyone on the Job*. San Francisco: Jossey-Bass.

Cobb, Charles. 2011. "Foreword." In *The Materiality of Freedom: Archaeologies of Postemancipation Life*, ed. Jodi A. Barnes, xi–xii. Columbia: University of South Carolina Press.

Coleman, Arica A. 2012. *That the Blood Stay Pure*. Bloomington: Indiana University Press.

Collins, Katherine Lavis. 2013. "An Anthropological and Archaeological Analysis of American Victorian (1876–1915) and Progressive Era (1900–1920) Medicine in San Diego, California." Master's thesis, San Diego State University.

Conkey, Margaret, and Joan Gero. 1991. "Tensions, Pluralities and Engendering Archaeology: An Introduction." In *Engendering Archaeology: Women and Prehistory*, ed. Joan Gero and Margaret Conkey, 3–30. New York: Basil Blackwell.

———. 1997. "Programme to Practice: Gender and Feminism in Archaeology." *Annual Review of Anthropology* 26: 411–37.

Conkey, Margaret, and Joan Spector. 1984. "Archaeology and the Study of Gender." *Advances in Archaeological Method and Theory* 7: 285–310.

Conrad, Cyler, Kenneth W. Gobalet, Kale Bruner, and Allen G. Pastron. 2015. "Hide, Tallow and Terrapin: Gold Rush-Era Zooarchaeology at Thompson's Cove (CA-SFR-186H), San Francisco, California." *International Journal of Historical Archaeology* 19: 502–51.

Conrad, Joseph. 1899. *Lord Jim*. New York: The Modern Library.

Courtemanche, Carl Joseph. 1982. "The Utilization of Water in San Diego County from 1890–1940: A Cultural Analysis." Master's thesis, San Diego State University.

Craine, Johnny. c. 1963. "Nathan Harrison." Unpublished biography, San Diego Historical Society Collection.

Crawford, Richard W. 1995. *Stranger Than Fiction: Vignettes of San Diego History*. San Diego: San Diego Historical Society.

Crouch, Herbert. 1965. *Reminiscences of HERBERT CROUCH 1869–1915*. N.p.: Self-published.

Davidson, James W., and Mark H. Lytle. 2000. *After the Fact: The Art of Historical Detection*, 4th ed. Vol. II. Boston: McGraw Hill.

Davidson, John. 1937. "Place Names in San Diego County: No. 191 – Nigger Grade." Unpublished manuscript written for *The San Diego Evening Tribune*, 12 November.

Davis, Abel. c. 1955. *The Memoirs of Abel M. Davis*. N.p.: Self-published.

Davis, Edward Harvey. 1932. "32-B Nate Harrison, Joshua Smith, Bill Nelson/ Image Ceremony at Palm Springs/Personalities/Palomar 1932." Unpublished manuscript, California State Parks Collection.

———. 1938. "Palomar Mountain History." Unpublished manuscript, California State Parks Collection.

———. 1982. "Palomar and the Stars." In *Palomar Mountain Views I*, ed. Bob Litchfield, 5–68. N.p.: Self-published.

————. n.d. "Edward H. Davis Papers." Box 3, Folder 29, San Diego History Center.

Davy, R. B., M. F. Price, and John L. Davis. 1890. *Proceedings of the Southern California Medical Society, Fourth Semi-Annual Meeting*. Los Angeles: Times-Mirror Printing and Binding House.

Day, Richard. 1981a. "Interview with Bessie Ormsby Helsel, " 5 September. Unpublished interview, Kirby Collection.

————. 1981b. "Interview with Max Peters, Pauma Valley." Unpublished interview, Kirby Collection.

————. 1981c. "Interview with Jim Wood." Unpublished interview, Kirby Collection.

Day, Richard, and Robert Melvin. 1981. "Interview with Chris Forbes at Pauma Reservation," 19 November. Unpublished interview, Kirby Collection.

De Graaf, Lawrence B., and Quintard Taylor. 2001. "Introduction: African Americans in California History, California in African American History." In *Seeking El Dorado: African Americans in California*, ed. Lawrence B. De Graaf, Kevin Mulroy, and Quintard Taylor, 3–71. Los Angeles: Autry Museum of Western Heritage.

Deagan, Kathleen A. 1983. *Spanish St. Augustine: The Archaeology of a Colonial Creole Community*. New York: Academic Press.

Deetz, James. 1977. *In Small Things Forgotten: The Archaeology of Early American Life*. New York: Doubleday, Anchor Press.

————. 1983. "Scientific Humanism and Humanistic Science: A Plea for Paradigmatic Pluralism in Historical Archaeology." In *Geoscience and Man*. Vol. 23: *Historical Archaeology of the Eastern United States: Papers from the R. J. Russell Symposium*, ed. Robert W. Neuman, 27–34. Baton Rouge: Louisiana State University Press.

————. 1987. "Harrington Histograms Versus Binford Mean Dates as a Technique for Establishing the Occupational Sequence of Sites at Flowerdew Hundred, Virginia." *American Archeology* 6(1): 62–67.

————. 1993. *Flowerdew Hundred*. Charlottesville: University Press of Virginia.

Deetz, James, and Edwin Dethlefsen. 1965. "The Doppler Effect and Archaeology: A Consideration of the Spatial Aspects of Seriation." *Southwestern Journal of Anthropology* 21: 196–206.

Deloria, Philip J. 1998. *Playing Indian*. New Haven: Yale University Press.

Dixon, Kelly. 2011. "'A place of recreation of our own': Archaeology of the Boston Saloon." In *The Materiality of Freedom: Archaeologies of Postemancipation Life*, ed. Jodi A. Barnes, 115–35. Columbia: University of South Carolina Press.

————. 2014. "Historical Archaeologies of the American West." *Journal of Archaeological Research* 22: 177–228.

Dixon, Kelly, Julie Schablitsky, and Shannon Novak, eds. 2011. *An Archaeology of Desperation: Exploring the Donner Party's Alder Creek Camp*. Norman: University of Oklahoma Press.

Dorsey, Leroy G. 2007. *We Are All Americans, Pure and Simple: Theodore Roosevelt and the Myth of Americanism*. Tuscaloosa: University of Alabama Press.

Dorson, Richard M. 1954. "Negro Tales." *Western Folklore* 13(2/3): 77–97.

Douglas, Mary. 1966. *Purity and Danger: An Analysis of Concepts of Pollution and Taboo*. London: Routledge and Keegan Paul.

Douglass, Frederick. 1861. "Pictures and Progress." In *The Frederick Douglass Papers*. Ser. 1, vol. 3, ed. John W. Blassingame. 452–58. New Haven: Yale University Press.

Droessler, Rachel Michele. 2015. "Reconstruction of San Diegan Food Culture through Nineteenth and Twentieth Century Faunal Remains, San Diego, California." Master's thesis, San Diego State University.

Du Bois, W. E. B. 1903. *The Souls of Black Folk*. New York: Dover Publications.

Dunbar, Paul Laurence. 1896. *Lyrics of Lowly Life*. New York: Dodd, Mead, and Company.

Ebron, Paulla A. 1998. "Enchanted Memories of Regional Difference in African American Culture." *American Anthropologist* 100(1): 94–105.

Edwards, Malcolm. 1977. "The War of Complexional Distinction: Blacks in Gold Rush California and British Columbia." *California Historical Quarterly* 56(1): 34–45.

Einstein, Albert. 1905. "On the Electrodynamics of Moving Bodies." In *The Principle of Relativity*, ed. H. A. Lorentz, 42–43. New York: Dover Publications Inc.

Ellison, Ralph. 1952. *Invisible Man*. New York: Vintage International.

Engelhardt, Fr. Zephyrin, O.F.M. 1920. *San Diego Mission*. San Francisco: The James H. Barry Company.

Engstrand, Iris H. W. 1993. *Document Sets for California and the West in US History*. Lexington: D.C. Heath and Company.

Fanon, Franz. 1968. *Wretched of the Earth*. New York: Grove Press.

Faulkner, William. 1951. *Requiem for a Nun*. New York: Random House.

Fennell, Christopher. 2011. "Examining Structural Racism in the Jim Crow Era of Illinois." In *The Materiality of Freedom: Archaeologies of Postemancipation Life*, ed. Jodi A. Barnes, 173–89. Columbia: University of South Carolina Press.

Fessenden, Reginald A. 1909. Means for Cleaning Guns. Patent Application US938836A, filed 2 November 1909.

Fike, Richard E. 1987. *The Bottle Book: A Comprehensive Guide to Historic Embossed Medicine Bottles*. Caldwell: Blackwell Press.

Fink, Gary. 1979. "Cultural Resource Assessment for Three Roads on Palomar Mountain; South Grade Road; Cafield Road; Nate Harrison Grade Road." Unpublished report. San Diego: South Coastal Information Center.

Fink, W. C. c. 1931. "Nigger Nate." Unpublished manuscript, San Diego Historical Society Collection.

Fisher, James A. 1966. "A Social History of the Negro in California, 1860–1900." Master's thesis, Sacramento State College.

Fleisher, Robert C. c. 1963. "Short History of Nathan Harrison: Better Known as Nigger Nate." Unpublished manuscript, Kirby Collection.

Flores, Richard R. 2002. *Remembering the Alamo: Memory, Modernity, and the Master Symbol*. Austin: University of Texas Press.

Fontana, Bernard L., J. Cameron Greenleaf, Charles W. Ferguson, Robert A. Wright, and Doris Frederick. 1962. "Johnny Ward's Ranch: A Study in Historic Archaeology." *Kiva* 28(1/2): 1–115.

Forbes, Jack D. 1969. *Native Americans of California and Nevada*. Healsburg: Naturegraph.

————. 2001. "The Early African Heritage of California." In *Seeking El Dorado: African Americans in California*, ed. Lawrence B. De Graaf, Kevin Mulroy, and Quintard Taylor, 73–97. Los Angeles: Autry Museum of Western Heritage.

Forbis, William H. 1973. "A Sweaty Little Man, Tall in the Saddle." In *The Cowboys*, ed. William H. Forbis, 13–37. Alexandria: Time-Life.

Foucault, Michel. 1975. *Discipline and Punish: The Birth of the Prison*. New York: Random House.

Franklin, Maria. 1997. "Out of Site, Out of Mind: The Archaeology of an Enslaved Virginia Household, ca. 1740–1776." PhD diss., University of California at Berkeley.

————. 2001. "The Archaeological Dimensions of Soul Food." In *Race and the Archaeology of Identity*, ed. Charles E. Orser, Jr., 88–107. Salt Lake City: The University of Utah Press.

Frazee-Worsley, Elizabeth. c. 1960. "Letter to Frances Beven Ryan." Ryan Collection, Pioneer Room of the Escondido Public Library.

"Front Pages: Did You Know?" 2002. *San Diego Magazine*, November.

Fucini, Joseph, and Suzy Fucini. 1985. *Entrepreneurs: The Men and Women Behind Famous Brand Names and How They Made It*. Boston: G.K. Hall & Co.

Gates, Henry Louis, Jr. 1990. "The Face and Voice of Blackness." In *Facing History: The Black Image in American Art, 1710–1940*, ed. Guy C. McElroy, xxix–xix. San Francisco: Bedford Arts.

Geertz, Clifford. 1979. "From the Native's Point of View: On the Nature of Anthropological Understanding." In *Interpretive Social Science: A Reader*, ed. Paul Rabinow and William M. Sullivan, 225–41. Berkeley: University of California Press.

Genovese, Eugene D. 1972. *Roll, Jordan, Roll: The World the Slaves Made*. New York: Vintage.

Gero, Joan M. 2015. *Yutopian: Archaeology, Ambiguity, and the Production of Knowledge in Northwest Argentina*. Austin: University of Texas Press.

Gladwell, Malcolm. 2000. *The Tipping Point: How Little Things Can Make a Big Difference*. New York: Little, Brown.

Glassie, Henry. 1963. "The Appalachian Log Cabin." *Mountain Life and Work* 39(4): 5–14.

————. 1968. "The Types of the Southern Mountain Cabin." In *The Study of American Folklore*, ed. Jan Harold Brunvand, 338–70. New York: Norton.

————. 1971. *Pattern in the Material Folk Culture of the Eastern United States*. Philadelphia: University of Pennsylvania Press.

————. 1975. *Folk Housing in Middle Virginia: A Structural Analysis of Historic Artifacts*. Knoxville: University of Tennessee Press.

————. 2000. *Vernacular Architecture*. Bloomington: Indiana University Press.

————. 2010. *Prince Twins Seven-Seven: His Art, His Life in Nigeria, His Exile in America*. Bloomington: Indiana University Press.

————. 2016. *The Stars of Ballymenone*. Bloomington: Indiana University Press.

Gonzales, Christian. 2014. "'Their Souls Are Equally Precious': Edward Henry Davis, Benevolence, Racial Logic, and the Colonization of Indigeneity." *Journal of San Diego History* 60(3): 181–206.

Goode, Kenneth G. 1973. *California's Black Pioneers*. Santa Barbara: McNally & Loftin Publishers.

Goodrich, Chauncey S. 1926. "Legal Status of the California Indian." *California Law Review* 14: 83–100.

Goss, Linda, and Marian E. Barnes, eds. 1989. *Talk That Talk*. New York: Simon & Schuster.

Gould, Stephen Jay. 1991. *Bully for Brontosaurus: Reflections in Natural History.* New York: W.W. Norton and Co.

Graburn, Nelson H. H. 1977. "Tourism: The Sacred Journey." In *Hosts and Guests: The Anthropology of Tourism,* ed. Valene Smith, 17–32. Philadelphia: University of Pennsylvania Press.

———. 1983. "The Anthropology of Tourism." *Annals of Tourism Research* 10(1): 9–33.

Gray, Paul Bryan. 2002. *Forster vs. Pico: The Struggle for the Rancho Santa Margarita.* Spokane: The Arthur H. Clark Company.

Greene, Brian. 2004. *The Fabric of the Cosmos.* New York: Vintage Books.

Gregory, Chris. 1982. *Gifts and Commodities.* London: Academic Press.

Groom, Winston. 1986. *Forrest Gump.* Garden City: Doubleday.

Gulbrandsen, Don. 2010. *Edward Sheriff Curtis: Visions of the First Americans.* Edison: Chartwell Books.

Gunderman, Shelby M. 2010. "'The First White Man on the Mountain': Archaeological, Historical, and Cultural Examinations of Nate Harrison's Cultural Identity." Master's thesis, San Diego State University.

Guralnik, David B., ed. 1986. *Webster's New World Dictionary of the American Language.* 2nd college ed. New York: Prentice Hall Press.

Gustavson, Todd. 2011. *500 Cameras, 170 Years of Photographic Innovation.* New York: Sterling Signature.

Hale, Grace E. 1998. *Making Whiteness: The Culture of Segregation in the South, 1890–1940.* New York: Pantheon Books.

Hallett, Anthony, and Diane Hallett. 1997. *Entrepreneur Magazine Encyclopedia of Entrepreneurs.* New York: John Wiley and Sons.

Handler, Richard, and Eric Gable. 1997. *The New History in an Old Museum: Creating the Past at Colonial Williamsburg.* Durham: Duke University Press.

Hardesty, Donald L. 1997. *The Archaeology of the Donner Party.* Reno: University of Nevada Press.

Harrington, J. C. 1954. "Dating Stem Fragments of Seventeenth and Eighteenth Century Clay Tobacco Pipes." *Quarterly Bulletin, Archaeological Society of Virginia* 9(1): 10–14.

———. 1955. "Archeology as an Auxiliary Science to American History." *American Anthropologist* 57(6): 1121–30.

Harrington, John P. 1932. *Explorations and Field-work of the Smithsonian Institution in 1932.* Washington, DC: Smithsonian Institution.

———. 1986. *The Papers of John Peabody Harrington in the Smithsonian Institution 1907–1957.* Microfilm Vol. 3, Reel 119, Frames 153–55. White Plains: Kraus International Publications.

Harris, LeRoy E. 1974. "The Other Side of the Freeway: A Study of Settlement Patterns of Negroes and Mexican-Americans in San Diego, California." PhD diss., Carnegie Melon University.

Harrison, Donald H. 2004. *Louis Rose, San Diego's First Jewish Settler and Entrepreneur.* San Diego: Sunbelt Publications.

Harrison, Lowell H., and James C. Klotter. 1997. *A New History of Kentucky*. Lexington: University of Kentucky Press.

Harvey, David. 1990. *The Condition of Postmodernity*. London: Blackwell Publishers.

Hastings, Edgar F. 1959a. "An Interview with Adalind S. Bailey," 14 May. Oral History Program, San Diego Historical Society.

———. 1959b. "An Interview with Louis Shannon Salmons," 17 June. Oral History Program, San Diego Historical Society.

———. 1960a. "An Interview with Harry P. Jones," 10 March. Oral History Program, San Diego Historical Society.

———. 1960b. "An Interview with Joseph B. Reece," 1 April. Oral History Program, San Diego Historical Society.

Heath, Barbara J., and Amber Bennett. 2000. "'The little Spots allow'd them': The Archaeological Study of African-American Yards." *Historical Archaeology* 34(2): 38–55.

Heath, J. H. 1919. "Aged Negro, Owner of Mountain Spring, Enters County Hospital For the Remainder of His Days." *The San Diego Union*, 22 October, 8.

———. 1921. "'Uncle Nate' Memorial." *Oceanside Blade*, 17 September.

Heighton, Robert F., and Kathleen A. Deagan. 1971. "A New Formula for Dating Kaolin Clay Pipestems." *The Conference on Historic Site Archaeology Papers* 6: 220–29.

Heizer, Robert, ed. 1974. *"They Were Only Diggers": A Collection of Articles from California Newspapers, 1851–1866, on Indian and White Relations*. Socorro: Ballena Press.

———. 1978. *Handbook of North American Indians*. Vol. 8. Washington, DC: Smithsonian Institution.

Helsel, Bessie Ormsby. 1998. "Ormsby Story." *Village News*, 17, 24, and 31 December.

Hemingway, Ernest. 1935. *Green Hills of Africa*. New York: Charles Scribner's Sons.

Henry, O. 1905. *The Gift of the Magi*. New York: Caedmon.

Henry, Susan L. 1987. "Factors Influencing Consumer Behavior in Turn-of-the-Century Phoenix, Arizona." In *Consumer Choice in Historical Archaeology*, ed. Suzanne M. Spencer-Wood, 359–82. New York: Plenum Press.

Hess, Gertrude Utt. n.d. "Charles Edward Utt: His Life and Times." Unpublished manuscript, San Diego History Center.

Hill, Joseph John. 1927. *The History of Warner's Ranch and its Environs*. Los Angeles: Private printing.

Hill, Richard W., Sr. 1998. "Developed Identities." In *Spirit Capture*, ed. Tim Johnson, 139–60. Washington, DC: Smithsonian Institution Press.

Hinsley, Curtis M., and David R. Wilcox, eds. 2015. *Coming of Age in Chicago: The 1893 World's Fair and the Coalescence of American Anthropology*. Lincoln: University of Nebraska Press.

"Historic Quotes." 1993. *Daily Times-Advocate*, 11 August.

Hodder, Ian. 1985. "Postprocessual Archaeology." *Advances in Archaeological Method and Theory* 8: 1–26.

———. 1986. *Reading the Past: Current Approaches to Interpretation in Archaeology*. Cambridge, UK: Cambridge University Press.

———. 1999. *The Archaeological Process: An Introduction*. Oxford, UK: Blackwell Publishers.

———. 2000. "Developing a Reflexive Method in Archaeology." In *Towards Reflexive Method in Archaeology: The Example at Çatalhöyük*, ed. Ian Hodder, 3–14. Cambridge, UK: Cambridge University Press.

———. 2004. *At the Trowel's Edge: An Introduction to Reflective Field Practices in Archaeology*. London: Routledge.

Holm, Cecelia. 2018. "Museums and Community Engagement." Master's thesis, San Diego State University.

Holmes, Mary J. 1855. *Homestead on the Hillside*. New York: Carleton Publisher.

Hoover, Robert L. 1978. "Final Report: Archaeological Survey and Cultural Resources Evaluation, Pauma Reservation, San Diego County, California." Unpublished report. San Diego: South Coastal Information Center.

Horn, James, William Kelso, Douglas Owsley, and Beverly Straube. 2013. *Jane: Starvation, Cannibalism, and Endurance at Jamestown*. Williamsburg: The Colonial Williamsburg Foundation and Preservation.

Horning, Audrey J. 2001. "Of Saints and Sinners: Mythic Landscapes of the Old and New South." In *Myth, Memory, and the Making of the American Landscape*, ed. by Paul A. Shackel, 21–46. Gainesville: University Press of Florida.

———. 2002. "Myth, Migration, and Material Culture: Archaeology and the Ulster Influence on Appalachia." *Historical Archaeology* 36(4): 129–49.

Horr, David Agee. 1974. "The Luiseño." In *American Indian Ethnohistory: California Indians I–VI*, ed. David Agee Horr, 97–205. New York: Garland Publishing Company.

Horwitz, Tony. 2008. *A Voyage Long and Strange*. New York: Henry Holt & Company.

Hubka, Thomas. 1986. "Just Folks Designing: Vernacular Designs and the Generation of Form." In *Common Places: Readings in American Vernacular Architecture*, ed. Dell Upton and John Michael Vlach, 426–32. Athens, GA: The University of Georgia Press.

Hudson, Tom. 1964. *Three Paths along a River: The Heritage of the Valley of the San Luis Rey*. Palm Desert: Desert-Southwest Publishers.

Hughes, Elizabeth. 1981. *The Big Book of Buttons: The Encyclopedia of Button History, Design, and Identification*. Green Forest: New Leaf Press.

Hughes, Karen, Barbara J. Little, and Roy Ballantyne. 2013. "Integrating Education and Entertainment in Archaeological Tourism: Complementary Concepts or Opposite Ends of the Spectrum." In *Tourism and Archaeology: Sustainable Meeting Grounds*, ed. Cameron Walker and Neil Carr, 65–90. Walnut Creek: Left Coast Press.

Hurst-Thomas, David. 1989. *Archaeology*, 2nd ed. New York: Holt, Rinehart, and Winston.

Hurston, Zora Neale. 1935. *Mules and Men*. Philadelphia: J.B. Lippincott Co.

———. 2001. *Every Tongue Got to Confess: Negro Folk-tales from the Gulf States*. New York: Harper-Collins Publishers.

Hutchins-Keim, Karen A. 2018. "The Plurality of Parting Ways: Landscapes of Dependence and Independence and the Making of a Free African American Community in Massachusetts." *Historical Archaeology* 52: 85–99.

Hyde, Villiana. 1971. *An Introduction to the Luiseño Language*. Banning: Malki Museum Press.

Isaac, Rhys. 1982. *The Transformation of Virginia, 1740–1790*. Chapel Hill: University of North Carolina Press.

———. 1993. "The First Monticello." In *Jeffersonian Legacies*, ed. Peter S. Onuf, 77–108. Charlottesville: University Press of Virginia.

Jackson, Barbara J. 1971. "Palomar: Its Past." *The High Country* 16(Spring): 23–24.

Jackson, Helen Hunt. 1884. *Ramona*. Boston: Little, Brown.

Jacobs, Tom. 1976. "Hawaiian Gardens: An Informal History." Retrieved 23 January 2017 from http://hgcity.org/History/HG%20History%202.pdf.

James, Laura M. 1958. "Palomar's Friendly Hermit." *The Journal of San Diego History* 4(1): 5–8.

Jarvis, Norman. 1988. "Curing and Canning of Fishery Products: A History." *Marine Fisheries Review* 50(4): 180–85.

Jasper, James A. c. 1934. "Trail-Breakers and History-Makers of Jullian-Ballena-Mesa Grande-Oak Grover-Warner Ranch-Banner-Cuyamaca in San Diego County California, History-Biography-Reminiscences." Unpublished memoirs, Julian Historical Society.

Jayme, Luis. 1772. "Letter of Luis Jayme, O.F.M., San Diego, October 17, 1772." In *Baja Travel Series*, ed. Maynard Geiger, 43–44. Los Angeles: Dawson's Book Shop.

Johnson, Matthew. 1995. *Archaeology of Capitalism*. Oxford, UK: Wiley-Blackwell.

Johnson, Samuel. 1755. "Preface to the Dictionary." In *A Dictionary of the English Language*, ed. Samuel Johnson. London: Published by consortium of Strahan, Knapton, Longman, Hitch, Hawes, Millar, and Dodsley.

Johnson, Susan Lee. 2000. *Roaring Camp: The Social World of the California Gold Rush*. New York: W.W. Norton & Company.

Joyce, Rosemary A. 2013. "Confessions of an Archaeological Tour Guide." *International Journal of Archaeological Method and Theory* 14(3): 328–58.

Joyce, Rosemary A., and Ruth E. Tringham. 2007. "Feminist Adventures in Hypertext." *Journal of Historical Archaeology* 17: 296–314.

Kabat-Zinn, Jon. 2012. *Mindfulness for Beginners*. Boulder: Sounds True.

Kanazawa, Mark T. 1998. "Efficiency in Western Water Law: The Development of the California Doctrine, 1850–1911." *The Journal of Legal Studies* 27(1): 159–84.

Katz, William Loren. 1987. *The Black West: A Pictorial History*, 3rd ed. Seattle: Open Hand.

Kazantzakis, Nikos. 1965. *Report to Greco*. New York: Touchstone.

Keeler, Robert W. 1978. "The Homelot on the Seventeenth-Century Chesapeake Tidewater Frontier." PhD diss., University of Oregon.

Kelly, Allan O. 1978. "North County Panorama: Return to the Mountain." *The San Diego Union*, 17 August.

Kern, Stephen. 1983. *The Culture of Time and Space 1880–1918*. Cambridge, MA: Harvard University Press.

King, B.B. 1975. "Lucille Talks Back." ABC Records.

King, Julia. 2012. *Archaeology, Narrative, and the Politics of the Past: The View from Southern Maryland*. Knoxville: University of Tennessee Press.

King, Joyce E. 1991. "Dysconcious Racism: Ideology, Identity, and the Miseducation of Teachers." *The Journal of Negro Education* 60(2): 133–46.

Knauft, Bruce M. 2006. "Anthropology in the Middle." *Anthropological Theory* 6(4): 407–30.

Knott, Beatrice Frichette. 1991. "Reading between the Lines: Social History of San Diego During the Early American Period as Derived from Public and Business Records." Master's thesis, University of San Diego.

Knudson, Kelly J., Lisa Frank, Brian W. Hoffman, and T. Douglas Price. 2004. "Chemical Characterization of Arctic Soils: Activity Area Analysis in Contemporary Yup'ik Fish Camps Using ICP-AES." *Journal of Archaeological Science* 31(4): 443–56.

Kopytoff, Igor. 1986. "The Cultural Biography of Things: Commoditization as Process." In *The Social Life of Things*, ed. Arjun Appadurai, 64–94. Cambridge, UK: Cambridge University Press.

Kroeber, Alfred L. 1976. *Handbook of the Indians of California*. New York: Dover Publications, Inc.

Kurashige, Scott. 2008. *The Shifting Grounds of Race: Black and Japanese Americans in the Making of Multiethnic Los Angeles*. Princeton: Princeton University Press.

LaFee, Scott. 2008. "Mind's Lie: Human memory routinely makes fact from fiction." *San Diego Union-Tribune*, 23 October.

Lambert, Joseph B. 1997. *Traces of the Past: Unraveling the Secrets of Archaeology through Chemistry*. Reading: Addison-Wesley.

Landon, David B. 1996. "Feeding Colonial Boston: A Zooarchaeological Study." *Historical Archaeology* 30(1): 1–153.

Lapham, Heather A. 2005. *Hunting for Hides: Deerskin Status and Cultural Change in the Protohistoric Appalachians*. Tuscaloosa: University of Alabama Press.

Lapp, Rudolph M. 1977. *Blacks in Gold Rush California*. New Haven: Yale University Press.

———. 1979. *Afro-Americans in California*. San Francisco: Boyd & Fraser Pub. Co.

Larsen, Clark S., Joseph Craig, Leslie E. Sering, Margaret J. Schoeninger, Katherine F. Russell, Dale H. Hutchinson, and Matthew A. Williamson. 1995. "Cross Homestead: Life and Death on the Midwestern Frontier." In *Bodies of Evidence: Reconstructing History through Skeletal Analysis*, ed. Anne L. Grauer, 139–60. New York: Wiley-Liss.

Lawlor, Laurie, and Edward S. Curtis. 2005. *Shadow Catcher: The Life and Work of Edward S. Curtis*. Lincoln: University of Nebraska Press.

LeMenager, Charles R. 1992. *Julian City and Cuyamaca Country*. Ramona: Eagle Peak Publishers.

Lennox, Jaime. 2008. "Archaeological History: Seriation of Nate Harrison Narratives." Master's thesis, San Diego State University.

Leone, Mark P. 1977. "The New Mormon Temple in Washington, DC." In *Historical Archaeology and the Importance of Material Things*, ed. Leland Ferguson, 43–61. California, PA: Society for Historical Archaeology.

———. 1982. "Some Opinions about Recovering Mind." *American Antiquity* 47(4): 742–60.

———. 2010. *Critical Historical Archaeology*. Walnut Creek: Left Coast Press.

Leriou, Natasha. 2004. "Constructing an Archaeological Narrative: The Hellenization of Cyprus." *Stanford Journal of Archaeology*. https://web.stanford.edu/dept/archaeology/journal/newdraft/leriou/paper.pdf.

Lerner, Bob. 2017. "Palomar's Black Pioneer Featured at History Museum." *Valley Roadrunner*, 24 April.

Lévi-Strauss, Claude. 1969. *The Elementary Structures of Kinship*. Boston: Beacon Press.

Levine, Lawrence W. 1977. *Black Culture and Black Consciousness: Afro-American Folk Though from Slavery to Freedom*. Oxford, UK: Oxford University Press.

Lewis, David. 2008. *Last Known Address: The History of the Julian Cemetery*. Julian: Headstone Publishing.

Lightfoot, Kent G. 1995. "Culture Contact Studies: Redefining the Relationship between Prehistoric and Historical Archaeology." *American Antiquity* 60(2): 199–217.

———. 2005. *Indians, Missionaries, and Merchants: The Legacy of Colonial Encounters on the California Frontiers*. Berkeley: University of California Press.

Lightfoot, Kent G., Antoinette Martinez, and Ann M. Schiff. 1998. "Daily Practice and Material Culture in Pluralistic Social Settings: An Archaeological Study of Culture Change and Persistence from Fort Ross, California." *American Antiquity* 63(2): 199–222.

Lightfoot, Kent G., and Otis Parrish. 2009. *California Indians and their Environment*. Berkeley: University of California Press.

Lindsay, Brendan C. 2012. *Murder State: California's Native American Genocide, 1846–1873*. Lincoln: University of Nebraska Press.

Litchfield, Bob. 1982a. "About Edward H. Davis." In *Palomar Mountain Views I*, ed. Bob Litchfield, 68. N.p.: Self-published.

———. 1982b. "George Doane Beard Growing Contest." In *Palomar Mountain Views I*, ed. Bob Litchfield, 90. N.p.: Self-published.

Litchfield, Nona. 1982. "Luiseno Lines." In *Palomar Mountain Views I*, ed. Bob Litchfield, 97–98. N.p.: Self-published.

Little, Barbara. 1994. "'She was. . . an example to her sex': Possibilities for a Feminist Historical Archaeology." In *Historical Archaeology of the Chesapeake*, ed. Paul Shackel and Barbara Little, 189–204. Washington, DC: Smithsonian Institution Press.

———. 2004. "Is the Medium the Message? The Art of Interpreting Archaeology in the US National Parks." In *Marketing Heritage: Archaeology and the Consumption of the Past*, ed. Yorke M. Rowan and Uzi Baram, 269–84. Lanham: AltaMira Press.

Lockwood, Herbert. 1967. *Fallout from the Skeleton's Closet: A Light Look at San Diego History*. La Mesa: Bailey and Associates.

Loewen, James W. 2005. *Sundown Towns: A Hidden Dimension of American Racism*. New York: The New Press.

Lomnitz, Claudio. 2001. *Deep Mexico, Silent Mexico: An Anthropology of Nationalism*. Minneapolis: University of Minnesota Press.

Lucas, Marion B. 2003. *A History of Blacks in Kentucky from Slavery to Segregation 1760–1891*. Lexington: University Press of Kentucky.

Luksic, Nik, and Jennifer Kendziorski. 1999. "The Use of Presidio Hill." *The Journal of San Diego History* 45(3): 5.

Lynch, Neil. c. 1990. "Off The Beaten Path: Try It Again, Sam." *The Front Page*, 6.

Mac Con Iomaire, M., and P. Gallagher. 2011. "Irish Corned Beef: A Culinary History." *Journal of Culinary Science and Technology* 9(1): 27–43.

Madley, Benjamin. 2016. *An American Genocide: The United States and the California Indian Catastrophe, 1846–1873*. New Haven: Yale University Press.

Madyun, Gail, and Larry Malone. 1981. "Black Pioneers in San Diego: 1880–1920." *The Journal of San Diego History* 27(2): 91–114.

Majewski, Teresita, and Michael J. O'Brian. 1987. "The Use and Misuse of Nineteenth-Century English and American Ceramics in Archaeological Analysis." In *Advances in Archaeological Method and Theory*, ed. Michael Schiffer, 97–209. New York: Academic Press.

Mallios, Seth. 1999. "At the Edge of the Precipice: Frontier Ventures, Jamestown's Hinterland, and the Archaeology of 44JC802." Richmond: Association for the Preservation of Virginia Antiquities.

———. 2000. "Archaeological Excavations at 44JC568, the Reverend Richard Buck Site." Richmond: Association for the Preservation of Virginia Antiquities.

———. 2005a. "Back to the Bowl: Using English Tobacco Pipe Bowls to Calculate Mean Site Occupation Dates." *Historical Archaeology* 39(2): 89–104.

———. 2005b. "Homo Regalos: A Call for Applied Gift Exchange in a Time of Global Commodification, Symbolic Violence, and Bloodshed." *International Journal of the Humanities* 1: 1485–90.

———. 2006a. *The Deadly Politics of Giving: Exchange and Violence at Ajacan, Roanoke, and Jamestown*. Tuscaloosa: University of Alabama Press.

———. 2006b. "Lucas Jackson and Post-Modernism: Are Current Scholars Playing a 'Cool Hand'?" *International Journal of the Humanities* 3(1): 31–36.

———. 2007. "The Apotheosis of Ajacan's Jesuit Missionaries." *Ethnohistory* 54(2): 223–44.

———. 2009. "Scientific Excavations at Palomar Mountain's Nate Harrison Site: The Historical Archaeology of a Legendary African-American Pioneer." *The Journal of San Diego History* 55(3): 141–60.

———. 2012. *Hail Montezuma! The Hidden Treasures of San Diego State*. San Diego: Montezuma Publishing.

———. 2013. "On the Fiftieth Anniversary of President John F. Kennedy's Visit to San Diego State." *The Journal of San Diego History* 59(1/2): 41–64.

———. 2014. "Spatial Seriation, Vectors of Change, and Multi-Centered Modeling for Cultural Transformations among San Diego's Historical Gravestones: 50 Years after Deetz and Dethlefsen's Archaeological Doppler Effect." *Journal of Anthropological Research* 70(1): 69–106.

———. 2016. "An Archaeology of San Diego Art, Identity, and Community: Confluent Uses of Historic Preservation in Research, Teaching, and Local Engagement." In *Heritage 2016—Proceedings of the 5th International Conference on Heritage and Sustainable Development*, ed. Rogério Amoêda, Sérgio Lira, and Cristina Pinheiro. Retrieved 21 January 2018 from https://greenlines-institute.org/en/products/publications/heritage-2016-proceedings-of-the-5th-international-conference-on-heritage-and-sustainable-development.

Mallios, Seth, and Donna Byczkiewicz. 2008. "Conserving WPA-Era Art at San Diego State University: The Removal, Restoration, and Re-Installation of

Genevieve Burgeson's 1936 NRA Packages." *The San Diego State University Occasional Archaeological Papers* 2(1): 47–67.

Mallios, Seth, Brenda Cabello, David M. Caterino, Erika Kleinhaus, Jaime Lennox, David Lewis, Lauren Lingley et al. 2017b. "Archaeological Excavations at the Nate Harrison Site in San Diego County, California: Final Report for the 2004–13 Field Seasons (Decade I)." San Diego: Montezuma Publishing.

Mallios, Seth, and Breana Campbell. 2015. "On the Cusp of an American Civil Rights Revolution: Dr. Martin Luther King, Jr.'s Final Visit and Address to San Diego in 1964." *The Journal of San Diego History* 61(2): 375–410.

Mallios, Seth, and David M. Caterino. 2006. "The Evolution of San Diego Cemeteries and Gravestones." *Proceedings of the Society for California Archaeology* 19: 57–59.

———. 2007a. *Cemeteries of San Diego*. Charleston, SC: Arcadia Publishing Company: Charleston.

———. 2007b. "Transformations in San Diego County Gravestones and Cemeteries." *Historical Archaeology* 41(4): 50–71.

———. 2011. "Mortality, Money, and Commemoration: Social and Economic Factors in Southern California Grave-Marker Change during the Nineteenth and Twentieth Centuries." *International Journal of Historical Archaeology* 15(3): 429–60.

Mallios, Seth, and Jaime Lennox. 2014. "Nate Harrison as Person, Myth, and Legend: Archaeological History and the Apotheosis of a Nineteenth-Century African-American in San Diego County." *Journal of African Diaspora Archaeology and Heritage* 3(1): 51–80.

Mallios, Seth, Jaime Lennox, James Turner, Melissa Allen, Micaela Applebaum, Jamie Bastide, Meagan Brown et al. 2018. "Archaeological Excavations at the Nathan Harrison Site in San Diego County, California: An Interim Technical Report for the 2018 Field Season." San Diego: Montezuma Publishing.

Mallios, Seth, Jaime Lennox, James Turner, Cece Holm, Jamie Bastide, Brandon Booth, Elyse Bradley et al. 2017a. "Archaeological Excavations at the Nate Harrison Site in San Diego County, California: An Interim Technical Report for the 2017 Field Season." San Diego: Montezuma Publishing.

Mallios, Seth, and Nicole J. Purvis. 2006. "Uncovering Local Art and Industry: The Discovery of Hidden WPA Murals at San Diego State University." *The San Diego State University Occasional Archaeological Papers* 1: 17–30.

Mallios, Seth, and Sarah Stroud. 2006. "Preliminary Excavations at the Nate Harrison Site." *Proceedings of the Society for California Archaeology* 19: 71–74.

Mallios, Seth, Sarah Stroud, Lauren Lingley, Jaime Lennox, Hillary Sweeney, Jason Maywald, and David M. Caterino. 2005. "Archaeological Excavations at the Nate Harrison Site in San Diego County, California: An Interim Technical Report for the Inaugural 2004 Field Season." San Diego: San Diego State University Department of Anthropology.

Mallios, Seth, Sarah Stroud, Lauren Lingley, Jaime Lennox, Hillary Sweeney, Olivia Smith, and David M. Caterino. 2006. "Archaeological Excavations at the Nate Harrison Site in San Diego County, California: An Interim Technical Report for the 2005 Field Season." San Diego: San Diego State University Department of Anthropology.

Mallios, Seth, Hillary Sweeney, David M. Caterino, Jaime Lennox, Destiny Larberg, Scott Mattingly, and David Lewis. 2009. "Archaeological Excavations at the Nate Harrison Site in San Diego County, California: An Interim Technical Report for the 2008 Field Season." San Diego: San Diego State University Department of Anthropology.

Mallios, Seth, Hillary Sweeney, Jaime Lennox, Kimberly Scott, Robert Tews, David M. Caterino, Anne Miller, Matthew Maxfeldt, and Sarah Stroud. 2007. "Archaeological Excavations at the Nate Harrison Site in San Diego County, California: An Interim Technical Report for the 2006 Field Season." San Diego: San Diego State University Department of Anthropology.

Mallios, Seth, Matthew Tennyson, Hillary Sweeney, Jaime Lennox, Brenda Cabello, Erika Kleinhans, and David M. Caterino. 2008. "Archaeological Excavations at the Nate Harrison Site in San Diego County, California: An Interim Technical Report for the 2007 Field Season." San Diego: San Diego State University Department of Anthropology.

Manders, Eric I., and Wayne A. Colwell. 1966. "California Battalion of Mounted Riflemen, 1846." *Military Collector and Historian* 18: 11–27.

"Marriage Notices." 1904. *San Diego Weekly Union*, 13 October.

Marston, Mary G. 1959. "Childhood Recollections of the Agua Tibia Ranch." *The Journal of San Diego History* 5(2): 29–31.

Martin, Gretchen. 2017. *Dancing on the Color Line: African American Tricksters in Nineteenth-Century American Literature*. Jackson: University Press of Mississippi.

Martinez, Natasha Bonilla. 1998. "An Indian Americas." In *Spirit Capture*, ed. Tim Johnson, 29–58. Washington, DC: Smithsonian Institution Press.

Martinez, Natasha Bonilla, and Rose Wyaco. 1998. "Camera Shots." In *Spirit Capture*, ed. Tim Johnson, 77–106. Washington, DC: Smithsonian Institution Press.

Marx, Karl. 1977. *Capital*. Vol. 1. New York: Vintage Books.

Mauss, Marcel. 1990. *The Gift*. New York: W.W. Norton.

May, Ronald V. 1986. "Dog-Holes, Bomb-Lances and Devil-Fish: Boom Times for the San Diego Whaling Industry." *The Journal of San Diego History* 32(2): 73–91.

———. 1987–1989. *Fort Guijarros Quarterly*. Vol. 1–3.

———. 2001. "'A Dead Whale or a Stove Boat': The History of Archaeology of the Ballast Point Whaling Station." *Mains'l Haul* 37(1): 4–10.

McAlester, Virginia, and Lee McAlester. 1984. *A Field Guide to American Houses*. New York: Alfred A. Knopf.

McCartney, Carole. 2006. *Forensic Identification and Criminal Justice*. Devon, UK: Willan.

McConnell, Stuart. 1992. *Glorious Contentment: The Grand Army of the Republic, 1865–1900*. Chapel Hill: The University of North Carolina Press.

McDougal, Dennis. 2002. *Privileged Son: Otis Chandler and the Rise and Fall of the L.A. Times Dynasty*. Cambridge, MA: Perseus Publishing.

McGriff-Payne, Sharon. 2009. *John Grider's Century: African Americans in Solano, Napa, and Sonoma Counties from 1845 to 1925*. N.p.: iUniverse.

McHenry, Anita Don. 1997. "The History of Valley Center, California: The Homestead Years, 1860–1900." Master's thesis, University of San Diego.

Melvin, Robert. 1981a. "Correspondence #1 with Richard Day," 1 September. Unpublished letter, Kirby Collection.

———. 1981b. "Correspondence #2 with Richard Day," 2 November. Unpublished letter, Kirby Collection.

———. 1981c. "Correspondence #3 with Richard Day," 7 November. Unpublished letter, Kirby Collection.

———. 1981d. "Correspondence #4 with Richard Day," 13 November. Unpublished letter, Kirby Collection.

———. 1981e. "Correspondence #5 with Richard Day," 24 November. Unpublished letter, Kirby Collection.

———. 1982a. "Correspondence #6 with Richard Day," 29 January. Unpublished letter, Kirby Collection.

———. 1982b. "Correspondence #7 with Richard Day," 27 May. Unpublished letter, Kirby Collection.

"Memorial Fountain." 1921. *Oceanside Blade*, 27 August.

Meredith, Howard V. 1983. "Compilation and Comparison of Averages for Standing Height at Late Childhood Ages on United States Boys of Several Ethnic Groups Studied between 1875 and 1980." *American Journal of Physical Anthropology* 61: 111–24.

Middleton, Joyce I. 1993. "Orality, Literacy, and Memory in Toni Morrison's *Song of Solomon*." *College English* 55(1): 64–75.

Miles, Robert. 1989. *Racism*. London: Routledge.

Miller, Anne J. 2012. *The Southern Emigrant Trail through Riverside County*. Bloomington: AuthorHouse.

Miller, Courtney A., and J. David Sweatt. 2007. "Covalent Modification of DNA Regulates Memory Formation." *Neuron* 53: 857–69.

Miller, George L. 1980. "Classification and Economic Scaling of Nineteenth Century Ceramics." *Historical Archaeology* 14: 1–40.

"Model 1873." N.d. The Winchester Arms Collectors Association. Retrieved 20 October 2018 from https://winchestercollector.org/models/model-1873/.

Momaday, N. Scott, Joseph D. Horse Capture, and Anne Makepeace. 2005. *Sacred Legacy: Edward S. Curtis and the North American Indian*. Burlington: Verve.

Monroe, J. Cameron, and Seth Mallios. 2004. "A Seventeenth-Century Chesapeake Cottage Industry." *Historical Archaeology* 38(2): 68–82.

Moore, Bertram. n.d. "Harrison- (Nathaniel) (Uncle Nate)." Ryan Collection, Pioneer Room of the Escondido Public Library.

Moore, Shirley Ann Wilson. 2016. *Sweet Freedom's Plains: African Americans on the Overland Trails 1841–1869*. Norman: University of Oklahoma Press.

Moratto, Michael J. 1984. *California Archaeology*. Orlando: Academic Press, Inc.

Morril, Rosa Neil. 1942. *Mary Jane Pioneer*. Venice, CA: Self-published.

Morris, Rick. 1988. *What The Horse Left Behind: The Archeological Study of Horseshoes*. Reno: Proquest.

Morrison, A. C. 1907. *The Baking Powder Controversy*. 2 vols. New York: American Baking Powder Association.

Mullins, Paul R. 1999. *Race and Affluence: An Archaeology of African America and Consumer Culture*. New York: Kluwer Academic/Plenum Publishers.

Mullins, Paul R., Modupe Labode, Lewis C. Jones, Michael E. Essex, Alex M. Kruse, and G. Brandon Muncy. 2011. "Consuming Lines of Difference: The

Politics of Wealth and Poverty along the Color Line." *Historical Archaeology* 43(3): 140–50.

"Murderer, Insane, Asks to be Hanged." 1907. *Los Angeles Herald*, 14 August.

"Negro Pioneer is Removed to Hospital." 1909. *San Diego Union*, 27 December.

Noël Hume, Ivor. 1964. "Archaeology: Handmaiden to History." *The North Carolina Historical Review* 41(2): 214–25.

———. 1979. *Martin's Hundred*. Charlottesville: University Press of Virginia.

"North County Yesterday." 1986. *Daily Times-Advocate*, 17 August.

O'Crouley, Don Pedro Alonso. 1774. *A Description of the Kingdom of New Spain by Señor Don Pedro Alonso O'Crouley*. London: John Howell Books.

Obeyesekere, Gananath. 1990. *The Work of Culture*. Chicago: University of Chicago Press.

———. 1992. *The Apotheosis of Captain Cook: European Myth-Making in the Pacific*. Princeton: Princeton University Press.

Olmsted, Frederick Law. 1862. *The Cotton Kingdom: A Traveler's Observations on Cotton and Slavery in the American Slave States*. New York: Mason Brothers.

Orange County (OC) Almanac. 1963. Orange County: OCUSA Press.

Orser, Charles E., Jr. 2001. "The Anthropology in American Historical Archaeology." *American Anthropologist* 103(3): 621–32.

———. 2007. *The Archaeology of Race and Racialization in Historic America*. Gainesville: University Press of Florida.

Oster, Harry. 1990. "Negro Humor: John & Old Master." In *Mother Wit: From the Laughing Barrel*, ed. Alan Dundes, 549–60. Jackson: University Press of Mississippi.

Palmer, Barbara. 2006. *The Civil War Veterans of San Diego California*. Westminster, MD: Heritage Books.

"Palomar Mountain." 1958. Unpublished manuscript, Kirby Collection.

Patterson, Orlando. 1985. *Slavery and Social Death*. Cambridge, MA: Harvard University Press.

Pauketat, Timothy R., and Diana D. Loren. 2005. "Alternative Histories and North American Archaeology." In *North American Archaeology*, ed. Timothy R. Pauketat and Diana D. Loren, 1–29. Malden: Blackwell Publishing.

Peacock, Primrose. 2009. *Discovering Old Buttons*. London: Shire Publications.

Pearce, Mark. 2011. "Have Rumours of the 'Death of Theory' Been Exaggerated?" In *The Death of Archaeological Theory?*, ed. John Bintliff and Mark Pearce, 80–89. Oxford, UK: Oxbow.

Pearsall, Susan. 1997. "In Waterbury, Buttons Are Serious Business." *New York Times*, 3 August.

Penner, Bruce R. 1997. "Old World Traditions, New World Landscapes: Ethnicity and Archaeology of Swiss-Appenzellers in the Colonial South Carolina Backcountry." *International Journal of Historical Archaeology* 1(4): 257–321.

Perkins, Elizabeth A. 1991. "The Consumer Frontier: Household Consumption in Early Kentucky." *The Journal of American History* 78(2): 486–510.

Perkins, Eloise. 1971. "Wayside Shrine Honors Former Slave who Lived on Palomar Mountain." *Daily Times-Advocate*, 2 May, 1–5.

———. 1972. "North County Nuggets: Marker Placed." *Daily Times-Advocate*, 10 August, B-6.

Petrie, W. M. Flinders. 1899. "Sequences in Prehistoric Remains." *The Journal of the Anthropological Institute of Great Britain and Ireland* 29(3/4): 295–301.

"Philip Sparkman Obituary." 1907. *The Escondido Times*, 24 May.

Phillips, George H. 1990. *The Enduring Struggle*. San Francisco: Boyd & Fraser Publishing Company.

"Pillar of Palomar." 1982. *Daily Times-Advocate*, 14 March.

"Pioneer's Grave to Have Marker." 1972. Unattributed newspaper article, Kirby Collection.

Pirkle, Arthur. 1994. *Winchester lever action repeating firearms: the models of 1866, 1873 & 1876*. Tustin: North Cape Publications.

Pitcaithley, Dwight T. 2001. "Abraham Lincoln's Birthplace Cabin: The Making of an American Icon." In *Myth, Memory, and the Making of the American Landscape*, ed. Paul A. Shackel, 240–54. Gainesville: University Press of Florida.

Pitt, Leonard. 1966. *The Decline of the Californios*. Berkeley: University of California Press.

Plane, Mark R. 2010. "Colonial Discourse, the Market Economy, and Catawba Itinerancy, 1760–1820." In *American Indians and the Market Economy, 1775–1850*, ed. Lance Greene and Mark R. Plane, 33–52. Tuscaloosa: University of Alabama Press.

Pogue, Dennis J. 1988. "Anthrosols and the Analysis of Archaeological Sites in a Plowed Context: The King's Reach Site." *Northeastern Historical Archaeology* 17: 1–15.

Pool, Bob. 2010. "Pioneer Gets Proper Tribute: Negrohead Mountain is Renamed after John Ballard, a Former Slave." *Los Angeles Times*, 24 February, AA3.

Posnansky, Merrick. 1999. "West Africanist Reflections on African-American Archaeology." In *"I, Too, Am America": Archaeological Studies of African-American Life*, ed. Theresa A. Singleton, 21–38. Charlottesville: University Press of Virginia.

Praetzellis, Adrian, and Mary Praetzellis. 2001. "Mangling Symbols of Gentility in the Wild West: Case Studies in Interpretive Archaeology." *American Anthropologist* 103(3): 645–54.

Praetzellis, Mary, and Adrian Praetzellis. 1992. "'We Were There, Too': Archaeology of an African-American Family in Sacramento, California." Unpublished archaeological report. Submitted to Facilities Management Division, General Services Department, City of Sacramento, Job No. PA11. Rohnert Park: Anthropological Studies Center.

———. 2004. "Putting the 'There' There: Historical Archaeologies of West Oakland: I-880 Cypress Freeway Replacement Project." Distributed by Department of Transportation, District 4, Cultural Resource Studies Office. Rohnert Park: Anthropological Studies Center.

Praetzellis, Mary, Adrian Praetzellis, and Marley R. Brown III. 1988. "What Happened to the Silent Majority? Research Strategies for Studying Dominant Group Material Culture in Late Nineteenth-Century California." In *Documentary Archaeology in the New World*, ed. Mary C. Beaudry, 192–202. Cambridge, UK: Cambridge University Press.

Purser, Margaret. 2017. "Boomtimes and Boomsurfers: Toward a Material Culture of Western Expansion." In *Historical Archaeology through a Western*

Lens, ed. Mark Warner and Margaret Purser, 3–31. Lincoln: University of Nebraska Press.

Raibmon, Paige. 2005. *Authentic Indians: Episodes of Encounter from the Late Nineteenth Century Northwest Coast*. Durham: Duke University Press.

Railton, Ben. 2007. *Contesting the Past, Reconstructing the Nation: American Literature and Culture in the Gilded Age, 1876–1893*. Tuscaloosa: University of Alabama Press.

Ramos, Jorge. 2007. *The Gift of Time: Letters from a Father*. New York: HarperCollins Publishers.

Ransom, John Crowe. 1941. *The New Criticism*. Norfolk, CT: New Directions.

Rawls, James J. 1984. *Indians of California: The Changing Image*. Norman: University of Oklahoma Press.

Reader, Joshua. 2009. *A Collection of Essays and Articles Pertaining to the History of Mariposa County, California*. N.p.: Self-published.

Reich, Peter. 2000. "The 'Pueblo Water Right' in California." In *Law in the Western United States*, ed. G.M. Bakken, 131–36. Norman: University of Oklahoma Press.

Reid, David. 2003. "Foreword." In *Under the Perfect Sun: The San Diego Tourists Never See*, ed. Mike Davis, Kelly Mayhem, and Jim Miller, 5–16. New York: The New Press.

Reisert, Sarah. 2018. "Baking up a Storm: When Crime and Politics Influenced American Baking Habits." *Distillations* 4(3): 46–47.

Rindge, Frederick. 1898. *Happy Days in Southern California*. Cambridge, MA and Los Angeles, CA: Self-published.

Robinson, Beverly. 1989. "Historical Arenas of African American Storytelling." In *Talk That Talk*, ed. Linda Goss and Marian E. Barnes, 211–16. New York: Simon & Schuster Inc.

Robinson, W. W. 1948. *Land in California*. Berkeley: University of California Press.

Rogers, Fred B. 1950. "Rosters of California Volunteers in the Service of the United States, 1846–1847." *Society of California Pioneers*. 17–25.

Rohrbach, Augusta. 2012. "Shadow and Substance." In *Pictures and Progress*, ed. Maurice O. Wallace and Shawn Michelle Smith, 83–100. Durham: Duke University Press.

Rosaldo, Renato. 1989. "Imperialist Nostalgia." *Representations* 26: 107–22.

Ross, David. 1998. "Making the Grade, Parts I–V." *Valley Roadrunner*.

———. 2005. "Nate Harrison Grade: Take a Ride Back in Time on a Historic Road." *Valley Roadrunner*.

Rucker, Edmund. 1951. "Nigger Nate Saga Mountain Memory." Unidentified newspaper, Kirby Collection. 22 February, A12.

Ruiz de Burton, María Amparo. 1992. *The Squatter and the Don*. Houston: Arte Público Press.

Rush, Philip S. 1952a. "The Story of 'Nigger Nate.'" *Southern California Rancher* 17(5): 18.

———. 1952b. "The Agua Tibia Ranch." *Southern California Rancher* 17(5): 29.

Russell, Charles, and Elena Quinn, eds. n.d. *Edward H. Davis and the Indians of the Southwest United States and Northwest Mexico*. Downey: Privately published by Elena Quinn.

Ryan, Frances Beven. 1964a. "Telephone interview with Clarence Rand," 17 October. Ryan Collection, Pioneer Room of the Escondido Public Library.

———. 1964b. "Notes from Mary Peet's scrapbook regarding interview with Louis Salmons," 4 November. Ryan Collection, Pioneer Room of the Escondido Public Library.

———. 1964c. "Interview with Clyde S. James," 24 November. Ryan Collection, Pioneer Room of the Escondido Public Library.

———. 1964d. "Telephone interview with Thekla James Young," 7 December. Ryan Collection, Pioneer Room of the Escondido Public Library.

———. 1964e. "Telephone interview with Frank Jones," 11 December. Ryan Collection, Pioneer Room of the Escondido Public Library.

———. 1964f. "Telephone interview with Wallace Stewart," 11 December. Ryan Collection, Pioneer Room of the Escondido Public Library.

———. 1964g. "Interview with Donald Jamison," 11 December. Ryan Collection, Pioneer Room of the Escondido Public Library.

———. 1964h. "Interview with Max Peters," 18 December. Ryan Collection, Pioneer Room of the Escondido Public Library.

———. 1964i. "Interview with M. J. Beemer," 19 December. Ryan Collection, Pioneer Room of the Escondido Public Library.

———. 1964j. "Interview with Fred Blum," 21 December. Ryan Collection, Pioneer Room of the Escondido Public Library.

Ryzewski, Krista. 2007. "Epidemic of Medicine: An Archaeological Dose of Popular Culture." *Barr International Series* 1677: 15–22.

Sachsman, David B., S. Kittrell Rushing, and Roy Morris. 2007. *Memory and Myth: The Civil War in Fiction and Film from* Uncle Tom's Cabin *to* Cold Mountain. West Lafayette: Purdue University Press.

Sahlins, Marshall. 1972. *Stone Age Economics*. Chicago: Aldine-Atherton.

———. 1985. *Islands of History*. Chicago: The University of Chicago Press.

———. 1995. *How "Natives" Think: About Captain Cook, for Example*. Chicago: The University of Chicago Press.

Said, Edward. 1978. *Orientalism*. New York: Vintage Books.

———. 1993. *Culture and Imperialism*. New York: Vintage Books.

Samford, Patricia. 1996. "The Archaeology of African-American Slavery and Material Culture." *The William and Mary Quarterly*. 3rd Series. 53(1): 87–114.

———. 2007. *Subfloor Pits and the Archaeology of Slavery in Colonial Virginia*. Tuscaloosa: The University of Alabama Press.

Sapirstein, Ray. 2012. "Out from Behind the Mask." In *Pictures and Progress*, ed. Maurice O. Wallace and Shawn Michelle Smith, 167–203. Durham: Duke University Press.

Savage, Sherman W. 1945. "The Negro on the Mining Frontier." *Journal of Negro History* 30: 34–46.

———. 1976. *Blacks in the West*. Westport: Greenwood Press.

Schomburg, Arthur. 1925. "The Negro Digs Up His Past." *The Survey*, 1 March, 670–72.

Schonberg, Jeffrey, and Philippe Bourgois. 2002. "Response: The Politics of Photographic Aesthetics: Critically Documenting the HIV Epidemic among

Heroin Injectors in Russia and the United States." *International Journal of Drug Policy* 13: 387–92.

Schumann, Rebecca. 2017. "Race and Agency in the Williamsburg Area's Free African American Population from 1723 to 1830." *Historical Archaeology* 51: 100–13.

Schwabe, Lars, Marian Joëls, Benno Roozendaal, Oliver T. Wolf, and Melly S. Oitzl. 2011. "Stress Effects on Memory: An Update and Integration." *Neuroscience and Biobehavioral Reviews* 36(7): 1740–49.

Schwarz, Ted. 1980. *A History of United States Coinage*. London: The Tantivy Press.

Shackel, Paul A. 2001. "Introduction: The Making of the American Landscape." In *Myth, Memory, and the Making of the American Landscape*, ed. Paul A. Shackel, 1–16. Gainesville: University Press of Florida.

Shackley, M. Steven. 1980. "Late Prehistoric Settlement Patterns and Biotic Communities in Cuyamaca Rancho State Park, San Diego Count, California." *Pacific Coast Archaeological Society Quarterly* 16(3): 37–52.

Shackley, M. Steven, ed. 2004. *The Early Ethnography of the Kumeyaay*. Berkeley: Phoebe Hearst Museum of Anthropology.

Shaffer, Marguerite S. 2001. *See America First: Tourism and the National Identity, 1880–1940*. Washington, DC: Smithsonian Institution Press.

Shaw, Gwendolyn DuBois, with contributions by Emily K. Shubert. 2006. *Portraits of a People: Picturing African Americans in the Nineteenth Century*. Seattle: University of Washington Press.

Shipek, Florence. 1977. "A Strategy for Change: The Luiseno of Southern California." PhD diss., University of Hawaii.

———. 1981. "A Native American Adaptation to Drought: The Kumeyaay as Seen in the San Diego Mission Records 1770–1798." *Ethnohistory* 28(4): 295–312.

———. 1993. "Kumeyaay Plant Husbandry: Fire, Water, and Erosion Management Systems." In *Before the Wilderness: Environmental Management by Native Californians*, ed. Thomas C. Blackburn and Kat Anderson. 379–88. Menlo Park: Ballena Press.

Shroder, Maurice. 1967. "The Novel as a Genre." In *The Theory of the Novel*, ed. Philip Stevick, 13–29. New York: Free Press.

Silliman, Stephen W. 2005. "Social and Physical Landscapes of Contact." In *North American Archaeology*, ed. Timothy R. Pauketat and Diana D. Loren, 273–96. Malden: Blackwell Publishing.

Simons, Dwight D. 1980. "Bird Remains." In *Historical Archaeology at the Golden Eagle Site*, ed. Mary Praetzellis, Adrian Praetzellis, and Marley R. Brown III, 1.1–1.12. Sonoma: Sonoma State University.

Slotkin, Richard. 1998. *The Myth of the Frontier in Twentieth-Century America*. Norman: The University of Oklahoma Press.

Smythe, William E. 1908. *History of San Diego: 1542–1908*. San Diego: The History Company.

Snodgrass, Mary Ellen. 2004. *Encyclopedia of Kitchen History*. New York: Fitzroy Dearborn.

Sontag, Susan. 1977. *On Photography*. New York: Farrar, Straus and Giroux.

Sorenson, Ted. 2009. *Counselor: A Life at the Edge of History*. New York: Harper Perennial.

Soulé, Frank, John H. Gihon, and James Nisbet. 1855. *Annals of San Francisco*. New York: Lewis Osborne, Publisher.

South, Stanley. 1964. *Analysis of the Buttons from Brunswick Town and Fort Fisher*. Gainesville: Florida Anthropological Society.

———. 1977. *Method and Theory in Historical Archaeology*. New York: Academic Press.

Sparkman, Philip S. 1905. "Sketch of the Grammar of the Luiseño Language of California." *American Anthropologist* 7: 656–62.

———. 1908a. "A Luiseño Tale." *Journal of American Folk-Lore* 21(80): 35–36.

———. 1908b. "The Culture of the Luiseño Indians." *University of California Publications in American Archaeology and Ethnology* 8(4): 187–234.

Spaulding, Albert C. 1960. "The Dimensions of Archaeology." In *Essays in the Science of Culture in Honor of Leslie A. White*, ed. Gertrude E. Dole and Robert L. Carneiro, 437–56. New York: Thomas Crowell and Co.

Spencer-Wood, Suzanne M., and Scott D. Heberling. 1987. "Consumer Choices in White Ceramics: A Comparison of Eleven Early Nineteenth-Century Sites." In *Consumer Choice in Historical Archaeology*, ed. Suzanne M. Spencer-Wood, 55–84. New York, Plenum.

Spier, Leslie. 1923. *Southern Diegueno Customs*. Berkeley: University of California Press.

Stanford, Leland. 1978. "Devil's Corner and Oliver S. Witherby." *Journal of San Diego History* 24(2): 236–53.

Stauffer, John, Zoe Trodd, and Celeste-Marie Bernier. 2015. *Picturing Frederick Douglass: An Illustrated Biography of the Nineteenth Century's Most Photographed American*. New York: Liveright.

Steinbeck, John. 1990. *Working Days: The Journals of* The Grapes of Wrath. New York: Penguin Books.

———. 1992. *The Grapes of Wrath*. New York: Penguin Classics.

Stone, Orra. 1930. *History of Massachusetts Industries*. Vol. 2. Boston: S. J. Clarke Publishing Co.

Stone, Joe. 1972. "Palomar Pioneer's Body Rests in Unmarked Grave." *The San Diego Union*, 31 May.

Stowe, Harriet Beecher. 1852. *Uncle Tom's Cabin, Or, Life Among the Lowly*. Boston: John P. Jewett & Co.

Strain, E. K. 1966. "Palomar Mountain State Park: Unit History." Unpublished manuscript, California State Parks Collection.

Strathman, Theodore A. 2005. "'Dream of a Big City': Water Politics and San Diego County Growth, 1910–1947." PhD diss., University of California, San Diego.

Strauss, David Levi. 2005. *Between the Eyes: Essays on Photography and Politics*. New York: Aperture.

Stroud, Sarah. 2005. "Scratching the Surface: Historical and Archaeological Investigations of Nate Harrison's Homestead." Master's thesis, San Diego State University.

Stuart, Gordon. 1966. *San Diego Back Country 1901*. Pacific Palisades: Self-published.

Szuter, Christine R. 1991. "Faunal Analysis of Home Butchering and Meat Consumption at the Hubbel Trading Post, Ganado, Arizona." *Animal Use and Culture Change* 8: 78–89.

Talbott, Tim. "Ham Brown Log Cabin." ExploreKYHistory. Retrieved 20 October 2017 from http://explorekyhistory.ky.gov/items/show/274.

Taye, George. c. 1940. "Palomar Mountain State Park, State Park No. 68." In *History of California State Parks*, ed. Aubrey Neasham. Sacramento: State of California, Department of Natural Resources, Division of Parks.

Tennesen, Kristin Norean. 2010. "Survival, Subsistence, and Industry at the Nate Harrison Historical Archaeology Site." Master's thesis, San Diego State University.

Tennyson, Matthew Patrick. 2007. "'Straight out of Dixie': An Analysis of the Architecture of the Nate Harrison Cabin." Master's thesis, San Diego State University.

Thomas, G. L. 1978. "The physics of fingerprints and their detection." *Journal of Physics E: Scientific Instruments* 11: 722–31.

Thomas, Julian. 2015a. "The Future of Archaeological Theory." *Antiquity* 89: 1277–86.

———. 2015b. "Why 'The Death of Archaeological Theory'?" In *Debating Archaeological Empiricism: The Ambiguity of Material Evidence*, ed. Charlotta Hillerdal and Johannes Siapkas, 11–31. London: Routledge.

Thompson, Nanette C. 1961. "Old Uncle Nate." *California Herald Publication of the Native Daughters of the Golden West*. Ryan Collection, Pioneer Room of the Escondido Public Library.

Thompson, Stephen. 1972. "Letter to the Editor." *Daily-Times Advocate*, 17 August.

Towne, Charles Wayland, and Edward Norris Wentworth. 1946. *Shepherd's Empire*. Norman: University of Oklahoma Press.

Trafzer, Clifford, and Joel Hayer. 1999. *Exterminate Them! Written Accounts of the Murder, Rape, and Enslavement of Native Americans during the California Gold Rush*. East Lansing: University of Michigan Press.

Trigger, Bruce G. 2006. *A History of Archaeological Thought*, 2nd ed. Cambridge, UK: Cambridge University Press.

True, D. L., C. W. Meighan, and Harvey Crew. 1974. "Investigations at Molpa, San Diego County, California." Unpublished archaeological report. San Diego: South Coastal Information Center.

Turner, Victor W. 1969. *The Ritual Process: Structure and Anti-Structure*. New York: Aldine de Gruyter.

———. 1992. *Blazing the Trail: Way Marks in the Exploration of Symbols*. Edited by Edith L. B. Turner. Tucson: University of Arizona Press.

Turner, Victor, and Edith L. B. Turner. 1978. *Image and Pilgrimage in Christian Culture: Anthropological Perspectives*. New York: Columbia University Press.

Twain, Mark. 1885. *The Adventures of Huckleberry Finn*. New York: Gabriel Wells.

———. [1873] 1969. *The Gilded Age: A Tale of Today*. New York: New American Library.

Ueber, Edward, and Alec MacCall. 1992. "The Rise and Fall of the California Sardine Empire." In *Climate Variability, Climate Change and Fisheries*, ed. Michael H. Glantz, 31–48. Cambridge, UK: Cambridge University Press.

Ulrich, Raul. 2018. *Farewell to the Horse: A Cultural History*. New York: Liveright Publishing.

Upton, Dell. 1982. "Vernacular Domestic Architecture in Eighteenth-Century Virginia." *Winterthur Portfolio* 17(2/3): 95–119.

———. 1986. "Introduction." In *America's Architectural Roots: Ethnic Groups that Built America*, ed. Dell Upton, 10–11. Washington, DC: The Preservation Press.

———. 1996. "Ethnicity, Authenticity, and Invented Traditions." *Historical Archaeology* 30(2): 1–7.

Upton, Dell, and John Michael Vlach, eds. 1986. *Common Places: Readings in American Vernacular Architecture*. Athens, GA: The University of Georgia Press.

US Congress. 1848. House Executive Document 41, Notes on a Military Reconnaissance from Fort Leavenworth in Missouri to San Diego, in California, by William H. Emory, 30th Cong., 1st sess.

Utt, James B. 1964. "Letter to Mrs. Frances B. Ryan," 24 November. Ryan Collection, Pioneer Room of the Escondido Public Library.

van Gennep, Arnold. 1961. *The Rites of Passage*. Chicago: University of Chicago Press.

Van R., J.T. 1912. "Palomar Notes." *Oceanside Blade*, 15 June.

Van Wormer, Stephen. R. 1996. "Revealing Cultural Status and Ethnic Differences Through Historic Artifact Analysis." *Proceedings for the Society for California Archaeology* 9: 310–23.

———. 2014. "Mexican and American Folk Architectural Traditions and Adaptations at Hedges: A Late Nineteenth–Early Twentieth-Century Mining Camp in the California Desert." *California Archaeology* 6(1): 95–118.

Vlach, John Michael. 1986. "The Shotgun House: An African Architectural Legacy." In *Common Places: Readings in American Vernacular Architecture*, ed. Dell Upton and John Michael Vlach, 58–78. Athens, GA: The University of Georgia Press.

———. 1993. *Back of the Big House: The Architecture of Plantation Slavery*. Chapel Hill: The University of North Carolina Press.

Vosoughi, Soroush, Deb Roy, and Sinan Aral. 2018. "The Spread of True and False News Online." *Science* 359(6380): 1146–51.

Voss, Barbara L. 2008. *The Archaeology of Ethnogenesis: Race and Sexuality in Colonial San Francisco*. Berkeley: University of California Press.

Waite, Barbara Anne. 2015. *Elsie's Mountain: Memories of Palomar & Southern California 1897–1987*. Vista: Palomar Mountain Bookworks.

Walker, Cameron, and Neil Carr. 2013. "Tourism and Archaeology: An Introduction." In *Tourism and Archaeology: Sustainable Meeting Grounds*, ed. Cameron Walker and Neil Carr, 11–36. Walnut Creek: Left Coast Press.

Walker, Dan. 2004. *Thirst for Independence: The San Diego Water Story*. San Diego: Sunbelt Publications.

Walker, Mark. 2017. "Approaching Transient Labor through Archaeology." In *Historical Archaeology through a Western Lens*, ed. Mark Warner and Margaret Purser, 85–110. Lincoln: University of Nebraska Press.

Wallace, Maurice O., and Shawn Michelle Smith. 2012. "Introduction." In *Pictures and Progress*, ed. Maurice O. Wallace and Shawn Michelle Smith, 1–17. Durham: Duke University Press.

Wallace, Michele. 2000. "Uncle Tom's Cabin: Before and After Jim Crow Era." *TDR* 44(1): 137–56.

Wallach, Jennifer Jensen. 2008. *Closer to the Truth Than Any Fact: Memoir, Memory, and Jim Crow*. Athens, GA: University of Georgia Press.

Wang, Sam, and Sandra Aamodtjune. 2008. "Your Brain Lies to You." *New York Times*, 29 June.

Warner, Mark, and Margaret Purser. 2017. "Introduction: Historical Archaeology through a Western Lens." In *Historical Archaeology through a Western Lens*, ed. Mark Warner and Margaret Purser, xii–xxx. Lincoln: University of Nebraska Press.

Warth, Gary. 2007. "Racial Slur Found on Cover Spurs Yearbook Recall: 1,000 Middle School Annuals Collected to Cover Offensive Word." *The San Diego Union-Tribune*, 8 June, B-10.

Washington, Booker T. 1903. *The Negro Problem*. New York: James Pott & Company.

———. 1986. *Up From Slavery*. New York: Penguin Books.

Weber, David J. 1973. *Foreigners in Their Native Land*. Albuquerque: University of New Mexico Press.

Weil, Simone. 1971. *The Need for Roots*. New York: Routledge.

"West Palomar Grade May Be Abandoned." 1938. *San Diego Union*, 8 February.

Wexler, Laura. 2012. "'A More Perfect Likeness': Frederick Douglass and the Image of the Nation." In *Pictures and Progress*, ed. Maurice O. Wallace and Shawn Michelle Smith, 18–41. Durham: Duke University Press.

Wheeler, B. Gordon. 1993. *Black California: The History of African-Americans in the Golden State*. New York: Hippocrene Books.

White, Phillip, and Stephen Fitt. 1998. *A Bibliography of the Indians of San Diego County: The Kumeyaay, Diegueno, Luiseño, and Cupeño*. Lanham: Scarecrow Press.

Wilken-Robertson, Michael. 2008. "Interview with Elizabeth Archaumbault," 29 July.

———. 2018. *Kumeyaay Ethnobotany: Shared Heritage of the Californias*. San Diego: Sunbelt Publications, Inc.

Wilkie, Laurie A. 2000. *Creating Freedom: Material Culture and African American Identity at Oakley Plantation, Louisiana, 1840–1950*. Baton Rouge: Louisiana State University Press.

———. 2014. *Strung Out on Archaeology*. Walnut Creek: Left Coast Press.

Willey, Gordon R., and Jeremy A. Sabloff. 1971. *A History of American Archaeology*. San Francisco: W.H. Freeman and Company.

Willis, Deborah. 2007. *Let Your Motto Be Resistance*. Washington, DC: Smithsonian Institution.

Wilson, Chris. 1997. *The Myth of Santa Fe: Creating a Modern Regional Tradition*. Albuquerque: University of New Mexico Press.

Winslow, Edward Winslow. 1918. *Clans and Moieties in Southern California*. Berkeley: University of California Press.

Wittfogel, Karl. 1957. *Oriental Despotism: A Comparative Study of Total Power*. Forge Village: Yale University Press.

Wood, Catherine. 1937. *Palomar: From Teepee to Telescope*. San Diego: Frye & Smith, Ltd.

Worster, Donald. 1985. *Rivers of Empire: Water, Aridity, and the Growth of the American West*. New York: Pantheon Books.

Wylie, Alison. 1989. "Archaeological Cables and Tacking: The Implications of Practice for Berstein's 'Options Beyond Objectivism and Relativism.'" *Philosophy of Social Sciences* 19: 1–18.

Yamaguchi, Elizabeth. 1998. "Black History and the US Census in Northern San Diego County: A Local Monument to Nathan Harrison." Unpublished manuscript, Fallbrook Historical Society.

Yentsch, Anne. 1988. "Legends, Houses, Families, and Myths: Relationships between Material Culture and American Ideology." In *Documentary Archaeology in the New World*, ed. Mary C. Beaudry, 5–19. Cambridge, UK: Cambridge University Press.

Yeoman, R. S. 1989. *A Guide Book of United States Coins*, 42nd ed. Edited by Kenneth Bressett. Racine: Western Publishing.

Ziegenbein, Linda M. 2013. "Inhabiting Spaces, Making Places: Creating a Spatial and Material Biography of David Ruggles." PhD diss., University of Massachusetts, Amherst.

💧 Index

CPSIA information can be obtained
at www.ICGtesting.com
Printed in the USA
JSHW060209030323
38370JS00016BA/487

9 781789 204308